MW01677053

An
ENGLISH-INDONESIAN-CHINESE
Dictionary

An
ENGLISH-INDONESIAN-CHINESE
Dictionary

•

英印汉词典

Yīng Yìn Hàn Cí Dǐan

黄礼枨

Wiliting

Penerbit PT Gramedia Pustaka Utama
Jakarta, 2004

An English - Indonesian - Chinese Dictionary

Oleh : Wiliting

GM 214 01.399

Jl. Palmerah Barat 33-37, lt. 2-3
Jakarta 10270

Desain sampul oleh Sofnir Ali
Setting oleh Wong Lok Dien

Edisi pertama diterbitkan oleh Penerbit Harapan, Pekalongan:
Cetakan pertama: Juli 1996
Cetakan kedua: November 1998

Edisi kedua (dengan revisi): Mei 2001
Cetakan kedua: Oktober 2004

Dicetak oleh Percetakan PT Ikrar Mandiri, Jakarta

Isi di luar tanggung jawab Percetakan

To the memory of my dear third son, Yuepeng

CONTENTS

FOREWORD

In 1998 the band to use Chinese language in Indonesia is lifted. People are free to use, write and communicate in the language. Chinese traditions and holidays are celebrated freely everywhere, e.g. the Chinese New Year, *barongsai,* the tradition of giving *ang pao*, etc. There are even newspapers and TV programmes in Chinese language. The language has been taught in some schools, as an extracurriculum- as well as a compulsory-program.

During these last three years, trade and business between Indonesia and China has grown very fast. Therefore, more and more people – not only those with ethnic Chinese background – want to study the language.

To cater the need of good and yet practical dictionary as a tool to study the language, we publish this second (revised) edition of *An English – Indonesian – Chinese Dictionary.* This edition includes more than 1200 new words than the first one. English is chosen as "entries" because we think that those who are interested in studying Chinese already have a good ability of English. Moreover, this dictionary could also be used by people whose first language is not Indonesian.

Jakarta, Mei 2001
The Publisher

THE SOUNDS OF CHINESE

Chinese Spelling 汉语拼音	International Phonetic Symbols 国际音标
b	[p]
p	[p']
m	[m]
f	[f]
d	[t]
t	[t']
n	[n]
l	[l]
g	[k]
k	[k']
h	[x]
j	[tɕ]
q	[tɕ']
x	[ɕ]
z	[ts]
c	[ts']
s	[s]
zh	[tʂ]
ch	[tʂ']
sh	[ʂ]
r	[ʐ]
y	[j]
w	[w]
a	[a]
o	[o]
e	[ə]
i	[i]
u	[u]
ü	[y]
-i	[ɿ][ʅ]*

Chinese Spelling 汉语拼音	International Phonetic Symbols 国际音标
e	[ɛ]
er	[ər]
ai	[ai]
ei	[ei]
ao	[au]
ou	[əu]
an	[an]
en	[ən]
ang	[aŋ]
eng	[əŋ]
ong	[uŋ]
ia	[ia]
ie	[iɛ]
iao	[iau]
iu, iou	[iəu]
ian	[ian]
in	[iŋ]
iang	[iaŋ]
ing	[iŋ]
iong	[yŋ]
ua	[ua]
uo	[uə]
uai	[uai]
ui, uei	[uei]
uan	[uan]
un, uen	[uən]
uang	[uaŋ]
üe	[yɛ]
üan	[yan]
ün	[yn]

* [ɿ] is used after *z c s*, [ʅ] is used after *zh ch sh r*.

DESCRIPTION OF CHINESE SOUNDS

a. Initials

b	like *p* in *spy*
c	like *ts* in *tsa* (strongly aspirated)
ch	like *ch* in *church* (strongly aspirated)
d	like *t* in *sty*
f	like *f* in *food*
g	like *k* in *sky*
h	like *h* in *her* (strongly gutturalized)
j	like *j* in *jeep* **or** like *tch* in *itching*
k	like *k* in *kind* (strongly aspirated)
l	like *l* in *land*
m	like *m* in *man*
n	like *n* in *nine*
p	like *p* in *par* (strongly aspirated)
q	like *ch* in *check* **or** in *cheap*
r	like *r* in *crew* (with the tongue tip curled far back)
s	like *s* in *sister*
sh	like *sh* in *shore*
t	like *t* in *ten*
w	like *w* in *way*
x	like *sh* in *she*
y	like *y* in *yet*
z	like *ds* in *deeds*
zh	like *j* in *jump*

b. Finals

a	like *a* in *father*
ai	like *ai* in *I* (1st person pronoun)
ao	like *ow* in *how*
an	like *un* in *unlikely* (**or** pronounced as *ahn*)
ang	*ahng*
e	like *er* in *her* (with silent *r*)
ei	like *ay* in *way*
en	like *en* in *learn* (with silent r)
eng	like *ung* in *lung*
i	like *ea* in *eat*

ia	*yah*
ie	like *ye* in *yes*
iao	like *yow* in *yowl*
iou	like *yee_oo* but close to *u* in *union*
ian	like *ien* in *lenient*
in	like *een* in *keen*
iang	*i_ahng*
ing	like *ing* in *sing*
iong	*y_oong*
o	like *aw* in *law*
ou	like *ow* in *low*
ong	*oo_ng*
u	like *oo* in "too"
ua, wa	*wah*
uo	like *wa* in *water*
uai	like *wi* in *wife*
uei	pronounced like *way*
uan	*oo_ahn*
uen	like *wen* in *Owen* **or** close to *won* in *wonder*
uang	*oo_ahng*
ueng	starts with a *w*-sound and ends like *ung* in *lung*
ü	as German *ü* in *über*; made by pronouncing the *i* of *machine* with the lips rounded as if to pronounce *oo* of *ooze*
üe	like ü plus *e*
üan	like ü plus *ahn*
ün	like ü followed by a final *n*

c. The Dividing Sign

If a word ends with a vocal sound followed by another word that begins with a vocal sound too, those two words are liable to run into each other in their Latin alphabet transcriptions. To avoid a confusion, the dividing sign ['] is used in the transcription. For example: *pi'ao* means 'furcoat'; without the dividing sign and written as *piao* it means *to float*.

d. Tone Mark

The Chinese language has four different tone marks for stressed syllables. These tones are compulsory in distinguishing different Chinese words which spelled the same in Latin alphabet. For example: Chinese *mǎ* means 'mother', while *mā* means 'horse'.

There are four basic tones and the tone marks are put above the main vowel of the syllable:

mā	má	mǎ	mà
妈	麻	马	骂
(mother)	(hemp)	(horse)	(scold)
→	↗	⤴	↘

- The first tone starts near the top of a speaker's voice range and continues on that level until the end.
  Example of first tone, high level:
  → mā 妈

- The second tone starts at mid-range, and rises rapidly to the top of the voice range.
  Example of second tone, high rising:
  ↗ má 麻

- The third tone starts below mid-range, dips to the lowest pitch, then rises above mid-range.
  Example of third tone, low dipping:
  ⤴ mǎ 马

- The fourth tone starts near the top of the range and falls very rapidly toward the bottom.
  Example of fourth tone, high falling to low:
  ↘ mà 骂

LIST OF ABBREVIATION

a.	adjective - kata sifat xíng róng cí 形容词
abbr.	abbreviation - singkatan suō xiě 缩写
adv.	adverb - kata keterangan fù cí 副词
art.	article - kata sandang (artikel) guàn cí 冠词
aux. v.	auxiliary verb - kata kerja bantu zhù cí 助词
conj.	conjunction - kata penghubung lián cí 连词
fr.	phrase - frase duǎn yǔ 短语
int.	interjection - kata seru tàn cí 叹词
n.	noun - kata benda míng cí 名词
pl.	plural - bentuk jamak fù shù 复数
pref.	prefix - awalan qián zhùi 前缀
prep.	preposition - kata depan qián zhì cí 前置词
pron.	pronoun - kata ganti dài cí 代词
v.	verb - kata kerja dòng cí 动词

A

a	(art.)	setiap, satu	měi yī 每一, yī 一
a.back	(adv.)	ke belakang	xiàng hòu 向后
ab.a.cus	(n.)	sipoa	suàn pán 算盘
a.baft	(adv.)	di buritan, di bagian belakang kapal	chuán wěi 船尾
a.ban.don	(v.)	meninggalkan	fàng qì 放弃, yí qì 遗弃
a.ban.doned	(a.)	yang ditinggalkan	bèi yí qì dė 被遗弃的
a.base	(v.)	merendahkan diri	jiàng dī shēn fèn 降低身份
a.bash	(v.)	memalukan	shǐ rén hài xiū 使人害羞
a.bate	(v.)	mereda, mengurang mengurangi	jiǎn tùi 减退, jiǎn qīng 减轻 jiǎn shǎo 减少, jiǎng dī 降低
ab.at.toir	(n.)	penjagalan, tempat pemotongan hewan	gōng gòng tú chǎng 公共屠场
ab.bess	(n.)	kepala biara wanita	nǚ xiù dào yuàn yuàn zhǎng 女修道院院长
ab.bey	(n.)	biara	xiù dào yuàn 修道院, sì yuàn 寺院
ab.bot	(n.)	kepala biara pria	xiū dào yuàn yuàn zhǎng 修道院院长, fāng zhàng 方丈
ab.bre.vi.ate	(v.)	memperpendek, menyingkat	sù xié 缩写
ab.bre.vi.a.tion	(n.)	kependekan, singkatan	sù xiě 缩写, jiǎn lùe 简略
ab.di.cate	(v.)	turun takhta	tùi wèi 退位
ab.do.men	(n.)	perut	dǔ zì 肚子, fù bù 腹部
ab.duct	(v.)	melarikan, menculik	guǎi zǒu 拐走, guǎi piàn 拐骗

a.bed	(adv.)	di tempat tidur	zài chuáng shàng 在床上
a.bet	(v.)	menghasut	suō shǐ 唆使
ab.hor	(v.)	benci akan, jijik pada	zēng wù 憎恶
a.bide	(v.)	tinggal (di), menetap	liú 留, jū zhù 居住
		mematuhi	zún shǒu 遵守
a.bil.i.ty	(n.)	kecakapan, keterampilan	néng lì 能力
a.ble	(a.)	cakap, sanggup	néng gàn dė 能干的
ab.nor.mal	(a.)	luar biasa	fǎn cháng dė 反常的
		tidak biasa	bù zhèng cháng dė 不正常的
a.board	(adv.)	di atas kapal	zài chuán shàng 在船上
a.bode	(n.)	tempat tinggal	zhù suǒ 住所
a.bol.ish	(v.)	menghapuskan	fèi chú 废除
a.bort	(v.)	gugur	duò tāi 堕胎, liú chǎn 流产
		gagal	shī bài 失败
a.bor.tion	(n.)	keguguran	liú chǎn 流产
		kegagalan	shī bài 失败
a.bound	(v.)	sangat banyak, kaya	fēng fù 丰富
a.bout	(prep.)	tentang, kira-kira	guān yú 关于, dà yuè 大约
a.bove	(prep.)	atas, di atas	zài shàng miàn 在上面
a.breast	(adv.)	berdampingan	bìng pái 並排, bìng jiān 並肩
a.bridge	(v.)	meringkaskan	sù duǎn 缩短
a.broad	(adv.)	di luar negeri	zài gúo wài 在国外
ab.ro.gate	(v.)	membatalkan, menghapuskan	fèi chú 废除, qǔ xiāo 取消
ab.scess	(n.)	bengkak bernanah, abses	nóng zhǒng 脓肿
ab.scond	(v.)	melarikan diri	táo pǎo 逃跑
ab.sence	(n.)	ketidakhadiran	quē xí 缺席
ab.sent	(a.)	tidak hadir	quē xí 缺席, bù zài chǎng 不在场
	(v.)	tidak hadir	quē xí 缺席

ab.sen.tee	(n.)	yang tidak hadir	quē xí zhě 缺席者
ab.sent-mind.ed	(a.)	ling lung	xīn bù zài yān 心不在焉
ab.so.lute	(a.)	mutlak	jué dùi dė 绝对的
ab.so.lute.ly	(adv.)	sama sekali	jué dùi di 绝对地
ab.solve	(v.)	mengampuni	shè miǎn 赦免
ab.sorb	(v.)	menyerap, mengisap	xī shōu 吸收
ab.stain	(v.)	berpantang	jiè chú 戒除
		tidak memberikan suara	qí quán 弃权
ab.stract	(a.)	abstrak	chōu xiàng dė 抽象的
ab.surd	(a.)	mustahil	huāng táng 荒唐
a.bun.dance	(n.)	kelimpahan	fēng fù 丰富
a.bun.dant	(a.)	berlimpah-limpah	fēng fù dė 丰富的
a.buse	(v.)	menyalahgunakan	làn yòng 滥用
		mencaci maki	màn mà 漫骂
a.but	(v.)	berbatasan	lín jiē 邻接
		berdampingan	jǐn kào 紧靠
a.cad.e.my	(n.)	akademi	zhuān mén xué xiào 专门学校
ac.cede	(v.)	menyetujui	dā yìng 答应
ac.cent	(n.)	aksen, tekanan ucapan	zhòng dú 重读
ac.cept	(v.)	menerima	jiē shòu 接受
		menyetujui	rèn kě 认可
ac.cept.able	(a.)	dapat diterima	kě jiē shòu dė 可接受的
			zhōng yì dė 中意的
ac.cess	(n.)	jalan masuk, terusan	tōng lù 通路
ac.ces.so.ry	(n.)	lampiran	fù jiàn 附件
		suku cadang	pèi jiàn 配件
		barang tambahan	fù shǔ pǐn 附属品
ac.ci.dent	(n.)	kecelakaan	shī shì 失事,
			yì wài shì gù 意外事故
ac.ci.den.tal	(a.)	kebetulan	ǒu rán dė 偶然的

ac.claim	(n.)	sorak sorai	huān hū 欢呼, hè cǎi 喝采
ac.cla.ma.tion	(n.)	aklamasi, suara bulat	yī zhì 一致
		sorakan, tepuk tangan	huān hū 欢呼, hè cǎi 喝采
ac.com.mo.date	(v.)	memuat, menampung	jiē nà 接纳, jiē dài 接待
		memberi akomodasi	gōng yìng 供应, gōng jǐ 供给
		menyesuaikan	shì yìng 适应
		mendamaikan	tiáo tíng 调停
ac.com.mo.dat.ing	(a.)	ramah	qīn qìe dė 亲切的
		baik hati	hǎo xīn dė 好心的
ac.com.mo.da.tion	(n.)	perlengkapan penginapan	zhù sù shè bèi 住宿设备
		penginapan	lǔ guǎn 旅馆
		peralatan	yòng jù 用具
		penyesuaian	tiáo jié 调节, shì yìng 适应
ac.com.pa.ny	(v.)	menemani	péi bàn 陪伴, péi tóng 陪同
ac.com.plice	(n.)	kaki tangan, antek	tóng móu 同谋, bāng xiōng 帮凶
ac.com.plish	(v.)	menyelesaikan	wán chéng 完成
ac.com.plish.ment	(n.)	prestasi, keberhasilan	chéng jī 成绩, chéng jìu 成就
		kepandaian	běn lǐng 本领
ac.cord	(n.)	keselarasan	yī zhì 一致, hé xié 和谐
	(v.)	cocok, sesuai	yī zhì 一致, fú hé 符合
ac.cord.ance	(n.)	sesuai, cocok	yì zhì 一致, fú hé 符合
ac.cord.ing	(adv.)	menurut, sesuai	àn zhào 按照
ac.cord.ing.ly	(adv.)	karena itu	yīn cǐ 因此, yú shì 于是
		sesuai dengan	shì dàng dí 适当地, xiāng yìng dí 相应地
ac.cor.di.on	(n.)	akordeon	shǒu fēng qín 手风琴
ac.cost	(v.)	menyapa	zhāo hū 招呼
ac.count	(n.)	rekening	zhàng 账, zhàng mù 账目, hù kóu 户口
		laporan, cerita	bào dǎo 报导, xù shù 叙述
		karena, alasan	yuán gù 缘故, lǐ yóu 理由

		pentingnya	zhòng yào xìng 重要性
		nilai	jià zhí 价值
		kegunaan, keuntungan	yòng chù 用处, lì yì 利益
		perhitungan	kăo lù 考虑, jì suàn 计算
	(v.)	menganggap	yĭ wéi 以为, rén wéi 认为
		memandang sebagai	shì wéi 视为
		menerangkan	shuō míng 说明, jiě shì 解释
ac.count.a.ble	(a.)	bertanggung jawab	yǒu zé rèn dė 有责任的
ac.count.ant	(n.)	akuntan	kuài jì yuán 会计员
ac.count.ing	(n.)	akuntansi	kuài jì xué 会计学
ac.cu.mu.late	(v.)	mengumpulkan	jí lěi 积累
		menghimpun	lěi jí 累积
ac.cu.ra.cy	(n.)	kecermatan	jīng mì xìng 精密性
		ketepatan	zhǔn què xìng 准确性
ac.cu.rate	(a.)	tepat, cermat, teliti	zhǔn qùe 准确, jīng mì 精密
ac.cursed	(a.)	terkutuk	ké zǔ zhòu dė 可诅咒的,
			kě zēng dė 可憎的
ac.cu.sa.tion	(n.)	tuduhan, penuduhan	kòng sù 控诉, gaò fà 告发
		kutukan	qiăn zé 谴责
ac.cuse	(v.)	mengutuk, menyalahkan	qiăn zé 谴责
		menuduh	zhĭ kòng 指控
		mengadukan	gào fā 告发
ac.cuser	(n.)	penuduh, pendakwa	kòng sù rén 控诉人,
			yuán gào 原告
ac.cus.tom	(v.)	membiasakan diri dengan	shĭ ... guàn yú 使…惯于
ache	(n.)	(rasa) sakit	tòng 痛
a.chieve	(v.)	mencapai	wán chéng 完成, dá dào 达到
a.chieve.ment	(n.)	prestasi, keberhasilan	chéng jī 成绩, chéng jiù 成就
a.cid	(n.)	asam	suān 酸
	(a.)	asam, masam	suān dė 酸的, suān xìng dė 酸性的

ac.know.ledge	(v.)	mengakui	chéng rèn 承认
ac.know.ledge.ment	(n.)	pengakuan	chéng rèn 承认
		pernyataan terima kasih	míng xiè 鸣谢
ac.quaint	(v.)	memperkenalkan	shǐ rèn shí 使认识, shǐ shú xí 使熟悉
		memberitahukan	tōng zhī 通知
ac.quaint.ance	(n.)	kenalan	shú rén 熟人
		tahu betul	xiāng shí 相识, shú xí 熟悉
ac.quire	(v.)	memperoleh	huò dé 获得
ac.quit	(v.)	membebaskan	.xuan gao wu zui 宣告无罪
a.cre	(n.)	ukuran luas tanah = 4072 m^2	yīng mǔ 英亩
ac.rid	(a.)	pedas, sengit	là 辣, xīn là 辛辣
ac.ro.bat	(n.)	akrobat	zá jì yǎn yuán 杂技演员
a.cross	(prep.)	melintang, menyeberang	héng qiē 横切, héng guò 横过
act	(v.)	bertindak	xíng dòng 行动
act.ing	(n.)	bermain sandiwara	biǎo yǎn 表演
ac.tion	(n.)	tindakan, perbuatan	xíng dòng 行动, dòng zùo 动作
ac.tive	(a.)	giat	huó pō dė 活泼的
		aktif	zhǔ dòng dė 主动的
ac.tiv.ist	(n.)	aktivis	jī jí fèn zǐ 积极分子, huó dòng jiā 活动家
ac.tiv.i.ty	(n.)	aktivitas	huó dòng 活动
ac.tor	(n.)	aktor, pemain sandiwara	yǎn yuán 演员
ac.tress	(n.)	pemain (wanita) sandiwara/film	nǔ yǎn yuán 女演员
ac.tu.al	(a.)	aktuil	xiàn shí dė 现实的
		sebenarnya	shí jì dė 实际的
a.cute	(a.)	tajam	jiān rùi 尖锐, mín rùi 敏锐
a.dapt	(v.)	menyesuaikan	shǐ ... shì yìng 使…适应
a.dapt.a.ble	(a.)	dapat menyesuaikan diri	kě shì yìng dė 可适应的, shì hé dė适合的

a.dapt.er	(n.)	penyadur	gǎi biān zhě 改编者
add	(v.)	menambah	jiā 加
ad.di.tion	(n.)	tambahan	jiā 加, tiān jiā wù 添加物
ad.dress	(v.)	berpidato	yǎn shūo 演说
	(n.)	pidato	yǎn shūo 演说
		alamat	dì zhǐ 地址
a.dept	(n.)	ahli	zhuān jiā 专家
ad.here	(v.)	melekat	nián zhù 黏住
ad.jec.tive	(n.)	kata sifat	xíng róng cí 形容词
ad.judge	(v.)	memutuskan perkara	pàn jú 判决
ad.just	(v.)	menyesuaikan	shǐ shì yìng 使适应
ad.ju.tant	(n.)	ajudan, pembantu	fù guān 付官, zhù shǒu 助手
ad.min.is.ter	(v.)	mengurus	guǎn lǐ 管理
ad.mi.ra.ble	(a.)	mengagumkan	kě jìng pèi dė 可敬佩的
ad.mir.al	(n.)	laksamana	hǎi jūn shàng jiàng 海军上将
ad.mire	(v.)	mengagumi	zàn tàn 赞叹
ad.mis.sion	(n.)	izin masuk, pengakuan	zhǔn rù 准入, xǔ kě 许可
ad.mit	(v.)	mengizinkan, mengaku	zhǔn xǔ 准许, xǔ kě 许可
ad.mit.tance	(n.)	hak masuk, boleh masuk	zhǔn rù 准入, rù chǎng xǔ kě 入场许可
ad.mix	(v.)	mencampurkan	hùn hé 混合
a.do	(n.)	ribut	máng luàn 忙乱
a.dopt	(v.)	mengangkat anak, adopsi	shōu yǎng 收养
		menerima untuk dipakai	cái nà 采纳
a.dor.a.ble	(a.)	patut dipuja	kě chóng bài dė 可崇拜的
a.dor.a.tion	(n.)	pemujaan, penyembahan	chóng bài 崇拜
a.dore	(v.)	memuja	chóng bài 崇拜
a.dorn	(v.)	menghias	zhuang shì 装饰
a.drift	(adv., a.)	terapung-apung	piāo liú 漂流
a.dult	(a.)	dewasa, akil balig	chéng nián dė 成年的
		masak, matang	chéng shú dė 成熟的
	(n.)	orang dewasa	chéng nián rén成年人

ad.vance	(v.)	maju, memberi persekot	jìn xíng 进行, yù fù 预付
ad.van.tage	(n.)	keuntungan	lì yì 利益
ad.vent	(n.)	kedatangan	lái lín 来临
ad.ven.ture	(n.)	petualangan	mào xiǎn 冒险
ad.verb	(n.)	kata keterangan	fù cí 副词
ad.ver.sa.ry	(n.)	lawan, musuh	dí shǒu 敌手, chóu rén 仇人
ad.ver.si.ty	(n.)	kemalangan	bù xìng 不幸, zāi huò 灾祸
ad.ver.tise	(v.)	memasang iklan	dēng guǎng gào 登广告
ad.ver.tise.ment	(n.)	iklan	guǎng gào 广告
ad.vice	(n.)	nasihat	zhōng gào 忠告
ad.vi.sa.ble	(a.)	patut	hé lǐ dė 合理的
ad.vise	(v.)	menasihatkan	zhōng gào 忠告, quàn gào 劝告
ad.vis.er	(n.)	penasihat	gù wèn 顾问
ad.vo.cate	(n.)	pembela	biàn hù rén 辩护人
aer.o.naut.ics	(n.)	ilmu penerbangan	háng kōng xué 航空学
aer.o.plane	(n.)	pesawat terbang	feī jī 飞机
a.far	(adv.)	jauh, tempat yang jauh	yuǎn 远, zài yuǎn chù 在远处
af.fair	(n.)	hal, urusan	shì wù 事务
af.fect	(v.)	mempengaruhi	yǐng xiǎng 影响
af.fected	(a.)	terpengaruh	shòu yǐng xiǎng dė 受影响的
af.fec.tion	(n.)	perasaan kasih sayang	gǎn dòng 感动, ài qíng 爱情
af.firm	(v.)	menegaskan, menguatkan	què rèn 确认, kěn dìng 肯定
af.fir.ma.tion	(n.)	penegasan	kěn dìng 肯定
af.fir.ma.tive	(a.)	bersifat membenarkan mengiyakan, yang positif	kěn dìng dė 肯定的 xǔ kě 许可
af.fix	(v.)	melampirkan	fù jiā 附加
	(n.)	tambahan, imbuhan	fù jiā yǔ 附加语, zhùi yǔ 缀语
af.flict	(v.)	menyebabkan sakit, menyebabkan derita	shǐ (rén) kǔ nǎo 使(人)苦恼, shǐ (rén) tòng kǔ 使(人)痛苦
af.ford	(v.)	menghasilkan	shēng chǎn 生产

af.fray	(n.)	pertengkaran	chǎo jià 吵架
		perkelahian	dǎ jià 打架
af.fright	(v.)	menakutkan	shǐ kǒng bù 使恐怖
a.fire	(adv.)	terbakar	zhúo hǔo 着火
a.float	(adv.)	terapung-apung	piāo fú dė 漂浮的
a.foot	(adv.)	berjalan kaki	bù xíng 步行
a.fraid	(a.)	takut	hài pà 害怕
a.fresh	(adv.)	mulai lagi, sekali lagi	chóng xīn 重新, zài 再
aft	(adv.)	bagian belakang kapal, buritan	chuán wěi 船尾
af.ter	(prep.)	di belakang, setelah	zài hòu在后, zhi hòu 之后
af.ter.noon	(n.)	sore	xià wǔ 下午
af.ter.wards	(adv.)	setelah itu	hòu lái 后来, yǐ hòu 以后
a.gain	(adv.)	lagi	zài 再
a.gainst	(prep.)	bertentangan,	dùi 对, fǎn dùi 反对,
		berlawanan dengan	xiāng fǎn 相反
agar-agar	(n.)	agar-agar	yáng cài 洋菜, shí huā cài 石花菜
age	(n.)	usia, zaman	nián líng 年龄, shí dài 时代
a.gen.cy	(n.)	perwakilan, agen	dài lǐ chù 代理处
a.gen.da	(n.)	agenda	jì shì bù 记事簿
a.gent	(n.)	agen	dài lǐ zhě 代理者
ag.gres.sion	(n.)	penyerbuan	qīn luè 侵略
ag.gres.sive	(a.)	bersifat menyerang	hào qīn luè dė 好侵略的
ag.gres.sor	(n.)	penyerbu, penyerang	qīn luè zhě 侵略者
ag.i.tate	(v.)	mengaduk	jiǎo dòng 搅动
		menghasut	shān dòng 煽动
ag.i.ta.tor	(n.)	pengaduk	jiǎo dòng qì 搅动器
		penghasut	shān dòng zhě 煽动者
a.go	(adv.)	yang lalu	gùo qù dė 过去的
ag.o.ny	(n.)	sengsara	tòng kǔ 痛苦

a.gra.ri.an	(a.)	agraris	tŭ dì dė 土地的
a.gree	(v.)	setuju	tóng yì 同意
a.gree.a.ble	(a.)	menyenangkan	yùe yì dė 悦意的
a.gree.ment	(n.)	perjanjian, persetujuan	xié dìng 协定
ag.ri.cul.ture	(n.)	pertanian	nóng yè 农业
a.head	(adv.)	di muka, di depan	zài qián 在前
aid	(v.)	membantu	bāng zhù 帮助
aim	(n.)	tujuan	mù dì 目的
	(v.)	membidik	miáo zhŭn 瞄准
air	(n.)	udara	kōng qì 空气
air.craft	(n.)	pesawat terbang	feī jī 飞机
air.drome	(n.)	lapangan terbang	feī jī chăng 飞机场
air force	(n.)	angkatan udara	kōng jūn 空军
air.mail	(n.)	pos udara	háng kōng yóu dì 航空邮递
air.man	(n.)	penerbang	feī jī jia shī yuán 飞机驾驶员, háng kōng yuán 航空员
air.plane	(n.)	pesawat	feī jī 飞机
air.port	(n.)	lapangan terbang	feī jī chăng 飞机场
a.larm	(n.)	kecemasan, tanda bahaya	jīng huāng 惊慌, jĭng bào 警报
al.bum	(n.)	album	xiàng bù 像簿, jí yóu bù 集邮簿
al.co.hol	(n.)	alkohol	jiŭ jīng酒精
al.ge.bra	(n.)	aljabar	dài shù 代数
a.li.as	(n.)	alias	bié míng 别名
a.lien	(a.)	asing	wài gúo dė 外国的
	(n.)	orang asing	wài gúo rén 外国人
a.light	(v.)	turun	xià lái 下来
		menyala	zhúo hŭo 着火, fā yàn 发焰
a.like	(a.)	sama	xiāng sì 相似
a.live	(a.)	hidup	húo dė 活的
all	(a.)	semua	suŏ yŏu dė 所有的, quán bù 全部

al.ley	(n.)	gang, jalan kecil	hú tóng 胡同, xiǎo lù 小路
al.li.ance	(n.)	persekutuan	lián méng 联盟
al.li.ga.tor	(n.)	buaya	è yú 鳄鱼
all out	(adv.)	dengan seluruh tenaga	jìn lì 尽力
al.low	(v.)	membiarkan	zhǔn xǔ 准许
		mengizinkan	yǔn xǔ 允许
al.low.ance	(n.)	tunjangan	jīn tiē 津贴
all-round	(a.)	serba bisa	wàn nén dė 万能的
al.ly	(v.)	bergabung	lián hé 联合
al.ma.nac	(n.)	almanak, penanggalan	lí shū 历书
al.most	(adv.)	hampir	jī hū 几乎
a.loft	(adv.)	di atas	zài gāo chù 在高处
a.lone	(a.)	sendiri	dú zì de 独自的
a.long	(adv.)	sepanjang	yán 沿
a.long.side	(adv.)	di sisi	zài páng biān 在旁边
		berdampingan	bìng jiān 並肩
a.loud	(adv.)	dengan keras	dà shēng dí 大声地
al.pha.bet	(n.)	abjad	zì mǔ 字母
al.read.y	(adv.)	telah, sudah	yǐ jīng 已经
al.so	(adv.)	juga	yě 也
al.tar	(n.)	tempat pemujaan, altar	jì tán 祭坛
al.ter	(v.)	mengubah	gǎi biàn 改变
al.ter.a.tion	(n.)	perubahan	gǎi biàn 改变
al.ter.nate	(a.)	ganti-berganti	lún liú 轮流, jiāo tì 交替
al.ter.na.tive	(a.)	bersifat ganti-berganti	jiaō tì dė 交替的
	(n.)	pilihan	xuǎn zhé dė 选择的
al.though	(conj.)	walaupun, meskipun	sŭi rán 虽然
al.ti.tude	(n.)	ketinggian	gāo dù 高度
al.to.geth.er	(adv.)	sama sekali	wán quán 完全
a.lum.nus	(n.)	alumni	xiào yǒu 校友

al.ways	(n.)	selalu	cháng cháng 常常, yǒng yǔan 永远
a.mass	(v.)	menumpuk mengumpulkan	dūi jī 堆积 chǔ xù 储蓄
am.a.teur	(n.)	amatir	yè yú dė 业余的
a.maze	(v.)	mengherankan	chī jīng 吃惊
am.bas.sa.dor	(n.)	duta besar	dà shǐ 大使
am.bi.tion	(n.)	ambisi	yě xīn 野心
am.bu.lance	(n.)	ambulans	jiù hù ché 救护车
a.mend	(v.)	mengubah, memperbaiki	xiū zhèng 修正
a.mid, a.midst	(prep.)	di tengah	zài dāng zhōng 在当中
a.miss	(a.)	salah	cùo wù dė 错误的
am.i.ty	(n.)	persahabatan	yǒu yí 友谊
am.nes.ty	(n.)	amnesti, pengampunan	dà shè 大赦
a.moe.ba	(n.)	amuba	biàn xíng chóng 变形虫
a.mong	(prep.)	di antara	zài qí jiān 在其间, zhi jian 之间
a.mount	(n.)	jumlah	zǒng shù 总数
am.ple	(a.)	besar	jù dà dė 巨大的
am.pli.fy	(v.)	memperbesar menguraikan dengan pan- jang lebar	fàng dà 放大 xiáng shù 详述
a.muse	(v.)	menghibur	yú lè 娱乐
an	(art.)	satu	yī gè 一个
a.nal.o.gy	(n.)	persamaan	xiāng sì 相似
a.na.ly.sis	(n.)	uraian, analisa, kupasan	fēn xī 分析, fēn jiě 分解
an.ar.chy	(n.)	kekacauan, kekalutan tak ada pemerintah	hùn lùan 混乱 wú zhèng fǔ zhuàng tài 无政府状态
a.nat.o.my	(n.)	ilmu urai tubuh, anatomi	jiě pōu xué 解剖学
an.ces.tor	(n.)	nenek moyang	zǔ zōng 祖宗
an.chor	(n.)	jangkar, sauh	máo 锚

an.cient	(a.)	dahulu kala, kuno	gǔ dài dė 古代的
and	(conj.)	dan	hé 和
a.new	(adv.)	mulai lagi dengan cara lain	zài 再, chóng xīn 重新
an.gel	(n.)	malaikat, bidadari	tiān shǐ 天使
an.ger	(n.)	kemarahan	nù 怒, qì fèn 气愤
an.gle	(n.)	sudut	jiǎo 角
	(v.)	memancing	diào yú 钓鱼
an.gler	(n.)	pemancing ikan	diào yú zhě 钓鱼者
an.gry	(a.)	marah	shēng qì 生气
an.guish	(n.)	penderitaan	tòng kǔ 痛苦
an.i.mal	(n.)	binatang	dòng wù 动物
an.i.mous	(n.)	rasa permusuhan	dí yì 敌意
an.kle	(n.)	mata kaki	huà 踝
an.ni.ver.sa.ry	(n.)	hari ulang tahun	zhōu nián jì niàn rì 周年记念日
an.nounce	(v.)	mengumumkan	xuān gào 宣告
an.nounce.ment	(n.)	pengumuman	bù gào 布告
an.noy	(v.)	mengganggu	fán rǎo 烦扰, fán nǎo 烦恼, sāo rǎo 骚扰
an.noy.ance	(n.)	gangguan	fán nǎo 烦恼, sāo rǎo 骚扰
an.nu.al	(a.)	tahunan, tiap tahun	měi nián dė 每年的
a.noth.er	(a.)	yang lain	bié dė 别的
an.swer	(n.)	jawaban	húi dá 回答
ant	(n.)	semut	mǎ yí 蚂蚁
an.ten.na	(n.)	antena	tiān xiàn 天线
an.ti.ci.pate	(v.)	mengharapkan	qī wàng 期望
		mengetahui lebih dulu	yù liào 预料
an.ti.ci.pa.tion	(n.)	antisipasi	xiān wéi 先为, yù liào 预料
an.tip.a.thy	(n.)	antipati	yàn wù 厌恶
an.tique	(a.)	kuno, antik	gǔ jiù dė 古旧的, gǔ dài dė 古代的
an.xi.e.ty	(n.)	kecemasan	jiāo jí 焦急, yōu lù 忧虑

anx.ious	(a.)	cemas, ingin tahu	yōu lǜ dė 忧虑的, kě wàng渴望
an.y	(a.)	sesuatu, apa saja	móu 某, rèn hé yī gè 任何一个
an.y.bod.y	(n.)	siapa pun,	rèn hé yī gè rén 任何一个人,
		siapa saja	wú lùn shúi 无论谁
an.y.how	(adv.)	bagaimanapun	wú lùn rú hé 无论如何
an.y.one	(pron.)	siapa pun,	rèn hé rén 任何人,
		siapa saja	wú lùn shúi 无论谁
an.y.thing	(pron., n.)	barang siapa pun	rèn hé dōng xī 任何东西,
			wú lǔn shén mė 无论什么
an.y.way	(adv.)	biarpun demikian	wú lùn rú hé 无论如何
an.y.where	(adv.)	di mana saja	wú lùn nǎ lǐ 无论哪里
an.y.wise	(adv.)	bagaimana juga	wǔ lùn rú hé 无论如何
a.pace	(adv.)	dengan cepat	kuài 快
a.part	(adv.)	terpisah	fēn kaī 分开
a.part.ment	(n.)	apartemen	fáng jiāng 房间, gōng yù 公寓,
			yī tào fáng jiān 一套房间
ap.a.thy	(n.)	apati	lěng mò 冷漠
		masa bodoh	mò bù guān xīn 漠不关心
ape	(n.)	kera	yuán 猿
	(v.)	meniru	mó fǎng 摹仿
a.pol.o.gize	(v.)	minta maaf	dào qiàn 道歉
a.pol.o.gy	(n.)	maaf	dào qiàn 道歉
ap.pa.ra.tus	(n.)	alat	yí qì 仪器, qì jù 器具
ap.par.ent	(a.)	jelas	xiǎn rán dė 显然的
ap.peal	(n.)	permohonan	kěn qiú 恳求, shàng sù 上诉
	(v.)	memohon	kěn qiú 恳求
ap.pear	(v.)	muncul	chū xiàn 出现
ap.pear.ance	(n.)	penampilan, rupa	chū xiàn 出现, wài mào 外貌
ap.pen.dix	(n.)	usus buntu	máng cháng 盲肠
		lampiran	fù lù 附录
ap.pe.tite	(n.)	nafsu makan, selera	shí yù食欲

ap.plaud	(v.)	bertepuk tangan, bersorak	gŭ zhăng 鼓掌, hè căi 喝采
ap.ple	(n.)	buah apel	píng gŭo 苹果
ap.pli.cant	(n.)	pelamar	shēn qíng zhě 申请者
ap.pli.ca.tion	(n.)	pemakaian, lamaran	yìng yòng 应用, shēn qíng 申请
ap.plied	(a.)	terpakai	yìng yòng dė 应用的
ap.ply	(v.)	menggunakan, melamar	fū 敷, qíng qiú 请求, shēn qíng 申请
ap.point	(v.)	menentukan, mengangkat	dìng 定, rèn mìng 任命
ap.point.ment	(n.)	pengangkatan, perjanjian	rèn mìng 任命, yùe dìng 约定
ap.pre.ci.ate	(v.)	menghargai	shăng shí 赏识
ap.pre.ci.a.tion	(n.)	penghargaan	zūn zhòng 尊重
ap.prise	(v.)	memberitahukan	tōng zhī 通知
ap.proach	(v.)	mendekati	jiē jìn 接近
	(n.)	pendekatan	jiē jìn 接近
ap.prov.al	(n.)	persetujuan, pengesahan	pī zhŭn 批准
ap.prove	(v.)	menyetujui, mengesahkan	pī zhŭn 批准
ap.prox.i.mate	(a.)	kira-kira	dà yuè dė 大约的
A.pril	(n.)	April	sì yuè 四月
a.pron	(n.)	celemek	wéi qún 围裙
apt	(a.)	cocok	hé yí dė 合宜的, qia dang dė 恰当的
ap.ti.tude	(n.)	bakat	cái néng 才能
a.quar.i.um	(n.)	akuarium	shŭi cú guăn 水簇馆
arch.bish.op	(n.)	uskup agung	dà zhŭ jiào 大主教
ar.chi.tect	(n.)	arsitek	jiàn zhù jiā 建筑家
ar.chi.tec.ture	(n.)	ilmu bangunan, arsitektur	jiàn zhù shù 建筑术
ar.dour	(n.)	semangat, hasrat	rè qíng 热情
a.re.a	(n.)	wilayah, daerah	qū yù 区域
		areal	miàn jī 面积
		bidang	dì miàn 地面
a.ren.a	(n.)	tempat pertandingan, arena	jìng jì chăng 竞技场
ar.gue	(v.)	berdebat	biàn lùn 辩论

ar.gu.ment	(n.)	perdebatan	biàn lùn 辩论
		dalil	lǐ yóu 理由
a.right	(adv.)	betul, benar	bù cuo 不错, zhèng que di 正确地
a.rise	(v.)	bangkit, bangun	qǐ laí 起来
		timbul	chū xiàn 出现, fā shēng 发生
ar.is.toc.ra.cy	(n.)	kaum ningrat	gùi zú 贵族
a.rith.me.tic	(n.)	ilmu hitung	suàn shù 算术
arm	(n.)	lengan	shǒu bì 手臂
ar.ma.da	(n.)	armada	jiàn dùi 舰队
ar.ma.ment	(n.)	tentara	jūn dùi 军队
		persenjataan	jūn bèi 军备
arm.chair	(n.)	kursi berlengan	ān lè yǐ 安乐椅
ar.mi.stice	(n.)	gencatan senjata	xiū zhàn 休战, tíng zhàn 停战
ar.mour	(n.)	baju baja	gāng jiǎ 钢甲
arms	(n.)	senjata	wǔ qì 武器
ar.my	(n.)	tentara	jūn dùi 军队
a.ro.ma	(n.)	bau harum	fēn fāng 芬芳
ar.o.mat.ic	(a.)	yang harum	fāng xiāng dė 芳香的
a.round	(adv.)	sekeliling, sekitar	zhōu wéi 周围, sì zhōu 四周
a.rouse	(v.)	membangunkan	huàn xǐng 唤醒
ar.range	(v.)	mengatur	zhěn lǐ 整理, bù zhì 布置
ar.range.ment	(n.)	penyelenggaraan	chóu bèi 筹备
		susunan	zhěng lǐ 整理, bù zhì 布置
ar.ray	(v.)	menghiasi, membariskan	zhuāng shì 装饰, pái lìe 排列
ar.rest	(v.)	menahan, menangkap	jū liú 拘留, dǎi bǔ 逮捕
ar.ri.val	(n.)	kedatangan	lái dào 来到, dào lái 到来, dào dá 到达
ar.rive	(v.)	datang, tiba	dào dá 到达
ar.ro.gant	(a.)	congkak, sombong	aò màn 傲慢
ar.row	(n.)	anak panah	jiàn 箭

ar.se.nal	(n.)	gudang senjata	bīng gōng chǎng 兵工厂
art	(n.)	seni	yì shuì 艺术
ar.ter.y	(n.)	urat nadi	dòng mài 动脉
ar.ti.cle	(n.)	benda, karangan	wù jiàn 物件, wén zhāng 文章
		ayat	tiáo kǔan 条款
ar.ti.fi.cial	(a.)	buatan	rén zào dė 人造的
		palsu	jiǎ dė 假的
ar.til.ler.y	(n.)	artileri	pào bīng 炮兵
ar.ti.san	(n.)	tukang	gōng jiàng 工匠
ar.tist	(n.)	seniman	yì shù jiā 艺术家
ar.tis.tic	(a.)	yang bersifat seni	yì shù dė 艺术的
as	(conj.)	seperti, sebagai	hǎo xiàng 好象
		karena	yīn wèi 因为
as far as	(adv.)	sepanjang	yuǎn zhì 远至
as for	(conj.)	tentang, mengenai	zhì yú 至于
as good as	(adv.)	sama dengan	gēn ... yī yàng 跟…一样
as if	(conj.)	seperti, bagaikan	hǎo xiàng 好象, fãng fú 仿佛
as it is	(fr.)	apa adanya	bǎo chí yuán zhuàng 保持原状, zhào jiù 照旧
as it were	(fr.)	seperti, bagaikan	hǎo xiàng 好象, fãng fú 仿佛
as soon as	(adv.)	secepat mungkin	yuè kuài yuè hǎo 越快越好
as to	(conj.)	mengenai	zhì yú 至于, guān yú 关于
as.cend	(v.)	naik	shàng shēng 上升
		mendaki	pān dēng 攀登
as.cent	(n.)	hal naik	shàng shēng 上升
		pendakian	dēng gāo 登高
ash	(n.)	abu	huī 灰
a.shamed	(a.)	malu	xiū chǐ 羞耻
a.shore	(adv.)	di darat	zài àn shàng 在岸上
		ke darat	xiàng àn 向岸

ash-tray	(n.)	asbak, tempat abu rokok	yān huī hé 烟灰盒
A.sia	(n.)	benua Asia	Yà zhōu 亚洲
A.sian	(n.)	orang Asia	Yà zhōu rén 亚洲人
	(a.)	yang berhubungan dengan Asia	Yà zhōu dė 亚洲的
A.sian.ness	(n.)	yang bersifat Asia	Yà zhōu xìng 亚洲性
a.side	(adv.)	di sisi,	zài yī biān 在一边,
		di samping	zài páng biān 在旁边
ask	(v.)	bertanya	wèn 问
a.skew	(a.)	miring	wāi xié 歪斜
a.sleep	(a.)	tidur	shùi zhė dė 睡着的
as.par.a.gus	(n.)	asparagus	lú sŭn 芦笋
as.pect	(n.)	aspek, segi	fāng miàn 方面
as.phalt	(n.)	aspal	bó yóu 柏油, lì qīng 沥青
as.pi.ra.tion	(n.)	keinginan, cita-cita, hasrat, aspirasi	yuàn wàng 愿望
as.pire	(v.)	bercita-cita	xiàng wăng 向望, rè wàng 热望
ass	(n.)	keledai	lú 驴
		orang bodoh	dāi rén 呆人, bèn rén 笨人
as.sail	(v.)	menyerang	gōng jī 攻击
as.sem.ble	(v.)	berkumpul	jí hé 集合
as.sem.bly	(n.)	sidang, majelis	jí hùi 集会, yì hùi 议会
as.sent	(v., n.)	menyetujui, persetujuan	zàn chéng 赞成, tóng yì 同意
as.sert	(v.)	menyatakan	xuān chèng 宣称
		mempertahankan	jiān chí 坚持
as.sess	(v.)	menilai, menaksir	píng dìng 评定, gū jì 估计
as.set	(n.)	aset	zī chăn 资产
as.sign	(v.)	menugaskan	zhĭ pài 指派
as.sign.ment	(n.)	tugas, penyerahan	rèn wù 任务, ràng dù 让渡
as.sim.i.late	(v.)	menyamakan, menyesuaikan	tóng hùa 同化

as.sim.i.la.tion	(n.)	asimilasi, percampuran	tóng hùa 同化
as.sist	(v.)	membantu	bāng zhù 帮助
as.sist.ant	(n.)	pembantu, asisten	zhù shǒu 助手
as.so.ci.ate	(n.)	kawan	péng yǒu 朋友
	(v.)	menggabungkan, meng-hubungkan, bergaul	lián hé 联合, jié hè 结合 jiaō jì 交际, jié jiaō 结交
as.so.ci.at.ion	(n.)	persekutuan, perkumpulan pergaulan	xié hùi 协会, tuán tǐ 团体 jiāo jì 交际
as.sume	(v.)	mengandaikan, menduga	jiǎ dìng 假定, yì duàn 臆断
as.sur.ance	(n.)	asuransi, jaminan	bǎo xiǎn 保险, bǎo zhèng 保证
as.sure	(v.)	menjamin, menanggung	bǎo zhèng 保证
asth.ma	(n.)	asma	qì chǔan bìng 气喘病
a.ston.ish	(v.)	mengherankan, heran	lìng rén jīng qí 令人惊奇
a.stray	(adv.)	kesasar, tersesat	mí lù 迷路
as.tro.naut	(n.)	astronaut, angkasawan	tài kōng rén 太空人
as.tro.nau.tess	(n.)	angkasawati	nǚ tài kōng rén 女太空人
as.tron.o.mer	(n.)	ahli falak	tiān wén xué jiā 天文学家
as.tron.o.my	(n.)	astronomi, ilmu falak	tiān wén xué 天文学
as.tro.space	(n.)	ruang angkasa	yu zhou kōng jian 宇宙空间
at	(prep.)	di, pada	zài 在
a.the.ism	(n.)	ateisme	wú shén lùn 无神论
a.the.ist	(n.)	orang yang tak menga-kui adanya Tuhan, ateis	wú shén lùn zhě 无神论者, bù xìn shén zhě 不信神者
ath.lete	(n.)	olahragawan, atlet	yùn dòng jiā 运动员
ath.let.ics	(n.)	olahraga, atletik	yùn dòng 运动
at.las	(n.)	buku peta, atlas	dì tú 地图
at.mos.phere	(n.)	udara, atmosfer	kōng qì 空气, dà qì 大气
at.om	(n.)	atom	yuán zi 原子
a.tom.ic	(a.)	yang berhubungan dengan atom	yuán zi dė 原子的
a.top	(adv.)	di puncak	zài dǐng shàng 在顶上

at.tach	(v.)	menghubungkan	jié hé 结合
		menggabungkan diri	jié hé 结合
		mengikat	xì láo 系牢
at.tack	(v.)	menyerang	gōng jī 攻击, xí jī 袭击
at.tain	(v.)	mencapai	dá dào 达到, dé 得
at.tempt	(n.)	percobaan	chăng shì 尝试
		usaha	nŭ lì 努力
	(v.)	berusaha	chăng shì 尝试, qĭ tú 企图
at.tend	(v.)	merawat, menghadiri	fú shì 服侍, chū xí 出席
at.ten.dant	(n.)	pelayan	fú wù yuán 服务员
		hadirin	chū xí zhě 出席者
at.ten.tion	(n.)	perhatian	zhù yì 注意
at.ten.tive	(a.)	penuh perhatian	liú xīn dė 留心的, zhù yì dė 注意的
at.ti.tude	(n.)	sikap	tài dù 态度, zī shì 姿势
at.tract	(v.)	menarik	xī yĭn 吸引
at.trac.tion	(n.)	daya tarik	xī yĭn lì 吸引力
		atraksi	jīng căi jié mù 精采节目
at.trac.tive	(a.)	menarik hati	dòng rén dė 动人的, yŏu xī yĭn lì dė 有吸引力的
auc.tion	(n.)	lelang	paī mài 拍卖
auc.tion.eer	(n.)	juru lelang	paī mài zhě 拍卖者
au.dit	(v.)	memeriksa pembukuan	zhàng mù jī hé 帐目稽核 chá zhàng 查帐
au.di.tor	(n.)	pendengar	tīng zhòng 听众
		pemeriksa buku	chá zhàng yuán 查帐员
au.di.to.ri.um	(n.)	aula	dà lĭ táng 大礼堂
Au.gust	(n.)	Agustus	bā yuè 八月
au.then.tic	(a.)	sah, asli, otentik	quán weī dė 权威的, zhēn zhèng dė 真正的, zhēn shí dė 真实的

au.thor	(n.)	pengarang	zùo zhě 作者, zuò jiā 作家
au.thor.ess	(n.)	pengarang wanita	nǔ zuò jiā 女作家
au.thor.i.ty	(n.)	kekuasaan	quán lì 权力, quán weī 权威
au.thor.ize	(v.)	memberi kuasa	shòu quán 授权
au.to	(n.)	mobil	qì chē 汽车
au.to.bi.og.ra.phy	(n.)	otobiografi	zì zhuàn 自传
aut.o.crat	(n.)	autokrat	dú cái zhě 独裁者
au.to.graph	(n.)	tanda tangan	qiān hào 签号, qiān míng 签名
		tulisan sendiri	qīn bǐ 亲笔
au.to.mat.ic	(a.)	otomatis	zì dòng dė 自动的
au.to.mat.i.cal ly	(adv.)	secara otomatis	zi dòng di 自动地
aut.o.mo.bile	(n.)	mobil	qì chē 汽车
au.ton.o.my	(n.)	otonomi	zi zhì 自治
au.top.sy	(n.)	pemeriksaan mayat, otopsi	yàn shī 验尸
au.tumn	(n.)	musim gugur	qiū tiān 秋天
aux.il.ia.ry	(a.)	pembantu, penolong	fū zhù dė 辅助的
a.vail	(n.)	guna, faedah	yòng chù 用处, yì chù 益处
	(v.)	berfaedah, membantu	yǒu yì 有益, yǒu bāng zhù 有帮助
a.vail.a.ble	(a.)	tersedia, terpakai	kě yòng dė 可用的
a.venge	(v.)	membalas dendam	bào chóu 报仇
aveng.er	(n.)	penuntut balas	bào chóu zhě 报仇者
av.e.nue	(n.)	jalan besar	dà lù 大路
av.er.age	(a.)	rata-rata	ping jūn dė 平均的
a.void	(v.)	menghindarkan	bì miǎn 避免
a.vow	(v.)	mengakui	gǒng kaī chéng rèn 公开承认
a.wait	(v.)	menunggu	děng hòu 等候, děng dài 等待
a.wake	(a.)	bangun, jaga	xǐng 醒, qīng xǐng 清醒
	(v.)	membangunkan	hùan xǐng 唤醒
a.ward	(n.)	hadiah	jiǎng pǐn 奖品
	(v.)	menghadiahkan	shòu jiǎng 授奖, jiǎng shǎng 奖赏

a.ware	(a.)	sadar	zhī jué dė 知觉的, zhī xī dė 知悉的
a.way	(adv.)	jauh, pergi jauh dari	zài yuǎn chù 在远处, yuǎn lí 远离
aw.ful	(a.)	hebat	feī cháng 非常, lì hài 厉害
		menakutkan	kě wèi dė 可畏的
a.while	(adv.)	sebentar	yī huì ėr 一会儿
awk.ward	(a.)	kaku, canggung	bèn zhuō dė 笨拙的
ax(e)	(n.)	kapak	fǔ tóu 斧头
ax.is	(n.)	poros, sumbu	zhóu 轴

B

ba.by	(n.)	bayi	yīng hái 婴孩
ba.by-sit	(v.)	menjaga bayi	zhào kàn yīng hái 照看婴孩
ba.by-sit.ter	(n.)	penjaga bayi	bǎo mǔ 保姆
bach.e.lor	(n.)	bujang, jejaka	dān shén hàn 单身汉, guāng gùn 光棍
back	(n.)	punggung	bèi 背
back.bone	(n.)	tulang punggung	jí gǔ 脊骨
back.er	(n.)	penyokong	zhī chí zhě 支持者
back.ground	(n.)	latar belakang	bèi jǐng 背景
back.ward	(a.)	terbelakang, cacat mental	lùo hòu 落后
back.wards	(adv.)	mundur	xiàng hòu 向后
ba.con	(n.)	daging asin/asap	xián ròu 咸肉
bac.te.ria	(n.)	bakteri	xì jūn 细菌
bad	(a.)	buruk, jelek	bù hǎo dė 不好的, huái dė 坏的
bad.ly	(adv.)	jelek parah	è liè dė 恶劣的 yán zhòng dė 严重的
bag	(n.)	kantung, tas	dài zǐ 袋子
bag.gage	(n.)	bagasi, barang bawaan	xíng lǐ 行李
bake	(v.)	memanggang	hōng 烘
bak.er	(n.)	tukang roti	miàn bāo shī 面包帅
bak.er.y	(n.)	kamar roti toko roti	miàn bāo fáng 面包房 miàn bāo diàn 面包店
bal.ance	(n.)	neraca, timbangan	píng héng 平衡, tiān píng 天平

bald	(a.)	botak	tū tóu dė 秃头的
ball	(n.)	bola	qiú 球
		pesta dansa	tiào wǔ hùi 跳舞会
bal.let	(n.)	balet	bā lěi wǔ 芭蕾舞
bal.loon	(n.)	balon	qì qiú 气球
ball-point	(n.)	bolpoin, pena atom	yuán zhū bǐ 圆珠笔, yuán zǐ bǐ 原子笔
ball-room	(n.)	ruangan dansa	tiào wǔ chǎng 跳舞场, wǔ tīng 舞厅
bam.boo	(n.)	bambu	zhú 竹
ban	(n.)	larangan	jìn zhǐ 禁止
ba.na.na	(n.)	pisang	xiāng jiāo 香蕉
band	(n.)	tali, pita	dài 带
		sekumpulan pemain musik	yuè dùi 乐队
ban.dage	(n.)	perban	běng dài 绷带
ban.dit	(n.)	penjahat, perampok	tǔ fěi 土匪, qiáng dào 强盗
bank	(n.)	bank	yín háng 银行
		tepi sungai	àn 岸
bank-book	(n.)	buku deposito	cún kuǎn bù 存款簿
bank.er	(n.)	bankir	yín háng jiā 银行家
bank.ing	(n.)	perbankan	yín háng yè 银行业
bank-note	(n.)	uang kertas	chāo piào 钞票
bank.rupt	(v.)	bangkrut	pò chǎn 破产
ban.ner	(n.)	bendera, spanduk	qí zhì 旗帜
ban.quet	(n.)	pesta makan	yàn hùi 宴会
bar	(n.)	batang, palang	tiáo 条, héng mù 横木
		tempat minum-minum	jiǔ bā 酒吧
bar.ba.ri.an	(n.)	orang biadab	yě mán rén 野蛮人
bar.ber	(n.)	tukang cukur	lǐ fà shī 理发师

bare	(a.)	telanjang	chì lǔo dė 赤裸的
bare.faced	(a.)	tidak tahu malu	bù yào liǎn 不要脸
bare.foot	(adv.)	dengan kaki telanjang	chì jiǎo dė 赤脚的
bare.ly	(adv.)	hampir tidak	qìa hǎo 恰好, jǐn jǐn 仅仅, jī hū méi yǒu 几乎没有
bar.gain	(n.)	menawar, tawar-menawar	jiāo yì 交易
		persetujuan	xié yì 协议
bark	(n.)	kulit kayu	shù pí 树皮
		gonggongan	fèi shēng 吠声
	(v.)	menggonggong, menyalak	gǒu fèi 狗吠
barn	(n.)	kandang kuda	mǎ fáng 马房
ba.rom.e.ter	(n.)	barometer	qì yā biǎo 气压表
bar.rack	(n.)	barak	bīng yíng 兵营, yīng fáng 营房
bar.rel	(n.)	tong	dà tǒng 大桶
		laras bedil	qiāng shēn 枪身, qiāng guǎn 枪管
bar.ren	(a.)	mandul, tandus, gersang	pín jí dė 贫瘠的, bù máo dė 不毛的
bar.ri.er	(n.)	rintangan	zǔ ài 阻碍
bar.ter	(v.)	barter, tukar-menukar barang	wù wù jiao huàn 物物交换
base	(n.)	alas, dasar	dǐ 底, jī chǔ 基础
ba.sic	(a.)	pokok, dasar	jī chǔ dė 基础的
ba.sin	(n.)	baskom	shǔi pén 水盆
ba.sis	(n.)	dasar	jī chǔ 基础
bask.et	(n.)	keranjang	lán zi 篮子
bask.et-ball	(n.)	(bola) basket	lán qiú 篮球
bass	(n.)	bas	nán dī yīn 男低音
bas.tard	(n.)	anak haram	sī shēng zi 私生子
bat	(n.)	kelelawar	biān fú 蝙蝠
		bet	qiú pò 球拍

bath	(n.)	mandi	xǐ zǎo 洗澡, mù yù 沐浴
bathe	(v.)	mandi	xǐ zǎo 洗澡, mù yù 沐浴
bath-room	(n.)	kamar mandi	xǐ zǎo fáng 洗澡房, yù shì 浴室
bat.tal.ion	(n.)	batalion	yíng 营
bat.ter.y	(n.)	baterai	diàn chí 电池
		sekelompok meriam	pào bīng lián 炮兵连
bat.tle	(n.)	peperangan	zhàn zhēng 战争
bat.tle.field	(n.)	medan perang	zhàn chǎng 战场
bat.tle.ship	(n.)	kapal perang	zhàn jiàn 战舰
bay	(n.)	teluk	hǎi wān 海湾
bay.o.net	(n.)	bayonet	cì dāo 刺刀
ba.zaar	(n.)	pasar amal, bazar	yì mài shì chàng 义卖市场
be	(v.)	ada	shì 是
beach	(n.)	pantai	shā tàn 沙滩, hǎi tàn 海滩, hǎi bīn 海滨
beak	(n.)	paruh burung	niǎo zhúo 鸟啄, niǎo hùi 鸟喙
beam	(n.)	balok kayu	héng liáng 横梁
		sinar	guāng xiàn 光线
bean	(n.)	kacang	dòu 豆
bean-curd	(n.)	tahu	dòu fǔ 豆腐
bear	(n.)	beruang	xióng 熊
	(v.)	melahirkan	shēng yù 生育, shēng chǎn生产
		menahan	rěn shòu 忍受
beard	(n.)	janggut, jenggot	hú zi 胡子, hú xù 胡须
beast	(n.)	binatang buas	shòu 兽
beat	(v.)	memukul	dǎ 打
beau.ti.ful	(a.)	cantik	měi lì 美丽
beau.ti.fy	(v.)	memperindah	měi hùa 美化, zhuāng shì 装饰
beau.ty	(n.)	kecantikan	měi 美, měi lì 美丽
be.cause	(conj.)	sebab, karena	yīn wèi 因为

be.come	(v.)	menjadi	chéng wéi 成为
bed	(n.)	tempat tidur	chuáng 床
bed.bug	(n.)	kutu busuk	chòu chóng 臭虫
bed.room	(n.)	kamar tidur	qǐn shì 寝室, shùi fáng 睡房
bed.spread	(n.)	penutup tempat tidur	chuáng dān 床单
bed-time	(n.)	waktu tidur	shùi jiào shí jiān 睡觉时间
bee	(n.)	tawon, lebah	mì fēng 蜜蜂
beef	(n.)	daging lembu	niú ròu 牛肉
beef.steak	(n.)	bistik	niú pái 牛排, niú ròu pái 牛肉排
beer	(n.)	bir	pí jǐu 啤酒
beet	(n.)	bit	tián cài 甜菜
bee.tle	(n.)	kumbang	jiǎ chóng 甲虫
be.fit	(v.)	cocok	shì hé 适合
be.fore	(prep.)	sebelum, di muka	yǐ qián 以前, zài qiá miàn 在前面, zǎo yú 早于, xiān yú 先于
be.fore.hand	(a.)	dahulu, di muka	yǐ qián 以前, zài qián 在前
be.friend	(v.)	berlaku seperti sahabat menolong	yǒu hǎo dài rén 友好待人 bāng zhù 帮助
beg	(v.)	meminta, memohon	qǐ qiú 祈求, kěn qiú 恳求
beg.gar	(n.)	pengemis	qǐ gài 乞丐
be.gin	(v.)	mulai	kaī shǐ 开始
be.gin.ner	(n.)	pemula	chū xuè zhě 初学者, shēng shǒu 生手
be.gin.ning	(n.)	permulaan	kaī shǐ 开始
be.grime	(v.)	mengotori	nòng zāng 弄脏
be.grudge	(v.)	iri	jí dù 嫉妒
be.half	(n.)	atas nama	dài biǎo 代表
be.have	(v.)	berkelakuan	jǔ dòng 举动, jǔ zhǐ 举止
be.hav.iour	(n.)	kelakuan	xíng wéi 行为, pǐn xíng 品行

be.head	(v.)	memotong kepala	zhǎn shǒu 斩首, kǎn tóu 砍头
be.hind	(adv.)	di belakang	zài hòu 在后, lùo hòu落后
be.hold	(v.)	melihat, memandang	kàn 看, zhù shì 注视
be.hold.er	(n.)	penonton	páng guān zhě 旁观者
be.ing	(n.)	makhluk, wujud	shēng wù 生物, shí zài 实在
be.lief	(n.)	kepercayaan	xìn yǎng 信仰
be.lieve	(v.)	percaya, mempercayai	xiāng xìn 相信, xìn rèn 信任
be.lit.tle	(v.)	menganggap kecil, meremehkan	xiǎo kàn 小看, qīng shì 轻视
bell	(n.)	lonceng, bel	zhōng 钟, líng 铃
bel.low	(v.)	melenguh	niú hǒu 牛吼
		berteriak	hào jiào 号叫
bel.lows	(n.)	puputan, embusan	fēng xiāng 风箱
bel.ly	(n.)	perut	dǔ zī 肚子
be.long	(v.)	kepunyaan, termasuk	shǔ yú 属于
be.long.ings	(n.)	harta benda	cái chǎn 财产
		barang kepunyaan	sǔo yǒu wù 所有物
be.lov.ed	(a.)	tercinta, kekasih	xīn ài dė 心爱的
be.low	(adv.)	di bawah	zài xià 在下, xià 下
belt	(n.)	ikat pinggang	yāo dài 腰带
bench	(n.)	bangku	cháng dēng 长凳
bend	(v.)	membengkokkan	shǐ wān qū 使弯曲
		membungkuk	wān yāo 弯腰
be.neath	(adv.)	di bawah	zài xià 在下
ben.e.fit	(n.)	keuntungan, manfaat	lì yì 利益
be.queath	(v.)	mewariskan	yí xià 遗下, chuán xià 传下
be.quest	(n.)	warisan	yí chǎn 遗产, yí wù 遗物
ber.i-ber.i	(n.)	beri-beri	jiǎo qì bìng 脚气病
be.seech	(v.)	memohon	kěn qiú 恳求, āi qiú 哀求
be.set	(v.)	mengepung	bāo wéi 包围, wéi gōng 围攻

be.side	(prep.)	di sisi	zài páng biān 在旁边
be.sides	(prep.)	di samping itu,	... yǐ wài …以外,
		lain dari itu	chú lė ... yǐ wài 除了…以外
best	(a.)	terbaik	zùi hǎo 最好
bet	(n.)	pertaruhan, taruhan	dǎ dǔ 打赌, dǔ bó 赌博
be.tray	(v.)	mengkhianati	bèi pàn 背叛
bet.ter	(a.)	lebih baik	gèng hǎo 更好
bet.ter.ment	(n.)	perbaikan	gǎi liáng 改良
be.tween	(prep.)	antara	zài qí zhōng 在其中,
			zài ... zhī jiān 在…之间
be.ware	(v.)	awas, berhati-hati	liú xīn 留心, jǐn fáng 谨防,
			xiǎo xīn 小心
be.yond	(prep.)	di seberang, jauh	zài nà biān 在那边,
			zài yuǎn chù 在远处,
			zài ... yǐ wài 在…以外
Bi.ble	(n.)	Kitab Injil	shèng jīng 圣经
bi.cy.cle	(n.)	sepeda	jiǎo chē 脚车
bid	(v.)	menyuruh, menawar	mìng lìng 命令, chū jià 出价
big	(a.)	besar	dà 大
bill	(n.)	paruh	niǎo zǔi 鸟咀, niǎo hùi 鸟喙
bill	(n.)	daftar, rekening	dān zi 单子, zhàng dān 帐单
		uang kertas	chāo piaò 钞票
bil.liards	(n.)	bilyar	tái qiú 台球
bind	(v.)	mengikat	kǔn 捆, fú 缚, bǎng 绑
		menjilid	zhuāng dìng 装订
bind.cr	(n.)	penjilid buku	zhuāng dìng gōng rén 装订工人
bi.og.ra.phy	(n.)	riwayat hidup, biografi	zhuàn jì 传记
bi.ol.o.gy	(n.)	biologi	shēng wù xúe 生物学
bird	(n.)	burung	niǎo 鸟
birth	(n.)	kelahiran	chū shēng 出生, dàn shēng 诞生

birth.day	(n.)	hari lahir	shēng rì 生日
birth-place	(n.)	tempat lahir	chū shēng dì 出生地
bis.cuit	(n.)	biskuit	bǐng gān 饼干
bish.op	(n.)	uskup	zhǔ jiào 主教
bit	(n.)	sedikit	yī diǎn 一点
bite	(v.)	menggigit	yǎo 咬
bit.ter	(a.)	pahit	kǔ 苦
black	(a.)	hitam	heī 黑, heī sè 黑色
black.board	(n.)	papan tulis	heī bǎn 黑板
black-list	(n.)	daftar hitam	hèi míng dān 黑名单
black.smith	(n.)	pandai besi	tiě jiàng 铁匠
blad.der	(n.)	kandung kemih	páng guāng 膀胱
blade	(n.)	mata pisau	dāo piàn 刀片
blame	(v.)	menyalahkan, mencela	zé bèi 责备, zé guài 责怪
blame.less	(a.)	tidak bersalah	wú zùi 无罪
blank	(a.)	blanko, kosong	kōng bǎi dė 空白的
blan.ket	(n.)	selimut	máo zhān 毛毡, bèi gài 被盖
bleed	(v.)	berdarah	chū xuè 出血
bless	(v.)	memberkati	zhù fú 祝福
blind	(a.)	buta	máng mù 盲目
bloc	(n.)	blok	jí tuán 集团
block	(n.)	balok	mù tóu 木头
		kompleks	qū 区
		blok	jí tuán 集团
block.ade	(n.)	blokade	fēng sǔo 封锁
blood	(n.)	darah	xùe 血
blood.bath	(n.)	pembantaian	dà tú sā 大屠杀
blood.less	(a.)	tidak berdarah	wú xuè dė 无血的
		kurang darah	pín xuè 贫血
blood-suck.er	(n.)	lintah darat	xī xuè dòng wù 吸血动物, xī xuè gǔi 吸血鬼

bloom	(v.)	berbunga	kaī huā 开花
	(n.)	bunga	huā 花
blos.som	(n.)	bunga	huā 花
	(v.)	berbunga	kaī huā 开花
blot	(n.)	noda bintik	wū diǎn 污点
blot.ter	(n.)	pengering/pengisap tinta	xī mò zhǐ 吸墨纸
blouse	(n.)	blus	nǚ shàng yī 女上衣,
			nǚ chèn shān 女衬衫
blow	(v.)	meniup	chuī 吹
blue	(a.)	biru	lán 兰, lán sè 兰色
bluc.print	(n.)	cetakan biru, denah	lán tú 兰图
blunt	(a.)	tumpul	dùn dė 钝的
boar	(n.)	babi hutan	yě zhū 野猪
board	(n.)	papan	bǎn 板
		badan, dewan	wěi yuán hùi 委员会
boast	(v.)	membual	chuī niú 吹牛
		menyombongkan diri	zì kuā 自夸
boat	(n.)	kapal, sampan	xiǎo chuán 小船
bod.y	(n.)	badan, tubuh	shēn tǐ 身体
bod.y-guard	(n.)	pengawal	wèi dùi 卫队, wèi bīng 卫兵
boil	(v.)	mendidih, merebus	fèi 沸, zhǔ 煮
bold	(a.)	berani	dà dǎn dė 大胆的
bomb	(n.)	bom	zhà dàn 炸弹
bomb.er	(n.)	bomber, pembom	hōng zhà jī 轰炸机
bona fide	(a.)	jujur	zhēn chéng dė 真诚的
		dapat dipercaya	kě kào dė 可靠的
bond	(n.)	perjanjian	qì yùe 契约
		surat obligasi	gōng zài 公债
		hubungan, pertalian	guān xì 关系, lián jié 联结
bone	(n.)	tulang	gǔ 骨, gǔ gé 骨骼
bo.nus	(n.)	bonus	hóng lì 红利, jiǎng jīn 奖金

book	(n.)	buku	shū 书
	(v.)	mendaftarkan, memesan	dēng jì 登记
book-case	(n.)	almari buku	shū chú 书橱, shū jia 书架
book-keep.er	(n.)	pemegang buku	bù jì yuán 簿记员
book-keep.ing	(n.)	pembukuan	bù jì 簿记
book.let	(n.)	buku kecil	xiǎo cè zi 小册子
book-mark	(n.)	pembatas buku	shū qiān 书签
book.sell.er	(n.)	penjual buku	shū shāng 书商
book.shop	(n.)	toko buku	shū diàn 书店
book-stall	(n.)	stan buku	shū tàn zi 书摊子
book.store	(n.)	toko buku	shū diàn 书店
book.worm	(n.)	kutu buku	shū chóng 书虫, shū daī zi 书呆子
boot	(n.)	sepatu bot	cháng tǒng xuē 长统靴
bor.der	(n.)	batas, pinggir	biān jiè 边界, biān yuán 边缘
bore	(v.)	membor	zuàn kǒng 钻孔
		menjemukan	lìng rén yàn fán 令人厌烦
bor.row	(v.)	meminjam	jiè 借
bo.som	(n.)	dada	xīong 胸
boss	(n.)	majikan, bos	gōng tóu 工头, lǎo bǎn 老板
bot.a.nist	(n.)	ahli tumbuh-tumbuhan	zhí wù xué jiā 植物学家
bot.a.ny	(n.)	ilmu tumbuh-tumbuhan	zhí wù xué 植物学
both	(a.)	kedua-duanya	shuāng fāng 双方
both.er	(v.)	menyusahkan	shǐ rén fán nǎo 使人烦恼, dǎ rǎo 打扰
bot.tle	(n.)	botol	píng zi 瓶子
bot.tom	(n.)	dasar	dǐ 底
bot.tom.less	(a.)	tak berdasar	wú dǐ dė 无底的
bound	(v.)	melompat	tiào 跳
	(n.)	perbatasan	jiè xiàn 界限
bound.a.ry	(n.)	tapal batas	jiè xiàn 界限, biān jiè 边界

bound.less	(a.)	tak ada batasnya	wú xiàn dė 无限的
bour.geois	(n.)	borjuis	zī chǎn jiē jí fèn zi 资产阶级分子
bour.geoi.sie	(n.)	golongan borjuis	zī chǎn jiē jí 资产阶级
bow	(n.)	busur	gōng 弓
		tunduk kepala	jū gōng 鞠躬
	(v.)	menundukkan kepala	jū gōng 鞠躬
bow.el	(n.)	usus	cháng 肠
bowl	(n.)	mangkuk	wǎn 碗
box	(n.)	peti	xiāng 箱
box.er	(n.)	petinju	quán jī jia 拳击家, quán jī yuán 拳击员
box.ing	(n.)	tinju	quán jī 拳击, quán shù 拳术
boy	(n.)	anak laki-laki	nán hái zi 男孩子
boy.cott	(n.)	boikot	dǐ zhì 抵制
boy.hood	(n.)	masa kanak-kanak	tóng nián shí dài 童年时代
brag	(v.)	membual	chuī niú 吹牛
brag.gart	(n.)	pembual	chuī niú dà wáng 吹牛大王
brain	(n.)	otak	nǎo 脑
brain.less	(a.)	bodoh	yú bèn 愚笨, méi yǒu nǎo jīn dė 没有脑筋的
braise	(v.)	tim, mengetim	dùn 炖
brake	(n.)	rem	zhì dòng jī 制动机
branch	(n.)	dahan, cabang	zhī 枝
brand	(n.)	merek dagang	shāng biāo 商标
brass	(n.)	kuningan	huáng tóng 黄铜
brave	(a.)	berani	yǒng gǎn 勇敢
brave.ly	(adv.)	dengan berani	yǒng gǎn dī 勇敢地
bread	(n.)	roti	miàn bāo 面包
breadth	(n.)	lebarnya, luasnya	guǎng kùo 广阔
break	(v.)	pecah	pò liè 破裂

break.fast	(n.)	makan pagi	zǎo cān 早餐
break.wa.ter	(n.)	dinding pemecah ombak	fáng bō tí 防波堤
breast	(n.)	dada	xiōng 胸, xiōng táng 胸膛
breath	(n.)	napas	qì xī 气息, hū xī 呼吸
breathe	(v.)	bernapas	hū xī 呼吸
breed	(v.)	membiakkan, beternak	fán zhí 繁殖, sì yǎng 饲养
breeze	(n.)	angin sepoi-sepoi	wēi fēng 微风
bribe	(v.)	menyogok	xíng hùi 行贿, hùi lù 贿赂
	(n.)	uang sogok	hùi lù qián 贿赂钱
brib.er	(n.)	penyuap	xíng hùi rén 行贿人
brick	(n.)	bata	zhuān 砖, zhuān tóu 砖头
bride	(n.)	pengantin perempuan	xīn niáng 新娘
bride.groom	(n.)	pengantin laki-laki	xīn láng 新郎
brides.maid	(n.)	gadis pengiring pengantin	nǔ bīn xiāng 女傧相
brides.man	(n.)	pria pengiring pengantin	nan bīn xiāng 男傧相
bridge	(n.)	jembatan	qiáo 桥
brief	(a.)	pendek, singkat	jiǎn duǎn dė 简短的
brief.ing	(n.)	uraian ringkas	jiǎn bào 简报
bri.gade	(n.)	brigade	lǚ 旅
brig.a.dier	(n.)	brigadir jenderal	zhǔn jiàng 准将
bright	(adj.)	terang	guāng míng 光明
bright.en	(v.)	berkilau-kilauan	fā guāng 发光, shǐ guāng míng 使光明
bril.liant	(a.)	berkilauan	huī huáng dė 辉煌的, guāng huī dė 光辉的
brim	(n.)	tepi, pinggir	biān yuán 边缘
bring	(v.)	membawa	dài lái 带来, nǎ lái 拿来
broad	(a.)	luas	guǎng kùo 广阔
broad.cast	(v.)	menyiarkan	guǎng bō 广播, bō sòng 播送
	(n.)	siaran	guǎng bō 广播
broil	(v.)	memanggang	kǎo 烤

bro.ker	(n.)	makelar	qián kè 掮客, jíng jì rén 经纪人
bron.chi.tis	(n.)	bronkitis	zhī qì guǎn yán 支气管炎
bronze	(n.)	perunggu	qīng tóng 青铜
brooch	(n.)	bros, peniti	xiōng zhēn 胸针, shì zhēn 饰针
brook	(n.)	anak sungai	xiǎo xī 小溪, xiǎo hé 小河
broom	(n.)	sapu	sǎo zhǒu 扫帚
broom-stick	(n.)	gagang sapu	sào zhǒu bǐng 扫帚柄
broth.er	(n.)	saudara laki-laki	xiōng dì 兄弟
brow	(n.)	dahi	é 额, méi 眉
brown	(a.)	cokelat (warna)	hé sè 褐色, zōng sè 棕色
brush	(n.)	sikat	shuā zi 刷子
bru.tal	(a.)	kejam	cán rěn 残忍
bub.ble	(n.)	gelembung	pào 泡, shǔi pào 水泡
buck.et	(n.)	ember	diào tǒng 吊桶, shǔi tǒng 水桶
buck.le	(n.)	kancing, gesper	kòu zi 扣子
bud	(n.)	tunas	yá 芽
Bud.dha	(n.)	Budha	fú 佛
Bud.dhism	(n.)	agama Budha	fú jiào 佛教
Bud.dhist	(n.)	penganut Budha	fú jiào tú 佛教徒
bud.get	(n.)	anggaran (belanja)	yù suàn àn 预算案
buf.fa.lo	(n.)	kerbau	shǔi niú 水牛
bug	(n.)	kutu, kutu busuk	chòu chóng 臭虫
build	(v.)	mendirikan	jiān zhù 建筑
build.ing	(n.)	gedung, bangunan	jian zhù wù 建筑物
bulb	(n.)	bola lampu, umbi bunga	dēng pào 灯泡, qiú jīng 球茎
bull	(n.)	sapi jantan	gōng niú 公牛
bul.let	(n.)	peluru	zǐ dàn 子弹
bul.le.tin	(n.)	surat edaran, siaran kilat	gōng bào 公报, gào shì 告示
bump	(v.)	menabrak	pèng 碰, zhuàng 撞
bunch	(n.)	seikat, serangkaian	yī shù 一束, yī chuàn 一串
bun.dle	(n.)	seikat, seberkas	shù 束, kǔn 捆

bur.den	(n.)	beban	dàn zi 担子, zhòng dàn 重担
bu.reau	(n.)	biro	jú 局
bu.reau.cra.cy	(n.)	birokrasi	guān liáo zhǔ yì 官僚主义
bu.reau.crat	(n.)	birokrat	guān liáo 官僚
bur.glar	(n.)	pencuri	yè dào 夜盗
bur.i.al	(n.)	penguburan	mái zàng 埋葬
burn	(v.)	membakar	shāo 烧
burst	(n.)	letusan	baò zhà 爆炸, bào fā 爆发
bur.y	(v.)	mengubur	mái zàng 埋葬
bus	(n.)	bis	gōng gòng qì chē 公共汽车
bush	(n.)	semak belukar	xiǎo guàn mù 小灌木
busi.ness	(n.)	urusan	shì wù 事务
		perdagangan, bisnis	shēng yì 生意
bus.y	(a.)	sibuk	máng lù 忙碌
but	(conj.)	tetapi	dàn shì 但是, kě shì 可是
but.cher	(n.)	tukang jagal	tú fū 屠夫
but.ter	(n.)	mentega	nǎi yóu 奶油, niú yóu 牛油
but.ter.fly	(n.)	kupu-kupu	hú dié 蝴蝶
but.tock	(n.)	pantat	pì gǔ 屁股
but.ton	(n.)	kancing	niǔ kòu 钮扣
	(v.)	mengancingkan	kòu 扣, kòu shàng 扣上
but.ton.hole	(n.)	lubang kancing	niǔ kòu kǒng 纽扣孔
buy	(v.)	membeli	mǎi 买
by	(prep.)	dengan, dekat, oleh	yóu 由, yòng 用, kào jìn 靠近, bei 被
by.gone	(a.)	yang lalu, yang lampau	gùo qù dė 过去的
bye-bye	(n.)	selamat tinggal	zài jiàn 再见
by-path	(n.)	jalan kecil	xiǎo lù 小路, zhī lù 支路
by-stand.er	(n.)	penonton	páng guān zhě 旁观者

C

cab	(n.)	taksi	chū zū qì chē 出租汽车
cab.bage	(n.)	kubis, kol	juǎn xīn cài 卷心菜,
			bāo xīn cài 包心菜
cab.in	(n.)	kabin	chuán cāng 船舱, jī cāng 机舱
cab.i.net	(n.)	lemari, kabinet	chú zi 橱子, nèi gé 内阁
ca.ble	(n.)	kabel	diàn xiàn 电线
		surat kawat, telegram	diàn bào 电报
ca.ca.o	(n.)	pohon cokelat	kě kě shù 可可树,
		buah cokelat	kě kě zi 可可子
cad	(n.)	bajingan, bangsat	wú lài 无赖, liú máng 流氓
cad.re	(n.)	kader	gàn bù 干部
cage	(n.)	sangkar, kurungan	lóng 笼
cake	(n.)	kue	bǐng 饼, gāo 糕
ca.lam.i.ty	(n.)	bencana	zaī huò 灾祸
cal.cu.late	(v.)	menghitung	jì suàn 计算
cal.cu.la.tor	(n.)	kalkulator	jì suàn jī 计算机
		juru hitung	jì suàn zhě 计算者
cal.en.dar	(n.)	kalender	rì lì 日历
calf	(n.)	anak sapi	xiǎo niú 小牛
call	(v.)	memanggil	jiào 叫
		menelepon	dǎ diàn huà 打电话
		mengunjungi	fǎng wèn 访问
calm	(a.)	tenang	píng jìng 平静, zhèn jìng 镇静
cam.el	(n.)	unta	luò tūo 骆驼

cam.er.a	(n.)	kamera	zhào xiàng jī 照相机
cam.er.a-man	(n.)	juru potret	zhào xiàng shī 照相师
		juru kamera	shè yǐng shī 摄影师
camp	(n.)	perkemahan	yíng 营, yě yíng 野营
cam.paign	(n.)	perang	zhàn yì 战役
cam.pus	(n.)	kampus	xiào yuàn 校苑
can	(n.)	kaleng	guàn tóu 罐头
	(v.)	dapat, sanggup	néng 能, hùi 会
ca.nal	(n.)	terusan	yùn hé 运河
ca.na.ry	(n.)	burung kenari	jīn sī què 金丝雀
can.cel	(v.)	membatalkan	qǔ xiaō 取消
can.cer	(n.)	kanker	aí 癌
can.di.date	(n.)	kandidat	hòu xuǎn rén 候选人
can.dle	(n.)	lilin	là zhú 蜡烛
can.dy	(n.)	kembang gula, permen	táng gǔo 糖果
cane	(n.)	tongkat	shǒu zhàng 手杖
		rotan	téng tiaó 藤条
can.non	(n.)	meriam	dà pào 大炮
can.not	(v.)	tidak dapat	bù néng 不能
ca.noe	(n.)	perahu, kano	dú mù zhōu 独木舟
can.vas	(n.)	kain layar, kain terpal	fān bù 帆布
cap	(n.)	kopiah, peci	mào zi 帽子, biàn mào 便帽
ca.pa.ble	(a.)	sanggup, dapat	yǒu néng lì 有能力
ca.pac.i.ty	(n.)	kesanggupan	néng lì 能力
		muatan	róng liàng 容量
cape	(n.)	tanjung	hǎi jiǎo 海角
cap.i.tal	(n.)	modal	zī jīn 资金
		ibu kota	shǒu dù 首都
		huruf besar	dà xiě zì mǔ 大写字母
	(a.)	yang pokok	zhǔ yào dė 主要的

cap.i.tal.ism	(n.)	kapitalisme	zī běn zhǔ yì 资本主义
cap.i.tal.ist	(n.)	kapitalis	zī běn jiā 资本家,
			zī běn zhǔ yì zhě 资本主义者
cap.sule	(n.)	kapsul	kōng xīn jiāo wán 空心胶丸
cap.tain	(n.)	kapten	shàng wèi 上尉
		nakhoda	chuán zhǎng 船长
		pemimpin regu	dùi zhǎng 队长
cap.tive	(n.)	tawanan	fú lú 俘虏
cap.ture	(n.)	penangkapan	bǔ huò 捕获, bǔ huò wù 捕获物,
			zhàn lì pǐn 战利品
car	(n.)	mobil	qì chē 汽车
car.a.van	(n.)	kafilah	shāng dùi 商队, lǚ xíng dùi 旅行队
		(mobil) karavan	dà péng chē 大篷车
car.bon	(n.)	karbon	tàn 碳
card	(n.)	kartu	zhǐ pái 纸牌, kǎ pian 卡片
card.board	(n.)	karton, kardus	zhǐ bǎn 纸板, kǎ zhǐ 卡纸
car.di.nal	(a.)	utama	zhǔ yaò dė 主要的
	(n.)	kardinal	hóng yī zhǔ jiào 红衣主教,
			zhǔ jiaò 主教
care	(n.)	hati-hati	zhù yì 注意, xiǎo xīn 小心
		kesusahan	yōu lù 忧虑
		perawatan	hù lǐ 护理
ca.reer	(n.)	pekerjaan, karier	zhuān yè 专业, zhí yè 职业
		jalan hidup	jīng lì 经历
care.ful	(a.)	hati-hati	xiǎo xīn dė 小心的
care.less	(a.)	tidak hati-hati	bù xiǎo xīn 不小心
care.taker	(n.)	pengurus	guǎn lǐ yuán 管理员
car.go	(n.)	muatan	hùo wù 货物
		kapal barang	hùo chuán 货船
car.i.ca.ture	(n.)	karikatur	fěng cì huà 讽刺画

car.ni.val	(n.)	karnaval	kuang huān jié 狂欢节
car.pen.ter	(n.)	tukang kayu	mù jiàng 木匠
car.pet	(n.)	karpet, permadani	dì tān 地毯
car.riage	(n.)	kereta	chē liàng 车辆
car.ri.er	(n.)	pembawa, pengangkut	bān yùn rén 搬运人, bān yùn gōng rén 搬运工人
car.rot	(n.)	wortel	hū luó bō 胡萝卜
car.ry	(v.)	membawa	dài 带, xī dài 携带
cart	(n.)	kereta, pedati, gerobak	shǒu chē 手车
car.tel	(n.)	persatuan kaum pengusaha	lóng duàn zǔ zhī 垄断组织
car.ton	(n.)	kotak kardus	zhǐ bǎn hé 纸板盒
car.toon	(n.)	gambar kartun	màn hùa 漫画, kǎ tong 卡通
		film gambar	dòng huà piàn 动画片
car.toon.ist	(n.)	kartunis	màn huà jiā 漫画家
carve	(v.)	mengukir	diāo kè 雕刻
carv.er	(n.)	pengukir	diāo kè jiā 雕刻家
case	(n.)	peti, kotak	xiāng zi 箱子, hé zi 盒子
		hal, kejadian	wèn tí 问题, shì jiàn 事件
		perkara, kasus	àn jiàn 案件
		penyakit	bìng zhēng 病症
cash	(n.)	uang kontan	xiàn jìn 现金, xiàn kǔan 现款, xiàn qián 现钱
	(v.)	menguangkan	dùi xiàn 兑现, dùi huàn xiàn jīn 兑换现金
cash.ier	(n.)	kasir	chū nà yuán 出纳员
ca.si.no	(n.)	tempat berjudi, kasino	dǔ bó guǎn 赌博馆, yú lè chǎng 娱乐场
cast	(v.)	melemparkan	tóu 投, paō 抛
cas.tle	(n.)	benteng, kastil	chéng bǎo 城堡

cat	(n.)	kucing	māo 猫
cat.a.logue	(n.)	katalog, daftar buku	mù lù 目录, tú shū mù lù 图书目录
catch	(v.)	menangkap	zhuō 捉, bǔ zhuō 捕捉
cat.e.gor.y	(n.)	kategori, jenis	zhǒng lèi 种类
cat.er.pil.lar	(n.)	ulat	máo chóng 毛虫
Cath.o.lic	(a.)	Katolik	tiān zhǔ jiaò dė 天主教的
		orang Katolik	tiān zhǔ jiaò tu 天主教徒
Ca.thol.i.cism	(n.)	agama Katolik	tiān zhǔ jiaò 天主教
cat.tle	(n.)	binatang ternak	jiā chù 家畜
		sapi	niú 牛
cause	(n.)	sebab, lantaran	yuán yīn 原因, lǐ yóu 理由
		perkara	sù sòng 诉讼
	(v.)	menyebabkan	yǐn qǐ 引起
cau.tion	(n.)	hati-hati, peringatan	jǐn shèn 谨慎, xiǎo xīn 小心
			zhōng gào 忠告, jǐng gào 警告
cau.tious	(a.)	hati-hati	xiǎo xīn dė 小心的,
			jǐn shèn dė 谨慎的
cav.al.ry	(n.)	pasukan berkuda, kavaleri	qí bīng 骑兵
cave	(n.)	gua	dòng 洞, shān dòng 山洞
cease	(v.)	berhenti	tíng zhǐ 停止
cease-fire	(n.)	gencatan senjata	tíng zhàn 停战, tíng hǔo 停火
cease.less	(a.)	tak henti-hentinya,	bù tíng dė 不停的,
		terus-menerus	ji xu bù duan dė 继续不断的
cede	(v.)	menyerahkan, mengalah	gē ràng 割让, rùng bù 让步
ceil.ing	(n.)	langit-langit	tiān huā bǎn 天花板
cel.e.brate	(v.)	merayakan	qìng zhù 庆祝
cel.e.bra.tion	(n.)	perayaan	qìng zhù hùi 庆祝会
cell	(n.)	sel	láo fáng 牢房
cel.lar	(n.)	gudang di bawah tanah	dì xià shì 地下室
ce.ment	(n.)	semen	shuǐ ní 水泥

cem.e.tery	(n.)	pekuburan, tanah makam	fén mù 公墓
cen.ser	(n.)	pedupaan, anglo dupa	xiāng lú 香炉
cen.sor	(n.)	sensor	shěn chá 审查, jiǎn chá 检查
cen.sus	(n.)	sensus, cacah jiwa	hǔ kǒu diào chá 户口调查, pǔ chá 普查
cent	(n.)	sen	fēn 分
cen.ti.me.tre	(n.)	sentimeter	lí mǐ 厘米
cen.ti.pede	(n.)	kelabang	wú gōng 蜈蚣
cen.tral	(a.)	pusat	zhōng xīn dė 中心的, zhōng yāng dė 中央的
cen.tral.i.za.tion	(n.)	sentralisasi, pemusatan	zhōng yāng jí quán 中央集权, jí zhōng 集中
cen.tre	(n.)	pusat	zhōng xīn 中心
cen.tu.ry	(n.)	abad	shì jì 世纪
cer.e.mo.ny	(n.)	upacara	yí shì 仪式
cer.tain	(a.)	tentu	yī dìng 一定, bì rán 必然
cer.tain.ly	(adv.)	tentu saja	yī dìng 一定, bì rán 必然
cer.tif.i.cate	(n.)	sertifikat, surat keterangan	zhèng míng shū 证明书
cer.ti.fy	(v.)	mengesahkan	zhèng míng 证明
chain	(n.)	rantai	lián tiáo 链条, tiě lián 铁链
chair	(n.)	kursi	yǐ zi 椅子
chair.man	(n.)	ketua	zhǔ xí 主席, hùi zhǎng 会长
chair-wom.an	(n.)	ketua (wanita)	nǔ zhǔ xí 女主席
chalk	(n.)	kapur tulis	fěn bǐ 粉笔
chal.lenge	(n.)	menantang	tiáo zhàn 挑战
chal.leng.er	(n.)	penantang	tiáo zhàn zhě 挑战者
cham.ber	(n.)	kamar	shì 室, fáng jiān 房间
cham.pagne	(n.)	sampanye	xiāng bīn jiǔ 香槟酒
cham.pion	(n.)	juara, kampiun	guān jūn 冠军, yōu shèng zhě 优胜者
chance	(n.)	kesempatan	jī hùi 机会

change	(n.)	perubahan	biàn huà 变化
		uang kecil	xiǎo qián 小钱, líng qián 零钱
		uang kembali	zhǎo tóu 找头, zhǎo qián 找钱
	(v.)	mengubah	gǎi biàn 改变, gēng huàn 更换
change.a.ble	(a.)	berubah-ubah	yì biàn dė 易变的
chan.nel	(n.)	selat, saluran	hǎi xiá 海峡, shǔi dáo 水道
cha.os	(n.)	kekacauan	hùn luàn 混乱
chap.ter	(n.)	bab	zhāng 章
char.ac.ter	(n.)	watak	xìng gé 性格, tè xìng 特性
		huruf	wén zì 文字, zì tǐ 字体
char.coal	(n.)	arang	mù tàn 木碳
charge	(v.)	menuduh	kòng gào 控告, suǒ jià 索价
		menetapkan harga	dìng jià 定价
		memuati	zhuāng tián 装填
		menyerang	jìn gōng 进攻
char.i.ty	(n.)	kedermawanan	cí shàn 慈善
charm	(n.)	mantera	fú zhòu 符咒, hù shēn fù 护身符
		daya tarik	xī yǐn lì 吸引力, mó lì 魔力
chart	(n.)	peta	dì tuí 地图
chase	(v.)	memburu, mengejar	zhūi bǔ 追扑, zhūi gǎn 追赶
chas.sis	(n.)	casis	chē jià 车架
chat	(v.)	mengobrol	xián tán 闲谈
chauf.feur	(n.)	sopir	sī jì 司机
cheap	(a.)	murah	pián yí 便宜
cheap.en	(v.)	menurunkan harga	jiǎn jià 减价
cheat	(v.)	menipu	qī piàn 欺骗
check	(v.)	memeriksa, mengecek	jiǎo chá 校查, hē dùi 核对
		menahan, mengekang	zǔ zhǐ 阻止, zhì zhǐ 制止
	(n.)	cek	zhī piào 支票
check.book	(n.)	buku cek	zhī piào bù 支票簿
check-up	(n.)	pemeriksaan kesehatan	tǐ gé jiǎn chá 体格检查

cheek	(n.)	pipi	jiá 颊, miàn jiá 面颊
cheer	(v.)	menggembirakan	lìng rén gāo xìng 令人高兴
		bersorak	huān hū 欢呼
cheer.ful	(a.)	gembira	kuài lè 快乐, gāo xìng 高兴
cheese	(n.)	keju	gān luò 干酪
chem.i.cal	(n.)	kimiawi	huà xué pǐn 化学品
chem.ist	(n.)	ahli kimia	huà xué jiā 化学家
chem.is.try	(n.)	ilmu kimia	huà xué 化学
cheque	(n.)	cek	zhī piào 支票
chess	(n.)	catur	qì 棋
chest	(n.)	dada	xiong 胸
		peti	xiāng 箱
chew	(v.)	mengunyah	jiaó 嚼
chick.en	(n.)	anak ayam, daging ayam	xiǎo jī 小鸡, jī ròu 鸡肉
chick.en-pox	(n.)	cacar air	shǔi dòu 水痘
chief	(n.)	kepala, pemimpin	lǐng xìu 领袖, shǒu lǐng 首领
	(a.)	yang utama	zhǔ yaò dė 主要的
child	(n.)	anak	xiǎo hái 小孩
child.hood	(n.)	masa kanak-kanak	yòu nián shí dài 幼年时代
child.ish	(a.)	kekanak-kanakan	yòu zhì 幼稚, hái zi qì 孩子气
chil.dren	(n.)	anak-anak	hái zi mén 孩子们
chill	(n.)	udara dingin	hán léng 寒冷
chim.ney	(n.)	cerobong asap	yān cōng 烟囱
chin	(n.)	dagu	ké 颏, xià bā ké 下巴颏
chi.na	(n.)	porselen, tembikar	cí qì 瓷器
chis.el	(n.)	pahat	zaó 凿
choice	(n.)	pilihan	xuán zé 选择
choc.o.late	(n.)	cokelat (makanan)	qiǎo kè lì táng 巧克力搪
choir	(n.)	paduan suara	hé chàng duì 合唱队, gē yǒng duì 歌咏队
chol.e.ra	(n.)	penyakit kolera	hùo luàn 霍乱

choose	(v.)	memilih	xuǎn zé 选择
chop	(v.)	memotong	qiē sùi 切碎
chop.sticks	(n.)	sumpit	kuài zi 筷子
cho.rus	(n.)	koor	hé chàng dùi 合唱队
Christ	(n.)	Kristus	jī dū 基督
Chris.tian	(n.)	orang Kristen	jī dū jiào tú 基督教徒
Chris.tian.i.ty	(n.)	agama Kristen	jī dū jiào 基督教
Christ.mas	(n.)	hari Natal	shèng dàn jié 圣诞节
chron.ic	(a.)	kronis	màn xìng 慢性
church	(n.)	gereja	jiào táng 教堂
church.yard	(n.)	halaman gereja	jiào táng yuán dì 教堂园地
		tanah pekuburan	mù dì 墓地
ci.gar	(n.)	cerutu	xuě qié yān 雪茄烟
cig.a.rette	(n.)	rokok	xiāng yān 香烟
cin.e.ma	(n.)	bioskop	diàn yǐng 电影
cir.cle	(n.)	lingkaran	yuán quān 圆圈, yuán zhōu圆周
	(v.)	mengelilingi	huán rǎo 环绕
cir.clet	(n.)	lingkaran kecil	xiǎo quān 小圈, xiǎo huán 小环
cir.cuit	(n.)	keliling	huán xíng 环行, xún húi 巡迴
cir.cu.lar	(a.)	bulat	yuán dė 圆的
cir.cu.late	(v.)	beredar	xún huán 循环, liú tōng 流通
cir.cu.la.tion	(n.)	peredaran	xún huán 循环, liú tōng 流通
cir.cum.stance	(n.)	keadaan	qíng kuàng 情况, qíng xíng情形
cir.cus	(n.)	sirkus	mǎ xì 马戏
cit.i.zen	(n.)	warga negara	gōng mín 公民
cit.i.zen.ship	(n.)	hak warga negara	gōng mín quán 公民权
		kewarganegaraan	guó ji 国籍
cit.y	(n.)	kota	chéng shi 城市
civ.il	(a.)	sipil	shì mín dė 市民的
		perdata	mín shì dė 民事的
		sopan	yǒu lǐ mào dė 有礼貌的

ci.vil.ian	(n.)	orang sipil	píng mín 平民
civ.il.i.za.tion	(n.)	peradaban	wén míng 文明
civ.il.ize	(v.)	menjadikan beradab	kaī huà 开化, jiào huà 教化
claim	(n.)	tuntutan	yaò qiú 要求
clap	(v.)	bertepuk tangan	paī shǒu 拍手, gǔ zhǎng 鼓掌
clash	(v.)	berselisih	chōng tū 冲突
class	(n.)	kelas	bān 班, jí 级, bān jí 班级
		golongan	jiē jí 阶级, jiē céng 阶层
		jenis	zhǒng lèi 种类
clas.si.fi.ca.tion	(n.)	klasifikasi	fēn lèi 分类
clas.si.fy	(v.)	menggolongkan	fēn lèi 分类
class-mate	(n.)	kawan sekelas	tóng bān tóng xué 同班同学
clause	(n.)	anak kalimat	zǐ jù 子句
claw	(n.)	cakar	zhǎo 爪
clay	(n.)	tanah liat	nián tǔ 粘土
clean	(a.)	bersih	qīng jié 清洁, gān jìng 干净
	(v.)	membersihkan	nòng qīng jié 弄清洁, nòng gān jìng 弄干净
clear	(a.)	jelas, terang	qīng chǔ 清楚, qíng lǎng 晴朗
		jernih	qīng xī 清晰
clear.ly	(adv.)	dengan jelas	qīng chǔ di 清楚地, míng lǎng di 明朗地
cler.gy.man	(n.)	pendeta	mù shī 牧师
clerk	(n.)	juru tulis	shū jì 书记
clev.er	(a.)	pintar, pandai	cōng míng 聪明
cli.ent	(n.)	klien	dàng shì rén 当事人
		pelanggan	gù kè 顾客
		pembeli	mǎi zhǔ 买主
cliff	(n.)	tebing tinggi	yái 崖, xuán yái 悬崖
cli.mate	(n.)	hawa, iklim	qì hòu 气候

cli.max	(n.)	puncak	dǐng diǎn 顶点
climb	(v.)	memanjat	pān dēng 攀登
cling	(v.)	melekat	nián zhù 粘住
clin.ic	(n.)	klinik	zhěn liáo sǔo 诊疗所
clip	(n.)	penjepit	jiā zi 夹子
clip.ping	(n.)	guntingan koran	jiǎn bào 剪报
clique	(n.)	klik	jí tuán 集团, pài xì 派系
cloak	(n.)	mantel	wài tào 外套, wài yī 外衣
clock	(n.)	jam	zhōng 钟
clock.wise	(a.)	menurut arah jarum jam	shùn shí zhēn 顺时针
close	(v.)	menutup	guān 关
	(a.)	dekat	jiē jìn 接近
clos.et	(n.)	kamar kecil, kakus	cè sǔo 厕所, biàn sǔo 便所
cloth	(n.)	kain	bù 布
clothes	(n.)	pakaian	yī fu 衣服
cloud	(n.)	awan	yún 云
cloud.less	(a.)	tidak berawan	wú yún dė 无云的
cloud.y	(a.)	berawan, mendung	yǒu yún dė 有云的, dūo yún dė 多云的, yìn tiān 阴天
clown	(n.)	badut	xiǎo chǒu 小丑
club	(n.)	kelab, kumpulan	jù lè bù 俱乐部, shè tuán 社团
clum.sy	(a.)	kaku, kikuk	bèn zhūo 笨拙
clus.ter	(n.)	sekelompok	yī qún 一群
		berkelompok	chéng qún 成群
coach	(n.)	kereta	dà mǎ chē 大马车
		pelatih	jiáo liàn 教练, zhǐ dǎo yuán 指导员
coal	(n.)	batu bara	méi 煤
co.a.li.tion	(n.)	koalisi	lían hé 联合
coal-mine	(n.)	tambang batu bara	méi kùang 煤矿

coarse	(a.)	kasar	cū 粗, cū cāo 粗糙
coast	(n.)	tepi laut, pantai	hǎi sàn 海岸, hǎi bīn 海滨
coat	(n.)	mantel, jas	wài tào 外套, wài yī 外衣
cob.bler	(n.)	tukang sepatu	bǔ xié jiàng 补鞋匠
cob.ra	(n.)	kobra	yǎn jìng shé 眼镜蛇
cob-web	(n.)	sarang labah-labah	zhī zhū wǎng 蜘蛛网
cock	(n.)	ayam jantan, jago	xióng jī 雄鸡, gōng jī 公鸡
cock.tail	(n.)	koktil	jī wěi jiǔ 鸡尾酒
co.coa	(n.)	bubuk cokelat minuman cokelat	kě kě fěn 可可粉, kě kě chá 可可茶
co.co.nut	(n.)	buah kelapa	yé zi 椰子
cof.fee	(n.)	kopi	kā feī 咖啡
cof.fee-house	(n.)	warung kopi	kā fēi guǎn 咖啡馆
cof.fer	(n.)	peti simpanan	bǎo xiǎn xiāng 保险箱
cof.fin	(n.)	peti mati	guān cái 棺材, guān mù 棺木
coil	(v.)	membelit	pán rǎo 盘绕
coin	(n.)	mata uang, uang logam	hùo bì 货币, yìng bì 硬币
cold	(n.)	dingin	léng 冷
col.lapse	(v.)	runtuh, roboh	dǎo tā 倒塌, kǔa tái 垮台
col.lar	(n.)	kerah baju	lǐng zi 领子
col.league	(n.)	teman sekerja, rekan	tóng liáo 同僚, tóng shì 同事
col.lect	(v.)	mengumpulkan	shōu jí 收集
col.lec.tion	(n.)	kumpulan	shōu cáng 收藏, sōu jí 搜集
col.lec.tive	(a.)	kolektif	jí tǐ dė 集体的
col.lege	(n.)	perguruan tinggi	xué yuàn 学院
col.lo.qui.al	(a.)	bahasa sehari-hari	kǒu yǔ dė 口语的
co.lon	(n.)	titik dua	mǎo hào 冒号
colo.nel	(n.)	kolonel	shàng xiào 上校
co.lo.ni.al	(a.)	penjajahan, kolonial	zhí mín dė 殖民的, zhí mín dì dė 殖民地的

co.lo.ni.al.ism	(n.)	kolonialisme, penjajahan	zhí mín zhǔ yì 殖民主义
col.on.ist	(n.)	penjajah	zhí mín zhě 殖民者
col.o.ny	(n.)	koloni, daerah jajahan	zhí mín dì 殖民地
col.our	(n.)	warna	yán se 颜色
colt	(n.)	anak kuda	xiǎo mǎ 小马
col.umn	(n.)	tiang ruangan, kolom barisan	zhù zi 柱子, lán 栏 zòng dùi 纵队
co.ma	(n.)	koma, pingsan	hūn mí 昏迷
comb	(n.)	sisir	shū zi 梳子
com.bat	(n.)	pertempuran	zhàn dòu 战斗
com.bi.na.tion	(n.)	kombinasi, gabungan	lián hé 联合
com.bine	(v.)	menggabungkan, bergabung	lián hé 联合
come	(v.)	datang	lái 来
com.e.dy	(n.)	sandiwara yang menggembirakan	xǐ ju 喜剧
com.fort	(n.)	kenikmatan, kesenangan, hiburan	shū fú 舒服, ān wèi 安慰
com.fort.a.ble	(a.)	nikmat, senang	shū fú 舒服
com.ic	(a.)	lucu, yang gembira	huá jī 滑稽, xǐ jù dė 喜剧的
	(n.)	komik, cerita bergambar	lián huán huà 连环画
com.ma	(n.)	koma	dòu hào 逗号, dòu diǎn 逗点
com.mand	(n.)	perintah	mìng lìng 命令
	(v.)	memerintah	zhǐ hūi 指挥, mìng lìng 命令
com.man.der	(n.)	komandan	zhǐ hūi guān 指挥官
com.mem.o.rate	(v.)	memperingati	jì niàn 纪念
com.mence	(v.)	mulai	kaı shǐ 开始
com.mend	(v.)	mempercayakan, memuji	tuī jiàn 推荐, chēng zàn 称赞
com.ment	(v.)	memberi ulasan, mengkritik	píng lùn 评论, pī píng 批评

com.merce	(n.)	perdagangan	shāng yè 商业
com.mer.cial	(a.)	komersial	shāng yè dė 商业的
com.mis.sion	(n.)	komisi	wĕi tūo 委托, wĕi rèn 委任
com.mis.sion.er	(n.)	komisaris	zhuān yuán 专员, wĕi yuán委员
com.mit	(v.)	mempercayakan, menitipkan	fù tūo 付托, wĕi tūo 委托
com.mit.tee	(n.)	komite, panitia	wĕi yuán hùi 委员会
com.mod.i.ty	(n.)	barang dagangan, komoditi	shāng pĭn 商品
com.mo.dore	(n.)	komodor	hăi jūn zhŭn jiàng 海军准将
com.mon	(a.)	umum, biasa	gòng tóng dė 共同的, pŭ tóng dė 普通的
com.mon.er	(n.)	rakyat biasa	pìng mín 平民
com.mon.ly	(adv.)	biasanya	píng cháng 平常, tōng cháng 通常
com.mon.place	(a.)	biasa	píng fán 平凡, píng cháng 平常
com.mon.wealth	(n.)	persemakmuran	lián bāng 联邦
com.mu.ni.cate	(v.)	menyampaikan, mengkomunikasikan	chuán bu 传布, chuán dá 传达
com.mu.ni.ca.tion	(n.)	komunikasi	chuán bo 传播, tōng xìn 通信
com.mu.nism	(n.)	komunisme	gòng chăn zhŭ yì 共产主义
com.mu.nist	(n.)	komunis	gòng chăn zhŭ yì zhĕ 共产主义者
com.mu.ni.ty	(n.)	masyarakat	shè hùi 社会
com.pact	(a.)	kompak, bersatu	tuán jié yī zhì 团结一致, jĭn mì 紧密
com.pan.ion	(n.)	teman, kawan	bàn lŭ 伴侣, péng yŏu 朋友
com.pa.ny	(n.)	perseroan	gōng sī 公司
		rombongan	tuán 团, dùi 队
		tamu	kè rén 客人
com.par.a.tive	(a.)	dengan perbandingan	bĭ jiào 比较
com.pare	(v.)	memperbandingkan	bĭ jiaŏ 比较

com.par.i.son	(n.)	perbandingan	bǐ jiaǒ 比较
com.part.ment	(n.)	kompartemen	chē shì 车室
		ruang tidur	fáng jián 房间
com.pass	(n.)	kompas	luó pán 罗盘,
			zhǐ nán zhēn 指南针
com.pas.sion	(n.)	perasaan kasihan	lián mǐn 怜悯, tóng qíng 同情
com.pel	(v.)	memaksa	qiáng pò 强迫
com.pen.sa.tion	(n.)	ganti rugi, bayaran	pei cháng 赔偿, cháng fù 偿付
com.pen.sate	(v.)	mengganti kerugian	péi cháng 赔偿
com.pete	(v.)	bersaing	jìng zhēng 竞争
com.pe.tence	(n.)	kesanggupan	shèng rèn 胜任
		kemampuan	néng lì 能力
com.pe.tent	(a.)	mampu	yǒu néng lì dė 有能力的
		sanggup	shèng rèn dė 胜任的
com.pe.ti.tion	(n.)	persaingan, pertandingan	jìng zhēng 竞争, jìng sài 竞赛
com.pet.i.tive	(a.)	bersaing	jìng zhēng dė 竞争的
com.pile	(v.)	mengumpulkan dan menyusun	biān zuǎn 编纂, biān jí 编辑
com.plain	(v.)	mengeluh, mengadu	sù kǔ 诉苦, kòng gào 控告
com.plaint	(n.)	keluhan, pengaduan	bào yuàn 抱怨, shēn sù 申诉
com.ple.ment	(n.)	pelengkap	bǔ chōng 补充
com.plete	(a.)	lengkap, sempurna	wán quán 完全
	(v.)	menyelesaikan	wán chéng 完成
com.plex	(a.)	kompleks	fù zá 复杂
com.plex.ion	(n.)	air muka, rupa	miàn sè 面色
com.pli.cate	(v.)	menyukarkan	fù zá hua 复杂化
		menyulitkan	shǐ fù zá 使复杂
com.pli.ca.tion	(n.)	komplikasi	fù zá 复杂,
			cùo zōng fù zá 错综复杂,
			bìng fā zhèng 并发症

com.ply	(v.)	menyetujui, mengizinkan	tóng yì 同意, dā yìng 答应
com.po.nent	(n.)	komponen, bagian	chéng fèn 成分, bù fèn 部分
com.pose	(v.)	mengarang	xiě zuò 写作
com.pos.er	(n.)	komposer	zuò qǔ jiā 作曲家
com.po.si.tion	(n.)	karangan, komposisi	zuò wén 作文, zuò qǔ 作曲
com.pound	(v.)	menggabungkan	zǔ hé 组合
com.pre.hend	(v.)	memahami	lǐ jiě 理解
		terdiri dari	bāo hán 包含
com.pre.hen.sion	(n.)	pengertian, pemahaman	lǐ jiě lì 理解力
com.press	(v.)	menyingkat	yā sù 压缩
		kompres	yǎn 罨
com.prise	(v.)	meliputi, berisi	bāo gūa 包括, bāo hán 包含
com.pro.mise	(n.)	kompromi	tǔo xié 妥协
com.pul.sion	(n.)	paksaan	qiáng pò 强迫, qiáng zhì 强制
com.pul.so.ry	(a.)	terpaksa	qiáng pò dė 强迫的, qiáng zì dė 强制的
		wajib	bì xū dė 必须的
com.pute	(v.)	memperhitungkan	jì suàn 计算
		menaksir	gū jì 估计
		memakai komputer	shǐ yòng diàn nǎo 使用电脑
com.put.er	(n.)	komputer, mesin hitung	diàn nǎo 电脑, jì suàn jī 计算机
com.put.er.ese	(n.)	istilah komputer	diàn nǎo shù yǔ 电脑术语
		bahasa komputer	diàn nǎo yǔ yán 电脑语言
com.put.er.ite	(n.)	pekerja komputer	diàn nǎo rén yuán 电脑人员
		penggemar komputer	diàn nǎo mí 电脑迷
com.put.er.i.zation	(n.)	komputerisasi	diàn nǎo huà 电脑化
com.put.er.like	(a.)	seperti komputer	xiàng diàn nǎo dė 象电脑的
com.put.er.man	(n.)	ahli komputer	diàn nǎo xué jiā 电脑学家
		teknisi komputer	diàn nǎo jì shī 电脑技师
com.rade	(n.)	kawan, kamerad	tóng zhì 同志
con.ceal	(v.)	bersembunyi, menyembunyikan	yǐn cáng 隐藏

con.cede	(v.)	mengakui	chéng rèn 承认
con.ceit	(n.)	kesombongan	zì fù 自负, zì gāo 自高, zì dà 自大
con.ceive	(v.)	membayangkan, menggambarkan	xiǎng xiàng 想象
		hamil	huài yùn 怀孕
con.cen.trate	(v.)	memusatkan	jí zhōng 集中
con.cen.tra.tion	(n.)	konsentrasi, pemusatan	jí zhōng 集中
con.cept	(n.)	paham, pengertian, konsep	gài nián 概念
con.cep.tion	(n.)	pengertian, gambaran	gài niàn 概念, xiǎng xiàng 想象
		pembuahan konsepsi	gòu sī 构思
con.cern	(n.)	urusan, kemasygulan	shì wù 事务, guà niàn 挂念
		perusahaan	qì yè 企业, shāng háng 商行
con.cern.ing	(prep.)	mengenai	guān yú 关于
con.cert	(n.)	konser	yīn yùe hùi 音乐会
	(v.)	mengatur, merencanakan	bù zhì 布置, jì huà 计划
con.ces.sion	(n.)	konsesi	ràng bù 让步, tè xǔ 特许, zū ràng 租让
con.cil.i.ate	(v.)	mendamaikan	tiáo jiě 调解, tiáo tíng 调停
con.cise	(a.)	ringkas, singkat	jiǎn míng dė 简明的, jiǎn yào 简要的
con.clude	(v.)	menyudahi	jié shù 结束
		menyimpulkan	zǒng jié 总结
con.clu.sion	(n.)	kesimpulan	jié lùn 结论
con.cord	(n.)	persesuaian	hé xié 和谐
con.crete	(a.)	konkret	jù tǐ dė 具体的
		berwujud	yǒu xíng dė 有形的
con.cu.bine	(n.)	selir, gundik	qiė 妾
con.cur	(v.)	setuju	tóng yì 同意
con.demn	(v.)	mengutuk	qiǎn zé 谴责, zhǐ ze 指责
		menghukum	chǔ jué 处决
con.di.ment	(n.)	bumbu masak	tiáo wèi pǐn 调味品

con.di.tion	(n.)	keadaan, syarat	qíng xíng 情形, tiáo jiàn 条件
con.duct	(n.)	kelakuan	xíng wéi 行为
	(v.)	memimpin, menuntun	zhǐ huī 指挥, yǐn dǎo 引导
con.duc.tor	(n.)	konduktor	shòu piaò yuán 售票员
		dirigen	yīn yuè zhǐ huī 音乐指挥
con.fer	(v.)	menganugerahkan	shòu yú 授予
		berunding	shāng liáng 商量
con.fer.ence	(n.)	konferensi	hùi yì 会议
		permusyawaratan	xié shāng hùi 协商会
		muktamar	dà hùi 大会
con.fess	(v.)	mengakui	gōng rèn 供认, chéng rèn 承认
		berterus terang	tǎn pǎi 坦白
con.fes.sion	(n.)	pengakuan	chéng rèn 承认
con.fi.dant	(n.)	teman karib	zhī xīn péng yǒu 知心朋友
con.fide	(v.)	mempercayakan	xìn rèn 信任, wěi tūo 委托
con.fi.dence	(n.)	kepercayaan	xìn rèn信任
con.fi.dent	(a.)	yakin	què xīn 确信, yǒu xīn xìn dė 有信心的
con.fi.den.tial	(a.)	rahasia	jī mì 机密
		intim	qìn xiá 亲狎, qīn mì 亲密
con.fine	(v.)	mengurung, membatasi	jiān jìn 监禁, xiàn zhí 限制
con.firm	(v.)	membenarkan	zhèng zhí 证实
con.flict	(n.)	konflik	chōng tū 冲突
con.front	(v.)	berhadapan muka	dùi kàng 对抗
		mempertemukan	dùi zhì 对质
con.fuse	(v.)	membingungkan	shǐ rén hūn luàn 使人混乱
con.fu.sion	(n.)	kebingungan	huāng luàn 慌乱, hūn luàn 混乱
con.fute	(v.)	membantah, menyangkal	fǎn bó 反驳, bó chì 驳斥
con.gen.i.tal	(a.)	bawaan	xiān tiān dė 先天的
con.grat.u.late	(v.)	mengucapkan selamat	zhù hè 祝贺, gōng xǐ 恭禧

con.grat.u.la.tion	(n.)	ucapan selamat	zhù he 祝贺 , daò xǐ 道喜
con.gress	(n.)	kongres	dà hùi 大会
		Dewan Perwakilan Rakyat	guó hùi 国会
con.junc.tion	(n.)	kata penghubung	lián jiē cí 连接词, lián cí 连词
con.nect	(v.)	menghubungkan	lián jiē 连接,lián xì 联系
con.nec.tion	(n.)	hubungan	gūan xì 关系
con.quer	(v.)	menaklukkan, me-ngalahkan	zhēng fú 征服, kè fú 克服
con.quer.or	(n.)	penakluk	zhàn shèng zhě 战胜者, zhèng fú zhě 征服者
con.quest	(n.)	kemenangan	zhēng fú 征服
con.science	(n.)	suara hati	liáng xīn 良心
con.scious	(a.)	sadar	zhī jué 知觉
con.sen.sus	(n.)	persetujuan, konsensus	yī zhì 一致
con.sent	(v.)	menyetujui	tóng yì 同意
con.se.quence	(n.)	akibat	jié gǔo 结果, hòu gǔo 后果
con.sid.er	(v.)	menganggap, mempertimbangkan	rèn wéi 认为, kǎo lù 考虑
con.sid.er.able	(a.)	penting	zhòng yào dė 重要的
con.sign	(v.)	menyerahkan	jiāo fù 交付
con.sign.ment	(n.)	konsinyasi	jì xiāo 寄销, jì mài 寄卖
con.sist	(v.)	terdiri dari	yóu...zǔ chéng 由…组成, yóu...gòu chéng 由…构成
con.sis.tent	(a.)	konsisten	qián hoù yī zhì 前后一致, yán xíng yī zhì 言行一致
con.sole	(v.)	menghibur	ān wèi 安慰, wèi wèn 慰问
con.sol.i.da.tion	(n.)	konsolidasi, penguatan	gǒng gù 巩固
con.so.nant	(n.)	huruf mati, konsonan	fǔ yīn 辅音
con.sort	(n.)	pasangan suami-istri	pèi ǒu 配偶
	(v.)	berteman	jié bàn 结伴

con.stant	(a.)	tetap	bu bìan dė 不变的
		tabah hati	jiān zhēn 坚贞, jiān dìng 坚定
con.sti.tu.tion	(n.)	undang-undang dasar, konstitusi	xiàn fa 宪法
con.struct	(v.)	membangun, mendirikan	jiàn zhù 建筑, jiàn shė 建设
con.struc.tion	(v.)	pembangunan, susunan	jiàn shė 建设, gòu zào 构造
con.struc.tive	(a.)	bersifat membangun, konstruktif	jiàn shė xìng dė 建设性的
con.sul	(n.)	konsul	lǐng shì 领事
con.su.late	(n.)	konsulat	lǐng shì guǎn 领事馆
con.sult	(v.)	minta nasihat, berunding	qíng jiào 请教, shàng liáng 商量
con.sul.tant	(n.)	konsultan	gù wén 顾问
con.sume	(v.)	memakai, menghabiskan	xiāo fĕi 消费, xiāo hào 消耗
con.sum.er	(n.)	konsumen	xiāo fèi zhě 消费者
		pemakai	yòng hù 用户
con.sump.tion	(n.)	konsumsi, pemakaian	xiāo fèi 消费
con.tact	(n.)	kontak, hubungan	jiē chù 接触
con.tain	(v.)	berisi, mengandung	hán yǒu 含有, bāo hán 包含
con.tainer	(n.)	wadah	róng qì 容器
con.temn	(v.)	memandang rendah	qīng mie 轻蔑
		meremehkan	miǎo shì 藐视
con.tem.po.ra.ry	(a.)	zaman sekarang	xiàn dài dė 现代的
		sezaman	tóng shí dài rén 同时代人
		sebaya	tóng bèi 同辈
con.tempt	(n.)	memandang rendah	qīng miè 轻蔑, miǎo shì 藐视
con.tend	(v.)	bersaing, berdebat	biàn lùn 辩论, tǎo lùn 讨论
con.tent	(a.)	puas, senang	mǎn zú 满足, mǎn yì 满意
con.tents	(n.)	isi	nèi róng 内容
con.test	(n.)	pertandingan	bǐ sài 比赛
con.test.ant	(n.)	kontestan	bǐ sài zhě 比赛者, jìng zhēng zhě 竞争者

con.text	(n.)	konteks	shàng xià wén 上下文, wén qì 文气
con.tin.ent	(n.)	kontinen, benua	dà lù 大陆
con.tin.ue	(v.)	berlangsung, meneruskan	jì xù 继续, lián xù 连续
con.tin.u.ous	(a.)	terus-menerus	jì xù bù duàn dė 继续不断的
con.tra.band	(n.)	selundupan, barang gelap	zǒu sī 走私, wéi jìn pǐn 违禁品
con.tra.cep.tion	(n.)	kontrasepsi	bì yùn 避孕
con.tract	(n.)	perjanjian, kontrak	qì yùe 契约, hé tóng 合同
	(v.)	susut, memendek	shōu su 收缩, sù duǎn 缩短
con.trac.tor	(n.)	kontraktor	dìng yùe rén 定约人, chéng bāo rén 承包人
con.tra.dict	(v.)	menyangkal, membantah	fǒu rèn 否认, fǎn bó 反驳
con.tra.dic.tion	(n.)	penyangkalan	fǎn bo 反驳
		kontradiksi	máo dùn 矛盾
con.tra.ry	(a.)	berlawanan	xiāng fǎn dė 相反的
con.trast	(n.)	kontras	dùi bǐ 对比, dùi zhào 对照
con.trib.ute	(v.)	menyokong, menyumbang	juān zhu 捐助
con.trol	(v.)	mengontrol, menguasai	kòng zhì 控制
con.tro.ver.sial	(a.)	kontroversial, yang menimbulkan persengketaan	yǐn qǐ zhēng lùn dė 引起争论的
con.tro.vert	(v.)	berdebat, berdiskusi	biàn lùn 辩论, tǎo lùn 讨论
con.ve.ni.ence	(n.)	kesenangan, kemudahan	ān yì 安逸, fāng biàn 方便
con.ve.ni.ent	(a.)	memudahkan	fāng bìan dė 方便的
		menyenangkan	ān yì dė 安逸的
con.ver.sa.tion	(n.)	percakapan	hùi hùa 会话, tán hùa 谈话
con.verse	(a.)	sebaliknya	xiāng fǎn dė 相反的
		yang terbalik	diān dǎo dė 颠倒的
con.ver.sion	(n.)	perubahan	zhuǎn biàn 转变, zhuǎn huà 转化
con.vert	(v.)	mengubah	gǎi biàn 改变
con.vex	(a.)	cembung	tú 凸
con.vey	(v.)	mengangkut	yùn sòng 运送
		menyampaikan	chuán dá 传达

con.vince	(v.)	meyakinkan	shuō fú 说服
con.voy	(n.)	pengawalan	hù sòng 护送, hù yùn 护运
cook	(v.)	memasak	zhǔ 煮
cool	(a.)	sejuk	liáng shǔang 凉爽
		dingin	léng dàn 冷淡
cool.ie	(n.)	kuli	kǔ lì 苦力
cool.ly	(adv.)	sejuk	liáng shuǎng 凉爽
coop	(n.)	sangkar	lóng 笼
co-op.er.a.tion	(n.)	kerja sama	hé zuò 合作
co-pilot	(n.)	asisten pilot, ko-pilot	fù jià shǐ yuán 副驾驶员, fù fēi xíng yuán 副飞行员
cop.per	(n.)	tembaga	tóng 铜
cop.y	(v.)	menyalin	chǎo xiě 抄写, téng xiě 誊写, fù xiě 复写
	(n.)	salinan	fù běn 付本, kǎo bèi 拷贝
cop.y.right	(n.)	hak cipta	bǎn quán 版权, zhù zùo quán 著作权
cord	(n.)	tali	shēng zi 绳子
cork	(n.)	sumbat botol, gabus	mù sè 木塞
corn	(n.)	jagung	yù shǔ shǔ 玉蜀黍
cor.ner	(n.)	sudut	jiǎo 角
corpse	(n.)	mayat	shī tǐ 尸体
cor.rect	(v.)	membetulkan	gaǐ zhèng 改正
	(a.)	benar	zhèng qùe 正确
cor.re.spond	(v.)	surat-menyurat	tōng xìn 通信
cor.re.spon.dent	(n.)	wartawan, koresponden	tōng xùn yuán 通讯员, jì zhě 记者
cor.ri.dor	(n.)	lorong dalam rumah, koridor	zǒu láng 走廊
cor.rupt	(a.)	korup	tān wū 贪污
cor.rup.tion	(n.)	korupsi	tān wū 贪污

cor.rupt.or	(n.)	koruptor	tān wū zhě 贪污者
cos.met.ic	(n.)	kosmetik	huà zhuāng pǐn 化装品
cost	(v.)	berharga	zhí 值
	(n.)	biaya	fèi yòng 费用
cost.ly	(a.)	mahal	áng gùi dė 昂贵的
cos.tume	(n.)	pakaian	fú zhuāng 服装
cot.tage	(n.)	pondok kecil, gubuk	xiǎo wu 小屋, máo wū 茅屋
cot.ton	(n.)	kapas	mián huā 棉花
cot.ton-mill	(n.)	pabrik pemintal	mián fǎng chǎng 棉纺厂, shā chǎng 纱厂
cough	(n.)	batuk	ké sòu 咳嗽
coun.cil	(n.)	dewan, majelis	wěi yuán hùi 委员会, lǐ shì hùi 理事会, píng yì hùi 评议会
coun.sel	(n.)	perundingan	hùi tán 会谈
coun.sel.lor	(n.)	penasihat	gù wèn 顾问
count	(v.)	menghitung	jì suàn 计算
coun.ter	(n.)	meja tempat pembayaran	gùi tái 柜台
	(adv., v.)	berlawanan	xiāng fǎn dė 相反的
coun.ter.feit	(a.)	palsu, tiruan	wěi zào dė 伪造的, jiǎ mào dė 假冒的
count.less	(a.)	tak terhitung	wú shù dė 无数的, shù bù qīng 数不清
coun.try	(n.)	desa, negeri	xiāng cūn 乡村, gúo jiā 国家
coun.try.man	(n.)	orang desa orang sebangsa orang sekampung	xiāng xià rén 乡下人 tóng bāo 同胞 tóng xiāng 同乡
coun.try.side	(n.)	desa, daerah luar kota	xiāng cūn 乡村
coun.ty	(n.)	kabupaten, daerah	xiàn 县, dì qū 地区
coup.le	(n.)	sepasang suami-istri	yī dùi 一对 fū fu 夫妇, fū qī 夫妻
cou.pon	(n.)	kupon	pèi jǐ piào 配给票

cour.age	(n.)	keberanian	yǒng qì 勇气
course	(n.)	perjalanan	lù chéng 路程
		pelajaran	kè chéng 课程
court	(n.)	istana, pengadilan	gōng diàn 宫殿, fǎ yuàn 法院
court.eous	(a.)	sopan	yǒu lǐ mǎo dė 有礼貌的
cour.te.sy	(n.)	kesopanan	lǐ maò 礼貌
court.yard	(n.)	halaman, pelataran	yuàn zi 院子
cous.in	(n.)	saudara sepupu (pria)	táng xiōng dì 堂兄弟,
			biǎo xiōng dì 表兄弟
		saudara sepupu (wanita)	táng jiě mèi 堂姐妹,
			biǎo jiě mèi 表姐妹
cov.er	(v.)	menutup	gài 盖, zhē gài 遮盖, yǎn gài 掩盖
	(n.)	tutup	gài zi 盖子, zhē gài wù 遮盖物
		bungkus	fēng pí 封皮
cov.et.ous	(a.)	tamak	tān xīn dė 贪心的
cow	(n.)	sapi betina, sapi	mǔ niú 母牛, niú 牛
cow.ard	(n.)	penakut, pengecut	nuò fū 懦夫
cow.boy	(n.)	koboi	niú láng 牛郎, niú zǎi 牛仔
crab	(n.)	kepiting	páng xiè 螃蟹
crack	(n.)	retak, celah	liè féng 裂缝
	(v.)	retak	pò liè 破裂
crack.er	(n.)	petasan, mercon	baò zhú 爆竹
		kue kering	bǐng gān 饼干
cra.dle	(n.)	buaian, ayunan	yáo lán 摇篮
craft	(n.)	keterampilan tangan	shǒu yì 手艺
		kemahiran	jì qiǎo 技巧
crash	(n.)	tubrukan, tabrakan	pèng zhuàng 碰撞
crawl	(v.)	merangkak, merayap	pá xíng 爬行
cray.on	(n.)	krayon	là bǐ 蜡笔
cra.zy	(a.)	gila	fēng kuáng dė 疯狂的

cream	(n.)	kepala susu, krim	rŭ yóu 乳油
cre.ate	(v.)	menciptakan	chuàng zào 创造
cre.a.tion	(n.)	ciptaan	chuàng zào wù 创造物, chuàng zùo pĭn 创造品
cre.a.tive	(a.)	kreatif	yŏu chuàng zào lì dė有创造力的
cre.a.tor	(n.)	pencipta	chuàng zào zhě 创造者
crea.ture	(n.)	makhluk	shēng wù 生物
cred.i.ble	(a.)	dapat dipercaya	kě kào dė 可靠的
cred.it	(n.)	kepercayaan	xìn yòng 信用
		utang	jì zhàng 记账, dài kuăn 贷款
		nama baik	róng yù 荣誉, shēng wàng 声望
cred.it.a.ble	(a.)	yang dapat dipuji	zhí dé zàn yáng dė 值得赞扬的
cred.i.tor	(n.)	piutang, kreditor	zhài quán rén 债权人, dài fāng 贷方
creep	(v.)	merangkak	pá 爬
creep.er	(n.)	binatang melata	pá chóng 爬虫
cre.mate	(v.)	membakar mayat	hŭo zàng 火葬
cre.ma.tor.i.um	(n.)	krematorium, tempat pembakaran mayat	hŭo zàng chăng 火葬场
cres.cent	(n.)	bulan muda, bulan sabit	xīn yùe 新月, méi yuè 眉月
crew	(n.)	anak buah (kapal)	chuán yuán 船员
crick.et	(n.)	jengkerik	xī shuài 蟋蟀
crime	(n.)	kejahatan	zùi xíng 罪行
crim.i.nal	(a.)	jahat	fàn zúi dė 犯罪的
	(n.)	penjahat	zùi fàn 罪犯, zùi rén 罪人
crim.son	(n.)	merah padam	shēn hóng sè 深红色
crip.ple	(n.)	orang pincang	bŏ zi 跛子
cri.sis	(n.)	krisis, kemelut	wēi jī 危机, kŏng huang 恐慌
crit.ic	(n.)	kritikus	pī píng jiā 批评家, pìng lùn jiā 评论家

crit.i.cal	(a.)	genting, gawat	weī jí 危急
		bersifat kritikan	pī píng dė 批评的,
			pī pàn dė 批判的
crit.i.cism	(n.)	kritikan	pī pìng 批评
crit.i.cize	(v.)	mengkritik	pī píng 批评
croc.o.dile	(n.)	buaya	è yú 鳄鱼
cro.ny	(n.)	teman karib	lǎo péng yǒu 老朋友
		kroni	zhì yǒu 挚友
crook	(n.)	lekuk	wān qū 弯曲
crop	(n.)	panen	shōu hùo 收获, shōu chéng 收成
cross	(n.)	salib, tanda silang	shí zì jià 十字架,
			shí zì xíng 十字形
	(v.)	menyeberang	héng dù 横渡, dù guò 渡过
		menyilang	jiāo chǎ 交叉
cross-roads	(n.)	perempatan, persimpangan	shí zì jiē 十字街
crow	(n.)	burung gagak	wū yā 乌鸦
	(v.)	berkokok	tí 啼
crowd	(n.)	orang banyak, khalayak ramai	rén qún 人群, qún zhòng 群众
crown	(n.)	mahkota	huáng guàn 皇冠, wáng guàn 王冠
	(v.)	menobatkan	jiā miǎn 加冕
cru.cial	(a.)	kritis, gawat	jué dìng dė 决定的
		penting sekali	jǐn yào guān tóu 紧要关头
crude	(a.)	kasar	cū cāo 粗糙
cru.el	(a.)	kejam	cán rěn 残忍
crumb	(n.)	remah-remah	sùi piàn 碎片
crum.ble	(v.)	meremukkan	nòng sùi 弄碎
crush	(v.)	memeras, menghancurkan	yā zhà 压榨, yā sùi 压碎
cry	(v.)	menangis, berteriak	kū 哭, jiào hǎn 叫喊
crys.tal	(n.)	kristal	shǔi jīng 水晶

crys.tal.li.za.tion	(n.)	kristalisasi	jié jīng 结晶
cube	(n.)	kubus	lì fāng xíng 立方形, lì fāng tǐ 立方体
cu.bic	(a.)	kubik	lì fāng dė 立方的, lì fāng tǐ dė 立方体的
cu.cum.ber	(n.)	ketimun	huáng guā 黄瓜
cuff	(n.)	manset	xiù kǒu 袖口
cul.ti.vate	(v.)	mengolah tanah memelihara	gēng zhòng 耕种, gēng zùo耕作 zāi péi 栽培, yǎng zhí 养殖
cul.ti.va.tor	(n.)	petani, pemelihara	gēng zhòng zhě 耕种者, zāi péi zhě 栽培者
cul.ture	(n.)	kebudayaan	wén huà 文化
cun.ning	(a.)	cerdik, licik	líng qiǎo 灵巧, jiǎo húa 狡猾
cup	(n.)	cangkir	bèi zi 杯子
cup.board	(n.)	lemari makanan	shí chú 食橱
cup-ful	(n.)	secangkir penuh	mǎn bēi 满杯
cure	(v.)	menyembuhkan, meng-obati	yī zhì 医治, zhì liáo 治疗
cu.ri.os.i.ty	(n.)	rasa ingin tahu	haó qí xīn 好奇心
cu.ri.ous	(a.)	ingin tahu, aneh	haò qí 好奇
curl	(n.)	ikal, keriting	juǎn fa 卷发
cur.ren.cy	(n.)	mata uang	huò bì 货币
cur.rent	(n.)	arus (listrik, air)	diàn liú 电流
curse	(v.)	mengutuk	zǔ zhòu 诅咒, zhòu mà 咒骂
cur.tain	(n.)	korden, tirai	chuāng lián 窗廉, mù 幕
curve	(n.)	garis lengkung, kurva	qū xiàn 曲线
cush.ion	(n.)	bantal, alas duduk	zhěn tóu 枕头, zùo diàn 坐垫
cus.tom	(n.)	adat, kebiasaan	fēng sú 风俗, xí gùan 习惯
cus.toms	(n., pl.)	pabean, bea, cukai	guān shùi 关税, hǎi guān 海关
cus.tom.er	(n.)	langganan	gù kè 顾客
cut	(n.)	memotong	gē 割, qiē 切

cy.cle	(n.)	putaran, peredaran	zhōu qī 周期, xún huán 循环
		sepeda	zì xíng chē 自行车, jiǎo chē 脚车
cyl.in.der	(n.)	silinder	yuán zhù tǐ 园柱体, yuán tǒng 园筒
cyst.itis	(n.)	radang kandung kemih	páng guāng yán 膀胱炎

D

dad	(n.)	ayah	bā bā 爸爸
dag.ger	(n.)	pisau, belati	bí shǒu 匕首
dai.ly	(a.)	sehari-hari, tiap hari	rì cháng dė 日常的, měi rì dė 每日的
	(adv.)	tiap hari	měi rì 每日, tiān tiān 天天
	(n.)	surat kabar harian	rì bào 日报
dair.y	(n.)	perusahaan susu	niú nǎi chǎng 牛奶场, niú nǎi fáng 牛奶房
dair.y.maid	(n.)	wanita pemerah susu	jǐ nǎi nǔ gōng 挤奶女工
dair.y.man	(n.)	pria pemerah susu	jǐ nǎi gōng rén 挤奶工人
dam	(n.)	tanggul	bà 坝, shǔi zhá 水闸
dam.age	(n.)	kerusakan	sǔn huài 损坏
damp	(a.)	lembab	cháo shī 潮湿
damp.en	(v.)	membasahi	nòng shī 弄湿
dance	(n.)	dansa	wǔ dǎo 舞蹈
	(v.)	berdansa, menari	tiào wǔ 跳舞
danc.er	(n.)	penari	wǔ dǎo yuán 舞蹈员, wǔ nǔ 舞女
dan.dy	(n.)	pria pesolek	huā huā gōng zi 花花公子
dan.ger	(n.)	bahaya	wēi xiǎn 危险
dan.ger.ous	(a.)	berbahaya	weī xiǎn dė 危险的
dare	(v.)	berani	gǎn 敢
		menantang	tiaó zhàn 挑战
dark	(a.)	gelap	àn 暗, hēi àn 黑暗
dark.en	(v.)	menggelapkan	nòng hēi 弄黑
		menjadi hitam	biàn hēi 变黑

dark-room	(n.)	kamar gelap	àn fáng 暗房
dar.ling	(a.)	tercinta	qīn ài dė 亲爱的
	(n.)	kekasih	ài rén 爱人
date	(n.)	tanggal	rì qī 日期
		kurma	zǎo zí 枣子
daugh.ter	(n.)	anak perempuan	nǔ ěr 女儿
dawn	(n.)	fajar	lí míng 黎明
day	(n.)	hari	rì 日, tiān 天
		siang hari	bǎi tiān 白天
day-break	(n.)	fajar menyingsing	pò xiǎo 破晓, lí míng 黎明
day-dream	(n.)	lamunan, khayalan, mimpi di siang bolong	mèng xiǎng 梦想, bái rì mèng 白日梦
	(v.)	bermimpi di siang bolong	bái rì zùo mèng 白日做梦
day.light	(n.)	siang hari	bǎi tiān 白天
day-off	(n.)	hari libur	xiū xī rì 休息日
day-time	(n.)	siang hari	bái tiān 白天
daze	(v.)	memusingkan, membingungkan	shǐ rén yǎn huā 使人眼花, shǐ rén hú tú 使人糊涂
dead	(a.)	mati	sǐ 死
dead.line	(n.)	saat batas terakhir, teng-gat waktu	jié zhǐ shí jiān 截止时间, qī xiàn 期限
dead.lock	(n.)	macet, jalan buntu	tíng zhì 停滞, jiāng jú 僵局
dead.ly	(a.)	mematikan	zhì mìng dė 致命的
deaf	(a.)	tuli	lóng 聋
deaf.en	(v.)	menulikan	zhèn lóng 震聋, shǐ ěr lóng 使耳聋
deaf.ness	(n.)	tuli	ěr lóng 耳聋
deal	(v.)	berdagang	maǐ mài 买卖, jiāo yì 交易
		membagikan	fēn gěi 分给, fēn fā 分发
	(n.)	banyaknya, jumlah	fēn liàng 分量
		perjanjian	qì yuè 契约

deal.er	(n.)	pedagang	shāng rén 商人
		distributor	fēn pèi zhě 分配者
		pembagi kartu	fēn pài zhě 分牌者, zhuáng jiā 庄家
dear	(a.)	yang tercinta	qīn ài dė 亲爱的
		mahal	àng guì 昂贵
death	(n.)	kematian	sǐ 死
death.less	(a.)	abadi	bù sǐ dė 不死的, bù xiǔ dė 不朽的
de.bar	(v.)	menghalangi, merintangi	zǔ ài 阻碍
de.base	(v.)	merendahkan, menurunkan	jiàng dī 降低
de.bate	(v.)	berdebat, bertukar pikiran	biàn lùn 辩论, tǎo lùn 讨论
de.bat.er	(n.)	pendebat	biàn lùn zhě 辩论者
deb.it	(n.)	debet, hutang	jiè fāng 借方
debt	(n.)	hutang	zài 债, jiè kuǎn 借款
debt.or	(n.)	orang yang berhutang, debitur	jiè fāng 借方, zhài wù rén 债务人
dec.ade	(n.)	masa sepuluh tahun, dasawarsa	shí nián 十年
de.cay	(v.)	membusuk	fǔ làn 腐烂
		mundur	shuāi tùi 衰退
de.cease	(n.)	meninggal, kematian	sǐ wáng 死亡, sǐ 死
de.ceit	(n.)	tipu muslihat	jiān jì 奸计, qī piàn 欺骗
de.ceive	(v.)	menipu	qī piàn 欺骗
de.ceiv.er	(n.)	penipu	piàn zi 骗子
De.cem.ber	(n.)	Desember	shí èr yuè 十二月
de.cent	(a.)	sopan, patut, pantas	zhèng pài dė 正派的, xiàng yàng dė 象样的
de.cide	(v.)	memutuskan	jué dìng 决定
de.ci.sion	(n.)	keputusan	jué dìng 决定, jué yì 决议
de.ci.sive	(a.)	yang menentukan	jué dìng xìng dė 决定性的

deck	(n.)	geladak	jiă băn 甲板
de.claim	(v.)	mendeklamasikan	lăng sòng 朗诵, xuān dú 宣读
dec.la.ma.tion	(n.)	deklamasi	lăng sòng 朗诵, xuān dú 宣读
dec.la.ra.tion	(n.)	pernyataan, deklarasi	xuān yán 宣言
de.clare	(v.)	menyatakan	xuān bù 宣布
de.cline	(v.)	menolak	xiè jué 谢绝, tuī què 推却
		turun, mundur	xià jiàng 下降, shuāi tùi 衰退
		miring	qīng xié 倾斜
de.coct	(v.)	merebus (jamu)	jiān (yào) 煎(药)
de.con.trol	(v.)	menghapuskan pengon-trolan	jiě chú guăn zhì 解除管制
dec.o.rate	(v.)	menghias	zhuāng shì 装饰
dec.o.ra.tion	(n.)	hiasan, penghiasan, dekorasi	zhuāng shǐ pǐn 装饰品, zhuāng shì 装饰
dec.o.ra.tor	(n.)	penghias, ahli menghias	zhuāng shì zhě 装饰者, zhuāng shì jiā 装饰家
de.crease	(v.)	berkurang	jiăn shăo 减少
de.cree	(n.)	perintah	mìng lìng 命令
de.cry	(v.)	merendahkan, meremehkan	biăn dī 贬低
		memfitnah	hŭi bàng 毁谤
ded.i.cate	(v.)	mempersembahkan	fèng xiàn 奉献, xiàn shēn 献身
de.duct	(v.)	memotong, mengurangi	kòu chú 扣除, jiăn qù 减去
deed	(n.)	perbuatan	xíng wéi 行为
deep	(a.)	dalam	shēn 深
deep.en	(v.)	memperdalam	jiā shēn 加深, shēn huà 深化
deep.fry	(v.)	menggoreng dengan mi-nyak yang banyak	zhà 炸
deer	(n.)	rusa, menjangan	lù 鹿
de.fame	(v.)	memfitnah	fĕi bàng 诽谤
de.fault	(n.)	kegagalan, kelalaian	shī baì 失败, hū luè 忽略
	(v.)	lalai	hū luè 忽略, bù fù zé 不负责

de.feat	(n.)	kekalahan	zhàn bài 战败, bài běi 败北
	(v.)	mengalahkan	jī bài 击败, zhàn shèng 战胜
de.fect	(n.)	cacat, kekurangan	quē xiàn 缺陷, quē diǎn 缺点
de.fec.tion	(n.)	penyeberangan, pengkhianatan	bèi pàn 背叛, biàn jié 变节
de.fend	(v.)	membela	bǎo wèi 保卫, biàn hù 辩护
de.fen.dant	(n.)	terdakwa	běi gào 被告
de.fense	(n.)	pertahanan	fáng yù 防御
de.fen.sive	(a.)	defensif, bersifat mem-bela	fáng yù xìng dė 防御性的, shǒu shì 守势
de.fer	(v.)	menunda, menangguhkan	tuī chí 推迟, yán qī 延期
de.fi.ance	(n.)	tantangan	tiāo zhàn 挑战
def.i.cit	(n.)	defisit	kuī kōng 亏空, chì zì 赤字
de.file	(n.)	jurang	xiá gǔ 峡谷
	(v.)	mengotorkan	nòng zāng 弄脏
de.fine	(v.)	memberi definisi	xìa dìng y i 下定义
		menentukan batas-batas	xiàn dìng 限定
def.i.nite	(a.)	pasti, tentu	què dìng dė 确定的, yī dìng dė 一定的
de.fi.ni.tion	(n.)	definisi	dìng yì 定义
de.fla.tion	(n.)	pengempesan	fàng qì 放气
		deflasi	tōng huò jǐn suō 通货紧缩
de.fy	(v.)	menentang	fǎn xàng 反抗
de.gradc	(v.)	merendahkan, menurunkan	jiàng dī 降低, jiàng jí 降级
de.gree	(n.)	derajat	dù 度, chéng dù 程度
		gelar	děng jí 等级, xué wèi 学位
de.i.ty	(n.)	dewa	shén 神
de.lay	(n.)	memperlambat, menunda	tuō yán 拖延, yán qī 延期
del.e.gate	(n.)	utusan	daì biǎo 代表
	(v.)	mengutuskan	paì daì biǎo 派代表, wěi pài 委派

del.e.ga.tion	(n.)	delegasi, perutusan	dài biǎo túan 代表团
de.lib.er.ate	(a.)	mempertimbangkan dengan cermat	zǐ xì kǎo lù 仔细考虑
del.i.cate	(a.)	enak, lezat	hǎo chī 好吃, měi wèi 美味
		halus, bagus	jīng xì 精细, you měi 优美
de.li.cious	(a.)	lezat	hǎo chī dė 好吃的, mèi wèi dė 美味的
de.light	(n.)	kenikmatan, kegembiraan	kuài lè 快乐, gāo xìng 高兴
	(v.)	menyenangkan	shǐ kuài lè 使快乐
de.liv.er	(v.)	menyampaikan	chuán dá 传达
		menyerahkan	jiāo fú 交付
de.liv.er.ance	(n.)	pelepasan, pembebasan	shí fàng 释放,jiè fàng 解放
de.liv.er.y	(n.)	pengiriman	dì sòng 递送
		penyerahan barang	jiāo huò 交货
		pengekstradisi	yǐn dù 引渡
del.ta	(n.)	delta	sān jiǎo zhōu 三角洲
de.lude	(v.)	menipu	qī piàn 欺骗
de.luxe	(a.)	mewah	háo huá dė 豪华的
de.mand	(v.)	menuntut, meminta	yào qiú 要求
		memerlukan	xū yào 需要
de.mise	(n.)	kematian	sǐ wáng 死亡
de.mis.sion	(n.)	pengunduran diri	cí zhí 辞职
		pembebasan tugas	miǎn zhí 免职
de.mo.bi.lize	(v.)	mendemobilisasikan	fù yuán 复员
		membubarkan	qiǎn sàn 遣散
de.moc.ra.cy	(n.)	demokrasi	mín zhǔ 民主
dem.o.crat	(n.)	demokrat	mín zhǔ zhǔ yì zhě 民主主义者, mín zhǔ rén shì 民主人士
de.moc.ra.tism	(n.)	demokratisme	mín zhǔ zhǔ yì 民主主义, mín zhǔ zhǐ dù 民主制度
de.moc.ra.ti.za.tion	(n.)	demokratisasi, pendemokrasian	mín zhǔ huà 民主化

dem.on.stra.tion	(n.)	demonstrasi, unjuk rasa	shì wēi 示威
		pertunjukan	shì fàn 示范, biǎo yǎn 表演
dem.on.stra.tor	(n.)	orang yang mempe-ragakan, demonstran	shì wēi zhě 示威者 shì fàn zhě 示范者
den	(n.)	lubang (di tanah/pohon)	dòng 洞
de.ni.al	(n.)	penyangkalan	fǒu rèn 否认
de.note	(v.)	menunjukkan	zhǐ shì 指示
		menyatakan	biǎo shì 表示
de.nounce	(v.)	mengadukan	gào fā 告发
		mencela	feī nàn 非难, zhǐ zé 指责
dense	(a.)	padat	mì 密, chóu mì 稠密
		tebal	hòu 厚, nóng hòu 浓厚
		lebat	mào mì 茂密
den.ti.frice	(n.)	pasta/tapal gigi	yá gāo 牙膏
den.tist	(n.)	dokter gigi	yá kē yī shēng 牙科医生
de.ny	(v.)	menyangkal	fǒu rèn 否认
de.part	(v.)	berangkat	chū fā 出发
de.part.ment	(n.)	departemen	bù 部
de.pend	(v.)	bergantung pada	yī kào 依靠
de.pen.dent	(a.)	tergantung pada	yī kào 依靠
de.pos.it	(v.)	menaruh, menyimpan	cún fàng 存放
	(n.)	uang simpanan	cún kuǎn 存款
de.pos.i.tor	(n.)	orang yang menyimpan uang	cún kǔan rén 存款人
de.pre.ci.ate	(v.)	menurun, jatuh nilainya	biǎn zhí 贬值
de.pre.ci.a.tion	(n.)	merosotnya nilai	biǎn zhí 贬值
de.press	(v.)	menurunkan, menekan	jiàng dī 降低, yā yì 压抑
de.pres.sion	(n.)	kemasygulan	qíng xù dī lùo 情绪低落
		depresi	xiaō tiáo 肖条, bù jǐng qì 不景气

de.prive	(v.)	merampas	bō dúo 剥夺, duó qǔ 夺取
depth	(n.)	kedalaman	shēn dù 深度
dep.uta.ti.on	(n.)	deputasi, utusan, perutusan	dài lǐ 代理, dài biǎo 代表
de.pute	(v.)	mengutuskan, mewakilkan	wěi pài 委派
dep.u.ty	(n.)	wakil, deputi	dài biǎo 代表
de.ride	(v.)	mengejek	cháo xiào 嘲笑
de.rive	(v.)	berasal dari	yuān yuán 渊源, pài shēng 派生
		memperoleh	qǔ dé 取得, dé lái 得来
de.scend	(v.)	turun	xià jiàng 下降, xià lái 下来
de.scend.ant	(n.)	keturunan	zǐ sūn 子孙, hoù yì 后裔
de.scribe	(v.)	menjelaskan, meng-uraikan	xù shù 叙述
		menggambarkan	miáo xiě 描写
des.ert	(n.)	gurun, padang pasir	shā mò 沙漠
	(a.)	tandus	huāng wú dė 荒芜的, bù máo dė 不毛的
de.sert	(v.)	meninggalkan	yí qì 遗弃, pāo qì 抛弃
		melarikan diri	táo pǎo 逃跑
de.serve	(v.)	pantas menerima	yìng shòu 应受, yìng dé 应得
		patut mendapat	zhí dé 值得
de.sign	(n.)	rencana, gambar, desain	shè jì 设计, tú àn 图案
	(v.)	merencanakan, merancang	jì huà 计划, shè jì 设计
de.sign.er	(n.)	perencana, perancang	shè jì yuán 设计员
de.sire	(n.)	keinginan, hasrat	yuàn wàng 愿望, yù wàng 欲望
	(v.)	ingin	yào qiú 要求
desk	(n.)	meja tulis	shū zhuō 书桌, xiě zì tái 写字台
des.pair	(n.)	putus asa	jué wàng 绝望
	(v.)	berputus asa	shī wàng 失望
des.per.ate	(a.)	putus asa	jué wàng dė 绝望的

des.pise	(v.)	memandang rendah	qīng shì 轻视
des.poil	(v.)	merampas, merampok	duó qǔ 夺取, luè duó 掠夺
des.sert	(n.)	makanan pencuci mulut	tián diǎn xīn 甜点心, cān hòu diǎn xīn 餐后点心
des.ti.na.tion	(n.)	tempat yang dituju	mù dì dì 目的地
des.ti.ny	(n.)	nasib, takdir	mìng yùn 命运
de.stroy	(v.)	membinasakan, merusak	pò huài 破坏
de.stroy.er	(n.)	kapal perusak	qū zhú jiàn 驱逐舰
		perusak	pò huài zhě 破坏者
de.struc.tion	(n.)	kerusakan, kehancuran	pò huài 破坏, hǔi miè 毁灭
de.tach	(v.)	memisahkan	fēn kāi 分开
de.tail	(v.)	menceritakan dengan panjang lebar	xiáng shù 详述
	(n.)	bagian-bagian yang kecil	xì jié 细节
de.tain	(v.)	menahan	liú zhù 留住, kòu liú 扣留
de.tect	(v.)	mendapati, mendeteksi	fā xiàn 发现, zhēn chá 侦查, tàn cè 探测
de.tec.tion	(n.)	deteksi	tàn cè 探测, zhēn chá 侦查
de.tec.tive	(n.)	detektif	zhēn tàn 侦探
de.ter.mi.na.tion	(n.)	ketentuan	jué dìng 决定
de.ter.mine	(v.)	menentukan	jué dìng 决定
de.test	(v.)	benci	tòng hèn 痛恨
de.vel.op	(v.)	berkembang	fā zhǎn 发展
de.vel.op.ment	(n.)	perkembangan	fā zhǎn 发展
dev.il	(n.)	iblis, setan	mó gǔi 魔鬼
de.vise	(v.)	merancang	shè jì 设计
de.vis.er	(n.)	perancang	shè jì yuán 设计员
de.vote	(v.)	mengabdikan diri	fèng xiàn 奉献, gòng xiàn 贡献
de.vour	(v.)	menelan	tūn 吞
dew	(n.)	embun	lù 露

di.ag.nose	(v.)	menetapkan penyakit, mendiagnosa	zhěn duàn 诊断
di.a.gram	(n.)	bagan, grafik	tú jiě 图解, tú biǎo 图表
di.al	(n.)	muka jam	zhōng miàn 钟面
	(v.)	memutar nomor telepon	bō diàn huà haò mǎ 拨电话号码, dǎ diàn huà gěi 打电话给
di.a.lect	(n.)	dialek	fāng yán 方言
di.a.logue	(n.)	dialog, percakapan	hùi huà 会话, dùi huà 对话
di.am.e.ter	(n.)	garis tengah, diameter	zhì jìng 直径
di.a.mond	(n.)	intan	jīn gāng zuān 金钢钻, jīn gāng shí 金刚石
dia-rrhea	(n.)	diare, sakit berak-berak	lì jí 痢疾
di.a.ry	(n.)	buku harian	rì jì 日记
dice	(n.)	dadu	shǎi zi 骰子
dic.tate	(v.)	dikte, mengimlakan	tīng xiě 听写
		memerintahkan	mìng lìng 命令
dic.ta.tion	(n.)	imla	tīng xiě 听写
dic.ta.tor	(n.)	diktator	dú cái zhě 独裁者, zhuān zhèng zhě 专政者
dic.tion.a.ry	(n.)	kamus	zì diǎn 字典
die	(v.)	mati	sǐ 死
die-hard	(n.)	orang yang keras kepala	wán gù 顽固, wán gù fèn zi 顽固分子
	(a.)	keras kepala, kolot	wán gù dė 顽固的, sǐ yìng dė 死硬的
di.et	(n.)	diet, makan berpantang	jì shí 忌食
dif.fer	(v.)	berbeda	chà bié 差别, bù tóng 不同
dif.fer.ence	(n.)	perbedaan	chà bié 差别
dif.fer.ent	(a.)	berlainan, berbeda	bù tóng dė 不同的
dif.fi.cult	(a.)	sukar, sulit	kùn màn dė 困难的
dig	(v.)	menggali	júe 掘, wā 挖
di.gest	(v.)	mencerna	xiāo hùa 消化

dig.it	(n.)	jari tangan/kaki	shǒu shǐ 手指, zhǐ 趾
		digit, letak angka/bilangan	zì wèi 字位
dig.ni.ty	(n.)	kemuliaan	gāo gùi 高贵, zūn gùi 尊贵
di.lem.ma	(n.)	dilema	liǎng nán 两难
		dalam keadaan serba sulit	jìn tuì liǎng nán 进退两难
dil.i.gent	(a.)	rajin	qín láo 勤劳
dim	(a.)	samar-samar, kabur	àn dàn 暗淡, mó hú 模糊
di.men.sion	(n.)	ukuran panjang lebar dan tinggi	tǐ jī 体积
		dimensi	kuān dù 宽度
di.min.ish	(v.)	mengurangi	jiǎn shǎo 减少
dine	(v.)	makan	yòng fàn 用饭, jìn cān 进餐
din.ning-car	(n.)	restorasi, kereta makan	cān chē 餐车
din.ing-room	(n.)	kamar makan	cān tíng 餐厅
din.ing-table	(n.)	meja makan	cān zhuō 餐桌, fàn zhuō 饭桌
din.ner	(n.)	makan malam	wǎn cān 晚餐, wǎn fàn 晚饭
dip	(v.)	mencelupkan	jìn 浸
diph.the.ri.a	(n.)	difteri	bǎi hóu 白喉
di.plo.ma	(n.)	ijazah, diploma	wén píng 文凭, bì yè zhèng shū 毕业证书
di.plo.ma.cy	(n.)	diplomasi	waì jiāo 外交, wài jiāo shǒu wàn 外交手腕
dip.lo.mat	(n.)	diplomat	wài jiāo jiā 外交家, wài jiāo guān 外交官
di.plom.a.tist	(n.)	diplomat	wài jiāo jiā 外交家
di.rect	(a.)	langsung	zhí jiē dė 直接的
	(v.)	menunjukkan, memimpin, mengarahkan	zhǐ shì 指示, zhǐ dǎo 指导
di.rec.tion	(n.)	arah	fāng xiàng 方向
		petunjuk	zhǐ dǎo 指导

di.rect.ly	(adv.)	dengan langsung	zhí jiē di 直接地
di.rec.tor	(n.)	direktur	lǐng dǎo zhě 领导者
		pengurus	lǐ shì 理事
		sutradara	dǎo yǎn 导演
dirt	(n.)	kotoran	zāng wù 脏物
dir.ty	(a.)	kotor	āng zāng 肮脏
dis.a.bil.i.ty	(n.)	ketidakmampuan	wú néng 无能
dis.ac.cord	(v.)	tidak sesuai, tidak cocok,	bù yī zhì 不一致,
		tidak setuju	bù fú hé 不符合
dis.ad.van.tage	(n.)	kerugian	bú lì 不利
dis.af.fec.tion	(n.)	ketidakpuasan	bù mǎn 不满
dis.a.gree	(v.)	berselisih paham	yì jiàn bù tóng 意见不同
		tak setuju	bù tóng yì 不同意
dis.a.gree.a.ble	(a.)	mengesalkan	tǎo yàn 讨厌
dis.ap.pear	(v.)	menghilang	xiāo shī 消失
dis.ap.point	(v.)	mengecewakan	lìng rén shī wàng 令人失望
dis.ap.point.ment	(n.)	kekecewaan	shī wàng 失望
dis.ap.prove	(v.)	menolak, tidak menye-tujui	bù zàn chéng 不赞成
dis.arm	(v.)	melucuti senjata	jiǎo xiè 缴械,
			jiě chú wǔ zhuāng 解除武装
dis.ar.range	(v.)	mengacaukan	rǎo luàn 扰乱
dis.ar.ray	(v.)	memberantakkan,	luàn qī bā zāo 乱七八糟
		mengacaukan	
dis.as.ter	(n.)	bencana, malapetaka	zaī nàn 灾难
dis.band	(v.)	membubarkan, bubar	jiě sàn 解散
dis.be.lieve	(v.)	tidak mempercayai	bù xiāng xìn 不相信
dis.burse	(v.)	membayar	zhī chū 支出
		mengeluarkan uang	bō kuǎn 拨款
dis.card	(v.)	membuang	diū 丢, pāo qì 抛弃

dis.cern	(v.)	melihat, kenal	kàn chū 看出, rèn shí 认识
dis.charge	(v.)	melepaskan	fàng shì 放射
		membongkar muatan	xiè hùo 卸货
		memecat	miǎn chú 免除
dis.ci.ple	(n.)	murid	dì zi 弟子, mén tú 门徒
dis.ci.pline	(n.)	disiplin, tata tertib	jì lù 纪律
dis.close	(v.)	membuka rahasia	xiè lòu mì mì 泄漏秘密,
			jiē fā 揭发, bào lù 暴露
dis.con.tent	(n.)	ketidakpuasan	bù mǎn 不满
dis.con.tin.ue	(v.)	berhenti, menghentikan	tíng zhǐ 停止
dis.cord	(n.)	perselisihan	bù hé 不和
dis.count	(v.)	memotong harga	dǎ zhě kòu 打折扣
	(n.)	potongan, rabat, diskon	zhě kòu 折扣
dis.cour.age	(v.)	menawarkan hati,	shǐ rén qì něi 使人气馁,
		melemahkan semangat	shǐ rén sàng qì 使人丧气
		menghalang-halangi	fāng ài 妨碍
dis.cov.er	(v.)	menemukan,	fā xiàn 发现
		mendapatkan	
dis.cov.er.y	(n.)	penemuan	fà xiàn 发现
dis.cred.it	(n.)	tidak dipercaya	wǔ xìn yòng 无信用
dis.creet	(a.)	berhati-hati	jǐn shèn 谨慎
dis.crim.i.nate	(v.)	membedakan	qì shì 歧视
dis.crim.i.na.tion	(n.)	pembedaan, diskriminasi	qí shì 歧视
dis.cuss	(v.)	membicarakan, merun-	tǎo lùn 讨论
		dingkan	
dis.cus.sion	(n.)	pembicaraan, diskusi	tǎo lùn 讨论
dis.dain	(v.)	meremehkan	miǎo shì 藐视
dis.ease	(n.)	penyakit	jí bìng 疾病
dis.em.bark	(v.)	mendarat	shàng àn 上岸, dēng lù 登陆
dis.en.chant	(v.)	menyadarkan	shǐ rén qīng xǐng 使人清醒

dis.fav.our	(n.)	tak disukai	shī chǒng 失宠
dis.grace	(n.)	noda, aib	chí rǔ 耻辱
dis.guise	(v.)	menyamar	jiǎ zhuāng 假装,
			wěi zhuāng 伪装
dis.gust	(n.)	perasaan jijik	yàn wù 厌恶
	(v.)	menjijikkan	lìng rén zuò ǒu 令人作呕,
			lìng rén tǎo yàn 令人讨厌
dish	(n.)	piring, hidangan	pán zi 盘子, cài yáo 菜肴
dish-cloth	(n.)	kain lap	mā bù 抹布
dis.hon.est	(a.)	tidak jujur	bù chéng shí 不诚实,
			bù lǎo shí 不老实
dis.hon.es.ty	(n.)	ketidakjujuran	bù chéng shí 不诚实,
			bù lǎo shí 不老实
dis.hon.our	(n.)	noda, aib	chì rǔ 耻辱, bù míng yù 不名誉
dis.in.te.grate	(v.)	menghancurkan	wǎ jiě 瓦解
		memecah belah	fēn liè 分裂
dis.like	(v.)	tidak suka, membenci	bù xǐ huān 不喜欢, yàn wù 厌恶
dis.loy.al	(a.)	tidak loyal, tidak setia	bù zhōng 不忠
dis.miss	(v.)	memecat	miǎn zhí 免职, kāi chú 开除
dis.mount	(v.)	turun	xià lái 下来
		membongkar muatan	xiè huò 卸货
dis.o.be.dience	(n.)	ketidakpatuhan	bù fú cóng 不服从
dis.o.be.dient	(a.)	membangkang, tidak patuh	bù fú cóng dė 不服从的
dis.o.bey	(v.)	tidak patuh	bù fú cóng 不服从
		melanggar perintah	bù tīng mìng lìng 不听命令
dis.or.der	(n.)	tidak teratur	méi yóu zhì xù 没有秩序,
			líng luàn 凌乱
dis.part	(v.)	memisahkan,	fēn liè 分裂
		menceraiberaikan	
dis.patch	(v.)	mengirim berita	jì fā xìn jiàn 寄发信件
		mengutus	pái qiǎn 派遣

dis.pense	(v.)	membagikan	fēn pèi 分配
dis.perse	(v.)	membubarkan	qū sàn 驱散
		bubar	sàn kāi 散开, fēn sàn 分散
dis.place	(v.)	memindahkan,	yí dòng 移动, zhuǎn yí 转移,
		menggantikan	tì daì 替代, qǔ daì 取代
dis.play	(v.)	mempertunjukkan,	chén liè 陈列
		memperagakan	
dis.please	(v.)	menyakitkan hati	shǐ rén shāng xīn 使人伤心
		tidak menyenangkan	shǐ rén bù gāo xìng 使人不高兴
dis.port	(v.)	berekreasi,	yú lè 娱乐,
		bermain-main	wán shǔa 玩耍
dis.po.sal	(n.)	pengaturan	ān pái 安排, chǔ lǐ 处理
		pembuangan	qīng chú 清除, chú qù 除去
dis.praise	(v.)	mencela	zhǐ zhé 指谪, qiǎn zé 谴责
dis.prove	(v.)	menyangkal, membantah	fǒu rèn 否认, fǎn bó 反驳
dis.pute	(n.)	perselisihan	zhēng lùn 争论
dis.re.gard	(v.)	mengabaikan	hū shì 忽视, hū luè 忽略
dis.re.spect	(n.)	tidak hormat	shī lǐ 失礼, shī jìng 失敬
dis.sat.is.fy	(v.)	tidak memuaskan	shǐ rén bù mǎn 使人不满
dis.solve	(v.)	melarutkan	róng jiě 溶解
dis.tance	(n.)	jarak	jù lí 距离
dis.tant	(a.)	jauh	yuǎn 远
dis.taste	(n.)	rasa tidak senang	yàn wù 厌恶
dis.taste.ful	(a.)	hambar	wú wèi dė 无味的
dis.til	(v.)	menyuling	zhēng liú 蒸馏
dis.til.ler	(n.)	penyuling	zhēng liú qì 蒸馏器
dis.tinct	(a.)	nyata, terang	qīng chǔ 清楚, míng xiǎn 明显
dis.tin.guish	(v.)	membedakan	qū bié 区别
dis.tin.guished	(a.)	termasyhur, terkemuka	jié chū dė 杰出的,
			yǒu míng dė 有名的

dis.tract	(v.)	membingungkan	shǐ rén mí luàn 使人迷乱
		mengalihkan perhatian	shǐ rén fēn xīn 使人分心
dis.tress	(n.)	keadaan menderita	tòng kǔ 痛苦
dis.trib.ute	(v.)	membagi-bagikan	fēn pèi 分配
dis.trib.u.tor	(n.)	penyalur, distributor	fēn pèi zhě 分配者
dis.trict	(n.)	daerah	dì fāng 地方, dì qū 地区
dis.trust	(n.)	ketidakpercayaan	bù xìn rèn 不信任
		kecurigaan	huái yí 怀疑
dis.turb	(v.)	mengganggu	dǎ rǎo 打扰, sāo rǎo 骚扰
dis.un.ion	(n.)	ketidakkompakan	bù tuán jié 不团结
		perpecahan	fēn liè 分裂
ditch	(n.)	selokan	shǔi gōu 水沟
dive	(v.)	menyelam	qián shǔi 潜水
div.er	(n.)	penyelam	qián shuǐ yuán 潜水员
di.vide	(v.)	membagi	fēn 分, huà fēn 划分
div.i.dend	(n.)	dividen, keuntungan	hóng lì 红利, gǔ xī 股息
di.vine	(a.)	bersifat ketuhanan	shén dė 神的
	(v.)	meramal	zhān bǔ 占卜, yù yán 预言
di.vin.er	(n.)	peramal	zhān bǔ zhě 占卜者
di.vorce	(n.)	perceraian	lí hūn 离婚
diz.zy	(a.)	pusing	tóu yùn 头晕
do	(v.)	melakukan, mengerjakan	zùo 做
dock	(n.)	pelabuhan	mǎ tóu 码头
		galangan kapal	chuán wù 船坞
dock.yard	(n.)	galangan kapal	zào chuán chǎng 造船厂
doc.tor	(n.)	dokter	yì shēng 医生
doc.trine	(n.)	ajaran, doktrin	jiào yì 教义, zhǔ yì 主义,
			xué shūo 学说
doc.u.ment	(n.)	dokumen	wén jiàn 文件
doe	(n.)	kijang betina	mǔ lù 母鹿

dog	(n.)	anjing	gǒu 狗
doll	(n.)	boneka	yáng wá wá 洋娃娃
dol.lar	(n.)	dolar	yuán 元
		mata uang Amerika Serikat	měi yuán 美元
do.mes.tic	(n.)	urusan rumah tangga	jiā tíng dė 家庭的
		dalam negeri, domestik	guó nèi dė 国内的
		(binatang) piaraan	jiā chù 家畜
dom.i.nance	(n.)	kekuasaan	tǒng zhì 统治
		pengaruh besar	yōu shì 优势
dom.i.nant	(a.)	dominan	tǒng zhì dė 统治的, zhàn yōu shì dė 占优势的
dom.i.nate	(v.)	menguasai	tǒng zhì 统治, kòng zhì 控制
do.min.ion	(n.)	dominion	zhǔ quán 主权, tǒng zhì quán 统治权
don.key	(n.)	keledai	lú zi 驴子
do.nor	(n.)	penderma	juān kuǎn rén 捐款人
		penyumbang darah	shū xuè zhě 输血者
doom	(n.)	kehancuran	miè wáng 灭亡
		nasib malang	ě yùn 厄运
door	(n.)	pintu	mén 门
door-bell	(n.)	bel pintu	mén ling 门铃
door-keep.er	(n.)	penjaga pintu	shǒu mén gōng rén 守门工人, mén fáng 门房
door-step	(n.)	ambang pintu	mén jiē 门阶
door.way	(n.)	pintu keluar masuk	mén lù 门路, jìn chū kǒu 进出口
dor.mi.to.ry	(n.)	asrama	sù shè 宿舍
dose	(n.)	dosis, takaran	yī fù 一服, yi tie 一帖
dot	(n.)	titik	diǎn 点
doub.le	(a.)	dobel, lipat/rangkap dua	shuāng bèi 双倍, liǎng bèi 两倍

doubt	(n.)	kesangsian, keraguan	huái yí 怀疑
	(v.)	meragukan	huái yí 怀疑
doubt.less	(adv.)	pasti, tentu	wú yí dė 无疑的, kěn dìng dė 肯定的
dove	(n.)	burung dara	gē zi 鸽子
down	(adv.)	ke bawah, turun	xiàng xià 向下, xià lái 下来
down.pour	(n.)	hujan lebat	qīng pén dà yǔ 倾盆大雨
down.stairs	(adv.)	di tingkat bawah	zaì lóu xià 在楼下
down.stream	(adv.)	hilir	xià liú dė 下流的
down.ward	(a.)	ke bawah	xiàng xià 向下
doze	(v.)	mengantuk	dǎ kē shùi 打瞌睡, dǎ dǔn ėr 打盹儿
doz.en	(n.)	lusin	dǎ 打
draft	(n.)	naskah, konsep	cǎo gǎo 草稿, cǎo àn 草案, cǎo tú 草图
		wesel	hùi piào 汇票
drag	(v.)	menyeret	tuō 拖
drag.on	(n.)	naga	lóng 龙
drag.on-fly	(n.)	capung	qīng tíng 蜻蜓
drain	(n.)	saluran, got	shǔi gōu 水沟
dra.ma	(n.)	drama, sandiwara	xì jù 戏剧
dra.mat.ic	(a.)	dramatis	xì jù xìng dė 戏剧性的
dram.a.tist	(n.)	penulis drama	jù zuò jiā 剧作家
draw	(v.)	menarik	lā 拉
		menggambar	huà 画
draw.er	(n.)	laci	chōu tì 抽屉
draw.ing	(n.)	gambar	tú huà 图画
		penarikan lotere	chōu qiān 抽签
		penarikan uang	tí cún 提存, tí kuǎn 提款
dread	(n.)	ketakutan	kǒng bù 恐怖
	(v.)	takut	hài pà 害怕
dream	(n.)	mimpi	mèng 梦
	(v.)	bermimpi	zuò mèng 作梦

dress	(n.)	pakaian	yī fú 衣服
	(v.)	berpakaian	chuān yī fú 穿衣服
		menghiasi	zhuāng shì 装饰
dress.maker	(n.)	penjahit	cái féng 裁缝
drib.ble	(v.)	menetes	dī xià 滴下
drift	(v.)	hanyut	piāo liú 漂流
		terombang-ambing	piāo bō 飘泊
drill	(n.)	latihan	cāo liàn 操练, liàn xí 练习
		bor	zuàn zi 钻子
		kain dril	xié wén bù 斜纹布
	(v.)	melatih	cāo liàn 操练, liàn xí 练习
		membor	zuàn kǒng 钻孔
drink	(v.)	minum	hē 喝
drip	(v.)	menetes	dī xià 滴下
drive	(v.)	mengemudikan	jià shǐ 驾驶
		mendorong, menghalau	tuī 推, gǎn 赶
driv.er	(n.)	sopir, pengemudi	shī jī 司机, chē fū 车夫
driz.zle	(n.)	gerimis	xì yǔ 细雨, máo máo yǔ 毛毛雨
drop	(v.)	menjatuhkan	tóu xià 投下, luò xià 落下
		menetes	dī xià 滴下
drown	(v.)	tenggelam	yān sǐ 淹死, nì sǐ 溺死
drowse	(v.)	mengantuk	dǎ kē shuì 打瞌睡
drudge	(v.)	membanting tulang, bekerja kasar	zuò kǔ gōng 做苦工
	(n.)	orang yang bekerja kasar	kǔ gōng 苦工
drug	(n.)	obat	yào pǐn 药品
		narkoba	má zùi yào 麻醉药
drum	(n.)	gendang, drum	gǔ 鼓
drum.mer	(n.)	pemain drum	gǔ shǒu 鼓手
drum.stick	(n.)	stik pemukul genderang	gǔ chúi 鼓槌
drunk	(a.)	mabuk	zùi 醉

drunk.ard	(n.)	pemabuk	jiǔ gǔi 酒鬼, zùi hàn 醉汉
dry	(a.)	kering	gān 干
duck	(n.)	itik, bebek	yā 鸭
due	(a.)	yang harus dibayar	yìng fù dė 应付的
		yang jatuh tempo	dào qī dė 到期的
du.el	(n.)	perang tanding, duel	júe dòu 决斗
dull	(a.)	tumpul	dùn 钝, chí dùn 迟钝
		bodoh	yú bèn 愚笨
dumb	(a.)	bisu	yǎ bā 哑吧
		diam	chén mò 沉默
du.pli.cate	(n.)	duplikat, salinan	fù běn 付本
du.ra.tion	(n.)	lamanya, selamanya	jiǔ zàn 久暂, qī jiān 期间
dur.ing	(prep.)	selama	zai...qí jiān 在…期间,
			zài...dė shí hòu 在…的时候
dusk	(n.)	senja	huáng hūn 黄昏
		gelap	yīn àn 阴暗
dust	(n.)	debu	huī chén 灰尘
dust.bin	(n.)	tempat sampah	lā jī tǒng 垃圾桶
dust.er	(n.)	penghapus debu	dǎn zi 掸子, chén fú 尘拂
dust.y	(a.)	berdebu	mǎn shì huī chén dė满是灰尘的
du.ti.ful	(a.)	patuh, menurut	fú cóng 服从, xiào shùn 孝顺
du.ty	(n.)	kewajiban	zé rèn 责任, yì wù 义务
		cukai	guān shùi 关税
du.ty-free	(a.)	bebas pajak	miǎn shùi dė 免税的
dwarf	(n.)	orang kerdil, katai	ǎi zi 矮子
dwell	(v.)	mendiami, bertempat tinggal	jū zhù 居住
dwell.er	(n.)	penghuni, penduduk	jū zhù zhě 居住者, jū mín 居民
dwell.ing	(n.)	tempat kediaman	zhù sǔo 住所
dye	(v.)	mencelup	rǎn sè 染色
	(n.)	bahan celup	rǎn liào 染料

dy.er	(n.)	tukang celup	rǎn gōng 染工
dye-stuff	(n.)	bahan celup	rǎn liào 染料
dy.ing	(a.)	hampir mati, sekarat	kuài yào sǐ dė 快要死的, chúi sǐ dė 垂死的
dy.nam.ic	(a.)	dinamis, dinamik	dòng lì dė 动力的
dy.na.mite	(n.)	bahan peledak	zhà yào 炸药
dy.na.mo	(n.)	dinamo	fā diàn jī 发电机
dyn.as.ty	(n.)	dinasti	wáng cháo 王朝
dys.en.tery	(n.)	disentri	lì jí 痢疾

E

each	(pron.)	tiap-tiap, masing-masing	měi gè 每个, gè gè 各个, gè zì 各自
ea.ger	(a.)	ingin sekali	kě wàng dė 渴望的
ea.gle	(n.)	burung garuda, rajawali	yīng 鹰
ear	(n.)	telinga	ěr dǔo 耳朵
ear.ly	(adv.)	pagi-pagi	zǎo 早
earn	(v.)	mendapat gaji	zhuàn dé 赚得
		memperoleh	huò dé 获得, bó dė 博得
ear.nest	(a.)	sungguh-sungguh	rèn zhēn 认真, chéng kěn 诚恳
ear-phone	(n.)	alat pendengar	ěr jì 耳机
ear-ring	(n.)	anting-anting	ěr huán 耳环
earth	(n.)	bumi, tanah	dì qiú 地球, tǔ dì 土地
earth.en	(a.)	terbuat dari tanah	tǔ zhì dė 土制的
	(n.)	barang tembikar	táo qì 陶器
earth.quake	(n.)	gempa bumi	dì zhèn 地震
earth.worm	(n.)	cacing tanah	qiū yǐn 蚯蚓
ear.wax	(n.)	tahi telinga	ěr shǐ 耳屎
ease	(n.)	kesenangan, ketenteraman	ān lè 安乐
east	(n.)	timur	dōng 东, dōng fāng 东方
east.ern	(a.)	timur, berarah timur	dōng fāng dė 东方的
eas.y	(a.)	mudah	róng yì 容易
		tenang	ān xīn 安心, zhèn dìng 镇定
eat	(v.)	makan	chī 吃
eat.able	(a.)	dapat dimakan	kě chī dė 可吃的
	(n.)	makanan	shí wù 食物

eaves	(n.)	tepi atap	wū yán 屋檐
ebb	(v.)	surut	tùi cháo 退潮
	(n.)	air surut	tùi cháo 退潮, dī cháo 低潮
ec.cen.tric	(a.)	aneh, eksentrik	gŭ guài 古怪
	(n.)	orang aneh, orang sinting	guài rén 怪人
ech.o	(n.)	gema	húi shēng 回声
	(v.)	menggema	xiǎng ying 响应, qĭ fǎn xiǎng 起反响, qĭ húi shēng 起回声
e.co.nom.ic	(a.)	mengenai ekonomi	jīng jì dė 经济的
e.co.nom.i.cal	(a.)	ekonomis	jīng jì dė 经济的
		hemat	jié shěng dė 节省的
e.co.nom.ics	(n.)	ilmu ekonomi	jīng jì xué 经济学
e.con.o.mist	(n.)	ahli ekonomi	jīng jì xué jiā 经济学家
		orang yang menghemat	jié yuè dė rén 节约的人
e.con.o.mize	(v.)	menghemat	jié jiǎn 节俭, jié shěng 节省
e.con.o.my	(n.)	ekonomi, penghematan	jīng jì 经济, jié jiǎn 节俭
edge	(n.)	pinggir	biān 边, biān yúan 边缘
		mata pisau	dāo kǒu 刀口
ed.it	(v.)	edit	biān jí 编辑
e.di.tion	(n.)	edisi	bǎn 版
ed.i.tor	(n.)	redaktur, editor	biān jí 编辑
ed.i.tor.i.al	(n.)	tajuk rencana	shè lùn 社论
ed.u.cate	(v.)	mendidik	jiào yù 教育
ed.u.ca.tion	(n.)	pendidikan	jiào yù 教育
ed.u.ca.tor	(n.)	pendidik	jiào yù zhě 教育者
ef.fect	(v.)	akibat, pengaruh	jié guǒ 结果, yǐng xiang 影响
		efek	xiào gŭo 效果
ef.fec.tive	(a.)	efektif, manjur	yǒu xiào dė 有效的, líng yàn dė 灵验的

ef.fi.cient	(a.)	efisien	yǒu xiào dė 有效的, xiào lù gāo dė 效率高的
ef.fi.cien.cy	(n.)	ketepatgunaan, efisiensi	xiào lù 效率, xiào néng 效能
ef.fort	(n.)	usaha, ikhtiar	nǔ lì 努力
egg	(n.)	telur	dàn 蛋
e.go	(n.)	diri sendiri	zì wǒ 自我
e.go.ism	(n.)	egoisme	lì ji zhǔ yì 利己主义, zì sī zì lì 自私自利
e.go.ist	(n.)	egois	lì ji zhǔ yì zhě 利己主义者
		orang yang mementing-kan diri sendiri	zì sī zì lì zhě 自私自利者
eight	(n.)	delapan	bā 八
eight.een	(n.)	delapan belas	shí bā 十八
eight.eenth	(n.)	kedelapan belas	dì shí bā 第十八
		tanggal delapan belas	shí bā rì 十八日, shí bā hào 十八号
eighth	(n.)	kedelapan	dì bā 第八
		tanggal delapan	bā rì 八日, bā hào 八号
eight.i.eth	(n.)	kedelapan puluh	dì bā shí 第八十
eight.y	(n.)	delapan puluh	bā shí 八十
ei.ther	(a.)	salah satu	rèn hé yī gè 任何一个
		tiap	měi yī gė 每一个, gè 各
	(pron.)	salah satu dari dua	liǎng zhě zhī yī 两者之一
	(adv.)	juga, pula	yì 亦, yě 也
e.ject	(v.)	mengusir, mengeluarkan	gǎn chū qù 赶出去, pái chì 排斥
e.lapse	(v.)	lewat, berlalu	gùo qù 过去
e.las.tic	(a.)	elastis	yǒu tán xìng dė 有弹性的
el.bow	(n.)	sikut	zhǒu 肘
el.der	(a.)	lebih tua	jiào lǎo dė 较老的, nián zháng dė 年长的
el.dest	(a.)	yang tertua	zùi lǎo dė 最老的

e.lect	(v.)	memilih	xuǎn jǔ 选举
e.lec.tion	(n.)	pemilihan	xuǎn jǔ 选举
general election	(n.)	pemilihan umum	dà xuǎn 大选, pǔ xuǎn 普选
e.lec.tor	(n.)	pemilih	xuǎn jǔ zhě 选举者, xuǎn mín 选民
e.lec.tric	(a.)	listrik	diàn dė 电的, dài diàn dė 带电的
e.lec.tri.ci.ty	(n.)	listrik	diàn 电
e.lec.tri.fi.ca.tion	(n.)	elektrifikasi	diàn qì huà 电气化
e.lec.tron	(n.)	elektron	diàn zi 电子
el.e.gant	(a.)	anggun, elok	yōu yǎ dė 优雅的, yōu měi dė 优美的
el.e.gy	(n.)	elegi, lagu kesedihan	aī gē 哀歌, wǎn gē 挽歌
el.e.ment	(n.)	unsur, elemen	chéng fēn 成分, fēn zi 分子
el.e.men.ta.ry	(a.)	elementer, dasar	chū bù dė 初步的,
			chū děng dė 初等的,
			jī běn dė 基本的
el.e.phant	(n.)	gajah	xiàng 象
el.e.vate	(v.)	mengangkat, menjunjung	tí gāo 提高, tái gāo 抬高, tí shēng 提升
e.lev.en	(n.)	sebelas	shí yī 十一
e.lev.enth	(n.)	kesebelas	dì shí yī 第十一
		tanggal sebelas	shí yī rì 十一日, shí yī hào 十一号
e.lim.i.nate	(v.)	meniadakan, menghapus	chú qù 除去, xiāo chú 消除
e.lite	(n.)	yang terkemuka	shè hùi míng liú 社会名流
		golongan atas	shàng céng shè huì 上层社会
el.lipse	(n.)	bulat panjang, elips	tǔo yuán xíng 椭园形
else	(adv.)	yang lain	qí tā 其他, bié dė 别的
else.where	(adv.)	di tempat lain	zaì bié chù 在别处
em.bar.go	(n.)	larangan dagang, embargo	jìn yùn 禁运
em.bark	(v.)	naik ke kapal	shàng chuán 上船
		menaikkan ke kapal	dā zài 搭载
em.bas.sy	(n.)	kedutaan	dà shǐ guǎn 大使馆
em.brace	(v.)	memeluk	yōng bào 拥抱

em.broi.der	(v.)	menyulam	cì xiù 刺绣
e.merge	(v.)	timbul, tampil	fú xiàn 浮现, chū xiān 出现
e.mer.gen.cy	(n.)	keadaan darurat	jǐn jí qíng kǔang 紧急情况, jǐn jí zhuàng tài 紧急状态
em.i.grant	(n.)	orang yang pindah ke negeri lain	qiáo mín 侨民
em.i.grate	(v.)	pindah ke negeri lain	qiáo jū 侨居, yí zhù wài gúo 移住外国
e.mo.tion	(n.)	emosi, perasaan	gǎn qíng 感情, qíng xù 情绪
em.per.or	(n.)	kaisar	huáng dì 皇帝
em.pha.sis	(n.)	tekanan	qiáng diào 强调, zhòng diǎn 重点
em.pha.size	(v.)	menekankan	qiáng diào 强调
em.pire	(n.)	kekaisaran, kerajaan	dì gúo 帝国
em.ploy	(v.)	memakai, mempekerjakan	shǐ yòng 使用, gù yòng 雇用
em.ploy.ee	(n.)	pegawai	gù yuán 雇员, zhí yuán 职员, gù gōng 雇工
em.ploy.er	(n.)	majikan	gù zhǔ 雇主, dōng jiā 东家
em.ploy.ment	(n.)	pekerjaan, mata penca-harian	zhí yè 职业, jiù yè 就业
em.pow.er	(v.)	memberi kuasa	shòu quán 授权
em.press	(n.)	ratu, kaisar perempuan	nǔ huáng 女皇, huáng hòu 皇后
emp.ty	(a.)	kosong	kōng 空, kōng xū 空虚
en.a.ble	(v.)	memungkinkan	shǐ néng gòu 使能够
en.chain	(v.)	mengunci, mengikat	sǔo zhù 锁住, shù fù 束缚
en.chant	(v.)	mempesona, menawan hati	shǐ rén mí hùo 使人迷惑, shǐ rén táo zuì 使人陶醉
en.chant.er	(n.)	penyihir	wū shì 巫士
en.chant.ress	(n.)	penyihir wanita	wū pó 巫婆
en.cir.cle	(v.)	mengelilingi	wéi rǎo 围绕, huán rǎo 环绕
en.close	(v.)	memagari, melampirkan	wéi zhù 围住, fēng rù 封入

en.coun.ter	(v.)	bertemu	yù jiàn 遇见
en.cour.age	(v.)	mendorong, membera-nikan	gŭ lì 鼓励
en.cy.clo.pe.dia	(n.)	ensiklopedia	băi kē quán shū 百科全书
end	(n.)	akhir, ujung pangkal, selesai	zhōng diăn 终点, mò duān 末端, zhōng jié 终结, wán bì 完毕
en.dan.ger	(v.)	membahayakan	weī hài 危害, weī jí 危及
en.deav.our	(v.)	berusaha mencoba	nŭ lì 努力, jìn lì 尽力 chăng shì 尝试
end.ing	(n.)	akhir, tamat	jié shù 结束, jié jú 结局
end.less	(a.)	tiada habisnya tak berujung pangkal	wú qióng dė 无穷的 wú xiàn dė 无限的
en.due	(v.)	menyerahkan mempercayakan	fù yŭ 赋予 shòu yŭ 授予
en.dure	(v.)	menahan, menderita sabar	rĕn shòu 忍受 rĕn nài 忍耐
en.e.my	(n.)	musuh	dí rén 敌人
en.er.gy	(n.)	tenaga	jīng lì 精力, néng li 能力
en.force	(v.)	melaksanakan, menja-lankan	zhí xíng 执行, shí xíng 实行
en.gage	(v.)	mempekerjakan mengikat janji mempertunangkan	gù yòng 雇用 yuè dìng 约定 dìng hūn 订婚
en.gaged	(a.)	berjanji bertunangan sibuk sedang dipakai	yŏu yuè dìng 有约定 dìng lė hūn 订了婚 máng 忙 zài shi yòng zhōng 在使用中
en.gine	(n.)	mesin	jī qì 机器
en.gi.neer	(n.)	insinyur	gōng chéng shī 工程师
en.gi.neer.ing	(n.)	ilmu teknik	gōng chéng xué 工程学

en.grave	(v.)	mengukir	diāo kè 雕刻
en.join	(v.)	menyuruh, memerintah	fēn fū 吩咐, mìng lìng 命令
en.joy	(v.)	menikmati	xiǎng shòu 享受, xīn shǎng 欣赏
en.kin.dle	(v.)	menyalakan api	diǎn hǔo 点火
en.large	(v.)	memperbesar	fàng dà 放大
		memperluas	kuò dà 扩大
en.light.en	(v.)	memberi penerangan	qǐ fā 启发
		memberi petunjuk	jiào dǎo 教导
en.mi.ty	(n.)	permusuhan	dí shí 敌视, chóu hèn 仇恨
en.no.ble	(v.)	memuliakan, mempermulia	shǐ gāo gùi 使高贵
e.nor.mous	(a.)	maha besar, sangat besar	jù dà dė 巨大的
e.nough	(a.)	cukup	zú gòu 足够
en.quire	(v.)	menanyakan	xún wèn 询问
		meminta keterangan	dǎ tīng 打听
en.rage	(v.)	membuat marah	shǐ rén fā nù 使人发怒
en.rich	(v.)	memperkaya	zhì fù 致富, shǐ fù yù 使富裕
en.roll	(v.)	mendaftarkan nama	zhù cè 注册, dēng jì 登记
en.slave	(v.)	memperbudak	nǔ yì 奴役
en.sure	(v.)	menjamin	bǎo zhèng 保证
		memastikan	qùe dìng 确定
en.tan.gle	(v.)	melibatkan	lián lěi 连累
en.ter	(v.)	memasuki	jìn rù 进入, zǒu jìn 走进
en.ter.prise	(n.)	perusahaan	qì yè 企业
en.ter.tain	(v.)	menjamu	kuǎn dài 款待
		menghibur	yú lè 娱乐
en.ter.tainer	(n.)	penghibur, pemain	kuān dài zhě 宽贷者, biǎo yǎn zhě 表演者
en.ter.tain.ment	(n.)	hiburan	yú lè 娱乐
		jamuan	zhāo dài hùi 招待会

en.throne	(v.)	naik takhta	jí wèi 即位
en.thu.si.asm	(n.)	semangat, antusiasme	rè xīn 热心, rè qíng 热情
en.tire	(a.)	seluruh, sama sekali	quán bù 全部, wán quán 完全
en.tit.le	(v.)	menamakan	gěi yǔ míng chēng 给与名称
		memberi hak	shòu quán 授权
en.trance	(n.)	pintu masuk	rù kǒu 入口
en.treat	(v.)	memohon	kěn qiú 恳求
en.trust	(v.)	mempercayakan	wěi tūo 委托
en.try	(n.)	jalan masuk, masuk	rù kǒu 入口, jìn rù 进入
		catatan	dēng jì 登记
en.vel.op	(v.)	membungkus	bāo zhù 包住
		menyelubungi	méng bì 蒙蔽
en.ve.lope	(n.)	amplop	xìn fēng 信封
en.vel.op.ment	(n.)	pembungkusan	bāo fēng 包封
		pengepungan	bāo wéi 包围
en.voy	(n.)	duta, utusan	shǐ jié 使节
en.vy	(n.)	iri hati	dù jì 妒忌
ep.i.sode	(n.)	episode, satu babak	yī duàn xì 一段戏
e.poch	(n.)	zaman, masa	shí daì 时代
e.qual	(a.)	sama, setara	xiāng děng 相等, tóng děng 同等
e.qua.tor	(n.)	khatulistiwa, ekuator	chì dào 赤道
e.quip	(v.)	memperlengkapi	zhuāng bèi 装备
e.quip.ment	(n.)	perlengkapan, peralatan	shè bèi 设备
eq.ui.ty	(n.)	keadilan	gōng zhèng 公正, gōng píng 公平
e.qui.va.lent	(a.)	senilai, seharga,	děng jià 等价,
		sama derajat,	tóng děng 同等,
		sepadan, ekivalen	xiāng tóng 相同, xiāng děng 相等
e.ra	(n.)	masa, zaman	shí dài 时代
e.rase	(v.)	menghapus	cā diào 擦掉
e.ras.er	(n.)	karet penghapus, setip	xiàng pí cā 橡皮擦

e.rect	(v.)	mendirikan, menegakkan	shù lì 竖立
	(a.)	berdiri, tegak	zhí lì 直立
err	(v.)	tersesat	tūo lí zhèng lù 脱离正路
		membuat kesalahan	fàn cùo wù 犯错误
er.rand	(n.)	suruhan	chāi shì 差事, chāi shǐ 差使, shǐ mìng 使命
er.ror	(n.)	kesalahan	cùo wù 错误
e.rupt	(v.)	meletus, meledak	(hǔo shān) bào fā (火山)爆发
e.rup.tion	(n.)	ledakan, letusan	(hǔo shān) bào fā (火山)爆发
es.cape	(v.)	lolos, melarikan diri	táo zǒu 逃走
es.pec.ial.ly	(adv.)	terutama, teristimewa	tè bié dė 特别的
es.pi.o.nage	(n.)	spionase, pengintaian	díe bào 谍报, díe bào huó dòng 谍报活动
es.say	(n.)	karangan pendek, esai	duǎn wén 短文, sǎn wén 散文
es.say.ist	(n.)	pengarang esai	sǎn wén jiā 散文家
es.sence	(n.)	pokok, intisari	běn zhì 本质, jīng huá 精华
es.sen.tial	(a.)	perlu, penting	bì xū dė 必需的, zhǔ yào dė 主要的
es.tab.lish	(v.)	mendirikan	chuàng lì 创立
es.tate	(n.)	tanah milik, estat	dì chǎn 地产
es.teem	(v.)	menghargai	zūn zhòng 尊重
es.ti.mate	(v.)	menaksir	gū jì 估计, gū jià 估价
es.trange	(v.)	menjauhkan	shū yuǎn 疏远
et cet.er.a	(adv.)	dsb., dll., dst.	děng děng 等等
e.ter.nal	(a.)	abadi	yǒng jiǔ dė 永久的
e.ter.ni.ty	(n.)	kekekalan, keabadian	yǒng yuǎn 永远, yǒng héng 永恒
e.vade	(v.)	menghindari, mengelak	duǒ bì 躲避
e.val.u.ate	(v.)	menilai, menaksir	gū jià 估价
		mengevaluasi	píng jià 评价
eve	(n.)	malam menjelang suatu kejadian	qián yè 前夜, qián xì 前夕

e.ven	(a.)	rata	píng 平, píng tăn 平坦
	(adv.)	bahkan	shén zhì 甚至
eve.ning	(n.)	petang, malam	bāng wăn 傍晚, wăn shàng 晚上
e.vent	(n.)	peristiwa	shì jiàn 事件, dà shì 大事
e.vent.ful	(a.)	banyak kejadian	dūo shì dė 多事的
e.ven.tu.al	(a.)	akhirnya	zùi hòu 最后
ev.er	(adv.)	pernah	céng jīng 曾经
		selalu	cháng cháng 常常
e.ver.green	(n.)	pohon yang selalu ber-daun hijau	cháng qīng shù 常青树
	(a.)	awet muda	cháng qīng dė 常青的
e.ver.last.ing	(a.)	kekal, abadi	yŏng jiŭ dė 永久的, bù xiŭ dė 不朽的
e.ver.more	(adv.)	selalu, selama-lamanya	yŏng yuăn 永远
e.ve.ry	(a.)	tiap-tiap, setiap	mĕi 每, mĕi gè 每个
e.ve.ry.body	(pron.)	tiap orang	mĕi gè rén 每个人, rén rén 人人
e.ve.ry.one	(pron.)	tiap-tiap orang, masing-masing	mĕi gè rén 每个人
e.ve.ry.thing	(pron.)	semuanya, segala-galanya	yī qiè dōng xī 一切东西, yī qiè shì qíng 一切事情
e.ve.ry.where	(adv.)	di mana-mana	chù chù 处处, dào chù 到处
e.vict	(v.)	mengusir	găn chū 赶出, qū zhú 驱逐
ev.i.dence	(n.)	bukti	zhèng jù 证据
e.vil	(a.)	jahat, busuk	xié è dė 邪恶的
	(n.)	kejahatan	huài shì 坏事, huò hài 祸害
e.voke	(v.)	menimbulkan	yĭn qĭ 引起
		membangkitkan	huàn qĭ 唤起
ewe	(n.)	domba betina	mŭ yáng 母羊
ex	(prep.)	bekas, eks, mantan	qián rèn dė 前任的, tùi xiū dė 退休的

ex.act	(a.)	tepat, saksama	zhèng què 正确, jīng què 精确
ex.am.i.na.tion	(n.)	ujian	kǎo shì 考试
ex.am.ine	(v.)	menguji, memeriksa	kǎo shì 考试, diào chá 调查
ex.am.i.nee	(n.)	orang yang diuji	kǎo shēng 考生
ex.am.in.er	(n.)	penguji	zhǔ kǎo rén 主考人
		pemeriksa	jiǎn chá yuán 检查员
ex.am.ple	(n.)	contoh, model, teladan	lì zi 例子, mó fàn 模范, bǎng yàng 榜样
ex.ceed	(v.)	melampaui, melebihi	chāo guò 超过, shèng gùo 胜过
ex.cel	(v.)	melampaui, mengungguli	shèng guò 胜过, yōu yú 优于
ex.cel.lent	(a.)	unggul	yōu xiù dė 优秀的
ex.cept	(v.)	mengecualikan	chú qù 除去, chú diào 除掉
	(prep.)	kecuali	chú wài 除外
ex.cep.tion	(n.)	kekecualian	lǐ wài 例外
ex.cess	(n.)	keterlaluan, berlebihan	gùo fēn 过分, guò shèng 过剩
ex.change	(v.)	menukar	jiāo huàn 交换
ex.cite	(v.)	menggairahkan, membangkitkan	cì jí 刺激, jí dòng 激动, shǐ rén xīng fèn 使人兴奋
ex.claim	(v.)	berseru, menyerukan	dà hǎn 大喊, dà jiào 大叫
ex.cla.ma.tion	(n.)	seruan	hū hǎn 呼喊, gǎn tàn 感叹
ex.clude	(v.)	mengesampingkan	pái chú 排除
		mengecualikan	chú qù 除去
ex.cuse	(v.)	memaafkan	yuán liàng 原谅
ex.e.cute	(v.)	melaksanakan	zhí xíng 执行, chǔ jué 处决
ex.e.cu.tion	(n.)	pelaksanaan hukuman, eksekusi	zhí xíng 执行, chǔ jué 处决
ex.ec.u.tor	(n.)	pelaksana	zhí xíng zhě 执行者
ex.empt	(v.)	membebaskan	miǎn chú 免除
ex.er.cise	(n.)	latihan, olahraga	liàn xí 练习, tǐ cāo 体操
ex.ert	(v.)	berusaha, mengusahakan	nǔ lì 努力, jìn lì 尽力

exh.ale	(v.)	menghembuskan	hū chū 呼出
		bernapas	hū qì 呼气
ex.haust	(v.)	melelahkan	shǐ pí láo 使疲劳
		menghabiskan	yòng wán 用完
ex.hib.it	(v.)	memamerkan	zhǎn lǎn 展览
ex.hi.bi.tion	(n.)	pameran	zhǎn lǎn hùi 展览会
ex.hort	(v.)	menasihati, mendorong	guī quàn 规劝, miǎn lì 勉励
ex.ile	(n.)	pengasingan	liú fàng 流放
		pembuangan	fàng zhù 放逐
ex.ist	(v.)	ada, hidup, eksis	cùn zài 存在, shēng cún 生存
ex.ist.ence	(n.)	ada, kehidupan, eksistensi	cún zài 存在, shēng cún 生存
ex.it	(n.)	pintu keluar	chū kǒu 出口
ex.pand	(v.)	meluas, melebar	kùo zhǎn 扩展
ex.pan.sion	(n.)	perluasan	kùo zhǎn 扩展
ex.pect	(v.)	mengharapkan	pàn wàng 盼望, xī wàng 希望
ex.pe.di.tion	(n.)	ekspedisi	yuǎn zhēng 远征
ex.pel	(v.)	mengusir	qū zhú 驱逐
ex.pend	(v.)	membelanjakan, menge-luarkan biaya	huā fèi 花费
ex.pense	(n.)	biaya, ongkos	fèi yòng 费用
ex.pen.sive	(a.)	mahal	áng gùi 昂贵
ex.pe.ri.ence	(n.)	pengalaman	jīng yàn 经验
ex.pe.ri.enced	(a.)	berpengalaman	yǒu jīng yàn dė 有经验的
ex.per.i.ment	(n.)	percobaan, eksperimen	shí yàn 实验, shì yàn 试验
ex.pert	(n.)	ahli, pakar	zhuān jia 专家
ex.pire	(v.)	habis waktunya, berakhir	mǎn qī 满期
ex.plain	(v.)	menerangkan	jiě shì 解释
		menjelaskan	shuō míng 说明
ex.plic.it	(a.)	terang	míng què dė 明确的
		jelas	míng bǎi dė 明白的

ex.plode	(v.)	meledak	bào zhà 爆炸
ex.ploit	(v.)	memeras	yā zhà 压榨, bō xuè 剥削
		mengeksploitasi	kaī fā 开发, kaī tuò 开拓
ex.ploi.ta.tion	(n.)	eksploitasi	kaī tuò 开拓, kaī fā 开发, bō xuè 剥削
ex.ploit.er	(n.)	pemeras	yā zhà zhě 压榨者, bō xuè zhě 剥削者
ex.plore	(v.)	menjelajahi	tàn xiǎn 探险, kān chá 勘查
ex.plo.sion	(n.)	ledakan, letusan	bào zhà 爆炸
ex.plo.sive	(a.)	mudah meledak	róng yì bào zhà dė 容易爆炸的, bào zhà xìng 爆炸性
	(n.)	bahan peledak	zhà yào 炸药
ex.po.nent	(n.)	orang yang menerangkan	shuō míng zhě 说明者
		contoh	diǎn xíng 典型
		lambang	dài biǎo 代表
ex.port	(v.)	mengekspor	shù chū 输出, chū kǒu 出口
	(n.)	ekspor	chū kǒu mào yì 出口贸易
		barang ekspor	chū kǒu shāng pǐn 出口商品
ex.pose	(v.)	membuka, menelanjangi	bào lù 暴露
ex.po.sure	(n.)	penyingkapan, penelanjangan	jiē lù 揭露, bào lù 暴露
		pencahayaan	shǐ lù guāng 使露光
ex.pound	(v.)	menjelaskan	jiě shuō 解说
ex.press	(v.)	menyatakan	biǎo dá 表达
		mengemukakan	biǎo míng 表明
	(a.)	cepat	tè bié kuài dė 特别块的
	(n.)	kereta api ekspres	tè bié kuài chē 特别块车
ex.pres.sion	(n.)	ungkapan, pernyataan	cí jù 词句, biǎo shì 表示
		air muka, ekspresi	liǎn sè 脸色
ex.tend	(v.)	memperluas	shēn zhǎn 伸展, kuò zhāng 扩张
		memperpanjang	shēn cháng 伸长
ex.ten.sion	(n.)	perluasan, perpanjangan	kuò zhǎn 扩展, shēn cháng 伸长

ex.ten.sive	(a.)	yang luas, ekstensif	guǎng kuò dė 广阔的, guǎng dà dė 广大的
ex.tent	(n.)	luas	liáo kuò 辽阔, guǎng dà 广大
		keluasan	fàn wéi 范围, dà xiǎo 大小
ex.te.ri.or	(a.)	di bagian luar	wài bù dė 外部的, wài miàn dė 外面的
ex.ter.mi.nate	(v.)	membasmi	pū miè 扑灭
		memusnahkan	xiāo miè 消灭
ex.ter.nal	(a.)	muka, luar	wài bù dė 外部的, biǎo miàn dė 表面的
ex.tin.guish	(v.)	memadamkan	pū miè 扑灭
ex.tin.guish.er	(n.)	alat pemadam	pū miė qì 扑灭器, miè huǒ qì 灭火器
ex.tort	(v.)	memaksa, memeras	bī pò 逼迫, lè suǒ 勒索
ex.tra	(a.)	tambahan, ekstra, istimewa	é wài dė 额外的, feī cháng dė 非常的
	(n.)	edisi tambahan	hào wài 号外
ex.tract	(n.)	sari, ikhtisar	tí yào 提要
	(v.)	mencabut	bá chū 拔出, zhāi lù 摘录
		mengambil sarinya	chōu chū jīng huá 抽出精华
ex.tra.dite	(v.)	mengekstradisi	yǐn dù zùi fàn 引渡罪犯
ex..tra.di.tion	(n.)	ekstradisi	yǐn dù zùi fàn 引渡罪犯
ex.traor.di.nar.y	(a.)	luar biasa	feī cháng de 非常的, tè bié dė 特别的
ex.treme	(a.)	ekstrem, luar biasa	jí duān 极端
ex.trem.ist	(n.)	ekstremis	jí duān pài 极端派
		kaum radikal	guò jí fèn zi 过极分子
ex.trude	(v.)	mendesak keluar	jǐ chū 挤出
		menerjang keluar	chōng chū 冲出
eye	(n.)	mata	yǎn jīng 眼睛
eye.ball	(n.)	bola mata	yǎn zhū 眼珠
eye.brow	(n.)	alis	méi máo 眉毛
eye.glass.es	(n.)	kaca mata	yǎn jìng 眼镜

eye.lash	(n.)	bulu mata	jié máo 睫毛
eye.lid	(n.)	pelupuk mata	yǎn pí 眼皮
eye.shot	(n.)	jarak pandangan	yǎn jiè 眼界, shì yě 视野
eye.sight	(n.)	penglihatan, pandangan	yǎn lì 眼力
eye.wash	(n.)	obat cuci mata	yǎn yào shǔi 眼药水
eye.wit.ness	(n.)	saksi mata	jiàn zhèng rén 见证人

F

fa.ble	(n.)	fabel	yù yán 寓言
face	(n.)	wajah	miàn kǒng 面孔, liǎn kǒng 脸孔
	(v.)	menghadap	miàn xiàng 面向
fa.cil.i.ty	(n.)	fasilitas, kemudahan	shè bèi 设备, biàn lì 便利
fact	(n.)	fakta, kenyataan	shì shí 事实
fac.tion	(n.)	golongan, faksi	zōng pài 宗派, dǎng pài 党派
fac.tor	(n.)	faktor, unsur	yīn sù 因素
fac.to.ry	(n.)	pabrik	gōng chǎng 工厂
fac.tu.al	(a.)	berdasarkan kenyataan, faktual	shì shí dė 事实的, què shí dė 确实的
fade	(v.)	layu, memucat	kū wěi 枯萎, tùi sè 退色
fag.ot	(n.)	seikat kayu bakar	yī shù mù chaí 一束木柴, chaí bǎ 柴把
fail	(v.)	gagal	shī bài 失败
fail.ure	(n.)	kegagalan	shī bài 失败
faint	(v.)	pingsan	hūn dǎo 昏倒
	(a.)	lemah	ruǎn rùo 软弱, shuāi rùo 衰弱
fair	(a.)	adil, jujur	gōng píng 公平, gōng zhèng 公正
fair.y	(n.)	peri	xiǎo xiān nǔ 小仙女
fair.y.land	(n.)	tempat tinggal peri	xiān jìng 仙境
fairy tale	(n.)	cerita tentang peri	shén huà 神话
		dongeng	tóng huà 童话
faith	(n.)	kepercayaan	xìn yòng 信用, xìn yǎng 信仰
		kesetiaan	zhōng chéng 忠诚

faith.less	(a.)	tidak setia	bù zhōng chéng 不忠诚
		tidak tulus	bù zhōng shí 不忠实
fall	(v.)	jatuh	diē dǎo 跌倒, lùo xià 落下, jiàng xià 降下
	(n.)	musim gugur	qiū jì 秋季
false	(a.)	palsu	jiǎ dė 假的
false.hood	(n.)	kebohongan	huǎng yán 谎言
fame	(n.)	kemasyhuran, nama harum	míng yù 名誉, míng wàng 名望
fa.mil.iar	(a.)	tahu, kenal, ramah, karib	shú xì 熟悉, qīn jìn 亲近
fam.i.ly	(n.)	keluarga	jiā tíng 家庭
fam.ine	(n.)	kelaparan	jī è 饥饿, jī huāng 饥荒
fa.mous	(a.)	terkenal	zhù mìng 著名
fan	(n.)	kipas angin	shàn zǐ 扇子
fa.nat.ic	(n.)	orang yang fanatik	kuáng rè zhě 狂热者, rù mì zhě 入迷者
fan.cy	(n.)	khayalan	huàn xiǎng 幻想
fan.tas.tic	(a.)	dalam khayalan	huàn xiǎng dė 幻想的
fan.ta.sy	(n.)	fantasi, khayalan	huàn xiǎng 幻想
far	(a.)	jauh	yuǎn 远, yáo yuǎn 遥远
fare	(n.)	ongkos kendaraan umum	chē fèi 车费
		penumpang	chèng kè 乘客
		makanan	shì wù 食物
fare.well	(int.)	sampai jumpa, selamat jalan, selamat tinggal	zài hùi 再会, zài jiàn 再见
	(n.)	perpisahan	gào bié 告别
farm	(n.)	tanah pertanian	nóng tián 农田, nóng chǎng 农场
farm.er	(n.)	petani	nóng fū 农夫, nóng mín 农民
farm-hand	(n.)	buruh tani	nóng chǎng gōng rén 农场工人
farm.house	(n.)	rumah pertanian	nóng shè 农舍

farm.yard	(n.)	pekarangan pertanian	nóng chǎng kōng dì 农场空地
far-see.ing	(a.)	berpandangan jauh	yǒu yǎn guāng dė有眼光的, yǒu xiān jiàn zhī míng有先见之明
far.ther	(adv.)	lebih jauh	gèng yuǎn 更远
far.ther.most	(a.)	paling jauh	zùi yuǎn 最远
far.thest	(adv.)	paling jauh	zùi yuǎn 最远
fash.ion	(n.)	mode pakaian, fesyen	fú zhuāng shì yàng 服装样式
fast	(a.)	cepat	kuài 快
		erat	jǐn 紧
	(v.)	berpuasa	jué shí 绝食
	(n.)	puasa	jué shí 绝食
fast.en	(v.)	mengikat, mengeratkan	kǔn jǐn 捆紧, kǔn láo 捆牢
fat	(a.)	gemuk	pàng 胖
	(n.)	lemak	zhī fáng 脂肪
fa.tal	(a.)	fatal, mematikan	zhì mìng dė 致命的
fate	(n.)	nasib	mìng yùn 命运
fated	(a.)	ditakdirkan	mìng dìng 命定, mìng yùn zhù dìng 命运注定
fath.er	(n.)	ayah	fù qīn 父亲
fa.ther-in-law	(n.)	mertua laki-laki	yùe fù 岳父, zhàng rén 丈人, gōng gōng 公公
fa.ther.land	(n.)	tanah air, tumpah darah	zǔ gúo 祖国
fa.tigue	(n.)	keadaan lelah	pí laó 疲劳
fat.ten	(v.)	menggemukkan	yǎng pàng 养胖
		menjadi gemuk	biàn pàng 变胖
fault	(n.)	kesalahan	guò shī 过失, cùo wù 错误
fault.finder	(n.)	orang yang mencari-cari kesalahan	chūi máo qiú cī dė rén 吹毛求疵的人
fault.find.ing	(a.)	mencari-cari kesalahan orang lain	chūi máo qiú cī dė 吹毛求疵的

fa.vour	(n.)	anugerah, karunia	ēn hùi 恩惠
		surat	xìn 信
	(v.)	lebih menyayangi	chóng ài 宠爱, piān ài 偏爱
		menguntungkan	yǒu lì yú 有利予
		menyokong	zhī chí 支持
fa.vour.ite	(a.)	kesayangan	chóng ér 宠儿, zùi bèi chóng ài dė rén 最被宠爱的人, zùi bèi xǐ ài dė gōng xī 最被喜爱的东西, zùi shòu huān yíng dė rén 最受欢迎的人
fay	(n.)	peri	xiān nǚ 仙女
fear	(n.)	rasa takut	hài pà 害怕, kǒng jù 恐惧
	(v.)	menakutkan	shǐ rén hài pà 使人害怕
fear.ful	(a.)	menakutkan	kě pà dė 可怕的
fear.less	(a.)	tidak takut	bù pà dė 不怕的
feast	(n.)	pesta	yàn hùi 宴会
feat	(n.)	prestasi	gōng jī 功绩
		tindakan yang hebat	wěi yè 伟业
		ketangkasan	jì yì 技艺
feath.er	(n.)	bulu ayam/burung	yǔ máo 羽毛
fea.ture	(n.)	raut muka, roman muka	miàn mào 面貌, xiàng mào 相貌
		ciri khas	tè sè 特色, tè zhēng 特征
Feb.ru.ar.y	(n.)	Februari	èr yùe 二月
fed.er.al	(a.)	federal	lián bāng dė 联邦的, lián méng dė联盟的
fed.er.ate	(v.)	berserikat, bersekutu	lián hé 联合, jié méng 结盟
fed.er.a.tion	(n.)	federasi, perserikatan	lián hé hùi 联合会, lián bāng联邦, lián méng 联盟

fee	(n.)	biaya	fèi 费
		uang sekolah	xué fèi 学费
		upah	chóu láo jìn 酬劳金, shăng qián赏钱
fee.ble	(a.)	lemah	shuāi ruò 衰弱
feed	(v.)	memberi makan	wèi 喂, wèi yăng 喂养
feel	(v.)	merasa, meraba	găn jué 感觉, chù mō 触摸
		berpendapat	yĭ wéi 以为, rèn wéi 认为
feel.ing	(n.)	perasaan	găn qíng 感情, găn jué 感觉
fel.low	(n.)	orang	rén 人, jiā hŭo 家伙
		anak	xiăo hŭo zi 小伙子
		teman	péng yŏu 朋友, hŭo bàn 伙伴
fel.low.ship	(n.)	persahabatan, persauda-raan	jiāo qíng 交情, yŏu ài 友爱
fe.male	(n.)	wanita, betina	nŭ xìng 女性, cí xìng 雌性
fem.i.nine	(a.)	bersifat wanita, feminin	nŭ xìng dė 女性的
fence	(n.)	pagar	lí bā 篱笆, wéi lán 围栏
fenc.ing	(n.)	anggar	jiàn shù 剑术
fer.ry	(n.)	perahu tambang	dù chuán 渡船
fer.tile	(a.)	subur	féi wò 肥沃
fer.ti.liz.er	(n.)	pupuk	féi liào 肥料
ferv.our	(n.)	semangat, kegairahan	rè qíng dė 热情的, rè liè dė 热烈的
fes.ti.val	(n.)	perayaan, festival	jié rì 节日
fetch	(v.)	mengambil	nă lái 拿来, dài lái 带来
		menjemput	yíng jiē 迎接, qĭng lái 请来
feu.dal	(a.)	feodal	fēng jiàn dė 封建的
feu.dal.ism	(n.)	feodalisme	fēng jiàn zhì dù 封建制度, fēng jiàn zhŭ yì 封建主义
fe.ver	(n.)	demam	fā rè 发热, fā shāo 发烧
few	(a.)	sedikit	shăo 少
few.ness	(n.)	jumlah sedikit	shăo shù 少数

fi.bre	(n.)	serat	xiān wéi 纤维
fic.tion	(n.)	fiksi	xiǎo shuō 小说
field	(n.)	ladang	tián dì 田地, tián yě 田野
		lapangan	chǎng 场
		medan	zhàn chǎng 战场
fierce	(a.)	galak, buas	xiōng bào 凶暴, xiōng měng 凶猛, xiōng è 凶恶
fife	(n.)	suling	dí zi 笛子
fif.teen	(n.)	lima belas	shí wǔ 十五
fif.teenth	(n.)	kelima belas	dì shí wǔ 第十五
		seperlima belas	shí wǔ fēn zhi yī 十五分之一
fifth	(n.)	kelima	dì wǔ 第五
		seperlima	wǔ fēn zhi yī 五分之一
fif.ti.eth	(n.)	kelima puluh	dì wǔ shí 第五十
		seperlima puluh	wǔ shí fēn zhi yi 五十分之一
fif.ty	(n.)	lima puluh	wǔ shí 五十
fight	(v.)	berkelahi, bertempur	dǎ jià 打架, dǎ zhàng 打仗
fight.er	(n.)	orang yang berkelahi	dǎ jià dė rén 打架的人
		orang yang bertempur	zhàn shì 战士
fig.ure	(n.)	bentuk, gambar	xíng zhuàng 形状, tú xíng 图形
		tokoh, angka	rén wù 人物, shù zì 数字
file	(n.)	kikir (perkakas)	cùo zí 锉子, cùo daō 锉刀
		arsip	dàng àn 档案
		tempat surat	wén jiàn jiā 文件荚
		barisan	dùi wǔ 队伍, paí dùi 排队
fill	(v.)	mengisi	tián mǎn 填满,chōng mǎn 充满
film	(n.)	film	jiāo piàn 胶片, ruǎn piàn 软片
		bioskop	yǐng piàn 影片, diàn yǐng 电影
fil.ter	(n.)	filter, saringan	gùo lù qì 过虑器
fi.nal	(n.)	final, yang terakhir	zùi hòu dė 最后的, jué sài 决赛
fi.nal.ist	(n.)	finalis	jué sai xuǎn shǒu 决赛选手

fi.nal.ly	(adv.)	akhirnya	zùi hòu 最后
fi.nance	(n.)	keuangan	cái zhèng 财政
fi.nan.cial	(a.)	mengenai keuangan	cái zhèng shàng dė 财政上的, jīn róng dė 金融的
fi.nan.ci.er	(n.)	ahli keuangan	cái zhèng jiā 财政家, jīn róng jiā 金融家
find	(v.)	menemukan	zhǎo dào 找到, fā xiàn 发现
fine	(a.)	bagus	yōu měi 优美, měi hǎo 美好
	(n.)	denda	fà kuǎn 罚款
fine.ness	(n.)	keindahan, keelokan	méi hǎo 美好, yōu liáng 优良
		kehalusan	jīng zhì 精致
fin.ger	(n.)	jari tangan	shǒu zhī 手指
fin.ish	(n.)	akhir, kesudahan	wán bì 完毕, jié shù 结束
	(v.)	menyudahkan, mengha-biskan, menyelesaikan	shì jié shù 使结束, shì wán chéng 使完成
fi.nite	(a.)	terbatas	yǒu xiàn dė 有限的, yǒu xiàn dìng dė 有限定的
fire	(n.)	api	hǔo 火
		kebakaran	hǔo zai 火灾, hǔo shao 火烧
	(v.)	menyalakan	diǎn hǔo 点火, shēng húo 生火
		menembakkan	kaī qiāng 开枪
fire-a.larm	(n.)	tanda bahaya kebakaran	hǔo jǐng 火警
fire-bri.gade	(n.)	pasukan pemadam ke-bakaran	xiāo fáng dùi 消防队
fire-en.gine	(n.)	mobil pemadam keba-karan	jiù hǔo jī 救火机, miè huǒ jī 灭火机
fire.fly	(n.)	kunang-kunang	yíng hǔo chóng 萤火虫
fire.man	(n.)	juru api	hǔo fū 火夫
		masinis	sī lǔ 司炉
		anggota pemadam ke-bakaran	jiù hǔo yuán 救火员, xiāo fáng yuán 消防员

fire-place	(n.)	perapian, tungku	bì lú 壁炉
fire-proof	(a.)	tahan api	nài hǔo dė 耐火的
fire.side	(n.)	di sisi perapian	lú biān 炉边
fire-water	(n.)	minuman keras	liè jiǔ 烈酒
fire.wood	(n.)	kayu bakar	mù chái 木柴
fir.ing	(n.)	menyalakan api	diǎn huǒ 点火
		menembakkan	shè jī 射击
firm	(n.)	firma, perusahaan	shāng hào 商号, gōng sī 公司
	(a.)	kokoh, teguh	jiān gù dė 坚固的, jiān dìng dė 坚定的
first	(a.)	pertama	dì yī 第一
first-hand	(a.)	langsung	zhí jiē dė 直接的
		tangan pertama	dì yī shǒu dė 第一手的
fis.cal	(a.)	mengenai keuangan	caì zhèng dė 财政的
fish	(n.)	ikan	yú 鱼
fish.er	(n.)	nelayan	yú fū 渔夫, yú mín 渔民
fish.ery	(n.)	perikanan	yú yè 渔业
fish-farm.ing	(n.)	pemeliharaan ikan	yǎng yú 养鱼
fish-hook	(n.)	mata kail, pancing	yú diào 鱼钓
fish.ing	(n.)	pemancingan/penang-kapan ikan	diào yú 钓鱼, bǔ yú 捕鱼
fish.mon.ger	(n.)	pedagang ikan	yú fàn 鱼贩, yú shāng 鱼商
fish.wife	(n.)	wanita penjual ikan	mài yú fù 卖鱼妇
fist	(n.)	tinju	quán tóu 拳头
fit	(a.)	cocok, patut	shì hé 适合, qià dàng 恰当,
		sehat	jiàn kāng 健康
	(v.)	menyesuaikan	shì shì hé 使适合, shì yìng 适应
five	(n.)	lima	wǔ 五
five.fold	(a.)	lipat lima	wǔ bèi dė 五倍的
fix	(v.)	memasang	zhuāng pèi 装配
		menentukan	jué dìng 决定
		membetulkan	xiū lǐ 修理

flag	(n.)	bendera	qì 旗
flag-pole	(n.)	tiang bendera	qí gān 旗杆
flam.boy.ant	(a.)	semarak	xiān yàn dė 鲜艳的,
			huā huā lù lù dė 花花碌碌的
		cemerlang	huá lì dė 华丽的,
			càn làn dė 灿烂的
flame	(n.)	nyala api	hŭo yàn 火焰
flash	(n.)	cahaya, nyala	shăn guāng 闪光, shăn liàng 闪亮
	(v.)	memberi cahaya, bersinar	fā shăn guāng 发闪光, fā liàng发亮
flat	(a.)	datar, ceper	píng 平, píng tăn 平坦
	(n.)	flat	gōng yù 公寓
flat.ter	(v.)	merayu	fèng chéng 奉承, taŏ hăo 讨好
fla.vour	(n.)	lezat, harum	mĕi wèi 美味, xiāng wèi 香味
flea	(n.)	kutu	zăo 蚤, tiào zăo 跳蚤
flee	(v.)	melarikan diri, kabur	táo zŏu 逃走
fleet	(n.)	armada	jiàn dùi 舰队
flesh	(n.)	daging	ròu 肉
flex.i.ble	(a.)	fleksibel	líng húo 灵活
flight	(n.)	penerbangan	feī xíng 飞行
float	(v.)	terapung, mengapung	piāo fú 漂浮, piāo líu 漂流
flock	(n.)	kelompok	qún 群
	(v.)	berkelompok, berkumpul	qún jí 群集
flood	(v.)	banjir	fàn làn 泛滥
	(n.)	banjir	hóng shŭi 洪水
floor	(n.)	lantai	dì băn 地板
flo.ra	(n.)	flora	zhí wù qún 植物群
		alam tumbuh-tumbuhan	zhí wù zhì 植物志
flour	(n.)	tepung terigu	miàn fĕn 面粉
flour.ish	(v.)	berkembang	fán róng 繁荣
		tumbuh subur	maò shèng 茂盛
		melambai-lambai	huī dòng 挥动

flow	(v.)	mengalir	líu dòng 流动
flow.er	(n.)	bunga, kembang	huā 花
flu.ent	(a.)	fasih, lancar	líu dòng 流动
flute	(n.)	suling	dí zi 笛子
fly	(v.)	terbang	feī 飞
	(n.)	lalat	cāng yíng 苍蝇
foam	(n.)	buih, busa	pào mò 泡沫
fo.cus	(n.)	fokus, titik api	jiāo diǎn 焦点
foe	(n.)	musuh	dí rén 敌人
fog	(n.)	kabut	wù 雾
fog.gy	(a.)	berkabut	yǒu wù dė 有雾的,
			duō wù dė 多雾的
fold	(n.)	kandang domba	yáng lán 羊栏
		lipatan	zhě dié 折迭, bèi 倍
	(v.)	melipat	zhě 折, hé lóng 合拢
folk	(n.)	orang-orang, rakyat	rén mén 人们, rén mín 人民
fol.low	(v.)	menurut, mengikut	gēn 跟, gēn sǔi 跟随
fol.low.er	(n.)	pengikut	gēn sǔi zhě 跟随者
fol.ly	(n.)	kebodohan	yú bèn 愚笨
fond	(a.)	suka	xǐ ài 喜爱, ài hǎo 爱好
food	(n.)	makanan	shí wù 食物, shí pǐn 食品
fool	(n.)	orang bodoh	bèn rén 笨人, shǎ guā 傻瓜
fool.ish	(a.)	bodoh, tolol	yú bèn 愚笨, yú chǔn 愚蠢
foot	(n.)	kaki	jiǎo 脚, zú 足
foot.ball	(n.)	sepak bola	zú qiú 足球
foot.note	(n.)	catatan kaki	jiǎo zhù 脚注
foot.path	(n.)	jalan kecil, lorong	rén xíng dào 人行道
foot.print	(n.)	jejak	zú jī 足迹, jiǎo yìn 脚印
foot.step	(n.)	langkah	jiǎo bù 脚步
for	(prep.)	untuk, karena	tì 替, wèi 为, yīn wèi 因为

for.bid	(v.)	melarang	jìn zhǐ 禁止
force	(n.)	kekuatan	lì liàng 力量, wǔ lì 武力
		angkatan perang	wǔ zhuāng bù dùi 武装部队
	(v.)	memaksa	qiáng pò 强迫
fore.cast	(n.)	prakiraan (cuaca)	yù cè 预测, yù baò 预报
fore.fa.ther	(n.)	nenek moyang	zǔ zōng 祖宗
fore.fin.ger	(n.)	jari telunjuk	shí zhǐ 食指
fore.front	(n.)	bagian paling depan	zùi qián bù 最前部, zùi qián xiàn 最前线
fore.head	(n.)	dahi, kening	é 额, qián é 前额
for.eign	(a.)	asing	wài guó dė 外国的
for.eign.er	(n.)	orang asing	wài guó rén 外国人
fore.know	(v.)	mengetahui sebelumnya	yù zhī 预知
fore.man	(n.)	mandor	gōng tóu 工头
fore.most	(a.)	terdepan	zùi qián dė 最前的
		paling awal	zùi chū dė 最初的
fore.noon	(n.)	pagi hari	shàng wǔ 上午
		sebelum tengah hari	wǔ qián 午前
fore.run.ner	(n.)	pelopor	xiān qū zhě 先驱者
fore.see	(v.)	mengetahui sebelumnya	yù jiàn 预见, yù zhī 预知
fore.shad.ow	(v.)	memberi pertanda	yù zhào 预兆
fore.sight	(n.)	tinjauan ke masa depan	yù jiàn 预见, xiān jiàn 先见
for.est	(n.)	hutan	sēn lín 森林
fore.tell	(v.)	meramalkan	yù yán 预言, yù gào 预告
for.ev.er	(adv.)	selama-lamanya	yǒng yǔan 永远
fore.warn	(v.)	memperingatkan sebe- lumnya	yù xiān jǐng gào 预先警告
fore.word	(n.)	prakata	qián yán 前言
for.get	(v.)	lupa, melupakan	wàng jì 忘记
for.get.ful	(a.)	pelupa	jiàn wàng 健忘

for.give	(v.)	memaafkan	yuán liàng 原谅
fork	(n.)	garpu	chă zi 叉子
form	(n.)	bentuk	xíng shì 形式, xíng zhuàng 形状
		formulir	biǎo gé 表格
	(v.)	membentuk	xíng chéng 形成, gòu chéng 构成
for.mal	(a.)	formil	xíng shì shàng dė 形式上的
		resmi	zhèng shì dė 正式的
for.mal.i.ty	(n.)	tata cara, formalitas	lǐ jié 礼节, xíng shì 形式
for.mat	(n.)	format	bǎn shì 版式
for.mer	(a.)	yang lebih dahulu,	qián zhě 前者,
		dahulu	yǐ qián 以前, cóng qián 从前
for.mu.la	(n.)	rumus, formula	gōng shì 公式
for.sake	(v.)	meninggalkan	yí qì 遗弃
fort	(n.)	benteng	bǎo lěi 堡垒
forth	(adv.)	maju, selanjutnya	xiàng qián 向前, yǐ hòu 以后
forth.with	(adv.)	dengan segera	lì jí 立即, lì kè 立刻
for.ti.eth	(n.)	keempat puluh	dì sì shí 第四十
		seperempat puluh	sì shí fēn zhī yī 四十分之一
fort.night	(n.)	dua minggu	liǎng xīng qī 两星期
for.tress	(n.)	benteng	bǎo lěi 堡垒
for.tu.nate	(a.)	berbahagia, beruntung	xìng fú 幸福, xìng yùn 幸运
for.tune	(n.)	peruntungan	xìng yùn 幸运
		nasib	mìng yùn 命运
for.ty	(n.)	empat puluh	sì shí 四十
fo.rum	(n.)	mimbar	lùn tán 论坛
for.ward	(adv.)	maju ke depan	xiàng qían 向前
	(v.)	mengirimkan	jì fā 寄发
fos.sil	(n.)	fosil	huà shí 化石
fos.ter	(v.)	mengasuh	fǔ yǎng 扶养
fos.ter-brother	(n.)	saudara angkat	yì xiōng dì 义兄弟

fos.ter-child	(n.)	anak angkat	yǎng zǐ 养子, yì zǐ 义子
fos.ter-father	(n.)	ayah angkat	yì fù 义父
fos.ter-mother	(n.)	ibu angkat	yì mǔ 义母
fos.ter-sister	(n.)	saudara angkat perem-puan	yì jiě mèi 义姐妹
foul	(a.)	kotor	āng zāng 肮脏
found	(v.)	mendirikan	jiàn lì 建立
foun.da.tion	(n.)	dasar	jī chǔ 基础
		dana	jī jīn 基金
		yayasan	jī jīn hùi 基金会
found.er	(n.)	pendiri	jiàn lì zhě 建立者, cuàng lì zhě 创立者
foun.tain	(n.)	air mancur	quán shǔi 泉水, pèn shǔi 喷水
foun.tain-head	(n.)	sumber air, asal	shùi yuán 水源, gen yuán 根源
four	(n.)	empat	sì 四
four.fold	(a.)	lipat empat	sì bèi 四倍
four.teen	(n.)	empat belas	shí sí 十四
four.teenth	(n.)	keempat belas	dì shí sì 第十四
		tanggal empat belas	shí sì rì 十四日, shí sì hào 十四号
fourth	(a.)	keempat	dì sì 第四
		tanggal empat	sì rì 四日, sì hào 四号
		seperempat	sì fēn zhī yī 四分之一
fowl	(n.)	unggas	jiā qín 家禽
fox	(n.)	rubah	hú lí 狐狸
fox.y	(a.)	licik	jiǎo huá 狡猾
frac.tion	(a.)	bagian kecil	xiǎo bù fēn 小部分
		pecahan	fēn shù 分数
frag.ment	(n.)	fragmen, pecahan	piàn duàn 片断, sùi piàn 碎片
fra.grance	(n.)	keharuman	xiāng wèi 香味
fra.grant	(a.)	harum	xiāng 香, fēn fáng 芬芳

frame	(n.)	kerangka, bingkai	gǔ jià 骨架, kuàng zi 框子
frame.work	(n.)	kerangka (rumah, dll.)	gǔ jià 骨架, jié gòu 结构
frank	(a.)	terus terang	tǎn bǎi 坦白
fraud	(n.)	penipuan	qī zhà 欺诈
free	(a.)	bebas, merdeka	zì yóu 自由
free.dom	(n.)	kebebasan, kemerdekaan	zì you 自由
freeze	(v.)	membeku	jié bīng 结冰, dōng jié 冻结
freight	(n.)	barang muatan	yùn hùo 运货
fre.quen.cy	(n.)	kekerapan, frekuensi	lǔ cì 屡次, cì shù 次数
fre.quent	(a.)	kerap, sering	cháng cháng 常常, jīng cháng 经常
fresh	(a.)	baru, segar	xīn xiān 新鲜
fric.tion	(n.)	pergesekan	mó cā 摩擦
Fri.day	(n.)	Jum'at	xīng qī wǔ 星期五
friend	(n.)	teman, kawan	péng yǒu 朋友
friend.less	(a.)	tak berteman	méi yǒu péng yǒu 没有朋友
friend.ly	(a.)	ramah-tamah	yǒu hǎo dė 友好的, yǒu shàn dė 友善的
friend.ship	(n.)	persahabatan	yǒu yì 友谊
fright	(n.)	ketakutan	hài pà 害怕, kǒng bù 恐怖
fright.en	(v.)	menakutkan menakut-nakuti	shǐ rén hài pà 使人害怕, xìa hǔ 吓唬
fright.ful	(a.)	menakutkan	kě pà dė 可怕的
frig.id	(a.)	dingin sekali	hán léng 寒冷, hěn léng 很冷
frog	(n.)	kodok, katak	qīng wā 青蛙
frog.man	(n.)	manusia katak	wā rén 蛙人, qián shǔi yuán 潜水员
frol.ic	(v., a.)	bermain-main, bersenang-senang	xǐ xì 嬉戏, huān lè 欢乐
from	(prep.)	dari, sejak	cóng 从
front	(n.)	depan, muka garis depan	qián miàn 前面 qián xiàn 前线

fron.tier	(n.)	tapal batas	biān jiè 边界
frost	(n.)	embun beku	shuāng 霜
frown	(v.)	mengerutkan dahi	zhòu méi tóu 皱眉头
	(n.)	kerut dahi	zhòu méi 皱眉
fruit	(n.)	buah-buahan	shŭi gŭo 水果
fruit.less	(a.)	tidak berbuah	bù jié gŭo 不结果
		tidak berhasil	mĕi yŏu jié gŭo 没有结果, mĕi yŏu shōu hùo 没有收获
frus.trate	(v.)	menggagalkan	cùo zhé 挫折
frus.tra.tion	(n.)	kegagalan, frustrasi	cùo zhé 挫折
fry	(v.)	menggoreng	jiān 煎
fu.el	(n.)	bahan bakar	rán liào 燃料
ful.fill	(n.)	memenuhi, menyelesai- kan	wán chéng 完成
full	(a.)	penuh	măn 满
fun	(n.)	senda gurau	wán xiào 玩笑
func.tion	(n.)	fungsi	jī néng 机能, zuò yòng 作用
func.tion.a.ry	(n.)	pejabat, pegawai, fung- sionaris	gōng wù yuán 公务员, gōng zùo rén yuán 工作人员
fund	(n.)	dana	jī jīn 基金, zī jīn 资金
fun.da.men.tal	(a.)	dasar	jī bĕn dė 基本的
fu.ner.al	(n.)	pemakaman, penguburan	zàng lĭ 葬礼
fun.nel	(n.)	corong, cerobong asap	lòu dŏu 漏斗, yān cōng 烟囱
fun.ny	(a.)	lucu, menggelikan	huá jī dė 滑稽的, hăo wán dė 好玩的, hăo xiào dė 好笑的
fur	(n.)	kulit berbulu, bulu halus	máo pí 毛皮, ruăn máo 软毛
fu.ri.ous	(a.)	sangat marah	kuáng nù dė 狂怒的,
		hebat, dahsyat	jī liè dė 激烈的
fur.nace	(n.)	perapian, tungku	lú zi 炉子
fur.ni.ture	(n.)	perabot rumah tangga	jiā jù 家具

fur.ri.er	(n.)	pedagang pakaian bulu	pí hùo shāng 皮货商
fur.ther	(adv.)	lebih jauh	gèng yuǎn 更远, gèng jìn yī bù 更进一步
fu.ry	(n.)	kemarahan, kegeraman	kuáng nù 狂怒, bào nù 暴怒
fu.ture	(n.)	masa depan	jiāng lái 将来, wèi lái 未来
fuzz	(n.)	bulu halus	xì máo 细毛
fuzz.y	(a.)	berbulu halus	yǒu xì máo dė 有细毛的

G

gai.ly	(adv.)	dengan gembira	kuài lè dė 快乐的
gain	(v.)	memperoleh	dé 得, huò dé 获得, zhuàn 赚
	(n.)	keuntungan, laba	lì yì 利益, zhuàn qián 赚钱
gain.say	(v.)	menyangkal	fǒu rèn 否认
gala	(n.)	pesta besar	dà jié rì 大节日
gale	(n.)	angin ribut	baò fēng 暴风
gal.lant	(a.)	megah	táng huáng 堂皇
		gagah berani	yǒng měng 勇猛
gal.ler.y	(n.)	serambi	zǒu láng 走廊
		galeri (seni)	měi shù guǎn 美术馆
gal.lop	(v.)	lari kencang (kuda)	(mǎ) feī pǎo 马飞跑, bèn chí 奔驰
gam.ble	(v.)	berjudi	dǔ bó 赌博
gam.bler	(n.)	penjudi	dǔ tú 赌徒, dǔ bó gǔi 赌博鬼
game	(n.)	permainan, pertandingan	yóu xì 游戏, bǐ sài 比赛
gan.der	(n.)	angsa jantan	xióng é 雄鹅
gang	(n.)	gerombolan	qún 群, bāng 帮
gang.ster	(n.)	penjahat	qiáng dào 强盗, dǎi tú 歹徒
gang.way	(n.)	gang, jalan sempit	tōng lù 通路, guò dào 过道
gap	(n.)	lubang, celah	kǒng xì 孔隙, quē kǒu 缺口
		jurang pemisah	hóng gòu 鸿沟, chā jù 差距
ga.rage	(n.)	garasi	qì chē fáng 汽车房
gar.bage	(n.)	sampah	lā jī 垃圾
gar.den	(n.)	kebun, taman	huā yuán 花园, gōng yuán 公园

gar.dener	(n.)	tukang kebun	yuán dīng 园丁
gar.dening	(n.)	berkebun	yuán yì 园艺
gar.lic	(n.)	dasun, bawang putih	dà suàn 大蒜
gar.ment	(n.)	pakaian	yī fú 衣服
gar.ri.son	(n.)	garnisun	zhù jūn 驻军
gas	(n.)	gas, bensin	qì tǐ 气体, qì yóu 汽油
gas.light	(n.)	lampu gas	méi qì dēng 煤气灯
gas mask	(n.)	kedok gas	fáng dú miàn jù 防毒面具
gas.o.lene	(n.)	bensin	qì yóu 汽油
gasp	(v.)	terengah-engah, megap-megap	chuǎn qì 喘气
gas-stove	(n.)	kompor gas	méi qì dēng 煤气灯
gate	(n.)	pintu gerbang	dà mén 大门, qiáng mén 墙门
gath.er	(v.)	berkumpul	jù jí 聚集, jí hé 集合
		mengumpulkan	cái jí 采集, sōu jí 搜集
gath.er.ing	(n.)	kumpulan	jí hùi 集会, jí hé 集合
gay	(a.)	gembira	kuāi lè 快乐
gaze	(v.)	memandang, menatap	zhù shì 注视, níng shì 凝视, dīng 盯
gem	(n.)	permata	bǎo shí 宝石
gen.der	(n.)	jenis kelamin	xìng bié 性别
gen.er.al	(a.)	umum, biasa	yī bàn dė 一般的
	(n.)	jenderal	jiāng jūn 将军
gen.er.a.tion	(n.)	generasi, angkatan	shì dài 世代, yī dài 一代
gen.er.a.tor	(n.)	generator, disel	fā diàn jī 发电机
gen.er.ous	(a.)	dermawan, murah hati	kāng kǎi 慷慨, kuān dà 宽大
ge.nius	(n.)	jenius	tiān cái 天才
gen.tle	(a.)	lemah lembut	sī wén 斯文, wén yǎ 文雅, wēn hé 温和
		sepoi-sepoi	hé fēng 和风, xì yǔ 细雨
		jinak	xún fú 驯服

gen.tle.man	(n.)	tuan	shēn shì 绅士, jūn zi 君子
		pria	nán rén 男人
	(pl.)	saudara-saudara, tuan-tuan	xiān shēng mėn 先生们
gen.u.ine	(a.)	tulen, asli	zhēn zhèng dė 真正的
ge.nus	(n.)	golongan, jenis	zhǒng lèi 种类
ge.og.ra.pher	(n.)	ahli ilmu bumi	dì lǐ xué jiā 地理学家, dì lǐ xué zhě 地理学者
ge.og.ra.phy	(n.)	ilmu bumi, geografi	dì lǐ xué 地理学
ge.ol.o.gy	(n.)	geologi	dì zhì xué 地质学
ge.om.e.try	(n.)	ilmu ukur, geometri	jǐ hé xué 几何学
germ	(n.)	kuman	xì jūn 细菌
ges.ture	(n.)	gerak, isyarat, sikap	shǒu shì 手势, zī tài 姿态, zī shì 姿势
ghost	(n.)	hantu	gǔi 鬼
gi.ant	(n.)	raksasa	jù rèn 巨人
gift	(n.)	hadiah, kado	lǐ wù 礼物
gin.ger	(n.)	jahe, halia	jiāng 姜
gir.dle	(n.)	ikat pinggang	yaō dài 腰带
girl	(n.)	gadis	nǔ hái zí 女孩子
give	(v.)	memberi	gěi 给
glad	(a.)	gembira	kuài lè 快乐
glance	(v.)	memandang sekejap	kàn yī yǎn 看一眼
		melihat sepintas lalu	piē yī yǎn 瞥一眼
glare	(n.)	cahaya yang menyilaukan	shǎn guāng 闪光
		pandangan marah	dèng yǎn 瞪眼
glass	(n.)	gelas, kaca	bō lí bèi 玻璃杯, bō lí 玻璃
		cermin	jìng zi 镜子
glasses	(n.)	kacamata	yan jing 眼镜
gleam	(n.)	sinar, kilau	guāng 光, shǎn guāng 闪光
glee	(n.)	kegembiraan	gāo xìng 高兴

glit.ter	(v.)	berkilat, berkilap-kilap	shăn shùo 闪烁
glo.bal	(a.)	global, sedunia	shì jiè dė 世界的,
			quán qiú dė 全球的
		keseluruhan	zǒng dė 总的, quán 全
globe	(n.)	bola, bola dunia	qiú 球, dì qiú 地球
gloom	(a.)	suram	yīn chén 阴沉, yīn àn 阴暗
glo.ri.ous	(a.)	mulia, jaya	guāng róng dė 光荣的,
			guāng róng dė chéng jiù 光荣的成就
glo.ry	(n.)	kemuliaan, kejayaan	guāng róng 光荣, fán róng 繁荣
glos.sa.ry	(n.)	daftar kosa kata	cí hùi biǎo 词汇表
glove	(v.)	sarung tangan	shǒu tào 手套
glue	(n.)	perekat	jiāo shǔi 胶水
gnaw	(v.)	menggerogoti	kěn 啃
go	(v.)	pergi	qù 去
goal	(n.)	tujuan	mù biǎo 目标
		gol	zú qiú qiú mén 足球球门
goat	(n.)	kambing	shān yáng 山羊
God	(n.)	Tuhan, dewa	shàng dì 上帝, shén 神
god.dess	(n.)	dewi	nǔ shén 女神
god.less	(a.)	tidak percaya kepada Tuhan	bù xìn shén dė 不信神的
gold	(n.)	emas	jīn 金, huáng jīn 黄金
gold.fish	(n.)	ikan mas	jīn yú 金鱼
gold-mine	(n.)	tambang emas	jīn kuàng 金矿
good	(a.)	baik, bagus	hǎo 好, liáng hǎo 良好
good-bye	(int.)	selamat jalan/tinggal	zài jiàn 再见, zài hùi 再会
good.ness	(n.)	kebaikan	shàn liáng 善良
goods	(n.)	barang-barang	hùo wù 货物
		harta benda	cái chǎn 财产
goose	(n.)	angsa	é 鹅

gos.sip	(n.)	gosip, bercakap angin	xián tán 闲谈, liáo tiān 聊天
		desas-desus	liú yán 流言, feī yǔ 蜚语
gov.ern	(v.)	memerintah	tǒng zhì 统治, guǎn lǐ 管理
gov.ern.ment	(n.)	pemerintah	zhèng fǔ 政府
gov.er.nor	(n.)	gubernur	shěng zhǎng 省长
grab	(v.)	mengambil, merampas	zhuā qǔ 抓取, qiáng duó 强夺
grace	(n.)	kemolekan	yōu yǎ 优雅, yōu měi 优美
		kurnia	ēn hùi 恩惠
grade	(n.)	tingkat, sederajat	děng jí 等级
grad.u.al	(a.)	berangsur-angsur	zhú jiàn 逐渐
grad.u.ate	(n.)	lulusan sekolah tinggi	dà xué bì yè shēng 大学毕业生
grain	(n.)	butir padi	gǔ lì 谷粒
gram.mar	(n.)	tata bahasa	yǔ fǎ 语法
gram.ma.ri.an	(n.)	ahli tata bahasa	yǔ fǎ xué jiā 语法学家
gram.o.phone	(n.)	gramofon	liú shēng jī 留声机
grand	(a.)	agung, besar	táng huáng 堂皇, hóng dà 宏大
		mulia	gāo gùi 高贵
grand.child	(n.)	cucu	sūn zi 孙子, wài sūn 外孙
grand.dad	(n.)	kakek	zǔ fù 祖父
grand.daught.er	(n.)	cucu perempuan	sūn nǚ 孙女, wài sūn nǚ 外孙女
grand.fath.er	(n.)	kakek	zǔ fù 祖父
grand.moth.er	(n.)	nenek	zǔ mǔ 祖母
grand.son	(n.)	cucu laki-laki	sūn zi 孙子, wài sūn 外孙
grant	(v.)	memberi izin	yǔn xǔ 允许, dā yìng 答应, tóng yì 同意
		memberi	gěi yú 给予
grape	(n.)	buah anggur	pú taó 葡萄
grasp	(v.)	mencengkeram	zhuā jǐn 抓紧
		menangkap	zhuā zhù 抓住
grass	(n.)	rumput	cǎo 草

grass.hop.per	(n.)	belalang	zhà měng 蚱蜢
grass.land	(n.)	padang rumput	cáo yuán 草原
grate.ful	(a.)	berterima kasih	gǎn xiè dė 感谢的
gra.tis	(adv.)	dengan gratis, dengan cuma-cuma	miǎn fèi 免费
grat.i.tude	(n.)	rasa terima kasih	gǎn xiè 感谢
grave	(n.)	kuburan	fén mù 坟墓
	(a.)	sungguh-sungguh	yán sù 严肃
gray	(a.)	abu-abu	huī sè dė 灰色的
graze	(v.)	merumput	chī caǒ 吃草
grease	(n.)	lemak	yóu zhī 油脂
great	(a.)	besar, agung	jù dà dė 巨大的, wěi dà dė 伟大的, zhòng dà dė 重大的
greed.y	(a.)	rakus	tān chī dė 贪吃的
		serakah	tān xīn dė 贪心的
green	(a.)	hijau	lù sè dė 绿色的
greet	(v.)	menyambut	yíng jiē 迎接
		memberi salam	wèn hòu 问候, zhì jìng 致敬
greet.ing	(n.)	salam	jìng lǐ 敬礼
		ucapan salam	zhù hè 祝贺, wèn hòu 问候
gre.nade	(n.)	granat	shǒu liú dàn 手榴弹
grey	(a.)	abu-abu	huī sè dė 灰色的
grief	(n.)	duka cita	beī tòng 悲痛, shāng xīn 伤心
grieve	(v.)	membuat orang sedih	shǐ rén shāng xīn 使人伤心
grim	(a.)	seram, kejam	léng kù dė 冷酷的, cán kù dė 残酷的
grind	(v.)	menggiling	mò 磨
grip	(v.)	mencengkeram	jǐn wò 紧握
		mengerti	lǐ jiě 理解
		menguasai	zhǎng wò 掌握

grit	(n.)	kerikil	shā lì 砂粒
groan	(v.)	mengaduh	shēn yín 呻吟
gro.cer	(n.)	penjual makanan dan minuman	shí pǐn shāng 食品商
		pedagang barang kelon-tong	zá húo shāng 杂货商
gro.cer.y	(n.)	toko makanan dan kelon-tong	shí pǐn zá huò diàn 食品杂货店
groom	(n.)	pengantin pria	xīn láng 新郎
		tukang kuda	mǎ fū马夫
gross	(a.)	kasar, kurang ajar	cū sú 粗俗, cú lǔ 粗鲁
		jumlah keseluruhan	zǒng shù dė 总数的, zǒng dė 总的
	(n.)	gros, dua belas lusin	lúo 罗
ground	(n.)	tanah	dì 地
ground.less	(a.)	tanpa dasar	méi yǒu gēn jù dė 没有根据的
		tanpa alasan	méi yǒu lǐ yoú dė 没有理由的
ground-nut	(n.)	kacang tanah	huā shēng 花生
ground.work	(n.)	dasar, fondasi	jī chǔ 基础
group	(n.)	kelompok	zǔ 组
		golongan	pài 派, jí tuán 集团
grow	(v.)	tumbuh	shēng zhǎng 生长
grudge	(n.)	dendam	yuàn hèn 怨恨
grum.ble	(v.)	menggerutu	fā laó sāo 发牢骚
guar.an.tee	(n.)	garansi	bǎo zhèng 保证, dān bǎo 担保
guar.an.tor	(n.)	penjamin	bǎo zhèng rén 保证人
guard	(n.)	pengawal	wèi bıng 卫兵, jing wèi yuán 警卫员
guard.ian	(n.)	wali	bǎo hù rén 保护人, jiān hù rén 监护人

gue(r).ril.la	(n.)	gerilya	yóu jī zhàn 游击战
		gerilyawan	yóu jī duì yuán 游击队员
guess	(v.)	menerka, menduga	cái cè 猜测, tuī cè 推测
guest	(n.)	tamu	kè rén 客人
guid.ance	(n.)	pembimbing, penunjuk	fū dǎo 辅导, xiàng dǎo 向导
		penuntun	zhǐ dǎo 指导
guide	(v.)	membimbing	yǐn dǎo 引导
		menunjukkan jalan	xiàng dǎo 向导
guilt	(n.)	rasa bersalah, rasa berdosa	fàn zùi 犯罪
guilt.less	(a.)	tak berdosa	wú zuì 无罪
gui.tar	(n.)	gitar	liù xián qín 六弦琴
gulf	(n.)	teluk	hǎi wān 海湾
gulp	(n.)	tegukan	tūn 吞
gun	(n.)	meriam, senapan	dà pào 大炮, qiāng 枪
gun.ner	(n.)	penembak	qiāng shǒu 枪手
gun.pow.der	(n.)	mesiu	huǒ yaò 火药
gun.stock	(n.)	batang senapan	qiāng tuō 枪托
gust	(n.)	badai	kuáng fēng 狂风
gut	(n.)	usus, isi perut	cháng 肠, nèi zàng 内脏
gut.ter	(n.)	selokan, parit	gōu 沟, shǔi gōu 水沟
gym.na.sium	(n.)	gedung olahraga	tǐ yù guǎn 体育馆
gym.nast	(n.)	pesenam	tǐ cāo yùn dòng yuán 体操运动员
		ahli senam	tǐ cāo zhuān jiā 体操专家
		olahragawan	tǐ yù jiā 体育家
		guru olahraga	tǐ yù jiào shī 体育教师
gym.nas.tic	(a.)	mengenai senam	tǐ cāo dė 体操的,
		mengenai olahraga	tǐ yù dė 体育的
gym.nas.tics	(n.)	senam, olahraga	tǐ cāo 体操, tǐ yù 体育

H

hab.it	(n.)	kebiasaan	xí guàn 习惯
hab.it.a.ble	(a.)	yang dapat ditinggali	kě jū zhù dė 可居住的
hab.i.ta.tion	(n.)	tempat tinggal	zhù sǔo 住所, zhù zhǎi 住宅
ha.bit.u.al	(a.)	biasa	xí guàn dė 习惯的
ha.bit.u.ate	(v.)	membiasakan	shǐ xí guàn 使习惯
hail	(n.)	hujan es	báo 雹
hair	(n.)	rambut	tóu fǎ 头发
		bulu	máo 毛
hair-breadth	(n.)	nyaris	chā yī diǎn 差一点, jī hū 几乎
hair.cut	(n.)	potong rambut	lǐ fǎ 理发, jiǎn fǎ 剪发
hair.dress.er	(n.)	penata rambut, tukang cukur	lǐ fǎ shī 理发师
hair.pin	(n.)	jepit rambut, tusuk konde	jiā fǎ zhēn 夹发针, zān zi 簪子
hairy	(a.)	berambut, berbulu	yǒu máo dė 有毛的
half	(n.)	setengah, separo	yī bàn 一半
half-way	(n.)	setengah jalan	bàn lù 半路, bàn tú 半途
hall	(n.)	ruangan besar	dà xià 大厦
		gedung pertemuan	lǐ táng 礼堂, hùi táng 会堂
halt	(n.)	penghentian	tǐng zhǐ 停止
halve	(v.)	membagi dua	dùi fēn 对分, píng fēn 平分
ham	(n.)	ham	hǔo tǔı 火腿
ham.let	(n.)	dusun kecil	xiaǒ cūn 小村
ham.mer	(n.)	palu	chúi 锤, tiě chúi 铁锤
hand	(n.)	tangan	shǒu 手
		jarum jam	zhǐ zhēn 指针

hand-bag	(n.)	tas tangan	shǒu tí dài 手提袋
hand.bill	(n.)	selebaran	chuán dān 传单
hand.book	(n.)	buku pedoman	shǒu cè 手册
hand.craft	(n.)	keterampilan tangan	shǒu yì 手艺
hand.cuff	(n.)	belenggu, borgol	shǒu kǎo 手铐
hand.ful	(n.)	segenggam	yī bǎ 一把
hand.ker.chief	(n.)	saputangan	shǒu jīn 手巾
han.dle	(n.)	tangkai	bǎ bǐng 把柄
hand-made	(a.)	buatan tangan	shǒu zhì dė 手制的, shǒu gōng dė 手工的
hand.shake	(n.)	jabatan tangan	wò shǒu 握手
hand.some	(a.)	ganteng, tampan	piào liàng 漂流, měi lì 美丽
hand-work	(n.)	pekerjaan tangan	shǒu gōng 手工
hand.y	(a.)	cekatan, ringan tangan	líng qiǎo 灵巧, qīng biàn 轻便
hang	(v.)	menggantung	xuán guà 悬挂
hang.er	(n.)	gantungan	guà gōu 挂钩, diào jià 吊架
hap.pen	(v.)	terjadi	fā shēng 发生
hap.py	(a.)	gembira, bahagia	kuài lè 快乐, xìng fú dė 幸福的
har.bour	(n.)	pelabuhan	gǎng kǒu 港口
hard	(a.)	keras	yìng dė 硬的
hard.en	(v.)	mengeras	yìng huà 硬化
hard.ship	(n.)	penderitaan, kesulitan	jiān kǔ 艰苦, jiān nán 艰难
hard.ware	(n.)	barang-barang dari logam	jīn shǔ qì 金属器, wǔ jīn 五金
har.dy	(a.)	tahan susah, tegar	nài kǔ 耐苦
hare	(n.)	terwelu	yě tù 野兔
harm	(n.)	kerugian, kerusakan	sǔn hài 损害, shāng hài 伤害
harm.ful	(n.)	berbahaya	yǒu hài dė 有害的
har.mon.ic	(a.)	selaras, serasi	hé xié dė 和谐的, tiáo hé dė 调和的
har.mon.i.ca	(n.)	harmonika	kǒu qín 口琴
har.mo.ny	(n.)	keselarasan, keserasian	tiáo hé 调和, hé xié 和谐

harsh	(a.)	kasar	cū cāo 粗糙
har.vest	(n.)	panen	shōu hùo 收获
haste	(n.)	kegopohan, ketergesaan	jí máng 急忙
hast.en	(v.)	bergegas, mempercepat	gǎn kuài 赶快, jiā shù 加速
hast.y	(a.)	terburu-buru	jí máng dė 急忙的
hat	(n.)	topi	mào zi 帽子
hatch	(v.)	menetas	fū huà 孵化
hate	(v.)	benci	hèn 恨, zēng hèn 憎恨
hate.ful	(a.)	penuh kebencian	kě hèn dė 可恨的
have	(v.)	mempunyai	yǒu 有
ha.ven	(n.)	tempat berlindung	bì nán sǔo 避难所
hawk	(n.)	rajawali	yīng 鹰
hawk.er	(n.)	penjaja	xiǎo fàn 小贩
hay	(n.)	rumput kering, jerami	gān cǎo 干草
hay.stack	(n.)	timbunan jerami	gān cǎo duī 干草堆
he	(pron.)	dia, ia (laki-laki)	tā 他
head	(n.)	kepala	tóu 头
head.ache	(n.)	sakit kepala	tóu tòng 头痛
head.line	(n.)	pokok berita	tóu tiáo xīn wén 头条新闻, zhǔ yào xīn wén 主要新闻
head.man	(n.)	mandor	gōng tóu 工头
head-mas.ter	(n.)	kepala sekolah	xiào zhǎng 校长
head.quar.ters	(n.)	markas besar	sī lìng bù 司令部, zǒng bù 总部
head.strong	(a.)	keras kepala, kepala batu	wán gù 顽固, gù zhí 固执
heal	(v.)	mengobati menyembuhkan	yī zhì 医治 zhì yù 治愈
health	(n.)	kesehatan	jiàn kāng 健康, wèi shēng 卫生
health.y	(a.)	sehat	jiàn kāng dė 健康的, hé hū wèi shēng dė 合乎卫生的
heap	(n.)	timbunan	duī 堆

hear	(v.)	mendengar	tīng 听
hear.er	(n.)	pendengar	tīng dė rén 听的人, páng tīng zhě 旁听者
hear.ing	(n.)	pendengaran	tīng jué 听觉
heart	(n.)	hati, jantung	xīn 心, xīn zàng 心脏
heart-ache	(n.)	sakit hati	xīn tòng 心痛
heart.less	(a.)	tanpa belas kasihan	bó qíng dė 薄情的, wú qíng dė 无情的
heart.y	(a.)	dengan sepenuh hati	qīn qìe dė 亲切的, rè qíng dė 热情的
heat	(n.)	panas	rè 热
heav.en	(n.)	surga, kayangan	tiān táng 天堂, tiān gúo 天国
heav.y	(a.)	berat	zhòng 重
hec.tare	(n.)	hektar	gōng qǐng 公顷
hedge	(n.)	pagar dari tanaman	lǐ bā 篱笆
heed	(v.)	memperhatikan	zhù yì 注意
	(n.)	perhatian	zhù yì 注意
heed.ful	(a.)	penuh perhatian	zhù yì dė 注意的
heed.less	(a.)	tidak perhatian	bù zhù yì 不注意
heel	(n.)	tumit	gēn 跟
he.ge.mo.ny	(n.)	hegemoni	bà quán 霸权
height	(n.)	tinggi	gāo dù 高度
height.en	(v.)	meninggikan	jiā gāo 加高
heir	(n.)	ahli waris	jì chéng rén 继承人
heir.ess	(n.)	ahli waris wanita	nǔ jì chéng rén 女继承人
hel.i.cop.ter	(n.)	helikopter	zhí shēng feī jī 直升飞机
hell	(n.)	neraka	dì yù 地狱
helm	(n.)	kemudi	duò 舵
hel.met	(n.)	topi baja, helm	kuī 盔, gāng kuī 钢盔
helms.man	(n.)	juru mudi	duò shǒu 舵手
help	(v.)	membantu	bāng zhù 帮助
help.er	(n.)	pembantu	zhù shǒu 助手

help.ful	(a.)	berguna	yǒu yòng dė 有用的
help.ing	(n.)	bantuan, pertolongan	bāng zhù 帮助
		porsi	fèn 份
help.less	(a.)	tak berdaya	wú kě nài hé 无可奈何
hen	(n.)	ayam betina	mǔ jī 母鸡
hence	(adv.)	sejak sekarang	jīn hòu 今后
		sebab itu, karenanya	yīn cǐ 因此
hep.a.tit.is	(n.)	hepatitis, radang hati	gān yán 肝炎
herb	(n.)	tanaman obat	yào cǎo 药草
herd	(n.)	kumpulan, kawanan	qún 群
herd.er	(n.)	penggembala	mù rén 牧人, mù mín 牧民
here	(adv.)	(di) sini	(zài) zhè lǐ (在)这里
here.af.ter	(adv.)	sejak sekarang	jīn hòu 今后
here.by	(adv.)	dengan ini	yīn cǐ 因此
he.ro	(n.)	pahlawan	yīng xíong 英雄
he.ro.ic	(a.)	heroik, bersifat kepahlawanan	yīng xióng dė 英雄的
he.ro.ine	(n.)	pahlawan wanita	nǔ yīng xióng 女英雄
her.o.in	(n.)	heroin, obat bius	mǎ fēi 吗啡
her.o.ism	(n.)	kepahlawanan, heroisme	yīng xióng qì gài 英雄气概
hers	(pron.)	kepunyaannya (perempuan)	tā dė 她的
her.self	(pron.)	ia sendiri (perempuan)	tā zì jǐ 她自己
hes.i.tate	(v.)	ragu-ragu	chí yí 迟疑, yóu yù 犹豫
hew	(v.)	menebang	kǎn 砍
hide	(v.)	bersembunyi	yǐn cáng 隐藏
		menyembunyikan	cáng qǐ lái 藏起来
high	(a.)	tinggi	gāo 高
high.road	(n.)	jalan raya	gōng lù 公路

high.speed	(a.)	kecepatan tinggi	gāo shù dė 高速的
high.tide	(n.)	air pasang	gāo cháo 高潮
high.way	(n.)	jalan raya	gōng lù 公路, dà lù 大路
hike	(v.)	berjalan kaki	bù xíng 步行, tú bù 徒步
hill	(n.)	bukit	xiǎo shān 小山, qiū líng 丘陵
hill.y	(a.)	berbukit-bukit	duō xiǎo shān dė 多小山的
him	(pron.)	dia, ia (laki-laki)	tā 他
him.self	(pron.)	ia sendiri (laki-laki)	tā zì jǐ 他自己
hind	(a.)	belakang	hòu miān 后面
hin.der	(v.)	menghalangi	fáng ài 妨碍, zǔ ài 阻碍
	(a.)	bagian belakang	hòu miàn dė 后面的
hind.er.most	(a.)	paling belakang	zùi hòu dė 最后的
hin.drance	(n.)	halangan, rintangan	fáng ài 妨碍, zhàng ài wù 障碍物
hinge	(n.)	engsel	jiǎo lián 铰链
hint	(n.)	isyarat	àn shì 暗示
hip	(n.)	pinggul	bì 髀, dà tǔi 大腿
hire	(v.)	menyewa	zū jiè 租借
		mempekerjakan	gù yòng 雇用
his	(pron.)	kepunyaannya (laki-laki)	tā dė 他的
his.to.ri.an	(n.)	ahli sejarah	lì shǐ xué jiā 历史学家
his.to.ry	(n.)	sejarah	lì shǐ 历史
hit	(v.)	memukul, mengenai	dǎ jī 打击, dǎ zhòng 打中
hith.er	(adv.)	ke sini, kemari	lái zhè lǐ 来这里, wǎng zhè lǐ 往这里
hith.erto	(adv.)	hingga sekarang ini	xiàng lái 向来, cóng lái 从来
hive	(n.)	sarang lebah	fēng fáng 蜂房
hob.by	(n.)	hobi, kegemaran	shì hào 嗜好, ài hào 爱好
hoe	(n.)	pacul, cangkul	chú tóu 锄头
hog	(n.)	babi	zhū 猪
hold	(n.)	memegang	nǎ zhù 拿住
		menggenggam	wò zhù 握住

hold.er	(n.)	pemilik, pemegang	chí yǒu zhě 持有者, zhàn yǒu zhě 占有者, bǎo chí zhě 保持者
		pegangan	bǎ bǐng 把柄, zhī jiā 支架
hole	(n.)	lubang	dòng 洞, kǒng 孔
hol.i.day	(n.)	hari libur	jià rì 假日
ho.li.ness	(n.)	kesucian	shén shèng 神圣
hol.low	(a.)	kosong, hampa	kōng dė 空的, kōng xū dė 空虚的
ho.ly	(a.)	suci	shén shèng 神圣的
hom.age	(n.)	penghormatan	zūn jìng 尊敬
home	(n.)	rumah, tempat tinggal	jiā 家
		kampung halaman	gù xiāng 故乡
home.land	(n.)	tanah air	zǔ guó 祖国
home.less	(a.)	tunawisma	wú jiā kě guī dė 无家可归的
home.work	(n.)	pekerjaan rumah	jiā tíng zùo yè 家庭作业
hon.est	(a.)	jujur	chéng shí 诚实
hon.ey	(n.)	madu	fēng mì 蜂蜜
hon.ey.moon	(n.)	bulan madu	mì yuè 蜜月
hon.our	(n.)	kehormatan	róng yù 荣誉
hon.our.a.ble	(a.)	yang terhormat	róng yù dė 荣誉的
		yang mulia	guāng róng dė 光荣的
hood	(n.)	kerudung kepala	toú jīn 头巾
		kap mobil	chē péng 车篷
hoof	(n.)	kuku kuda atau sapi	tí 蹄
hook	(n.)	kait, cantelan	gōu 钩, diào gōu 吊钩
hop	(v.)	meloncat	tiào 跳, tiào yuè 跳跃
hope	(n.)	harapan	xī wàng 希望
hope.ful	(a.)	penuh harapan	hěn yǒu xī wàng dė很有希望的
		besar harapan	dà yǒu xī wàng dė 大有希望的
hope.less	(a.)	tidak ada harapan	méi yǒu xī wàng 没有希望

ho.ri.zon	(n.)	horison	dì píng xiàn 地平线, shŭi píng xiàn 水平线
hor.i.zon.tal	(a.)	horisontal	dì píng dė 地平的, shŭi píng dė 水平的
horn	(n.)	tanduk	jiăo 角
		terompet	hào jiăo 号角, lā bā 喇叭
hor.ri.ble	(a.)	menakutkan, mengerikan	kĕ pà dė 可怕的
hor.ror	(a.)	horor	kŏng bù 恐怖
horse	(n.)	kuda	mă 马
horse.man	(n.)	penunggang kuda	qí mă zhĕ 骑马者, qí shŏu 骑手
horse.pow.er	(n.)	daya kuda	mă lì 马力
horse-race	(n.)	pacuan kuda	sài mă 赛马, păo mă 跑马
hos.pi.tal	(n.)	rumah sakit	yī yuàn 医院
hos.pi.tal.i.ty	(n.)	keramah-tamahan	hào kè 好客, yīn qín 殷勤
host	(n.)	tuan rumah	zhŭ rén 主人, wū zhŭ 屋主
hos.tage	(n.)	sandera	rén zhì 人质
hos.tel	(n.)	asrama, pondokan	sù shè 宿舍, zhāo dài sŭo 招待所
		losmen	kè diàn 客店
hos.tess	(n.)	nyonya rumah	nŭ zhŭ rén 女主人,
		pemilik penginapan (wanita)	lŭ guăn nŭ zhŭ rén 旅馆女主人
		pramugari	nŭ zhāo dài 女招待
hos.tile	(a.)	bermusuhan	dí duì dė 敌对的, dí shì dė 敌视的
hos.til.i.ty	(n.)	permusuhan	dí dùi 敌对, dí yì 敌意
hot	(a.)	panas	rè 热
ho.tel	(n.)	hotel	lŭ guăn 旅馆, fàn diàn 饭店
hound	(n.)	anjing pemburu	liè gŏu 猎狗
hour	(n.)	jam	xiăo shí 小时, zhōng diăn 钟点
house	(n.)	rumah	fáng wū 房屋
how	(adv.)	bagaimana	zĕn yàng 怎样, rú hé 如何
how.ev.er	(adv.)	bagaimanapun	wú lùn zĕn yàng 无论怎样, wú lùn rú hè 无论如何

huge	(a.)	sangat besar	jù dà dė 巨大的
hu.man	(a.)	mengenai manusia	rén dė 人的, rén lèi dė 人类的
hu.mane	(a.)	sifat kasih sayang	rén cí dė 仁慈的
		berperikemanusiaan	rén dào dė 人道的
hu.man.ism	(n.)	humanisme, perikemanusiaan	rén dào zhǔ yì 人道主义
hu.man.i.ta.ri.an	(n.)	orang yang berperikemanusiaan	rén dào zhǔ yì zhě 人道主义者
hu.man.i.ty	(n.)	umat manusia	rén lèi 人类, rén xìng人性
		perikemanusiaan, humanitas	rén dào 人道
hu.man.kind	(n.)	kemanusiaan	rén lèi 人类
hum.ble	(a.)	rendah hati	qiān xū dė 谦虚的,
		rendah	dī jiàn dė 低贱的
hu.mil.i.ty	(n.)	kerendahan hati	qiān xùn 谦逊
hu.mor.ist	(n.)	orang yang suka melucu	yōu mò jià 幽默家
		orang yang suka humor	huá jī jiā 滑稽家
hu.mour	(n.)	humor, lucu	yōu mò 幽默
hun.dred	(n.)	ratus	bǎi 百
hun.dredth	(n.)	keseratus	dì yī bǎi 第一百
		seperseratus, perseratus	bǎi fēn zhī yī 百分之一
hun.ger	(n.)	lapar, kelaparan	jī è 饥饿, jī huāng 饥荒
hun.gry	(a.)	lapar	è 饿, jī è dė 饥饿的
hunt	(v.)	berburu	dǎ liè 打猎
hun.ter	(n.)	pemburu	liè rén 猎人
hurl	(v.)	melemparkan	diū 丢, zhì 掷
hur.ry	(n.)	kegopohan, buru-buru	huāng máng 慌忙, jí máng 急忙
hurt	(v.)	melukai	shāng hài 伤害, shòu shāng受伤
	(n.)	luka	chuāng shāng 创伤
hus.band	(n.)	suami	zhàng fū 丈夫
hush	(n.)	diam	chén mò 沉默

hut	(n.)	gubuk kecil	xiǎo máo wū 小茅屋
hy.dro.gen	(n.)	hidrogen, zat cair	qīng 氢
hymn	(n.)	himne, nyanyian pujian	zàn měi gē 赞美歌
hy.phen	(n.)	tanda hubung	lián jiē hào 连接号
hyp.no.tism	(n.)	hipnotisme	cuī mián shù 催眠术, cuī mián 催眠

I

I	(pron.)	saya	wǒ 我
ice	(n.)	es	bīng 冰
ice.berg	(n.)	gunung es	bīng shān 冰山
ice-box	(n.)	lemari es, peti es	bīng xiāng 冰箱
ice-cream	(n.)	es krim	bīng qí lìn 冰淇淋
i.cy	(a.)	dingin seperti es	bīng léng dė 冰冷的
i.de.a	(n.)	gagasan, ide	yì jiàn 意见, zhǔ yì 主意
i.deal	(a.)	ideal, idaman	lǐ xiǎng dė 理想的
i.deal.ism	(n.)	idealisme	lǐ xiǎng zhǔ yì 理想主义, wéi xīn zhǔ yì 唯心主义
i.deal.ist	(n.)	seorang idealis	lǐ xiǎng zhu yì zhě 理想主义者, wéi xīn zhǔ yì zhě 唯心主义者
i.deal.ize	(v.)	mengidealkan	lī xiǎng hùa 理想化
i.den.ti.cal	(a.)	sama, serupa, identik	tóng yàng dė 同样的, yī yāng dė 一样的
i.den.ti.fi.ca.tion	(n.)	identifikasi, pengenalan	shí bié 识别, biàn rèn 辨认
i.den.ti.fy	(v.)	mengenali	biàn bié 辨别, biàn rèn 辨认
i.den.ti.ty	(n.)	identitas, ciri-ciri	běn xìng 本性, tè zhēng 特征
ide.ol.o.gist	(n.)	adicita	lǐ lùn jiā 理伦家, sī xiǎng jiā 思想家
id.e.ol.o.gy	(n.)	ideologi	sī xiǎng yì shí 思想意识
id.i.om	(n.)	idiom	chéng yǔ 成语
i.dle	(a.)	malas, bermalas-malasan	lǎn duò 懒惰, lǎn sàn 懒散
i.dol	(n.)	idola, berhala	ǒu xiàng 偶象
i.e.(*id est*) = that is	(abbr.)	ialah, yakni	jí 即, jiù shì 就是

if	(conj.)	jika, kalau	rú gǔo 如果, jiǎ shǐ 假使
ig.no.ble	(a.)	hina	dī jiàn dė 低贱的, beī bǐ dė 卑鄙的
ig.no.rance	(n.)	ketidaktahuan	wú zhī 无知
		kebodohan	yú mèi 愚昧
ig.no.rant	(a.)	ketidaktahuan	wú zhī dė 无知的
		bodoh	yú mèi dė 愚昧的
ig.nore	(v.)	tidak mengindahkan	bù lǐ cái 不理睬
		mengabaikan	hū shì 忽视
ill	(a.)	sakit	bìng 病, yǒu bìng dė 有病的
		buruk	è 恶, è liè dė 恶劣的
il.le.gal	(a.)	gelap, tidak sah, ilegal	feī fǎ dė 非法的, bù hé fǎ dė 不合法的
il.lit.er.a.cy	(n.)	tuna aksara	wén máng 文盲
ill.ness	(n.)	penyakit	bìng 病, jí bìng 疾病
il.log.i.cal	(a.)	tidak logis	bù hé lúo ji dė 不合逻辑的
		tidak masuk akal	bù hé lǐ dė 不合理的,
			bù tōng dė 不通的
ill-treat	(v.)	menganiaya	nuè dài 虐待
il.lu.sion	(n.)	ilusi, khayalan	huàn xiǎng 幻想
il.lus.trate	(v.)	menerangkan dng gambar	tú jié 图解
		menerangkan	shuō míng 说明
il.lus.tra.tion	(n.)	ilustrasi, gambar	chā tú 插图
		penjelasan	zhù jiǎ 注解
im.age	(n.)	gambar, patung	xiao xiàng 肖像, ǒu xiàng 偶象
		kesan	yín xiàng 印象, yǐng xiàng 影象
i.mag.i.na.tion	(n.)	imajinasi, daya khayal	xiǎng xiàng lì 想象力
im.ag.ine	(v.)	membayangkan	xiǎng xiàng 想象, shè xiǎng 设想
im.i.tate	(v.)	meniru	mó fǎng 模仿
im.i.ta.tion	(n.)	imitasi, tiruan	mó fǎng 模仿, fǎng zào pǐn 仿造品
im.i.ta.tor	(n.)	peniru	mó fǎng zhě 模仿者,
			fǎng zào zhě 仿造者

im.me.diate	(a.)	segera	lì jí 立即, lì kè 立刻
im.me.diate.ly	(adv.)	dengan segera	lì jí 立即, lì kè 立刻。mǎ shàng 马上
im.me.mo.ri.al	(a.)	sudah lama sekali	yuǎn gǔ dė 远古的, tài gǔ dė 太古的
im.mense	(a.)	besar sekali	jù dà 巨大, guǎng dà 广大,
			wú xiàn dė 无限的
im.merse	(v.)	membenamkan	jin mò 浸没, chén rù 沈入
		mencelupkan	jin ru 浸入
im.mi.grant	(n.)	imigran	yí mín 移民
im.mi.grate	(v.)	datang pindah dari	yí rù 移入
im.mi.gra.tion	(n.)	imigrasi	yí mín rù jìng 移民入境
im.mo.bile	(a.)	tak dapat bergerak	bù néng dòng dė 不能动的
im.mor.al	(a.)	imoral, tidak bermoral	bù dào dé dė 不道德的
im.mor.tal	(a.)	hidup selama-lamanya	yǒng shēng dė 永生的, bù sǐ dė 不死的
im.mo.va.ble	(a.)	tidak bergerak	bù dòng dė 不动的
		tidak dapat bergerak	bù néng dòng dė 不能动的
im.mune	(a.)	kebal	miǎn yì dė 免疫的
im.mu.ni.ty	(n.)	imunitas, kekebalan	miǎn yi 免疫, miǎn yi xìng 免疫性
im.mu.nize	(v.)	mengebalkan	shǐ miǎn yi 使免疫
im.mu.ni.za.tion	(n.)	imunisasi, pengebalan	miǎn yi 免疫
im.par.tial	(a.)	adil, tak memihak	dà gōng wú sī 大公无私
im.pass.a.ble	(a.)	tidak dapat dilalui	bù néng tōng xing dė 不能通行的
im.passible	(a.)	tanpa perasaan, mati rasa	má mù dė 麻木的
im.pas.sioned	(a.)	bersemangat, berapi-api	rè qíng dė 热情的, rė liė de 热烈的
im.pas.sive	(a.)	tanpa perasaan	wú gǎn júe dė 无感觉的
		dingin	léng dàn 冷冻
im.pa.tience	(n.)	ketidaksabaran	bù nài fán 不耐烦
im.pa.tient	(a.)	tidak sabar	bù nài fán dė 不耐烦的
im.pel	(v.)	memaksa, mendorong	pò shǐ 迫使, tuī jìn 推进
im.per.fect	(a.)	tidak sempurna	bù wán měi dė 不完美的
im.pe.ri.al	(a.)	mengenai kekaisaran	dì guó dė 帝国的

im.pe.ri.al.ism	(n.)	imperialisme	dì guó zhǔ yì 帝国主义
im.pe.ri.al.ist	(n.)	imperialis	dì guó zhǔ yì zhě 帝国主义者
im.per.il	(v.)	membahayakan	weī hài 危害
im.pe.ri.ous	(a.)	bersifat mutlak	zhūan hèng dė 专横的
		sombong, angkuh	aò màn dė 傲慢的
im.per.son.al	(a.)	tidak bersifat perorangan	feī gè rén dė 非个人的
im.ple.ment	(n.)	alat	gōng jù 工具
im.ple.menta.tion	(n.)	pelaksanaan	zhí xíng 执行
im.pli.cate	(v.)	melibatkan	qian shè 牵涉
im.plore	(v.)	memohon dengan sangat	kěn qiú 恳求, qǐ qiú 乞求
im.ply	(v.)	mengisyaratkan	àn shì 暗示
im.po.lite	(a.)	tidak sopan	bù lǐ mào dė 不礼貌的
im.port	(v.)	mengimpor	shù rù 输入, jìn kǒu 进口
im.por.tance	(n.)	pentingnya, kepentingan	zhòng yào 重要, zhòng dà 重大
im.por.tant	(a.)	penting	zhòng yào 重要, zhòng dà 重大
im.por.ta.tion	(n.)	pemasukan	shù rù 输入, jìn kǒu 进口
		barang masuk	shù rù pǐn 输入品, jìn kǒu huò 进口货
im.port.er	(n.)	importir	shù rù shāng 输入商, jìn kǒu shāng 进口商
im.pos.si.ble	(a.)	mustahil, tidak mungkin	bù kě néng 不可能
im.post	(n.)	pajak	shùi 税
im.pos.tor	(n.)	penipu	piàn zi 骗子
im.pos.ture	(n.)	penipuan	qī piàn 欺骗
im.po.tence	(n.)	ketidakmampuan, kelemahan	wú néng 无能, wú lì 无力
im.po.tent	(a.)	tidak mampu, lemah	wú néng dė 无能的, wú lì dė 无力的
im.press	(v.)	mengesankan	shǐ rén gǎn dòng 使人感动, gěi rén yìn xiàng 给人印象
		mencap, mencetak	gài yìn 盖印, yìn rù 印入
im.pres.sion	(n.)	kesan	yìn xiàng 印象

im.print	(v.)	menyetempel	gài yìn 盖印
im.pris.on	(v.)	memenjarakan	jiān jìn 监禁,
			guān jìn jiān láo 关禁监牢
im.prob.a.ble	(a.)	tidak mungkin	bù kě néng 不可能, wei bì 未必
im.prop.er	(a.)	tidak pantas	bù shì dàng dė 不适当的
		tidak senonoh	bù he shi dė 不合式的
im.prove	(v.)	memperbaiki	gǎi liáng 改良, gǎi shàn 改善
im.prove.ment	(n.)	perbaikan	gǎi liáng 改良, gǎi shàn 改善
im.pru.dence	(n.)	kecerobohan	qīng shuài 轻率, lǔ mǎng 卤莽
im.pru.dent	(a.)	tidak hati-hati, ceroboh	qīng shuài 轻率, lǔ mǎng 卤莽
		kurang ajar, tidak sopan	wú lǐ dė 无礼的
im.pulse	(n.)	gerak hati, impuls	chōng dòng 冲动
im.pu.ni.ty	(n.)	kebebasan dari hukum	miǎn zùi 免罪
im.pure	(a.)	tidak murni, cemar	bù chún jié dė 不纯洁的
in	(prep)	dalam, di	gaì lǐ miàn 在里面, zaì 在
in.a.bil.i.ty	(n.)	ketidakmampuan,	wú néng 无能
		ketidaksanggupan	
in.ac.cu.rate	(a.)	tidak saksama, tidak teliti	bù zhǔn què 不准确, bù jīng mì 不精密
in.ac.tion	(n.)	ketidakgiatan,	bù huó dòng 不活动,
		kelambanan	bù huó pō 不活泼
in.ac.tive	(a.)	tidak aktif	bù huó dòng 不活动
in.ar.tis.tic	(a.)	bukan seni	fēi yì shù dė 非艺术的
in.at.ten.tion	(n.)	ketidakpedulian	bù zhù yì 不注意
in.au.di.ble	(a.)	tidak terdengar	tīng bù jiàn 听不见
in.born	(a.)	pembawaan sejak lahir	shēng lái dė 生来的,
			tiān shēng dė 天生的
in.cal.cu.la.ble	(a.)	tidak terhitung	wǔ shù dė 无数的,
			suàn bù qīng dė 算不请的
in.ca.pa.ble	(a.)	tidak mampu,	wú néng dė 无能的
		tidak sanggup	

in.cau.tious	(a.)	tidak berhati-hati	bù xiǎo xīn 不小心, jǐn shèn 谨慎
in.cense	(n.)	dupa	xiāng 香
	(v.)	membakar dupa	shāo xiāng 烧香
		menjadikan marah	shǐ rén fā nù 使人发怒
in.cen.tive	(n.)	insentif, perangsang	cì ji 刺激, wù zhì gǔ lì 物质鼓励
inch	(n.)	inci	yīng cùn 英寸
in.ci.dent	(n.)	kejadian, peristiwa	shì jiàn 事件, shì biàn 事变
in.ci.den.tal	(a.)	kebetulan, sekali-sekali	ǒu rán xìng dė 偶然性的
in.cise	(v.)	mengiris	qiè 切
in.cite	(v.)	menghasut, mendorong	shān dòng 煽动, jī lì 激励, cuī cù 催促
in.cline	(v.)	cenderung, condong	qīng xié 倾斜, qīng xiàng 倾向
in.clude	(v.)	mencakup, termasuk	bāo guā 包括
in.come	(n.)	penghasilan, pendapatan	shōu rù 收入
in.com.pe.tence	(n.)	ketidakcakapan, ketidak-mampuan	wú néng lì 无能力, bù shèng rèn 不胜任
in.com.plete	(a.)	tidak lengkap	bù wán quán 不完全
in.con.clu.sive	(a.)	tidak meyakinkan	bù què dìng dė 不确定的
in.con.sid.er.a.ble	(a.)	sedikit, tidak berarti	weī xiǎo dė 微小的, bù zhòng yào dė 不重要的, bù zú dào dė 不足道的
in.con.sis.tent	(a.)	tidak konsisten	bù yī zhì dė 不一致的
in.con.stant	(a.)	tidak tetap	bù jiān dìng 不坚定
in.con.ve.nient	(a.)	tidak menyenangkan menyusahkan	bù fāng biàn dė 不方便的, má fán dė 麻烦的
in.cor.rect	(a.)	salah	cuò wù 错误
in.crease	(v.)	bertambah	zēng jiā 增加
in.deed	(adv.)	memang, benar-benar	dì què 的确, què shí 确实
in.def.i.nite	(a.)	tidak tentu	bù dìng dė 不定的
in.de.pend.ence	(n.)	kemerdekaan	dú lì 独立

in.de.pen.dent	(a.)	merdeka	dú lì dė 独立的
in.dex	(n.)	indeks, petunjuk	sŭo yĭn 索引
in.di.cate	(v.)	menunjukkan	zhĭ shì 指示
in.di.ca.tion	(n.)	petunjuk	zhĭ shì 指示
in.dif.fer.ence	(n.)	sikap acuh tak acuh	bù guān xīn 不关心
in.di.gent	(a.)	miskin	pín qióng 贫穷
in.dig.ni.ty	(n.)	penghinaan	wŭ rŭ 侮辱
in.di.rect	(a.)	tidak langsung	jiān jiē dė 间接的, bù zhí jiē 不直接
in.dis.tinct	(a.)	tidak jelas	bù qīng chŭ 不清楚
in.di.vid.ual	(a.)	perseorangan	gè rén dė 个人的
	(n.)	individu, perseorangan	gè rén 个人
in.di.vid.u.al.ism	(n.)	individualisme	gè rén zhŭ yì 个人主义, lì jĭ zhŭ yì 利己主义
in.di.vid.u.al.ist	(n.)	individualis	gè rén zhŭ yì zhě 个人主义者, lì jĭ zhŭ yì zhě 利己主义者
in.door	(a.)	di dalam rumah	zài wū lĭ 在屋里
in.doors	(adv.)	di dalam rumah	zài wū lĭ 在屋里
in.duce	(v.)	menyebabkan	yĭn qĭ 引起
		membujuk	quàn tòu 劝诱, yĭn yòu 引诱
in.dus.tri.al	(a.)	berhubungan dengan industri	gōng yè dė 工业的
in.dus.tri.al.iza.tion	(n.)	industrialisasi	gōng yè huà 工业化
in.dus.tri.al.ize	(v.)	industrialisasi	gong yè huà 工业化
in.dus.tri.ous	(a.)	rajin	qín laó dė 勤劳的
in.dus.try	(n.)	industri	gōng yè 工业
in.ef.fec.tive	(a.)	tidak efektif	wú xiào dė 无效的
in.ef.fi.cien.cy	(n.)	ketidakefisienan	xiào lù dī 效率低
in.ef.fi.cient	(a.)	tidak efisien	xiào lù dī dė 效率低的
in.ex.act	(a.)	tidak tepat	bù zhŭn què 不准确
in.ex.pen.sive	(a.)	murah	pián yí dė 偏宜的

in.ex.pe.ri.ence	(n.)	tidak berpengalaman	wú jīng yàn 无经验, wài háng 外行
in.ex.pert	(a.)	tidak ahli	bù shú liàn dė 不熟练的, wài háng dė 外行的
in.fant	(n.)	bayi	yīng hái 婴孩
in.fan.try	(n.)	infantri	bù bīng 步兵
in.fect	(v.)	menulari, menjangkitkan	chuán rǎn 传染
in.fec.tion	(n.)	infeksi, penularan	chuán rǎn 传染, gǎn rǎn 感染
in.fer.i.or	(a.)	lebih rendah, bawahan	xià jí dė 下级的, dī děng dė 低等的
in.fin.ite	(a.)	tak terbatas, tak terhingga	wú xiàn dė 无限的, wú qióng dė 无穷的
in.fin.i.tive	(n.)	infinitif	bù dìng shì 不定式
	(a.)	tidak tentu	bù dìng dė 不定的
in.fin.i.ty	(n.)	ketidakterbatasan	wú xiàn 无限, wú qióng 无穷
in.firm	(a.)	lemah	shuài rùo 衰弱, nùo rùo 懦弱
in.flu.ence	(n.)	pengaruh	yǐng xiǎng 影响
in.flu.en.tial	(a.)	berpengaruh	yǒu yǐng xiǎng dė 有影响的
in.flu.en.za	(n.)	influenza, flu	liú xíng xíng 流行性, gǎn mào 感冒
in.form	(v.)	memberitahukan	gào sù 告诉, tōng zhī 通知
in.for.mal	(a.)	tidak resmi, informal	feī zhèng shì dė 非正式的
in.for.ma.tion	(n.)	informasi	xiāo xī 消息, qíng bào 情报
in.for.mer	(n.)	pelapor	gào fā rén 告发人
		pengadu	jiǎn jǔ rén 检举人
in.fre.quent	(a.)	jarang-jarang	shǎo yǒu dė 少有的
		tidak sering	bù cháng dė 不常的
in.fuse	(v.)	infus	guàn rù 灌入, guàn shù 灌输
in.gen.u.ous	(a.)	berterus-terang	tǎn bái 坦白
		sederhana	dān chún 单纯
in.grat.i.tude	(n.)	sikap tidak berterima kasih	wàng ēn fù yì 忘恩负义
in.hab.it	(v.)	mendiami	jū zhù 居住
in.hab.it.ant	(n.)	penduduk	jū mín 居民

in.hale	(v.)	menghirup,	xī rù 吸入,
		menarik napas	xī qì 吸气
in.her.ent	(a.)	bersifat bawaan	shēng lái dė 生来的
in.her.it	(v.)	mewarisi	jì chéng 继承
in.her.it.ance	(n.)	warisan	yí chǎn 遗产
in.her.itor	(n.)	ahli waris	jì chéng rén 继承人
in.hu.man	(a.)	kejam, tidak manusiawi	cán rěn 残忍, bù rén dào 不人道
in.i.tial	(a.)	awal, pertama	zuī chū dė 最初的
	(n.)	huruf awal	kaī shǒu zì mǔ 开首字母
in.ject	(v.)	menyuntikkan	zhù shè 注射
in.jec.tion	(n.)	injeksi, suntikan	zhù shè 注射
in.jec.tor	(n.)	penyuntik	zhù shè zhě 注射者, zhù shè qī 注射器
in.jure	(v.)	melukai	shāng hài 伤害
in.jus.tice	(n.)	ketidakadilan	bù gong píng 不公平
ink	(n.)	tinta	mò shǔi 墨水
in.land	(n.)	pedalaman	nèi dì 内地
inn	(n.)	penginapan, losmen	lǚ diàn 旅店, xiǎo lǚ guǎn 小旅馆
in.ner	(a.)	dalam	nèi 内, nèi bù dė 内部的
in.no.cence	(n.)	keadaan tidak bersalah	wú zùi 无罪
in.no.cent	(a.)	tidak bersalah	wú zùi dė 无罪的
in.no.vate	(v.)	memperbarui	gǎi gé 改革, gé xīn 革新
in.no.va.tion	(n.)	inovasi, pembaruan	gǎi gé 改革, gé xīn 革新
in.no.va.tor	(n.)	pembaharu	gǎi gé zhě 改革者, gé xīn zhě 革新者
in.put	(n.)	pemasukan, input	shu rù 输入
in.quest	(n.)	pemeriksaan perkara	shěn wèn 审问
		pemeriksaan mayat	yàn shī 验尸
in.quire	(v.)	menanyakan	xún wèn 询问
		meminta keterangan	dǎ tīng 打听
in.sect	(n.)	serangga	kūn chóng 昆虫
in.se.cure	(a.)	tidak aman	bù ān quán 不安全

in.sen.si.ble	(a.)	tidak sadar	wú zhī jué dė 无知觉的, bù shěng rén shì dė 不省人事的
in.sert	(v.)	menyisipkan	chā rù 插入, qiàn rù 嵌入
in.side	(n.)	bagian dalam	nèi bù 内部, lǐ miàn 里面
in.sin.cere	(a.)	tidak jujur, tidak tulus	bù zhēn chéng 不真城, bù chéng kěn 不诚恳
in.sist	(v.)	bersikeras, mendesak	jiān chí 坚持, qiáng qíu 强求, qiáng yào 强要
in.spect	(v.)	memeriksa, menyelidiki	jiǎn chá 检查, diào chá 调查
in.spec.tor	(n.)	inspektur, pengawas	jiǎn chá yuán 检查员, jiān dū yuán 监督员
in.spi.ra.tion	(n.)	ilham, inspirasi	líng gǎn 灵感
in.spire	(v.)	mengilhami	gěi yú líng gǎn 给予灵感
in.spir.it	(v.)	membangkitkan semangat	gǔ wǔ 鼓舞, gǔ lì 鼓励
in.stance	(n.)	contoh	lì zi 例子
in.stant	(a.)	segera	lì kè dė 立刻的
in.stead	(adv.)	sebagai ganti	dài tì 代替
in.sti.gate	(v.)	menghasut	shān dòng 煽动
in.stig.ator	(n.)	penghasut	shān dòng zhě 煽动者
in.stinct	(n.)	naluri, insting	běn néng 本能, tiān xìng 天性
in.sti.tute	(n.)	institut, lembaga	xué yuàn 学院, xué hùi 学会
in.struct	(v.)	mengajar	jiào 教
in.struc.tion	(n.)	pengajaran, perintah petunjuk, instruksi	jiào dǎo 教导 zhǐ lìng 指令, zhǐ shì 指示
in.stru.ment	(n.)	alat, perkakas alat musik	gōng jù 工具, qì jù 器具 yuè qì 乐器
in.suf.fi.cient	(a.)	tidak cukup	bù zú dė 不足的
in.sult	(n.)	penghinaan	wǔ rǔ 侮辱
	(v.)	menghina	wǔ rǔ 侮辱
in.sur.ance	(n.)	asuransi	bǎo xiǎn 保险

in.sure	(v.)	mengasuransikan	bǎo xiǎn 保险
in.tel.lect	(n.)	daya pikir	zhì lì 智力, cái zhì 才智
		intelek	zhī shí fèn zi 知识分子
in.tel.lec.tu.al	(a.)	cerdik, pandai	zhì huì dė 智慧的, yǒu zhì lì dė 有智力的
	(n.)	cendekiawan	zhī shí fèn zi 知识分子
in.tel.li.gence	(n.)	kecerdasan	cōng míng 聪明
in.tel.li.gent	(a.)	cerdas	cōng míng dė 聪明的
in.tend	(v.)	bermaksud	xiǎng yào 想要, dǎ suàn 打算
in.ten.sive	(a.)	intensif, bersifat memberi tekanan	jiā qiāng 加强, jiā jǐn 加紧
in.ten.tion	(n.)	niat, maksud	yì tú 意图, qì tú 企图
in.ten.tion.al	(a.)	secara sengaja	gù yì dė 故意的
in.ter.est	(n.)	minat	xìng qù 兴趣
in.ter.est.ing	(a.)	menarik perhatian	yǐn rén zhǔ yì dė 引人注意的, yǒu qù wèi dė 有趣味的
in.ter.fere	(v.)	mencampuri, turut campur	gān shè 干涉
in.ter.im	(n.)	sementara	zàn shí dė 暂时的
in.te.ri.or	(a.)	bagian dalam	nèi bù dė 内部的, lǐ miàn dė 里面的
in.ter.me.di.ate	(a.)	tingkat menengah	zhōng děng dė 中等的
	(v.)	menengahi	tiáo tíng 调停
in.ter.nal	(a.)	dalam	nèi 内, nèi bù 内部
		dalam negeri	gúo nèi 国内
in.ter.na.tion.al	(a.)	internasional, antarbangsa	gúo jì dė 国际的, shì jiè dė 世界的
in.ter.na.tion.al.ism	(n.)	internasionalisme	gúo jì zhǔ yì 国际主义
in.ter.na.tion.al.ist	(n.)	internasionalis	gúo jì zhǔ yì zhě 国际主义者
in.ter.pol	(n.)	interpol	gúo jì xíng jǐng 国际刑警
in.ter.pret	(v.)	menerjemahkan	fān yì 翻译

in.ter.pret.er	(n.)	penerjemah	fān yì zhě 翻译者, fān yì yuán 翻译员
in.ter.ro.gate	(v.)	menanyai	zhì wèn 质问
in.ter.ro.ga.tion	(n.)	pemeriksaan, tanda tanya	shěn wèn 审问, wèn haò问号
in.ter.rog.a.tive	(a.)	bersifat bertanya	yì wèn dė 疑问的
		kalimat tanya	yì wèn jù 疑问句
in.ter.rupt	(v.)	mengganggu, menyela, memotong	dǎ rǎo 打扰, chā zǔi 插咀, dǎ duàn 打断
in.ter.val	(n.)	waktu istirahat	xiū xī shí jiān 休息时间
in.ter.vene	(v.)	campur tangan	gān yù 干预, gān shè 干涉
in.ter.view	(n.)	interviu, wawancara	jì zhě zhāo dài hùi 记者招待会, jì zhě fǎng wèn 记者访问
in.ti.mate	(a.)	karib, intim	qīn mì 亲密, mì qiè 密切
	(v.)	mengisyaratkan	àn shì 暗示
	(n.)	teman karib	zhī xīn péng yǒu 知心朋友
in.to	(prep.)	ke dalam	jìn rù 进入
		menjadi	biàn chéng 变成, huà wéi 化为
in.tol.er.ant	(a.)	tidak bertoleransi	bù néng róng rěn dė 不能容忍的
in.to.na.tion	(n.)	intonasi, nada suara	shēng diào 声调, yǔ diào 语调
in.tran.si.tive	(a.)	intransitif	bù jí wù dė 不及物的
in.trigue	(n.)	tipu daya	yīn móu 阴谋, guǐ jì 诡计
in.tro.duce	(v.)	memperkenalkan	jiè shào 介绍
		memasukkan	yǐn jìn 引进
in.tro.duc.tion	(n.)	perkenalan	jiè shào 介绍
		kata pengantar, pengantar	dǎo yán 导言, yǐn dǎo 引导
in.trude	(v.)	mengganggu	qīn rǎo 侵扰, qīn fàn 侵犯
in.tru.der	(n.)	pengganggu	qīn rǎo zhě 侵扰者, qīn fàn zhě 侵犯者
in.vade	(v.)	menyerbu	qǐn lùe 侵略
in.vad.er	(n.)	penyerbu	qǐn lùe zhě 侵略者

in.val.u.a.ble	(a.)	tidak ternilai harganya	wú fǎ gū jià dė 无法估价的, wú jià dė 无价的
in.va.sion	(n.)	penyerbuan	qǐn lüè 侵略
in.vent	(v.)	menemukan, menciptakan	fā míng 发明, chùang zào 创造
in.ven.tion	(n.)	penemuan	fā míng 发明, chùang zào 创造
in.ven.tor	(n.)	penemu, pencipta	fā míng zhě 发明者, chùang zào zhě 创造者
in.ven.to.ry	(n.)	inventaris, daftar barang	cái chǎn mù lù 财产目录
in.verse	(a.)	kebalikan	duì lǐ dė 对立的, xiāng fǎn dė 相反的
in.vert	(v.)	membalikkan	diān dǎo 颠倒, zhuǎn huà 转化
in.vest	(v.)	menanam modal	tóu zī 投资
in.ves.ti.gate	(v.)	menyelidiki	diào chá 调查
in.ves.ti.ga.tor	(n.)	pemeriksa	diào chá zhě 调查者
in.vest.ment	(n.)	penanaman modal	tóu zī 投资
in.vest.or	(n.)	penanam modal	tóu zī zhě 投资者
in.vis.i.ble	(a.)	tidak kelihatan	kàn bù jiàn dė 看不见的, wú xíng dė 无形的
in.vi.ta.tion	(n.)	undangan	yāo qǐng 邀请
in.vite	(v.)	mengundang	yāo qǐng 邀请
in.vit.ing	(a.)	menarik, memikat	xī yǐn rén dė 吸引人的
in.voice	(n.)	faktur	fā piào 发票, hùo dān 货单
in.voke	(v.)	meminta, memohon	qí qiú 祈求, kěn qiú 恳求
in.vol.un.ta.ry	(a.)	tidak sengaja	wú yì dė 无意的
in.volve	(v.)	melibatkan	juǎn rù 卷入
in.ward	(a.)	menuju ke dalam dalam batin	xiàng nèi dė 向内的, nèi xīn dė 内心的
i.ron	(n.)	besi	tiě 铁
i.ro.ny	(n.)	ironi, ejekan	fèng cì 讽刺
ir.reg.u.lar	(a.)	tidak teratur	bù guī zé dė 不规则的

ir.rel.e.vant	(a.)	tidak relevan	bù xiāng gān dė 不相干的
ir.rep.a.ra.ble	(a.)	tak dapat diperbaiki	bù néng xiū lǐ dė 不能修理的
ir.re.proach.a.ble	(a.)	tak tercela	wú kě zhǐ zé dė 无可指责的
		tak ada celanya	wú quē diǎn dė 无缺点的
ir.re.sist.i.ble	(a.)	tak dapat menahan	bú kě dǐ kàng dė 不可抵抗的
ir.re.spon.si.ble	(a.)	tidak bertanggung jawab	bù fù zé dė 不负责的
ir.ri.gate	(v.)	mengairi	guàng gài 灌溉
ir.ri.ga.tion	(n.)	irigasi, pengairan	guàng gài 灌溉
ir.ri.ta.ble	(a.)	lekas marah	yì nù dė 易怒的
ir.ri.tate	(v.)	menjengkelkan	shǐ rén shēng qì 使人生气
ir.ri.ta.tion	(n.)	kemarahan, kejengkelan	shēng qì 生气
is.land	(n.)	pulau	dǎo 岛
isle	(n.)	pulau kecil	xiǎo dǎo 小岛
i.so.late	(v.)	mengasingkan	gé lí 隔离, shǐ gū lì 使孤立
i.so.la.tion	(n.)	pengasingan, isolasi	gū lì 孤立, gé lí 隔离
is.sue	(n.)	persoalan	wèn tí 问题
		terbitan	fā xíng 发行
		hasil	jié gǔo 结果
		pengeluaran	liú chū 流出
it	(pron.)	dia, ini, itu	tā 它, zhè 这, nà 那
i.tal.ic	(n.)	huruf miring	xié tǐ zì 斜体字
itch	(n.)	penyakit kudis	jiè chuāng 疥疮
		keinginan yang besar	kě wàng 渴望
	(v.)	gatal	yǎng 痒, fā yǎng 发痒
i.tem	(n.)	item, hal	xiàng mù 项目
		berita	yī tiáo xīn wén 一条新闻, yī zé xīn wén 一则新闻
its	(pron.)	kepunyaannya	tā dė 它的
itself	(pron.)	ia sendiri	tā zì jǐ 它自己, tā běn shēn 它本身
i.vo.ry	(n.)	gading	xiàng yá 象牙

J

jab	(v.)	menusuk	cì 刺
jack	(n.)	kelasi, awak kapal	shǔi shǒu 水手
		pekerja	gōng rén 工人
		dongkrak	qǐ zhòng qì 起重器
jack.et	(n.)	jaket	wài tào 外套
jade	(n.)	batu zamrud	yù 玉
jail	(n.)	penjara	jiān láo 监牢
jail.er	(n.)	penjaga penjara	jiān láo kàn shǒu zhě 监牢看守者, yù lí 狱吏
jam	(v.)	macet, menyumbat	qiǎ zhù 卡住, sè zhù 塞住
	(n.)	selai	gǔo jiàng 果酱
Jan.uary	(n.)	Januari	yī yùe 一月, zhèng yùe 正月
jar	(n.)	kendi, botol	tán zi 坛子, píng zi 瓶子
jaw	(n.)	rahang	hàn 颔
jay	(n.)	sejenis burung	xǐ qùe 喜鹊
		orang bodoh	shǎ gùa 傻瓜
jeal.ous	(a.)	iri hati, cemburu	dù jì 妒忌
jeal.ous.y	(n.)	perasaan iri hati	dù jì xīn 妒忌心
jeans	(n.)	kain dril, jins	xié wén bù 斜纹布
jeep	(n.)	jip	jí pū chē 吉普车
jeer	(v.)	mengejek	jī xiào 讥笑
jest	(n.)	olok-olok, senda gurau	xiào hùa 笑话
		lelucon	huá jī 滑稽
jest.er	(n.)	pelawak	xiào jiàng 笑匠

jet	(n.)	pancaran	pēn shè 喷射
		jet	pēn shè fēi jī 喷射飞机,
			pēn shè jī 喷射机
jew.el	(n.)	permata	bǎo shí 宝石
jew.el.ler	(n.)	pedagang permata,	bǎo shí shāng 宝石商,
		tukang permata	bǎo shí gōng rén 宝石工人
jew.el.ler.y	(n.)	barang-barang perhiasan	guì zhòng shǒu shì 贵重首饰
job	(n.)	pekerjaan	zhí yè 职业, gōng zùo 工作
join	(v.)	menghubungkan	lián jiē 连接
		memasuki	jiā rù 加入
		ikut serta	cān jiā 参加
joint	(n.)	sambungan	jiē tóu 接头
		tulang sendi	guān jié 关节, gǔ jié 骨节
joke	(n.)	kelakar, senda gurau	xiào hùa 笑话, wán xiào 玩笑
jok.er	(n.)	pelawak	huá jī jiā 滑稽家
jol.ly	(a.)	riang gembira	kuài lè 快乐, gāo xìng 高兴
jour.nal	(n.)	surat kabar, majalah	rì bào 日报, zá zhì 杂志
		catatan harian	rì jì 日记
jour.nal.ist	(n.)	wartawan	xīn wén jì zhě 新闻记者
jour.ney	(n.)	bepergian jauh, perjalanan	lǚ xíng 旅行, lǚ chéng 旅程
jowl	(n.)	rahang bawah	è 颚, xià bā 下巴
joy	(n.)	kegembiraan, suka cita	huān lè 欢乐, gāo xìng 高兴
joy.ful	(a.)	bergembira	huān lè dė 欢乐的,
			xìng gāo cǎi liè 兴高采烈,
			gāo xìng dė 高兴的
joy.less	(a.)	tidak bergembira	bù gāo xìng dė 不高兴的
judge	(n.)	hakim	fǎ guān 法官
		wasit	cái pàn yuán 裁判员
judge.ment	(n.)	keputusan pengadilan	pàn jué 判决
		pendapat	yì jiàn 意见

jug	(n.)	kendi	dà hú 大壶
		penjara	jiān láo 监牢
jug.gle	(v.)	bermain sulap	biàn xì fǎ 变戏法
jug.gler	(n.)	pemain sulap	biàn xì fǎ zhě 变戏法者
juice	(n.)	air buah	gǔo zhì 果汁
juic.y	(a.)	banyak airnya	duō zhì dė 多汁的
Ju.ly	(n.)	Juli	qī yuè 七月
jump	(v.)	melompat	tiào 跳
junc.tion	(n.)	sambungan	jiē tóu 接头
		persimpangan	lián jiē diǎn 连接点,
			jiāo chā diǎn 交叉点
June	(n.)	Juni	liù yuè 六月
jun.gle	(n.)	rimba	sēn lín 森林
ju.nior	(a.)	lebih muda, lebih rendah	xiǎo yú 小于, dī yú 低于
	(n.)	tingkat bawah	dī jí 低级
		orang yang lebih muda	xià yī bèi 下一辈, wǎn bèi 晚辈,
			nián xiǎo zhě 年小者
ju.ry	(n.)	juri, dewan juri	péi shěn yuán 陪审员,
			péi shěn tuán 陪审团
just	(a.)	adil	gōng píng dė 公平的
		layak	hé lǐ dė 合理的
	(adv.)	tepat, pas	zhèng 正, qià hǎo 恰好
		baru saja	gāng cái 刚才, cái 才
		hanya	zhǐ shì 只是, bù guò 不过
jus.tice	(n.)	keadilan	gōng zhèng 公正, gōng píng 公平
		peradilan	sī fǎ 司法
		hakim	fǎ guān 法官
jus.ti.fy	(v.)	membenarkan, membela	zhèng shí 证实, biàn hù 辩护

K

kan.ga.roo	(n.)	kanguru	dài shǔ 袋鼠
ka.pok	(n.)	kapuk	mù mián 木棉
keen	(a.)	tajam	jiān rùi 尖锐, mǐn rùi 敏锐
		bersemangat, gemar	rè xīn 热心, xǐ huān 喜欢
keep	(v.)	memegang, memelihara	nă zhė 拿着, yăng 养,
		menjaga, menyimpan	fáng shǒu 防守, bǎo cún 保存
		meneruskan	bǎo chí 保持, jì xù 继续
keep.er	(n.)	penjaga	kàn shǒu rén 看守人,
			kàn hù rén 看护人
		pemelihara	bǎo guǎn rén 保管人,
			sì yǎng rén 饲养人
		pengurus	guǎn lǐ rén 管理人
keep.ing	(n.)	pemeliharaan	bǎo guǎn 保管, bǎo cún 保存
ken.nel	(n.)	kandang anjing	gǒu wō 狗窝
ker.nel	(n.)	biji, inti	rén 仁, hé 核, hé xīn 核心
ket.tle	(n.)	ceret	shǔi hú 水壶
key	(n.)	kunci, anak kunci	yào shì 钥匙
kick	(v.)	menendang	tī 踢
kid	(n.)	anak kambing	xiǎo yáng 小羊
kid.ney	(n.)	ginjal	shèn 肾
kill	(v.)	membunuh	sā 杀, sā sǐ 杀死
kill.er	(n.)	pembunuh	sā rén zhě 杀人者, sā shǒu 杀手
ki.lo	(n.)	kilogram	gōng jīn 公斤
ki.lo.me.tre	(n.)	kilometer	gōng lǐ 公里

ki.lo.ton	(n.)	seribu ton	qiān dūn 千吨
ki.lo.watt	(n.)	kilowat	qiān wǎ tè 千瓦特
kin	(n.)	sanak keluarga	qīn qī 亲戚
kind	(a.)	ramah, baik hati	qīn qiè 亲切, rén cí 仁慈
	(n.)	macam, jenis	zhǒng lèi 种类
kin.der.gar.ten	(n.)	taman kanak-kanak	yòu ér yúan 幼儿园
kin.dle	(v.)	menyalakan	diǎn hǔo 点火, rán shāo 燃烧
		membangkitkan	jí qǐ 激起, gǔ wǔ 鼓舞
kind.ness	(n.)	kebaikan hati	rén cí 仁慈, qīn qiè 亲切
king	(n.)	raja	wáng 王, guó wáng 国王
king.dom	(n.)	kerajaan	wáng gúo 王国
ki.osk	(n.)	kios	shū bào tíng 书报亭, shū bào tàn 书报摊
kiss	(v.)	mencium	jiē wěn 接吻, qīn zǔi 亲咀
kit	(n.)	anak kucing	xiāo maō 小猫
kit.chen	(n.)	dapur	chú fáng 厨房
kite	(n.)	layang-layang	fēng zhēng 风筝
kit.ten	(n.)	anak kucing	xiǎo maō 小猫
knave	(n.)	bangsat, penipu	wú lài 无赖, liú máng 流氓
knee	(n.)	lutut	xī 膝, xī gài 膝盖
kneel	(v.)	berlutut	gùi 跪
knife	(n.)	pisau, belati	xiǎo daō 小刀
knight	(n.)	kesatria	qí shì 骑士, wǔ shì 武士
knit	(v.)	merajut	biān zhī 编织
knob	(n.)	tombol, kenob, pegangan	yuán kuài 园块, niē shǒu 捏手
knock	(v.)	memukul, mengetok	qiaō 敲, qiaō dǎ 敲打, kòu 叩
knot	(n.)	simpul	jié 结
know	(v.)	mengetahui, mengenal	zhı daò 知道, rėn shi 认识
		mengerti	dǒng dé 懂得
know.ledge	(n.)	pengetahuan	zhī shí 知识, xué wèn 学问

L

la.bel	(n.)	label, etiket	biāo qiān 标签
lab.or.a.to.ry	(n.)	laboratorium	shí yàn shì 实验室
la.bour	(n.)	pekerjaan, buruh	gōng zùo 工作, láo dòng 劳动
la.bour.er	(n.)	pekerja, buruh	láo dòng zhě 劳动者
lace	(n.)	renda, tali sepatu	huā biān 花边, xié daì 鞋带
lack	(n.)	kekurangan	quē fá 缺乏
lad	(n.)	anak laki-laki	nán hái zi 男孩子
lad.der	(n.)	tangga, jenjang	tī zi 梯子, jiē tī 阶梯
lade	(v.)	memuat	zhuāng zài 装载
lad.en	(a.)	bermuatan	zhuāng mǎn dė 装满的
la.dy	(n.)	nyonya, wanita	nǚ shì 女士, fù nǚ 妇女
lair	(n.)	sarang binatang	chù wō 畜窝, chù kū 畜窟
lake	(n.)	danau	hú 湖
lamb	(n.)	anak domba	gāo yáng 羔羊, xiǎo yáng 小羊
lame	(a.)	pincang	bǒ jiǎo 跛脚
la.ment	(v.)	ratapan, keluh kesah	āi dào 哀悼, āi kū 哀哭, bēi tàn 悲叹
lamp	(n.)	lampu	dēng 灯
land	(n.)	tanah, daratan, negeri	tǔ dì 土地, lù dì 陆地, gúo tǔ 国土
land.ing	(n.)	pendaratan	dēng lù 登陆
land.la.dy	(n.)	wanita pemilik losmen wanita pemilik tanah istri tuan rumah	lǚ gǔan nǚ zhǔ rén 旅馆女主人 nǚ dì zhǔ 女地主 laǒ bǎn niáng 老板娘, nǚ fáng dōng 女房东

land.lord	(n.)	tuan tanah, pemilik tanah	dì zhǔ 地主, fáng dōng 房东
		pemilik losmen	lǚ guǎn lǎo bǎn 旅馆老板
land.own.er	(n.)	tuan tanah,	dì zhǔ 地主,
		pemilik tanah	tǔ dì sǔo yǒu rén 土地所有人
land.scape	(n.)	pemandangan alam	fēng jǐng 风景
lane	(n.)	jalan kecil/setapak	xiǎo xiàng 小巷
lan.guage	(n.)	bahasa	yǔ yán 语言
lan.tern	(n.)	lentera, lampion	tí dēng 提灯, dēng lóng 灯笼
lap	(v.)	menjilat	shì 舐
	(n.)	pangkuan	xī gài 膝盖, huái bào 怀抱
large	(a.)	besar, luas	dà 大, guǎng dà 广大, kuān dà 宽大
lark	(n.)	senda gurau	wán xiào 玩笑
		burung yg suka menyanyi	yún què 云雀, bǎi líng niǎo 百灵鸟
lar.va	(n.)	anak serangga	yòu chóng 幼虫
lass	(n.)	gadis	shǎo nǔ 少女
last	(a.)	terakhir, yang lalu	zùi hoù dė 最后的, qián 前
	(v.)	berlangsung, meneruskan	chí xù 持续, jì xù 继续
last.ing	(a.)	berlangsung lama, awet	chí jiǔ 持久, nài jiǔ 耐久
		abadi	yǒng héng dė 永恒的
last.ly	(adv.)	akhirnya	zùi hòu 最后
latch	(n.)	palang pintu, selot	mén shuān 门闩
late	(a.)	terlambat	chí 迟
late.ly	(adv.)	baru-baru ini	zùi jìn 最近, jìn lái 近来
la.tent	(a.)	tersembunyi,	qián fú dė 潜伏的,
		terpendam	qián zài dė 潜在的
later	(adv.)	kemudian	yǐ hòu 以后
latest	(a.)	yang terakhir	zùi hòu dė 最后的,
			zùi chí dė 最迟的
lathe	(n.)	mesin bubut	chē chuáng 车床
lath.er	(n.)	busa sabun	féi zào pào 肥皂泡

Lat.in	(n.)	bahasa Latin	lā tīng yǔ 拉丁语
lat.i.tude	(n.)	garis lintang	wěi dù 纬度
		ruang gerak	huó dòng yú dì 活动余地
		kebebasan	zì yóu 自由
lat.ter	(a.)	yang terakhir,	hoù miàn dė 后面的,
		yang belakangan	hoù zhě 后者
lat.ter.ly	(adv.)	akhir-akhir ini	jìn lái 近来, zuì jìn 最近
laugh	(v.)	tertawa	xiào 笑
laun.dry	(n.)	penatu, binatu	xǐ yī diàn 洗衣店
laun.dry-man	(n.)	tukang penatu	xǐ yī gōng rén 洗衣工人
la.va	(n.)	lahar	róng yán 熔岩
lav.a.to.ry	(n.)	kamar mandi, kamar kecil	guàn xǐ shì 盥洗室, cè sǔo 厕所
lave	(v.)	mencuci	xǐ dí 洗涤
		mandi	xí zǎo 洗澡, mù yù 沐浴
law	(n.)	undang-undang, hukum	fǎ lìng 法令, fǎ lù 法律
law-court	(n.)	pengadilan	fǎ yuàn 法院
law.ful	(a.)	sah, resmi	hé fǎ dė 合法的
law.less	(a.)	tidak sah	feī fǎ dė 非法的, bù fǎ dė 不法的
lawn	(n.)	halaman berumput	cǎo píng 草坪, cǎo dì 草地
law-suit	(n.)	perkara hukum	sù sòng 诉讼
law.yer	(n.)	pengacara	lù shì 律士
lax	(a.)	longgar	sōng 松, sōng xiè 松懈
lay	(v.)	meletakkan	fàng 放
		bertelur	shēng dàn 生蛋
lay.er	(n.)	lapisan	céng 层
la.zy	(a.)	malas	lǎn dùo 懒惰
lead	(v.)	memimpin	lǐng dǎo 领导, yǐn dǎo 引导
		mendahului	lǐng xiān 领先
lead.er	(n.)	pemimpin	lǐng xiù 领袖, lǐng dǎo 领导
leaf	(n.)	daun	yè zi 叶子, shù yè 树叶

leaf.let	(n.)	daun kecil	xiǎo ye 小叶
		selebaran	chuán dān 传单
leaf.y	(a.)	berdaun lebat	duō yè dė 多叶的
league	(n.)	liga, persekutuan	tóng méng 同盟, lián méng 联盟
leak	(a.)	bocor	lòu 漏
leak.proof	(a.)	tahan bocor, anti bocor	fáng lòu dė 防漏的, bù loù dė 不漏的
lean	(a.)	kurus	shòu 瘦
		miring	qīng xiè 倾斜
	(v.)	menyandarkan	yī kào 依靠
leap	(v.)	melompat	tiào 跳
learn	(v.)	belajar	xué xí 学习
		mendapat kabar	tīng shuō 听说, huò xī 获悉
learn.ed	(a.)	terpelajar	yǒu xúe wèn dė 有学问的, bó xué dė 博学的
learn.er	(n.)	pelajar	xué xí zhě 学习者
learn.ing	(n.)	pengetahuan	xué wèn 学问
lease	(n.)	kontrak sewa	zū yùe 租约
least	(a.)	paling sedikit	zùi shǎo 最少
leath.er	(n.)	kulit	pí gé 皮革
leave	(v.)	meninggalkan	lí kaī 离开, xǔ kě 许可
		menyisakan	liu xià 留下, sheng xià 剩下
		membiarkan	tīng rén 听任
	(n.)	izin cuti	zhǔn jià 准假
lec.ture	(n.)	kuliah, ceramah	jiǎng xué 讲学, jiǎng kè 讲课
lec.tur.er	(n.)	dosen, penceramah	jiǎng shī 讲师, jiǎng xué zhě 讲学者
left	(a.)	kiri	zuǒ 左
	(adv.)	ke kiri	xiàng zuǒ 向左
left.ism	(n.)	condong ke kiri	zuǒ cīng 左倾
left.ist	(n.)	golongan kiri	zuǒ pài 左派
leg	(n.)	kaki	tǔi 腿

le.gal	(a.)	legal, sah	hé fǎ dė 合法的
le.gal.i.ty	(n.)	keabsahan	hé fǎ 合法
le.gal.i.za.tion	(n.)	legalisasi	hé fǎ huà 合法化
le.gal.ize	(v.)	mensahkan, melegalisa-sikan	shǐ hé fǎ huà 使合法化
leg.end	(n.)	legenda, dongeng	zhuàn qí 传奇, chuán shuō 传说
leg.en.da.ry	(a.)	yang berhubungan de-ngan legenda	zhùan qí dė 传奇的, chuán shuō dė 传说的
leg.is.late	(v.)	membuat/mensahkan undang-undang	lì fǎ 立法
leg.is.la.tion	(n.)	perundang-undangan	lì fǎ 立法, fǎ guī 法规
leg.is.la.tive	(a.)	legislatif	lì fǎ dė 立法
	(n.)	legislatif	lì fǎ quán 立法权, lì fǎ jī guān 立法机关
leg.is.la.tor	(n.)	pembuat undang-undang	lì fǎ zhě 立法者
leg.is.la.ture	(n.)	badan pembuat undang-undang	lì fǎ jī guān 立法机关
le.git.i.ma.cy	(n.)	legitimasi, hak kekuasaan	hé fǎ xìng 合法性, zhèng tǒng 正统
le.git.i.mate	(a.)	sah	hé fǎ dė 合法的, zhèng tǒng dė 正统的
lei.sure	(n.)	waktu senggang	xián kōng 闲空
lem.on	(n.)	jeruk sitrun, jeruk limun	níng méng 柠檬
lem.on.ade	(n.)	limun	níng méng zhì 柠檬汁
lend	(v.)	meminjamkan	chū jiè 出借, jiè gěi 借给
lend.er	(n.)	orang yang meminjamkan orang yang mengkredit-kan uang	chū jiè zhě 出借者 gaō lì dài zhě 高利贷者
length	(n.)	panjang, panjangnya	cháng 长, cháng dù 长度
length.en	(v.)	memperpanjang	lā cháng 拉长, yán cháng 延长
lens	(n.)	lensa	jìng tóu 镜头, tòu jìng 透镜
leop.ard	(n.)	macan tutul	bào 豹

lep.er	(n.)	penderita penyakit kusta	má fēng bìng zhě 麻风病者
less	(a.)	tak sebanyak	gèng shǎo 更少
		lebih sedikit (daripada)	jiào shǎo 较少
less.en	(v.)	mengurangi	jiǎn shǎo 减少
les.son	(n.)	pelajaran	gōng kè 功课, jiào xùn 教训
lest	(conj.)	agar tidak	yǐ miǎn 以免, miǎn dé 免得
let	(v.)	membiarkan	ràng 让
		mengizinkan	róng xǔ 容许, yǔn xǔ 允许
let.ter	(n.)	huruf, surat	zì mǔ 字母, xìn 信
let.ter-box	(n.)	kotak surat	xìn xiāng 信箱
let.ter-pa.per	(n.)	kertas surat	xìn zhǐ 信纸
lev.el	(n.)	permukaan	shǔi píng miàn 水平面
		mutu	shǔi píng 水平, shǔi zhǔn 水准
	(a.)	rata, datar	shǔi píng dė 水平的
	(v.)	meratakan	lòng píng 弄平, pu píng 铺平
li.a.bil.i.ty	(n.)	pertanggungjawaban	yīng fù zé 应负责, yóu yì wù 有义务
li.a.ble	(a.)	bertanggung jawab	yǒu zè rèn dė 有责任的
li.ar	(n.)	pembohong	shuō huǎng zhě 说谎者
lib.er.al	(a.)	murah hati	kāng kǎi 慷慨, kuān dà 宽大
		bebas, liberal	zì yóu zhǔ yì dė 自由主义的
	(n.)	penganut liberalisme	zì yóu zhǔ yì zhě 自由主义者
lib.er.al.ism	(n.)	liberalisme	zì yóu zhǔ yì 自由主义
lib.er.al.ist	(n.)	liberalis	zì yóu zhǔ yì zhě 自由主义者
lib.er.ate	(v.)	membebaskan	jiě fàng 解放
		melepaskan	shì fàng 释放
lib.er.a.tion	(n.)	pembebasan	jiě fàng 解放
lib.er.a.tor	(n.)	pembebas	jiě fàng zhě 解放者
lib.er.ty	(n.)	kemerdekaan, kebebasan	zì yóu 自由
li.bra.ri.an	(n.)	pengurus perpustakaan	tú shū guǎn guǎn lǐ yuán 图书馆管理员

li.bra.ry	(n.)	perpustakaan	tú shū guǎn 图书馆
li.cence	(n.)	surat izin, lisensi, izin	xǔ kě zhèng 许可证,
			zhí zhào 执照, xǔ kě 许可
li.cense (li.cence)	(v.)	mengizinkan	zhǔn xǔ 准许, xǔ kě 许可
lick	(v.)	menjilat	shi 舐
lid	(n.)	tutup	gài zi 盖子
lie	(v.)	berbohong	shuō huāng 说谎
		terletak, berbaring	zài 在, tàng 躺
lieu.ten.ant	(n.)	letnan	zhōng wèi 中尉, shaō wèi 少尉
life	(n.)	kehidupan, jiwa	shēng cún 生存, shēng mìng生命
life.less	(a.)	tidak bernyawa	wú shēng mìng dė 无生命的
life-long	(a.)	sepanjang hidup,	zhōng shēng 终生,
		seumur hidup	bì shēng 毕生
life.time	(n.)	sepanjang hidup,	zhōng shēng 终生,
		seumur hidup	bì shēng 毕生
lift	(v.)	mengangkat	jǔ qǐ 举起
	(n.)	lift	dìan tī 电梯
light	(n.)	cahaya, lampu	guāng 光, diàn dēng 电灯
	(a.)	terang	guāng liàng dė 光亮的
		ringan	qīng dė 轻的
	(v.)	menyalakan, menerangi	diàn hǔo 点火, zhào liàng 照亮
light.en	(v.)	meringankan	jiǎn qīng 减轻
		menjadi terang, menyinari	fā liàng 发亮, zhào liàng 照亮
light.er	(n.)	tongkang, geretan	bó chuán 驳船, dă hǔo jī 打火机
light-house	(n.)	menara api, mercu suar	dēng tă 灯塔
light.ning	(n.)	kilat	shǎn diàn 闪电
lik.a.ble	(a.)	menggembirakan	kě xǐ dė 可喜的
		menyenangkan	kě ài dė 可爱的
like	(v.)	suka	xǐ huān 喜欢
	(a.)	seperti	xiāng xiàng dė 相象的
		sama	tóng yàng dė 同样的

	(prep.)	seperti, sama dengan	xiàng 象, gēn...yī yàng 跟…一样, hǎo xiàng 好象
like.li.hood	(n.)	kemungkinan	kě néng xìng 可能性
like.ly	(a.)	mungkin	kě néng 可能
like.ness	(n.)	kesamaan, persamaan	tóng yàng 同样, xiāng sì 相似
like.wise	(adv.)	sama, demikian juga	tóng yàng 同样, zhào yàng 照样
	(conj.)	juga, begitu juga	yě 也, ér qiě 而且
li.ly	(n.)	bunga bakung	bǎi hé huā 百合化
limb	(n.)	anggota badan	sì zhī 四肢
lim.ber	(a.)	lemah, lentur	róu ruǎn 柔软
lime	(n.)	kapur	shí huī 石灰
lim.it	(n.)	batas	jiè xiàn 界限
	(v.)	membatasi	xiàn zhì 限制
lim.i.ta.tion	(n.)	pembatasan	xiàn zhì 限制, xiàn dù 限度
lim.ited	(a.)	terbatas	yǒu xiàn dė 有限的
lim.it.less	(a.)	tak terbatas	wú xiàn dė 无限的
limp	(v.)	berjalan pincang	bō zhē zǒu 跛着走, bō xíng 跛行
	(a.)	lemah	ruǎn rùo 软弱
line	(n.)	garis, baris	xiàn 线, háng 行
		lin, jalur lalu lintas	jiāo tōng xiàn 交通线
		macam merk	hùo sè 货色, shāng pǐn zhǒng lèi 商品种类
lin.en	(n.)	kain linen	yà má bù 亚麻布
lin.gua	(n.)	bahasa	yü yán 语言
		lidah	shé 舌
lin.gual	(a.)	berhubungan dengan bahasa atau lidah	yǔ yán dė 语言的, shé dė 舌的
lin.guist	(n.)	ahli bahasa	yǔ yán xué jiā 语言学家
lin.guis.tic	(a.)	berhubungan dengan ilmu bahasa	yǔ yán xué dė 语言学的

lin.guis.tics	(n.)	ilmu bahasa	yǔ yán xué 语言学
link	(v.)	menghubungkan	lián jiē 连接
	(n.)	mata rantai	huán 环, lián huán 链环
li.on	(n.)	singa	shī zi 狮子
li.on.ess	(n.)	singa betina	cī shī 雌狮
lip	(n.)	bibir	chún 唇, zǔi chún 咀唇
lip-stick	(n.)	lipstik, gincu	kǒu hóng 口红
liq.uid	(n.)	benda cair	yì tǐ 液体
list	(n.)	daftar	biǎo 表, mù lù 目录, mǐn dān 名单
	(v.)	membuat daftar	liè biào 列表
		mendaftarkan	biān mù lù 编目录
lis.ten	(v.)	dengar, mendengarkan	tīng 听
lis.ten.er	(n.)	pendengar	tīng zhě 听者, shōu tīng zhě 收听者
list.less	(a.)	tidak bergairah, lesu	lǎn yāng yāng 懒洋洋, méi jīng dǎ cǎi 没精打采
lit.er.a.cy	(n.)	melek huruf	shí zì 识字
lit.er.al	(a.)	harfiah	zì miàn shàng dė 字面上的, zhú zì dė 逐字的
lit.er.al.ly	(adv.)	secara harfiah	zì miàn shàng 字面上, zhú zì di 逐字地
lit.er.ar.y	(a.)	berhubungan dengan kesusastraan	wén xué dė 文学的
lit.er.ate	(a.)	melek huruf	shí zì dė 识字的
	(n.)	orang terpelajar	shí zì zhě 识字者
lit.er.a.ture	(n.)	kesusastraan	wén xué 文学
lit.tle	(a.)	kecil, sedikit	xiǎo 小, shǎo 少
li.tre	(n.)	liter	shēng 升
live	(v.)	hidup	shēng cún 生存, huó zhē 活着
		tinggal	shēng húo 生活, zhù 住
	(a.)	yang hidup	húo dė 活的

live.li.hood	(n.)	mata pencarian	shēng húo 生活, shēng jì 生计
live.li.ness	(n.)	keaktifan, kelincahan	húo pō 活泼, líng húo 灵活
live.ly	(a.)	lincah	huó pō 活泼, huó yào 活跃
liv.er	(n.)	hati, limpa	gān 肝
live.stock	(n.)	ternak	jiā chù 家畜
liv.ing	(a.)	yang hidup	húo zhē dė 活着的, húo pō dė 活泼的
	(n.)	mata pencarian, nafkah	shēng jí 生计
load	(v.)	memuat	zhuāng zài 装载
	(n.)	muatan, beban	zài hè 载荷, dàn zi 担子
loaf	(n.)	sebatang roti tawar utuh	yī tiáo miàn bāo 一条面包
	(v.)	bermalas-malasan	hùn rì zi 混日子, yóu shǒu haò xián 游手好闲
loan	(n.)	pinjaman	dài jiè 贷借, dài kuǎn 贷款, jiè kuǎn 借款
lob	(n.)	pukulan bola tinggi-tinggi	diào gāo qiú 吊高球
	(v.)	memukul bola tinggi-tinggi	diào gāo qiú 吊高球
lob.by	(n.)	ruang tunggu	jiē dài shì 接待室
		ruang depan, lobi	qián tíng 前厅
lob.ster	(n.)	udang karang	lóng xia 龙虾
lo.cal	(a.)	setempat	běn dì dė 本地的, dì fāng dė 地方的
lo.cate	(v.)	menempatkan	shè zhì 设置
		menentukan tempatnya	què dìng dì diǎn 确定地点
lo.ca.tion	(n.)	tempat, lokasi	dì diǎn 地点
lock	(n.)	kunci	sǔo 锁
	(v.)	mengunci	sǔo shàng 锁上, shàng sǔo 上锁
		dikunci	bèi sǔo zhù 被锁住
lock.smith	(n.)	tukang kunci	sǔo jiàng 锁匠
lo.co.mo.tive	(n.)	lokomotif	hǔo chē tóu 火车头, jí chē 机车

lo.cust	(n.)	belalang	huáng chóng 蝗虫
lodge	(v.)	menginap	tóu sù 投宿
		memondok	jì sù 寄宿
	(n.)	tempat penginapan,	zhù suǒ 住所,
		losmen	yù suǒ 寓所
lodg.er	(n.)	pemondok	fáng kè 房客, jì sù zhě 寄宿者
lodg.ing	(n.)	penginapan, pondokan	zhù sǔo 住所, sù shè 宿舍
loft	(n.)	loteng	gé lóu 阁楼
lof.ty	(a.)	tinggi, mulia	gāo 高, gāo shàng 高尚
log	(n.)	balok kayu	dà mù liaò 大木料, yuán mù cái 圆木材
log.a.rithm	(n.)	logaritma	dùi shù 对数
log.ic	(n.)	logika	luó ji 逻辑, lùn lǐ xué 伦理学
log.i.cal	(a.)	logis	hé luó ji dė 合逻辑的
loin	(n.)	pinggang	yāo 腰
lone	(a.)	sendirian	dān dú 单独, gū dú 孤独
lone.ly	(a.)	sendirian, sunyi	gū dú dė 孤独的, jì mò dė寂寞的
long	(v.)	rindu, ingin sekali	kě wàng 渴望, xiǎng niàn 想念
	(a.)	panjang, jauh	cháng dė 长的, yuǎn dė 远的
	(adv.)	lama	jiǔ 久, cháng jiǔ 长久
long.ing	(n.)	rindu, keinginan	kě wàng 渴望, xiǎng niàn 想念
lon.gi.tude	(n.)	garis bujur	jīng dù 经度
long-term	(a.)	jangka panjang	cháng qī dė 长期的,
			cháng yuǎn dė 长远的
look	(v.)	melihat	kàn 看
look.er-on	(n.)	penonton	páng guān zhě 旁观者
look.ing-glass	(n.)	cermin, kaca	jìng zi 镜子
look.out	(a.)	waspada	tí fáng 提防, jǐng jiè 警戒
loose	(a.)	longgar, lepas	sōng 松, sàn 散
	(v.)	melepaskan	jiě kaī 解开
		melonggarkan	fàng sōng 放松

loos.en	(v.)	melepaskan	jiě kaī 解开
		melonggarkan	fàng sōng 放松
lop	(v.)	memotong	kǎn 砍
lord	(n.)	raja	gúo wáng 国王
		Tuhan, Kristus	shàng dì 上帝, zhǔ 主
		bangsawan	gùi zhú 贵族
lord.ly	(a.)	agung, mulia, angkuh	táng huáng 堂皇, háo huá 豪华
lose	(v.)	kehilangan	shī qù 失去, sāng shī 丧失
		kalah	shù 输, shī bài 失败
los.er	(n.)	orang yang kehilangan	shī zhǔ 失主
		orang yang kalah	shī bài zhě 失败者
loss	(n.)	kerugian, kehilangan	sǔn shì 损失, yí shī 遗失
		kekalahan	shī bài 失败
lost	(a.)	hilang	shī qù dė 失去的
		tersesat	mí shí dė 迷失的, mí lù 迷路
lot	(n.)	nasib, undian	mìng yùn 命运, chō qiān 抽签
		banyak, partai	xǔ duō 许多, pī 批
lot.ter.y	(n.)	lotere, undian	cǎi piaò 彩票
lo.tus	(v.)	teratai	hé huā 荷花
loud	(a.)	keras, nyaring	dà shēng 大声, xiǎng liàng 响亮
loud-speak.er	(n.)	pengeras suara	kùo yīn qì 扩音器, yáng shēng qì 扬声器
louse	(n.)	kutu, tuma	shī zi 虱子
lov.a.ble	(a.)	menarik, menyenangkan	kě ài dė 可爱的
love	(v.)	mencintai, menyayangi, menyukai	ài 爱, xǐ huān 喜欢
	(v.)	cinta, asmara, kekasih	ài 爱, ài qíng 爱情, ài rén 爱人
love.ly	(a.)	indah, cantik	méi lǐ dė 美丽的, kě ài dė 可爱的
lov.er	(n.)	kekasih, pacar	ài rén 爱人, qíng rén 情人
low	(a.)	rendah, hina	dī 低, ǎi 矮, xià jiàn dė 下贱的

low.er	(a.)	lebih rendah	gèng dī dė 更低的, dī jí dė 低级的
	(v.)	menurunkan	fàng dī 放低, jiàng dī 降低
low.li.ness	(n.)	kerendahan	xià jiàn 下贱, qiān xùn 谦逊
low.ly	(a.)	rendah rendah hati	xià jí dė 下级的, qiān xùn dė 谦逊的
loy.al	(a.)	setia	zhōng xīn dė 忠心的, zhōng chéng dė 忠诚的
loy.al.ist	(n.)	orang yang setia kepada pemerintah	zhōng chén 忠臣
loy.al.ty	(n.)	kesetiaan	zhōng chéng 忠诚, zhōng xīn忠心
luck	(n.)	nasib, nasib baik, kemujuran	yùn qì 运气, hǎo yùn qì 好运气, xìng yùn 幸运
luck.i.ly	(adv.)	untunglah	xìng kuī 幸亏
luck.less	(a.)	tidak mujur, sial	bù xìng dė 不幸的, dǎo méi dė 倒霉的
luck.y	(a.)	mujur, untung	xìng yùn dė 幸运的, jí xiáng dė 吉祥的
lug.gage	(n.)	bagasi	xíng lǐ 行李
lum.ber	(n.)	kayu	mù cái 木材
lump	(n.)	gumpalan	kuài 块
lunch	(n.)	makan siang	wǔ cān 午餐, wǔ fàn 午饭
lung	(n.)	paru-paru	feì 肺
lux.u.ry	(n.)	kemewahan	shē chǐ 奢侈, haó huá 豪华

M

ma.chine	(n.)	mesin	jī qì 机器
ma.chine-gun	(n.)	senapan mesin	jī guān qiāng 机关枪, jī qiāng 机枪
ma.chin.ist	(n.)	masinis, ahli mesin	jī shī 机师
mack.in.tosh	(n.)	plastik tahan air	fáng shǔi jiāo bù 防水胶布
		jas hujan terbuat dari plastik	jiāo bù yǔ yī 胶布雨衣
mad	(a.)	gila	fēng 疯
mad.am	(n.)	nyonya	fú rén 夫人
made	(a.)	yang dibuat	tè zhì dė 特制的, rén zào dė 人造的
mad.house	(n.)	rumah (perawatan orang) gila	fēng rén yuàn 疯人院
mad.man	(n.)	orang gila	fēng rén 疯人
mad.ness	(n.)	kegilaan	fēng kuáng 疯狂
mag.a.zine	(n.)	majalah	zá zhì 杂志
mag.got	(n.)	belatung	qū chóng 蛆虫
mag.ic	(n.)	sihir	mó shù 魔术
		sulap	biàn xì fǎ 变戏法
mag.i.cal	(a.)	yang berhubungan dengan ilmu sihir	mó shù dė 魔术的
		gaib	bù kě sī yì dė 不可思仪的
ma.gi.cian	(n.)	tukang sihir, tukang sulap	mó shù jiā 魔术家
mag.is.trate	(n.)	hakim	shěn pàn guān 审判官, fǎ guān 法官
mag.nate	(n.)	tokoh terkemuka	dà rén wù 大人物
mag.net	(n.)	magnet	cí tiě 磁铁

mag.nif.i.cence	(n.)	keagungan, keindahan	zhuàng lì dė 壮丽的, háo huá dė 豪华的
mag.nif.i.cent	(a.)	amat bagus, sangat indah	zhuàng lì dė 壮丽的
mag.ni.fy	(v.)	memperbesar	fàng dà 放大, kuā dà 夸大
mag.pie	(n.)	burung *magpie*	xǐ què 喜鹊
maid	(n.)	gadis	shào nǔ 少女
		pelayan perempuan	nǔ pú rén 女仆人
maid.en	(n.)	gadis, perawan	shǎo nǔ 少女, chǔ nǔ 处女
mail	(n.)	surat-surat pos	yòu jiàn 邮件
	(v.)	mengeposkan	yóu jì 邮寄
mail.box	(n.)	kotak pos, bis surat	xìn xiāng 信箱
mail.man	(n.)	tukang pos	yóu chāi 邮差
main	(a.)	utama	zhǔ yào dė 主要的
main.land	(n.)	benua, daratan	dà lù 大陆
main.ly	(adv.)	terutama	zhǔ yào 主要
		sebagian besar	dà bù fēn 大部分
main.tain	(v.)	mempertahankan	wéi chí 维持
maize	(n.)	jagung	yù mǐ 玉米, yù shǔ shǔ 玉蜀黍
maj.es.ty	(n.)	kemuliaan, kebesaran	zūn yán 尊严, gāo gùi 高贵
ma.jor	(a.)	lebih besar	jiǎo dà dė 较大的
		sebagian besar	dūo shù dė 多数的
		penting	zhǔ yào dė 主要的
	(n.)	mayor	shǎo jiao 少校
ma.jor.i.ty	(n.)	suara terbanyak,	duō shù 多数
		golongan terbesar	duō shù xí wèi 多数席位, duō shù pài 多数派
		dewasa	chéng nián 成年
make	(v.)	membuat	zùo 做, zhì zào 制造
mak.er	(n.)	pembuat	zhì zào zhě 制造者
make-up	(n.)	riasan wajah	huà zhuang 化妆
mak.ing	(n.)	pembuatan	zhì zào 制造

ma.lar.i.a	(n.)	malaria	nuè jí 疟疾
male	(a.)	laki-laki, jantan	nán dė 男的, xióng dė 雄的
	(n.)	laki-laki, jantan	nán zǐ 男子, nán xìng 男性, xióng xìng 雄性
mam.ma (ma.ma)	(n.)	ibu	mā mȧ 妈妈
mam.mal	(n.)	binatang menyusui	bǔ rǔ dòng wù 哺乳动物
mam.ma.lia	(n.)	binatang menyusui	bǔ rǔ dòng wù 哺乳动物
mam.mal.o.gy	(n.)	ilmu tentang binatang menyusui	bǔ rǔ dòng wù xué 哺乳动物学
man	(n.)	orang, orang laki-laki, manusia	rén 人, nán rén 男人, rén lèi 人类
man.age	(v.)	mengurus, mengatur, mengusahakan	guǎn lǐ 管理, jīng yíng 经营
man.age.ment	(n.)	pengelolaan	guǎn lǐ 管理, jīng yíng 经营
man.a.ger	(n.)	manajer, pengelola, pimpinan perusahaan	jīng lí 经理
man.date	(n.)	perintah, amanat, mandat	mìng lìng 命令, xùn lìng 训令 wěi rèn shū 委任书
man.da.rin	(n.)	pejabat tinggi pemerintah Cina dahulu	(qīng cháo) dà guān (清朝) 大官
		bahasa resmi (Mandarin)	guān huà 官话
mane	(n.)	surai kuda	zōng máo 鬃毛
man.ful	(a.)	berani	yǒng gǎn 勇敢
man.go	(n.)	mangga	máng guǒ 芒果
man.hood	(n.)	masa dewasa	chéng rén qī 成人期
		kejantanan	nán zi hàn 男子汉
man.i.fest	(v.)	menunjukkan, menyatakan	biǎo míng 表明, biǎo shì 表示
	(a.)	nyata, jelas	míng bǎi dė 明白的, xiǎn míng dė 显明的
man.i.fes.ta.tion	(n.)	manifestasi	biǎo míng 表明, biǎo shì 表示

man.i.fes.to	(n.)	manifesto	xuān yán 宣言
man.i.fold	(a.)	bermacam-macam	gè zhǒng gè yàng dė 各种各样的
ma.nip.u.late	(v.)	menjalankan	cāo zuò 操作
		menggerakkan	cāo zòng 操纵
man.kind	(n.)	umat manusia	rén lèi 人类
man.like	(a.)	seperti manusia	xiàng rén dė 象人的
man-made	(a.)	buatan tangan	rén zào dė 人造的
man.ner	(n.)	cara	fāng fǎ 方法
		sikap	tài dù 态度
		gaya	fēng gé 风格
man.ner	(n.)	tata krama	lǐ maò 礼貌, guī jǔ 规矩
man.ner.ly	(a.)	sopan	yǒu lǐ mào dė 有礼貌的
man-of-war	(n.)	kapal perang	zhàn jiàn 战舰
man.ser.vant	(n.)	jongos	nán pú rén 男仆人,
			nán yòng rén 男佣人
man.tle	(n.)	mantel	zhào yī 罩衣
		jubah longgar tanpa	pī fēng 披风
		lengan	
man.u.al	(a.)	pekerjaan tangan	yòng shǒu dė 用手的,
			shǒu gōng dė 手工的
	(n.)	buku pedoman	shǒu cè 手册
man.u.al.ly	(adv.)	dengan tangan	yòng shǒu 用手
man.u.fac.to.ry	(n.)	pabrik	gōng chǎng 工厂
man.u.fac.ture	(v.)	membuat	zhì zào 制造
	(n.)	pembuatan, usaha pabrik	zhì zào 制造, zhì zào yè 制造业
man.u.fac.tur.er	(n.)	pemilik pabrik	gōng chǎng zhǔ 工厂主
		pengusaha pabrik	zhì zào shāng 制造商,
			shēng chǎn zhě 生产者
ma.nure	(n.)	pupuk, rabuk	féi liào 肥料
man.u.script	(n.)	naskah	shǒu gǎo 手稿, dǐ gǎo 底稿

man.y	(a.)	banyak	duō 多, xǔ duō 许多
map	(n.)	peta, atlas	dì tú 地图
mar.ble	(n.)	marmer	dà lǐ shí 大理石
March	(n.)	Maret	sān yùe 三月
march	(n.)	perjalanan	xíng jìn 行进
		mars	jìn xíng qǔ 进行曲
		gerakan militer	xíng jūn 行军
	(v.)	berjalan berbaris	xíng jìn 行进, xíng jūn 行军
mare	(n.)	kuda betina	mǔ mǎ 母马
mar.gin	(n.)	garis pinggir, batas	biān xiàn 边线, biān yuán 边缘, jiè xiàn 界限
ma.rine	(a.)	tentang laut	hǎi dė 海的
		tentang kapal laut	chuán yòng dė 船用的
	(n.)	prajurit laut , kapal laut	hǎi bīng 海兵, chuán bo 船舶
mar.i.ner	(n.)	marinir, pelaut	hǎi yuàn 海员, chuán yuán 船员
mark	(n.)	tanda, bekas	jì hào 记号, hěn jī 痕迹
		sasaran	mù biāo 目标
		angka	fēn shù 分数
		ciri	tè zhèng 特征
marked	(a.)	nyata, mencolok	xiǎn zhù dė 显著的, yǐn rén zhù yì dė 引人注意的
mark.er	(n.)	penilai, penanda	jì fēn yuán 记分员
mar.ket	(n.)	pasar	shì chǎng 市场
mar.riage	(n.)	perkawinan	jié hūn 结婚, hūn yīn 婚姻
mar.ried	(a.)	yang sudah kawin	jié lē hūn dė 结了婚的
mar.ry	(v.)	kawin, mengawini	jié hūn 结婚, qǔ 娶, jià 嫁
mar.shal	(n.)	marsekal	yuán shuài 元帅
mart	(n.)	pusat perdagangan	shang yè zhōng xīn 商业中心
mar.vel	(n.)	keajaiban	qí jī 奇迹
mar.vel.lous	(a.)	menakjubkan	qí guài dė 奇怪的

marx.ism	(n.)	marxisme	mǎ kè sī zhǔ yì 马克思主义
marx.ist	(n.)	marxis	mǎ kè sī zhǔ yì zhě 马克思主义者
mas.cot	(n.)	jimat, maskot	jí rén 吉人, jí wù 吉物
mas.cu.line	(a.)	jantan, bersifat laki-laki	nán xìng dė 男性的, yang xìng dė 阳性的
mask	(n.)	kedok, topeng	miàn jù 面具, miàn zhào 面罩
ma.son	(n.)	tukang batu	shǚi ní jiàng 水泥匠
mass	(n.)	tumpukan	duī 堆
		banyak sekali	dà liàng 大量, duō shù 多数
		massa	qún zhòng 群众
mass.a.cre	(n.)	pembunuhan besar-besaran	dà tú shā 大屠杀
mas.sage	(n.)	pijit	àn mó 按摩
	(v.)	memijit, mengurut	àn mó 按摩
mast	(n.)	tiang layar	wéi gàn 桅干
mas.ter	(n.)	majikan	zhǔ rén 主人
		guru pria	nán jiào shī 男教师
	(v.)	menguasai	zhǎng wò 掌握, jīng tòng 精通
mas.ter.y	(n.)	penguasaan	kòng zhì 控制, zhǎng wò 掌握, jīng tòng 精通
mat	(n.)	tikar	xí zi 席子
match	(n.)	korek api	hǔo chái 火柴
		tandingan	dùi shǒu 对手
		pertandingan	bǐ sài 比赛
		pasangan	xiāng pèi zhě 相配者
match.less	(a.)	tiada bandingnya	wú bǐ dė 无比的
mate	(n.)	teman, kawan	péng yǒu 朋友, hǔo bàn 伙伴
ma.te.ri.al	(n.)	bahan, material	cái liào 材料
		kebendaan	wù zhì 物质
ma.te.ri.al.ism	(n.)	materialisme	wéi wù zhǔ yì 唯物主义, wéi wù lùn 唯物论

ma.te.ri.al.ist	(n.)	materialis	wéi wù zhǔ yì zhě 唯物主义者
			wéi wù lùn zhě 唯物论者
ma.ter.ni.ty	(n.)	sifat keibuan	mǔ xìng 母性
math.e.ma.ti.cian	(n.)	ahli matematika	shù xué jiā 数学家
math.e.mat.ics	(n.)	ilmu pasti, matematika	shù xué 数学
mat.ter	(n.)	benda	wù zhì 物质
		hal	shì qíng 事情
		persoalan	wèn tí 问题
mat.tress	(n.)	kasur	ru zi 褥子
ma.ture	(a.)	matang, dewasa	shú 熟, chéng shú 成熟
max.i.mum	(n.)	paling banyak	zuì duō shù 最多数, jí xiàn 极限
may	(aux v.)	mungkin, boleh	yě xǔ 也许, kě yǐ 可以
May	(n.)	Mei	wǔ yuè 五月
may.be	(adv.)	barangkali	yě xǔ 也许, dà gài 大概
may.or	(n.)	walikota	shì zhǎng 市长
ma.yor.ess	(n.)	istri walikota	shì zhǎng fū rén 市长夫人
		wanita yang menduduki jabatan walikota	nǚ shì zhǎng 女市长
me	(pron.)	saya	wǒ 我
mead.ow	(n.)	padang rumput	cáo yuán 草原
meal	(n.)	tepung	miàn fén 面粉
		makanan	shàn shí 膳食, yī cān 一餐
meal time	(n.)	jam makan	chī fàn shí jiān 吃饭时间
mean	(v.)	bermaksud, berarti	yòng yì 用意, yì sī 意思
	(a.)	hina, keji	bēi bǐ 卑鄙, xià liù 下流
	(n.)	pertengahan	zhōng jiān 中间
mean.ing	(n.)	arti	yì yì 意义
mean.ing.less	(a.)	tak berarti	wú yì yì dė 无意义的, méi yì sī dė 没意思的
mean.ly	(adv.)	secara licik, secara keji	bēi bǐ di 卑鄙的, xià liú di 下流的
mean.ness	(n.)	keburukan, kepicikan	bēi bǐ 卑鄙, xià liú 下流

means	(n.)	cara, alat	shǒu duàn 手段, gōng jù 工具
		harta	zī chǎn 资产
mean.time	(adv.)	sementara itu	dāng shí 当时, tóng shí 同时
mean.while	(adv.)	sementara itu	dāng shí 当时, tóng shí 同时
mea.sles	(n.)	campak, cacar air	má zhěn 麻疹
meas.ure	(n.)	ukuran	chě cùn 尺寸, dù liàng 度量
	(v.)	mengukur	liáng 量, cè liáng 测量
meat	(n.)	daging	ròu 肉
me.chan.ic	(n.)	ahli mesin	jī xiè shì 机械师, jì gōng 技工
me.chan.i.cal	(a.)	yang berhubungan dengan mesin	jī xiè dė 机械的
		yang memakai mesin	yòng jī xiè dė 用机械的
me.chan.ics	(n.)	ilmu mekanika	lì xué 力学
mech.a.nism	(n.)	alat mekanik, mekanisme	jī xiè 机械, jī gòu 机构
mech.a.nist	(n.)	ahli mesin, mekanik	jī xiè shī 机械师
mech.a.ni.za.tion	(n.)	mekanisasi	jī xiè huà 机械化
mech.a.nize	(v.)	memekanisasikan	shǐ jī xiè huà 使机械化
med.al	(n.)	medali	jiǎng zhāng 奖章, xūn zhāng 勋章
med.dle	(v.)	mencampuri, campur tangan	gàn shè 干涉, gàn yù 干预
me.dial	(a.)	di tengah-tengah	zài zhōng jiān dė 在中间的
me.dian	(a.)	yang di tengah-tengah	zhōng jiān dė 中间的
	(n.)	garis tengah, jalur tengah	zhōng xiàn 中线
me.di.ate	(v.)	menengahi	tiáo jiě 调解
me.di.a.tor	(n.)	penengah, pelerai	tiáo jiě rén 调解人
med.i.cal	(a.)	yang berkenaan dengan kedokteran/pengobatan	yī xué shàng dė 医学上的, yī yào shàng dė 医药上的
med.i.cine	(n.)	obat, ilmu kedokteran	yào 药, yī xué 医学
me.dium	(a.)	sedang, medium	shì zhōng dė 适中的, zhōng hào dė 中号的

	(n.)	tengah, perantara	zhōng jiān 中间, méi jiè 媒介
		alat	gōng jù 工具
meek	(a.)	lembut hati, penurut	wēn shùn 温顺
meet	(v.)	bertemu	yù jiàn 遇见, pèng jiàn 碰见
	(a.)	pantas	shì dàng 适当, shì hé 适合
meet.ing	(n.)	pertemuan	huì jiàn 会见, huì yì 会议
mega.ton	(n.)	satu juta ton	yì bǎi wàn dūn 一百万吨
mel.low	(a.)	ranum dan manis	tián měi 甜美
		masak, matang	shú tòu dė 熟透的
mel.o.dy	(n.)	lagu	yuè qǔ 乐曲, gē qǔ 歌曲
mel.on	(n.)	melon	tián guā 甜瓜
melt	(v.)	mencair	róng huà 融化, róng jiě 融解
mem.ber	(n.)	anggota	chéng yuán 成员, hùi yuán 会员
mem.ber.ship	(n.)	keanggotaan	huì yuán zī gé 会员资格, huì ji 会籍
mem.brane	(n.)	selaput	mó 膜, bó mó 薄膜
mem.oir	(n.)	buku kenang-kenangan	húi yì lù 回忆录
		riwayat hidup	zhuàn jì 传记
mem.o.ran.dum	(n.)	memorandum	bèi wàng lù 备忘录
me.mo.ri.al	(n.)	tanda peringatan	jì niàn pǐn 纪念品, jì niàn bēi 纪念碑
	(a.)	yang bersifat peringatan	jì niàn dė 纪念的
mem.o.ry	(n.)	ingatan	jì yì 记忆, jì xìng 记性
men.ace	(n.)	ancaman	weī xié 威胁
mend	(v.)	memperbaiki	xiū lǐ 修理
		membetulkan	gǎi zhèng 改正
men.tal	(a.)	mental	xīn lǐ dė 心理的, jīng shén dė 精神的
men.tion	(v.)	menyebutkan	tí qǐ 提起
men.u	(n.)	daftar makanan, menu	cài dān 菜单
mer.chan.dise	(n.)	barang dagangan	shāng pín 商品
mer.chant	(n.)	pedagang	shāng rén 商人
mer.chant.man	(n.)	kapal pedagang	shāng chuán 商船

mer.ci.ful	(a.)	penuh belas kasihan, bermurah hati	cí bēi 慈悲
mer.ci.less	(a.)	tak kenal belas kasihan	cán rěn dė 残忍的
mer.cy	(n.)	kemurahan hati	kuān dà 宽大
		belas kasihan	cí bēi 慈悲
mere	(a.)	hanya	zhǐ shì 只是, jǐn jǐn 仅仅
mere.ly	(adv.)	hanya	zhǐ shì 只是, jǐn jǐn 仅仅
merge	(v.)	menggabungkan, bergabung	guī bìng 归并, hé bìng 合并
merg.er	(n.)	penggabungan	hé bìng 合并
me.rid.i.an	(n.)	garis bujur	zǐ wǔ xiàn 子午线
mer.it	(n.)	jasa, kebaikan	gōng láo 功劳, yōu diǎn 优点
	(v.)	patut	zhí dé 值得, yìng dé 应得
mer.ry	(a.)	riang gembira	kuài lè dė 快乐的
mess	(v.)	mengotori, mengacaukan	nòng zāng 弄脏, nòng zāo 弄糟
mes.sage	(n.)	berita	xiāo xī 消息
mes.sen.ger	(n.)	utusan, pesuruh,	shǐ zhě 使者,
		pengantar surat	tōng xìn yuán 通信员
met.al	(n.)	logam	jīn shǔ 金属
me.tal.lic	(a.)	dari logam, seperti logam	jīn shǔ dė 金属的
me.teor	(n.)	meteor	liú xīng 流星
me.teor.o.log.i.cal	(a.)	berhubungan dengan meteorologi	qì xiàng dė 气象的
me.teor.ol.o.gist	(n.)	ilmu cuaca	qì xiàng xué jiā 气象学家
me.teor.ol.o.gy	(n.)	meteorologi, ilmu cuaca	qì xiàng xué 气象学
meth.od	(n.)	cara, metode	fāng fǎ 方法, fāng shì 方式
me.tre (me.ter)	(n.)	meter	gōng chǐ 公尺
me.trop.o.lis	(n.)	kota besar	dà dù shì 大都市, dà chéng shì 大城市
met.ro.pol.i.tan	(a.)	berhubungan dengan kota besar	dà dù shì dė 大都市的

mi.ca	(n.)	mika	yún mŭ 云母
mi.crobe	(n.)	kuman, mikroba	wēi shēng wù 微生物, xì jūn 细菌
mi.cro.phone	(n.)	mikrofon	kuò yīn qì 扩音器
mi.cro.scope	(n.)	mikroskop	xiăn weī jìng 显微镜
mid	(a.)	tengah	zhōng jiān dė 中间的
mid.day	(n.)	tengah hari	zhōng wŭ 中午
mid.dle	(n.)	(bagian) tengah	zhōng jiān 中间, zhōng bù 中部
mid.dle-aged	(a.)	setengah baya	zhōng nián 中年
mid.dle.man	(n.)	perantara	zhōng jiān rén 中间人, zhōng jiè rén 中介人
mid.most	(a.)	pas tengah	zhèng zhōng dė 正中的
mid.night	(n.)	tengah malam	wŭ yè 午夜, zĭ yè 子夜
midst	(n.)	tengah	zhōng jiān 中间
mid.way	(a.)	tengah jalan	zhōng tú dė 中途的
mid.wife	(n.)	bidan	zhù chăn shī 助产士, jiē shēng pó 接生婆
might	(n.)	kekuatan, tenaga	lì 力
might.y	(a.)	kuat	yŏu lì dė 有力的
mild	(a.)	lembut, sejuk, ringan	wēn hé dė 温和的, qīng dė 轻的
mile	(n.)	mil	yīng lĭ 英里
mil.i.tant	(a.)	militan	zhàn dòu xìng dė 战斗性的, hào zhàn dė 好战的
	(n.)	orang yang militan	jī jí fèn zi 积极份子, dòu shì 斗士
mil.i.ta.ry	(a.)	militer, ketentaraan	jun rén dė 军人的, jūn shì dė 军事的
	(n.)	tentara	jūn dùi 军队, jūn rén 军人
mi.li.tia	(n.)	milisi	mín bīng 民兵, mín jūn 民军
milk	(n.)	susu	niú năi 牛奶
mill	(n.)	penggilingan pabrik pemintalan	mó făng 磨房 făng shā chăng 纺纱厂
mil.len.ni.um	(n.)	masa seribu tahun	yī qiān nián 一千年

mil.liard	(n.)	miliar	shí yì 十亿
mil.li.gram	(n.)	miligram	háo kè 毫克
mil.li.litre	(n.)	mililiter	háo shēng 毫升
mil.li.metre	(n.)	milimeter	háo mǐ 毫米
mil.lion	(n.)	juta	bǎi wàn 百万
mil.lion.aire	(n.)	jutawan	bǎi wàn fù wēng 百万富翁
mim.ic	(a.)	bersifat tiruan	mó fǎng dė 模仿的,
			xué yàng dė 学样的
	(n.)	orang yang meniru	xué yàng zhě 学样者
		barang tiruan	mó fǎng pǐn 模仿品,
			fǎng zào pǐn 仿造品
mind	(n.)	pikiran, ingatan	xīn shén 心神, xīn sī 心思
	(v.)	berhati-hati	liú xín 留心, liú shén 留神
		memperhatikan, menjaga	zhù yì 注意, zhào liào 照料
mind.ful	(a.)	berhati-hati	liú xīn dė 留心的
		memperhatikan	liú yì dė 留意的
mind.less	(a.)	tidak hati-hati	bù liú xīn dė 不留心的
		tidak perhatian	bù zhù yì dė 不注意的
mine	(pron.)	punya saya	wǒ dė 我的, wǒ dė dōng xī 我的东西
	(n.)	tambang	kuàng shān 矿山, kuàng kēng 矿坑
	(v.)	menambang	kaī kuàng 开矿
min.er	(n.)	buruh tambang	kuàng gōng 矿工
min.er.al	(n.)	barang tambang, mineral	kuàng wù 矿物, wú jī wù 无机物
min.er.al.o.gy	(n.)	mineralogi	kuàng wù xué 矿物学
min.gle	(v.)	bercampur, bergabung	hùn hé 混合
min.imal	(a.)	yang paling sedikit	zùi shǎo dė 最少的
		yang paling rendah	zùi dī xiàn dù dė 最低限度的
min.i.mum	(n.)	paling sedikit	zùi shào 最少
		paling kecil, minimum	zùi dī xiān dù 最低限度
min.ing	(n.)	pertambangan	kuàng yè 矿业, cǎi kuàng 采矿

min.is.ter	(n.)	menteri	bù zhǎng 部长
		pendeta	jiào shì 教士
min.is.try	(n.)	kementerian	bù 部
mi.nor	(a.)	lebih kecil	jiào xiǎo dė 较小的, jiào shǎo dė 较少的
		kurang penting	cì yào dė 次要的
		di bawah umur	wèi chéng nián dė 未成年的
mi.nor.i.ty	(n.)	minoritas	shǎo shù 少数
		golongan kecil	shǎo shù pài 少数派
mi.nus	(a.)	kurang, minus	fù dė 负的
min.ute	(n.)	menit	fēn 分
mi.nute	(a.)	amat kecil	weī xiǎo 微小
		teliti	jīng mì 精密
	(n., pl.)	notulen, laporan rapat	hùi yì jì lù 会议记录
mir.a.cle	(n.)	keajaiban	qí jī 奇迹
mi.rac.u.lous	(a.)	ajaib	qí miào dė 奇妙的, shén qí dė 神奇的
mir.ror	(n.)	cermin	jìng zi 镜子
mirth	(n.)	keriangan, kegembiraan	gāo xìng 高兴, kuài lè 快乐
mis.ad.ven.ture	(n.)	nasib malang, musibah	bù xìng 不幸, zaī nàn 灾难
mis.ap.ply	(v.)	menyalahgunakan	wù yòng 误用, làn yòng 滥用
mis.be.have	(v.)	berbuat tidak baik	biǎo xiàn bù hǎo 表现不好, xíng wéi bù zhèng 行为不正
mis.car.ry	(v.)	gagal, gugur	shī bài 失败, liú chǎn 流产
mis.chance	(n.)	kemalangan, musibah	bù xìng 不幸, zaī nàn 灾难
mis.chief	(n.)	kenakalan, kerusakan	è zuò jù 恶作剧, sǔn hài 损害
mis.chic.vous	(a.)	nakal	tiáo pí dė 调皮的, taó qì dė 淘气的
mis.con.duct	(n.)	kelakuan tidak senonoh	xíng wéi bù zhèng 行为不正
	(v.)	kelakuan buruk	bū guī jǔ 不规矩
mis.count	(v.)	salah hitung	suàn cùo 算错
mis.deed	(n.)	perbuatan jahat	è xíng 恶行, zuì xíng 罪行

mis.do.ing	(n.)	perbuatan buruk	huaì shì 坏事
		perbuatan dosa	è xíng 恶行, zuì xíng 罪行
mi.ser	(n.)	orang kikir	lìn sè gǔi 吝啬鬼
mis.er.a.ble	(a.)	amat menyedihkan, sengsara	beī cǎn 悲惨
mis.er.y	(n.)	kesengsaraan	tòng kǔ 痛苦, beī cǎn 悲惨
mis.fit	(n.)	orang yang canggung	bù chèn zhí dė rén 不称职的人
		pakaian yang tidak cocok	bù shì hé dė fú zhuāng 不适合的服装
mis.for.tune	(n.)	kemalangan	bù xìng 不幸
mis.in.form	(v.)	memberi informasi yang salah	chuán cùo 传错
mis.in.ter.pret	(v.)	salah menafsirkan	wù jiě 误解
mis.lay	(v.)	salah meletakkan	cùo fàng 错放, fàng cùo lė 放错了
mis.lead	(v.)	menyesatkan	yǐn rù qí tú 引入歧途
mis.man.age	(v.)	salah mengurus	bàn cùo 办错, guǎn lǐ cùo wù 管理错误
mis.name	(v.)	salah memanggil/memberi nama	jiào cuò 叫错
mis.place	(v.)	salah meletakkan	fàng cùo 放错
mis.print	(v.)	salah cetak	yìn cùo 印错
mis.read	(v.)	salah membaca	dú cùo 读错
miss	(n.)	nona	xiǎo jiě 小姐
mis.shap.en	(a.)	berbentuk tidak serasi	jī xíng dė 畸形的
mis.sile	(n.)	benda yang dilepaskan	fā shè wù 发射物
		misil, peluru	fēi dàn 飞弹, dǎo dàn 导弹
miss.ing	(a.)	yang hilang	yí shì dė 遗失的, shī zōng dė 失踪的
mis.sion	(n.)	tugas	rèn wù 任务,
		perutusan, misi	dài biǎo tuán 代表团
		penyebaran agama Katolik	chuán jiào 传教, chuán dào 传道
mis-spell	(v.)	salah mengeja	cùo pīn 错拼

mis-spend	(v.)	membuang-buang	làng fèi 浪费, luàn huā 乱花
mis.state	(v.)	salah mengucapkan	shūo cùo 说错
mist	(n.)	kabut	wù 雾
mis.take	(n.)	kekeliruan, kesalahan	wù huì 误会, wù jiě 误解
mis.ter	(n.)	tuan	xiān shēng 先生
mis.treat	(v.)	menganiaya	nuè dài 虐待
mis.tress	(n.)	nyonya rumah, nyonya	jiā tíng zhǔ fù 家庭主妇, nǔ zhǔ rén 女主人
mis.trust	(v.)	tidak mempercayai	bù xìn rèn 不信任
		mencurigai	huái yí 怀疑
mist.y	(a.)	berkabut	yǒu wù dė 有雾的
mis.un.der.stand	(v.)	salah mengerti	wù jiě 误解, wù huì 误会
mis.use	(v.)	menyalahgunakan	wù yòng 误用, làn yòng 滥用
mix	(v.)	mencampurkan, meng-aduk	hùn hé 混合
		bergaul	jiāo jí 交际
		mempergaulkan	shǐ...jiāo wǎng 使…交往
mix.ture	(n.)	campuran	hùn hé 混合, hùn hé wù 混合物
mix-up	(n.)	kekacauan	hùn luàn 混乱
moan	(n.)	suara mengerang, rin-tihan	shēn yín shēng 呻吟声
mob	(n.)	orang banyak	mín zhòng 民众
		gerombolan, pengacau	wū hé zhī zhòng 乌合之众, bào tú 暴徒
mo.bile	(a.)	bergerak	yùn dòng dė 运动的
		aktif	huó dòng dė 活动的
mo.bil.i.za.tion	(n.)	mobilisasi, pengerahan	dòng yuán 动员
mo.bil.ize	(v.)	pengerahan	dòng yuán 动员
mock	(v.)	mengejek	jī xiào 讥笑, cháo xiào 嘲笑
mock.er	(n.)	orang yang mengejek	jī xiào zhě 讥笑者, cháo xiào zhě 嘲笑者

mo.dal	(a.)	berhubungan dng bentuk	xíng shì shàng dė 形式上的
		berhubungan dng perasaan	qíng tài dė 情态的
mode	(n.)	cara, ragam	fāng shì 方式, fēng dù 风度
		mode	shí zhuāng 时装
mod.el	(n.)	model	mó xíng 模型, mó tè ér 模特儿
		contoh	mó fan 模范
mod.er.ate	(a.)	sedang, moderat	shì zhōng dė 适中的,
			wēn hé dė 温和的
	(n.)	orang moderat	zhōng jiān pài 中间派
		golongan moderat	wēn hé pài 温和派
mod.er.a.tor	(n.)	ketua	zhǔ chí rén 主持人
		pelerai, penengah	tiáo jiě rén 调解人
mod.ern	(a.)	modern, mutakhir	xiàn dài dė 现代的
mod.ern.i.za.tion	(n.)	modernisasi	xiàn dài huà 现代化
mod.est	(a.)	rendah hati, sederhana	qiān xū 谦虚, pǔ sù 朴素
mod.i.fi.ca.tion	(n.)	modifikasi, perubahan	xiū gǎi 修改, gǎi biàn 改变
mod.i.fi.er	(n.)	kata yg menentukan sifat	xiū shì yǔ 修饰语
mod.i.fy	(v.)	mengubah, memodifikasi	xiū gǎi 修改, xiū shì 修饰
		membatasi, mengurangi	jiǎn qīng 减轻
mod.ish	(a.)	yang terbaru	liú xíng dė 流行的
		masa kini	shí máo dė 时髦的
moist	(a.)	lembap	cháo shī 潮湿
moist.en	(v.)	membasahi	nòng shī 弄湿
mois.ture	(n.)	uap lembap	shī qì 湿气
mole	(n.)	tahi lalat	heī zhi 黑痣
		tikus mondok	yǎn shǔ 鼹鼠
		tanggul pelabuhan	fáng bō tí 防波提
mo.ment	(n.)	saat, ketika	shí kè 时刻, qǐng kè 顷刻
mon.arch	(n.)	raja	guó wáng 国王
mon.as.ter.y	(n.)	biara	sì yuàn 寺院

Mon.day	(n.)	hari Senin	xīng qī yī 星期一
mon.e.ta.ry	(a.)	moneter	jīn róng dė 金融的, hùo bì dė 货币的
mon.ey	(n.)	uang	qián 钱, jīn qián 金钱, hùo bì 货币
mon.eyed	(a.)	memiliki banyak uang	yǒu qián dė 有钱的
		kaya	fù yǒu dė 富有
mon.ger	(n.)	pedagang	shāng rén 商人
mon.i.tor	(n.)	ketua kelas, monitor	bān zhǎng 班长, jiān tīng yuán 监听员
	(v.)	memantau, mengawasi	jiān shì 监视
mon.it.ress	(n.)	ketua kelas (perempuan)	nǔ bān zhǎng 女班长
monk	(n.)	rahib	hé shang 和尚
mon.key	(n.)	kera	hòu zi 猴子
mo.nop.o.list	(n.)	orang yang memonopoli	dú zhàn zhě 独占者, lóng dùan zhě 垄断者, zhuàn mài zhě 专卖者
mo.nop.o.lis.tic	(a.)	yang bersifat monopoli	dú zhàn dė 独占的, lóng duàn dė 垄断的
mo.nop.o.lize	(v.)	memonopoli	dú zhàn 独占, lóng duàn 垄断, zhuān mài 专卖
mo.nop.o.ly	(n.)	monopoli	dú zhàn 独占, lóng duàn 垄断, zhuān mài 专卖
mon.o.tone	(n.)	monoton	dān diào 单调
mon.ster	(n.)	makhluk menakutkan	guài wù 怪物
month	(n.)	bulan	yuè 月
month.ly	(a.)	tiap bulan, bulanan	měi yuè dė 每月的
	(n.)	majalah bulanan	yuè kān 月刊
mon.u.ment	(n.)	monumen, tugu peringatan	jì niàn beī 纪念碑
mood	(n.)	perasaan hati	xīn qíng 心情
		modus	yǔ qì 语气
moon	(n.)	bulan	yuè liàng 月亮
moon.beam	(n.)	sinar bulan	yuè guāng 月光

moon.light	(n.)	cahaya bulan	yuè guāng 月光
moon.shine	(n.)	sinar bulan	yuè guāng 月光
mor.al	(n.)	moril, akhlak	dào yì dė 道义的, daò dé shàng dė 道德上的, jīng shén shàng dė 精神上的, yǒu dào dé dė 有道德的
mo.rale	(n.)	semangat juang	shì qì 士气
mo.ral.i.ty	(n.)	kesusilaan, moralitas	dào dé 道德
more	(a.)	lebih banyak	gèng dūo dė 更多的
	(adv.)	lebih, lagi	gèng dūo 更多, zai 再, jiào dūo 较多
more.o.ver	(adv.)	lagi pula	ér qiě 而且, cǐ wài 此外
		selain itu, tambahan lagi	jiā zhī 加之
morn.ing	(n.)	pagi	zǎo shàng 早上, zǎo chén 早晨
mor.tal	(a.)	fana, dapat mati	hùi sǐ dė 会死的, yào sǐ dė 要死的, zhì mìng dė 致命的
mor.tal.i.ty	(n.)	kematian, keadaan dapat mati	zhì mìng xìng 致命性, bì sǐ xìng 必死性
mosque	(n.)	mesjid	huí jiào táng 回教堂, qīng zhēn sì 清真寺
mos.qui.to	(n.)	nyamuk	wén zi 蚊子
moss	(n.)	lumut	xiǎn tāi 藓苔, dì yī 地衣
most	(adv.)	paling banyak	zùi duō 最多, zùi 最
most.ly	(adv.)	umumnya	zhǔ yào di 主要地, yī bān di 一般地, dà bù fēn 大部分
moth	(n.)	ngengat	é 蛾
moth.er	(n.)	ibu	mǔ qīn 母亲
moth.er-in-law	(n.)	ibu mertua	yuè mù 悦目
moth.er.land	(n.)	tanah air, ibu pertiwi	zǔ guó 祖国

mo.tif	(n.)	motif, tema	zhŭ tí 主题
mo.tion	(n.)	gerak	dòng 动, yùn dòng 运动
		mosi, usul	dòng yì 动议
mo.tion.less	(a.)	tidak bergerak	bù dòng 不动
mo.tive	(n.)	alasan	dòng jī 动机
mo.tor	(n.)	motor, mesin	fā dòng jī 发动机
mo.tor-car	(n.)	mobil	qì chē 汽车
mo.tor-cy.cle	(n.)	sepeda motor	jī qì jiăo tà chē 机器脚踏车
mo.tor.way	(n.)	jalan mobil	qì chē dào 汽车道, qì chē lù 汽车路
mot.to	(n.)	semboyan	gé yán 格言
mould	(n.)	cetakan	mó xíng 模型
	(v.)	membentuk	sù zào 塑造
mount	(v.)	mendaki gunung	dēng shān 登山
		naik kuda	shàng mă 上马
	(n.)	gunung	shān 山
moun.tain	(n.)	gunung	shān 山
moun.tain.eer	(n.)	pendaki gunung	dēng shān yùn dòng yuán 登山运动员, pá shān jiā 爬山家
		penduduk pegunungan	shān dì rén 山地人
moun.tain.ous	(a.)	bergunung-gunung	duō shān dė 多山的
mourn	(v.)	berduka-cita, berkabung	bēi tòng 悲痛, āi dào 哀悼
mourn.er	(n.)	orang yang berkabung	bēi tòng dė rén 悲痛的人, shŏu sàng dė rén 守丧的人, sòng sàng dė rén 送丧的人
mouse	(n.)	tikus	lăo shŭ 老鼠
mouse-trap	(n.)	perangkap tikus	bŭ shŭ qì 扑鼠器
mous.tache	(n.)	kumis	zī 髭
mouth	(n.)	mulut	zuĭ 咀
move	(v.)	bergerak, menggerakkan	yí dòng 移动, kāi dòng 开动
move.ment	(n.)	gerakan, pergerakan	húo dòng 活动, yùn dòng 运动

mov.ie	(n.)	film	diàn yǐng 电影
mov.ing	(a.)	yang bergerak	húo dòng dė 活动的
mow	(v.)	memotong rumput	gē cǎo 割草
mow.er	(v.)	tukang potong rumput	gē cǎo gōng rén 割草工人
		mesin potong rumput	gē cǎo jī 割草机
much	(a.)	banyak	xǔ duō 许多
mud	(n.)	lumpur	ní jiāng 泥浆
mud.dy	(a.)	berlumpur	ní níng dė 泥泞的
mule	(n.)	keledai	lú zi 驴子
mul.ti.ply	(v.)	memperbanyak	zēng jiā 增加
		mengalikan	chéng 乘
mul.ti.tude	(n.)	banyak, orang banyak	duō 多, zhòng duō 众多, dà zhòng 大众
mur.der	(v.)	membunuh	sā hài 杀害, móu sā 谋杀
	(n.)	pembunuhan	mìng àn 命案
mur.der.er	(n.)	pembunuh	xiōng shǒu 凶手, sā rén fàn 杀人犯
mur.mur	(v.)	menggerutu	fā láo sāo 发牢骚
	(n.)	gerutu	yuàn yán 怨言, láo sāo 牢骚
mus.cle	(n.)	otot	jīn 筋, jī ròu 肌肉
muse	(v.)	merenung	mò xiǎng 默想
mu.se.um	(n.)	museum	bó wù guǎn 博物馆
mush.room	(n.)	jamur	yáng mó gū 羊蘑菇
mu.sic	(n.)	musik	yīn yùe 音乐
mu.si.cian	(n.)	ahli musik, musisi	yīn yuè jiā 音乐家
muss	(v.)	mengacaubalaukan	gǎo luàn 搞乱
		mengotorkan	lòng zāng 弄脏
must	(aux. v.)	harus, mesti	bì xū 必须, yī dìng yào 一定要
mute	(n.)	orang bisu	yǎ bā 哑 巴
mut.ton	(n.)	daging kambing	yáng ròu 羊肉
mu.tu.al	(a.)	saling	xiāng hù dė 相互的
		bersama	gòng tóng dė 共同的

my	(a.)	punyaku	wǒ dė 我的
myr.i.ad	(n.)	banyak sekali	wú shù 无数
my.self	(pron.)	saya sendiri	wǒ zì jǐ 我自己
mys.te.ri.ous	(a.)	aneh, gaib	shén mì dė 神秘的, ào miào dė 奥妙的
mys.ter.y	(n.)	kegaiban, misteri	shén mì 神秘, ào miào 奥妙
mys.tic	(a.)	mistik, gaib, ajaib	shén mì dė 神秘的, ào miào dė 奥妙的
	(n.)	ahli ilmu kebatinan	shén mì jiā 神秘家,
			shén mì zhǔ yì zhě 神秘主义者
mys.ti.cism	(n.)	paham/ilmu mistik	shén mì zhǔ yì 神秘主义
mys.ti.fy	(v.)	membingungkan	mí hùo 迷惑
		mempesonakan	shén mì huà 神秘化

N

nail	(n.)	paku, kuku	dìng zi 钉子, zhǐ jiǎ 指甲
na.ked	(a.)	telanjang	lǜo tǐ dė 裸体的
name	(n.)	nama	míng zi 名字
name.less	(a.)	tidak dikenal, tidak punya nama	wú míng dė 无名的
name.ly	(adv.)	yakni	jí shì 即是, jiù shì 就是
nap	(n.)	tidur sebentar	xiǎo shùi 小睡
		tidur siang	shùi wǔ jiào 睡午觉
nape	(n.)	tengkuk	jǐng bèi 颈背
nap.kin	(n.)	serbet	cān jīn 餐巾
nar.co.sis	(n.)	pembiusan, narkosis	má zuì 麻醉, má zùi fã 麻醉珐
nar.cot.ic	(n.)	obat bius, narkotik	má zùi jì 麻醉剂, má zùi yào 麻醉药
nar.row	(a.)	sempit	xiá zhǎi 狭窄
nar.row-mind.ed	(a.)	berpandangan sempit	qì liàng xiǎo dė 气量小的
		berpikiran sempit	xiǎo qì dė 小气的
nas.ty	(a.)	busuk, kotor	fã chòu dė 发臭的, ān zāng dė 肮脏的
na.tal	(a.)	yang berhubungan dengan kelahiran	chū shēng dė 出生的, dàn shēng dė 诞生的
na.tion	(n.)	bangsa	mín zú 民族
na.tion.al	(a.)	nasional	mín zú dė 民族的, gúo mín dė 国民的, gúo jiā dė 国家的
na.tion.al.ism	(n.)	nasionalisme	mín zú zhǔ yì 民族主义
na.tion.al.ist	(n.)	nasionalis	mín zú zhǔ yì zhě 民族主义者

na.tion.al.i.ty	(n.)	kebangsaan	gúo jí 国籍
na.tion.al.i.za.tion	(n.)	nasionalisasi	gúo yǒu hùa 国有化
na.tion.al.ize	(v.)	menasionalisasikan	shōu wéi gúo yǒu 收为国有, gúo yǒu huà 国有化
na.tion.al.ly	(adv.)	seluruh negara	quán gúo di 全国地
na.tion-wide	(a.)	nasional, seluruh negara	quán gúo dė 全国的, quán mín zú dė 全民族的, quán mín dė 全民的
na.tive	(n.)	penduduk asli	tǔ rén 土人, yuán jū mín 原居民
	(a.)	asli	tǔ zhù dė 土著的
		alamiah	xiān tiān dė 先天的, tiān rán dė 天然的
		asal	yuán lái dė 原来的
nat.ty	(a.)	rapi	zhěng jié 整洁
nat.u.ral	(a.)	lazim, wajar	zì rán dė 自然的, dāng rán dė 当然的
		mengenai alam	tiān rán dė 天然的, zì rán jiè dė 自然界的
nat.u.ral.ism	(n.)	naturalisme	zì rán zhǔ yì 自然主义
nat.u.ral.ist	(n.)	naturalis	zì rán zhǔ yì zhě 自然主义者, zì rán kē xué jiā 自然科学家
nat.u.ral.i.za.tion	(n.)	naturalisasi	guī huà 归化
nat.u.ral.ize	(v.)	menaturalisasikan	guī huà 归化, shǐ guī huà 使归化
na.ture	(n.)	alam	zì rán 自然
		tabiat	běn xìng 本性
		sifat	xìng zhì 性质
naught	(n.)	nol	líng 零
naugh.ti.ness	(n.)	kenakalan	wán pí 顽皮
naugh.ty	(a.)	nakal	wán pí dė 顽皮的
na.val	(a.)	mengenai angkatan laut	hǎi jūn dė 海军的
na.vel	(n.)	pusar, puser	dǔ qí yǎn 肚脐眼

nav.i.gate	(v.)	berlayar, mengemudikan	háng xíng 航行, jià shǐ 驾驶
nav.i.ga.tion	(n.)	pelayaran, navigasi	háng xíng 航行, háng hǎi 航海
		ilmu pelayaran	háng hǎi shù 航海术
nav.i.ga.tor	(n.)	navigator	lǐng háng zhě 领航者
		ahli pelayaran	háng hǎi zhě 航海者
na.vy	(n.)	angkatan laut	hǎi jūn 海军
near	(adv.)	dekat	jìn 近
near.by	(a. adv.)	dekat, tidak berapa jauh	fù jìn 附近, jiē jìn 接近
near.ly	(adv.)	hampir	jī hū 几乎, chā yī diǎn 差一点
neat	(a.)	rapi, bersih	zhěng jié 整洁
ne.ces.sa.ri.ly	(adv.)	pasti, mesti	bì dìng 必定, bì rán 必然, dāng rán 当然
nec.es.sa.ry	(a.)	perlu	bì yào dė 必要的, bì xū dė 必须的
ne.ces.si.ty	(n.)	keperluan	bì yào xìng 必要性
		keharusan	bì rán xìng 必然性
		kebutuhan	bì xū pǐn 必需品
neck	(n.)	leher	jǐng 颈, bó zi 脖子
neck.lace	(n.)	kalung	xiàng liàn 项链
neck.tie	(n.)	dasi	lǐng dài 领带
need	(n.)	keperluan, kebutuhan	bì xū 必需, bī xū pǐn 必需品
	(v.)	memerlukan, harus	xū yào 需要, bì xū 必须
need.ful	(a.)	yang diperlukan	xū yào dė 需要的, bì yào dė 必要的
nee.dle	(n.)	jarum	zhēn 针
need.less	(a.)	tidak perlu	bù bì yào dė 不必要的, bù xū yào dė 不须要的
nee.dle-wo.man	(n.)	tukang jahit wanita	nǚ cái féng 女裁缝
nee.dle-work	(n.)	jahitan tangan, sulam menyulam	zhēn xiàn húo 针线活
need.y	(a.)	miskin	pín qióng dė 贫穷的
ne.gate	(v.)	menyangkal	fǒu rèn 否认

neg.a.tive	(a.)	negatif	fǒu dìng dė 否定的
neg.lect	(v.)	mengabaikan, melalaikan	shū hū 疏忽, hū lùe 忽略
ne.go.ti.ate	(v.)	merundingkan, berunding	tán pàn 谈判, jiāo shè 交涉
ne.go.ti.a.tion	(n.)	perundingan	tán pàn 谈判, jiāo shè 交涉, shāng liáng 商量
ne.go.ti.a.tor	(n.)	perunding, orang yang berunding	tán pàn zhě 谈判者, jiāo shè zhě 交涉者
ne.gro	(n.)	orang negro	heī zhǒng rén 黑种人
neigh	(n.)	meringkik	mǎ sì shēng 马嘶声
neigh.bour	(n.)	tetangga	lín jù 邻居
nei.ther	(a.)	dua-duanya tidak	liǎng gè dù bú 两个都不, dù bù 都不
ne.on	(n.)	lampu neon	nī hóng dēng 霓虹灯
neph.ew	(n.)	keponakan laki-laki	zhì ér 侄儿, wài shēng 外甥
nerve	(n.)	urat saraf	shén jīng 神经
nerv.ous	(a.)	gugup, bingung	shén jìng bù ān dė 神经不安的, jiāo jí dė 焦急的
nerv.ous.ness	(n.)	kegugupan	shén jìng guò mǐn 神经过敏
nest	(n.)	sarang	chaó 巢, wō 窝
net	(n.)	jala, jaring	wǎng 网
	(a.)	bersih	chún jìng 纯净
	(n.)	menerima bersih	jìng dé 净得, jìng zhuàn 净赚
neu.ter	(a.)	netral	zhōng xìng dė 中性的
	(n.)	kata yang bersifat netral	zhōng xìng cí 中性词
neu.tral	(a.)	netral	zhōng lì dė 中立的
	(n.)	orang yang netral	zhōng lì zhě 中立者
		negara yang netral	zhōng lì gúo 中立国
nev.er	(adv.)	tak pernah	cóng lái bù 从来不, yǒng bù 永不
nev.er.more	(adv.)	tidak lagi	bù zài 不再
nev.er.the.less	(conj.)	sekalipun demikian namun	jìn guǎn rú cǐ 尽管如此 rán ér 然而

new	(a.)	baru	xīn 新
new.com.er	(n.)	pendatang baru	xīn lái zhě 新来者, mò shēng rén 陌生人
new.ly	(adv.)	baru saja	xīn jìn 新近, zùi jìn 最近
news	(n.)	berita	xīn wén 新闻, xiāo xī 消息
news.pa.per	(n.)	surat kabar, koran	bào zhǐ 报纸
news-stand	(n.)	kios koran	bào tàn 报摊, mài bào tàn 卖报摊
next	(a.)	berikutnya	jiē xià lái dė 接下来的, qí cì 其次
		lain	bié dė 别的
	(adv.)	berikutnya	xià cì 下次, xià yī cì 下一次
nib	(n.)	mata pena, ujung pena	bǐ jiān 笔尖
nib.ble	(v.)	menggerogoti, menggigiti	kěn 啃
nice	(a.)	cantik, baik, enak	měi lì 美丽, hǎo 好
nick.name	(n.)	nama panggilan	chùo hào 绰号, xiǎo míng 小名
niece	(n.)	keponakan perempuan	zhì nǚ 侄女, wài shēng nǚ 外甥女
night	(n.)	malam	yè 夜, wǎn shàng 晚上
night-club	(n.)	klub malam	yè zǒng hùi 夜总会
night.dress	(n.)	pakaian tidur	shùi yī 睡衣
night.fall	(n.)	senja	huáng hūn 黄昏, bāng wǎn 傍晚
night.gown	(n.)	pakaian tidur wanita	nǚ shùi yī 女睡衣
night.in.gale	(n.)	burung bulbul	yè yīng 夜莺
night.mare	(n.)	mimpi buruk	è mèng 恶梦
night-school	(n.)	sekolah malam	yè xiào 夜校
night.shirt	(n.)	baju tidur (pria)	(nán) shùi yī (男)睡衣
night-watch	(n.)	jaga malam	shǒu yè 守夜
ni.hil.ism	(n.)	nihilisme	xū wú zhǔ yì 虚无主义
ni.hil.ist	(n.)	penganut nihilisme, nihilis	xū wú zhǔ yì zhě 虚无主义者
nil	(n.)	nol	líng 零
nim.ble	(a.)	cepat, cekatan	mǐn jié 敏捷

nine	(n.)	sembilan	jiǔ 九
nine.fold	(a.)	lipat sembilan	jiǔ bèi 九倍
nine.teen	(n.)	sembilan belas	shí jiǔ 十九
nine.teenth	(n.)	kesembilan belas	dì shí jiǔ 第十九
		tanggal sembilan belas	shí jiǔ hào 十九号
		sepersembilan belas	shí jiǔ fēn zhī yī 十九分之一
nine.ti.eth	(n.)	kesembilan puluh	dì jiǔ shí 第九十
		sepersembilan puluh	jiǔ shí fēn zhī yī 九十分之一
nine.ty	(n.)	sembilan puluh	jiǔ shí 九十
ninth	(n.)	persembilan	jiǔ fēn zhī yī 九分之一
		kesembilan	dì jiǔ 第九
		tanggal sembilan	jiǔ hào 九号
nip	(v.)	mengigit, menjepit	yǎo 咬, jiā 夹
nip.ple	(n.)	puting susu, pentil	nǎi tóu 奶头, xiàng pí nǎi tóu 橡皮奶头
no	(a., adv.)	tidak, bukan	bù 不, bù shì 不是
no.ble	(a.)	mulia, ningrat	gaō gùi 高贵, gùi zú dė 贵族的
	(n.)	bangsawan	gùi zú 贵族
no.ble.man	(n.)	bangsawan	gùi zú 贵族
no.bod.y	(pron.)	tak seorang pun	méi yǒu rén 没有人, shúi yě bù 谁也不
nod	(n.)	mengangguk	diǎn tóu 点头
noise	(n.)	ribut, gaduh	chǎo zá 吵杂, chǎo nào 吵闹
	(v.)	menyiarkan kabar angin	yáo chuán 谣传
noise.less	(a.)	tak bersuara	méi yǒu shēng yīn 没有声音, ān jing 安静
nois.y	(a.)	ribut, gaduh	chǎo nào dė 吵闹的
nom.i.nal	(a.)	nominal, hanya namanya	míng yì shàng dė 名义上的,
		menurut yang tertulis saja	guà míng dė 挂名的,
			zì mìan shàng dė 字面上的
nom.i.nate	(v.)	mencalonkan	tí míng 提名
		mengangkat	rèn mìng 任命

nom.i.na.tion	(n.)	pencalonan, nominasi	tí míng 提名
		pengangkatan	rèn mìng 任命
non	(prefix)	tidak, bukan	bù 不, feī 非
non.age	(n.)	belum dewasa	wèi chéng nián 未成年
non.ag.gres.sion	(n.)	tidak menyerbu	bù qīn luè 不侵略
non.a.lign.ed	(a.)	non-blok, tidak bersekutu	bù jié méng 不结盟
non.a.lign.ment	(n.)	non-blok	bù jié méng 不结盟
none	(pron.)	tidak satu pun	shúi yě bù 谁也不,
		tak seorang pun	méi yǒu rén 没有人
non.es.sen.tial	(a.)	yang tidak penting	bù zhòng yào dė 不重要的
non.pa.reil	(a.)	tiada bandingannya	wú bǐ dė 无比的
		nomor satu	tiān xià dì yī 天下第一
non.par.ti.san	(a.)	tidak berpihak	bù piān xiàng 不偏向
non.par.ty	(a.)	tak berpartai	wú dǎng pài dė 无党派的,
			fēi dǎng dė 非党的
non.sense	(n.)	omong kosong	fèi huà 废话, hú shūo 胡说
non-stop	(a.)	tanpa berhenti	bù tíng dė 不停的
noon	(n.)	tengah hari	zhōng wǔ 中午
nor	(conj.)	juga tidak	yě bù 也不
nor.mal	(a.)	biasa, normal	zhèng cháng dė 正常的
north	(n.)	utara	běi 北, běi fāng 北方
	(adv.)	di utara	zài běi fāng 在北方
		ke utara	xiàng běi 向北
north-east	(n.)	timur laut	dōng běi 东北
	(adv.)	di timur laut	zài dōng běi 在东北
		ke timur laut	xiàng dōng běi 向东北
north.er.ly	(a.)	dari utara	cóng běi fāng lái dė 从北方来的
	(adv.)	dari utara	cóng běi fāng lái 从北方来
		ke utara	xiàng běi 向北
north.ern	(a.)	utara	běi fāng dė 北方的

north.ern.er	(n.)	orang (dari) utara	běi fāng rén 北方人
north.ward	(a., adv.)	ke arah utara	xiàng běi dė 向北的
	(n.)	bagian utara	běi bù 北部
north-west	(n.)	barat laut	xī běi 西北, xī běi bù 西北部
north-west.er	(n.)	angin barat laut	xī běi fāng 西北方
nose	(n.)	hidung	bí zi 鼻子
nos.tal.gia	(n.)	nostalgia	huái jiù 怀旧
nos.trill	(n.)	lubang hidung	bí kǒng 鼻孔
not	(adv.)	tidak	bù 不
no.ta.ble	(a.)	menarik perhatian	yǐn rén zhù yì dė 引人注意的, zhí dé zhù yì dė 值得注意的
	(n.)	orang terkemuka	zhī míng rén shì 知名人士, xián dá 贤达
no.ta.ry	(n.)	notaris	gōng zhèng rén 公证人
no.ta.tion	(n.)	notasi	biāo zhì 标志, jì hào 记号, yuè pǔ 乐谱
note	(n.)	catatan	bǐ jì 笔记
		surat pendek	biàn tiáo 便条, duǎn xìn 短信
		tanda bunyi	yīn fú 音符
		perhatian	zhù yì 注意
		uang kertas	chāo piào 钞票
note.book	(n.)	buku catatan	bǐ jì běn 笔记本
note-paper	(n.)	kertas surat	xìn zhǐ 信纸
noth.ing	(n.)	tidak ada apa-apa	méi yǒu dōng xī 没有东西, shén mē yě méi yǒu 什么也没有
		kosong	líng 零, kōng xū 空虚
	(adv.)	bukan apa-apa	méi yǒu shén mē 没有什么
		sama sekali tidak	háo bù 毫不, jué bù 决不
no.tice	(n.)	perhatian, pemberitahuan	zhù yì 注意, tōng gào 通告
	(v.)	memperhatikan	zhù yì 注意
no.ti.fy	(v.)	memberitahukan	tōng zhī 通知

no.tion	(n.)	pengertian, paham	gài niàn 概念, jiàn jiě 见解
no.to.ri.e.ty	(n.)	kemasyhuran (karena hal yang tidak baik)	chòu míng zhāo zhù 臭名昭著
no.tor.i.ous	(a.)	terkenal buruknya	chòu míng zhāo zhù 臭名昭著
not.with.stand.ing	(prep.)	meskipun	bù guǎn 不管, suī rán 虽然
nought	(n.)	nol	líng 零, wú 无
noun	(n.)	kata benda, nomina	míng cí 名词
nour.ish	(v.)	memelihara	yǎng yù 养育
nov.el	(n.)	novel	xiǎo shūo 小说
	(a.)	baru	xīn yǐng 新颖
nov.el.ist	(n.)	novelis	xiǎo shūo jiā 小说家
nov.el.ty	(n.)	baru, hal yang baru	xīn yǐng 新颖, xīn shì wù 新事物
No.vem.ber	(n.)	November	shí yī yùe 十一月
now	(adv.)	sekarang	xiàn zài 现在
now.a.days	(adv.)	sekarang	xiàn zài 现在
no.where	(adv.)	tidak di mana pun juga	nǎ li yě bù 哪里也不
no.wise	(adv.)	sama sekali tidak	jué bù 决不
		bagaimanapun tidak	yī diǎn yě bù 一点也不
nox.ious	(a.)	berbahaya	yǒu hài dė 有害的
nu.cle.ar	(n.)	nuklir	hé dė 核的, yuán zī hé dė 原子核的
nui.sance	(n.)	hal yang merepotkan	má fán dė shì 麻烦的事
num.ber	(n.)	nomor, angka	hào shù 号数, shù zì 数字, shù mù 数目
		jumlah	zǒng gòng 总共
num.ber.less	(a.)	tak terhitung	wǔ shù dė 无数的
		tidak bernomor	méi yǒu hào mǎ dė 没有号码的
nu.mer.al	(n.)	angka	shù zì 数字
nu.mer.ous	(a.)	banyak sekali	wú shù dė 无数的, hěn dūo 很多
nun	(n.)	biarawati	xiū nǔ 修女, ní gū 尼姑
nurse	(n.)	perawat, pengasuh	hù shì 护士, nǎi mā 奶妈
nurs.ery	(n.)	kamar anak-anak	bǎo yù shì 保育室
		kebun bibit	miáo pǔ 苗圃

nur.ture	(n.)	pengasuhan	yǎng yù 养育, péi yǎng 培养
nut	(n.)	buah berkulit keras	jiān gǔo 坚果
nu.tri.ment	(n.)	makanan yang mengandung banyak gizi	yíng yǎng pǐn 营养品, zī yǎng pǐn 滋养品
nutshell	(n.)	kulit keras dari buah-buahan	jiān gǔo ké 坚果壳
ny.lon	(n.)	nilon	ní lóng 尼龙
nymph	(n.)	bidadari, peri	xiān nǔ 仙女, měi nǔ 美女

O

oar	(n.)	dayung	jiǎng 桨
oars.man	(n.)	tukang dayung, penda-yung	huá shǒu 划手
o.a.sis	(n.)	daerah subur di tengah padang pasir	lù zhōu 绿洲, wò zhōu 沃洲
oat	(n.)	gandum	yàn mài 燕麦
oath	(n.)	sumpah	shì yán 誓言
oat.meal	(n.)	makanan gandum	mài piàn 麦片
		bubur gandum	mài piàn zhōu 麦片粥
o.be.dience	(n.)	kepatuhan	fú cóng 服从
o.be.dient	(a.)	patuh	fú cóng dė 服从的
o.bey	(v.)	mematuhi	fú cóng 服从
ob.ject	(n.)	benda, tujuan	wù tǐ 物体, mù dì 目的
		pelengkap, objek	bīn yǔ 宾语
	(v.)	menolak, keberatan	fǎn dùi 反对
ob.jec.tion	(n.)	keberatan	fǎn dùi 反对
ob.jec.tive	(a.)	menurut kenyataan, objektif	kè guān dė 客观的
	(n.)	tujuan, sasaran	mù dì 目的, mù biaō 目标
ob.jec.tiv.ism	(n.)	keobjektifan, objektivisme	kè guān zhǔ yì 客观主义, kè guān xìng 客观性
ob.li.ga.tion	(n.)	kewajiban	yì wù 义务
o.blige	(v.)	mengharuskan, mewajib-kan	qiáng pò 强迫, zé chéng 责成

ob.long	(n.)	empat persegi panjang	cháng fāng xíng 长方形
ob.scure	(a.)	gelap, samar-samar	àn 暗, mó hú 模糊
ob.ser.va.tion	(n.)	pengamatan	guān chá 观察
ob.serve	(v.)	mengamati	guān chá 观察
ob.serv.er	(n.)	pengamat	guān chá zhě 观察者
ob.sta.cle	(n.)	rintangan	zhàng ài 障碍
ob.struct	(v.)	merintangi	fáng ài 妨碍, zǔ aì 阻碍
ob.tain	(v.)	memperoleh	dé dào 得到, qǔ dé 取得
ob.vi.ous	(a.)	nyata, jelas	míng xiǎn dė 明显的,
			míng bǎi dė 明白的
oc.ca.sion	(n.)	kesempatan	shí jī 时机
oc.ca.sion.al	(a.)	kadang-kadang	yǒu shí 有时
		kebetulan	ǒu rán dė 偶然的
oc.ca.sion.al.ly	(adv.)	kadang-kadang	yǒu shí 有时
oc.cu.pant	(n.)	yang menduduki	zhàn yǒu zhě 占有者
		penghuni, penumpang	jū zhù zhě 居住者
oc.cu.pa.tion	(n.)	pendudukan	zhàn lǐng 占领, zhàn jù 占据
		pekerjaan	zhí yè 职业, zhuān yè 专业
oc.cu.py	(v.)	menduduki	zhàn lǐng 占领, zhàn jū 占居
		menempati	zhù jìn 住进
		memakan waktu	zhàn shí jiān 占时间
		memiliki	zhàn yǒu 占有
oc.cur	(v.)	terjadi	fā sheng 发生
oc.cur.rence	(n.)	kejadian, peristiwa	fā shēng 发生, shì jian 事件
o.cean	(n.)	lautan, samudra	hǎi yáng 海洋
o'clock	(adv.)	jam, pukul	diǎn zhōng 点钟
oc.ta.gon	(n.)	segidelapan	bā biān xíng 八边形
Oc.to.ber	(n.)	Oktober	shí yuè 十月
oc.u.list	(n.)	dokter mata	yǎn kē yī shēng 眼科医生
odd	(a.)	ganjil, aneh	qí guài 奇怪

o.dour	(n.)	bau	qì wèi 气味
o.dour.less	(adj.)	tak berbau	méi yǒu qì wèi dė 没有气味的
of	(prep.)	dari, kepunyaan	dė 的
off	(adv.)	jauh dari, dari,	yáo yuǎn 遥远, cóng 从,
		pergi dari, putus	lí kaī 离开, duàn 断
of.fence	(n.)	pelanggaran	fàn guī 犯规, fàn zùi 犯罪
		penyerangan	gōng jī 攻击
		penghinaan	qī wǔ 欺侮
of.fend	(v.)	mengganggu	mào fàn 冒犯
		menyakiti hati	shāng gǎn qíng 伤感情
		melakukan kesalahan	fàn cùo wù 犯错误
		melanggar	wéi fǎn 违反
of.fend.er	(n.)	orang yang berdosa	zùi fàn 罪犯
of.fen.sive	(n.)	serangan	gōng shì 攻势, gōng jī 攻击
	(a.)	bersifat menyerang	gōng jī xìng dė 攻击性的
		menjijikkan	kě yàn dė 可厌的
		menyakitkan	shāng gǎn qíng dė 伤感情的
of.fer	(v.)	menawarkan	tí gōng 提供
		mengemukakan	tí chū 提出
of.fice	(n.)	jabatan	zhí wù 职务
		kantor	bàn gōng tíng 办公厅,
			bàn gōng shì 办公室
of.fi.cer	(n.)	perwira, pejabat	jūn guān 军官, gōng wù yuán 公务员
of.fi.cial	(a.)	resmi	guān fāng dė 官方的,
			zhēng shì dė 正式的
	(n.)	pejabat	guān yuán 官员
off.set	(v.)	menutup kerugian	mí bǔ 弥补
		mengimbangi	dǐ xiāo 抵销
	(n.)	cetakan offset	jiāo yìn 胶印, tòu yìn 透印,
			chuán yìn 传印

off.spring	(n.)	anak cucu	ĕr nǔ儿女, zǐ sūn 子孙
of.ten	(adv.)	sering	cháng cháng 常常, jīng cháng 经常
oil	(n.)	minyak	yóu 油
oil-col.our	(n.)	cat minyak	yóu cǎi 油彩
oil-field	(n.)	daerah pertambangan minyak	yóu tián 油田
oil-paint.ing	(n.)	lukisan cat minyak	yóu huà 油画
oil.y	(a.)	berminyak	dūo yóu dė 多油的
old	(a.)	tua, lama, usang	lǎo 老, jiù 旧
old.en	(a.)	kuno, dahulu	gǔ lǎo dė 古老的, gǔ dài dė 古代的
o.men	(n.)	pertanda, alamat	yù zhào 预兆
o.mis.sion	(n.)	penghilangan, kelalaian	shĕng luè 省略, yí loù 遗漏
o.mit	(v.)	menghilangkan	shěng luè 省略
		tak memasukkan	yí lòu 遗漏
om.ni.bus	(n.)	bis umum	gōng gòng qì chē 公共汽车
on	(prep.)	pada, atas, di	zài 在, shàng miàn 上面, zài...shàng 在…上
once	(adv.)	sekali	yī cì 一次
one	(pron.)	satu	yī 一
one.self	(pron.)	diri sendiri	zì jǐ 自己
one-sid.ed	(a.)	sepihak	yī biān dė 一边的, dān miàn dė 单面的
on.ion	(n.)	bawang merah	yáng cōng 洋葱
on.look.er	(n.)	penonton	páng guān zhĕ 旁观者
on.ly	(a.)	satu-satunya, tunggal	wéi yī 唯一, dān dú 单独
on.set	(n.)	serangan	gōng jī 攻击
on.ward	(a.)	yang menghadap ke depan	xiàng qián dė 向前的
on.wards	(adv.)	ke depan, maju	xiàng qián 向前, qiàn jìn 前进
o.pen	(v.)	membuka	kaī 开, dă kaī 打开
	(a.)	terbuka	kaī dė 开的, kaī zhė dė 开着的, gōng kāi dė 公开的

o.pen-air	(a.)	tempat terbuka	lù tiān 露天
o.pen-hand.ed	(a.)	murah hati	kāng kǎi dė 慷慨的
o.pen-heart.ed	(a.)	jujur	kěn qiè dė 恳切的
o.pen.ing	(n.)	permulaan, pembukaan	kaī shǐ 开始, kaī mù 开幕
		lubang, lowongan	kōng 空, dòng 洞, kōng dì 空地
o.pen.ly	(adv.)	secara terbuka	gōng kāi dì 公开地
		berterus terang	tǎn bǎi dì 坦白地
op.er.a	(n.)	opera	gē jù 歌剧
op.er.ate	(v.)	bekerja, menjalankan	gōng zùo 工作, cāo zùo 操作
		membedah	kāi dāo 开刀
op.er.a.tion	(n.)	pembedahan, operasi	dòng shǒu shù 动手术
		penyelenggaraan	shí shī 实施
		pekerjaan, berlaku	gōng zùo 工作, shēng xiào 生效
		gerakan	xíng dòng 行动
op.er.a.tion.al	(a.)	mengenai pekerjaan sehari-hari, operasional	yè wù shǎng dė 业务上的
		mengenai cara bekerja	cāo zùo shàng dė 操作上的
op.er.a.tor	(n.)	operator, petugas	cāo zùo zhě 操作者, qín wù yuán 勤务员
o.pin.ion	(n.)	pendapat, opini	yì jiàn 意见, kàn fǎ 看法
o.pium	(n.)	candu	yā piàn 鸦片
op.po.nent	(n.)	lawan	dùi shǒu 对手
op.por.tune	(a.)	tepat pada waktunya	jí shí dė 及时的
		kebetulan	còu qiǎo 凑巧, qià hǎo 恰好
op.por.tun.ism	(n.)	oportunisme	jī huì zhǔ yì 机会主义
op.por.tun.ist	(n.)	oportunis	jī hùi zhǔ yì zhě 机会主义者
op.por.tu.ni.ty	(n.)	kesempatan	jī hùi 机会
op.pose	(v.)	menentang, melawan	fǎn dùi 反对, fǎn kàng 反抗
op.po.site	(a.)	berhadapan, berlawanan	xiāng dùi dė 相对的, xiāng fǎn dė 相反的

	(adv.)	di depan	zài dùi miàn 在对面
	(prep.)	berhadapan dengan	zài...dùi miàn 在…对面
		di hadapan	xiāng dùi 相对
op.po.si.tion	(n.)	perlawanan	fǎn dùi 反对, dùi lì 对立
		oposisi	fǎn dùi pài 反对派
op.press	(v.)	menindas	yā pò 压迫
op.pres.sion	(n.)	penindasan	yā pò xíng wéi 压迫行为
op.pres.sor	(n.)	penindas	yā pò zhě 压迫者
op.ti.cal	(a.)	berhubungan dengan penglihatan	shì jué dė 视觉的
op.ti.cian	(n.)	ahli kacamata	yǎn jìng zhuān jiā 眼镜专家
		pedagang kacamata	yǎn jìng shāng 眼镜商
op.tics	(n.)	optik	guāng xué 光学
op.ti.mism	(n.)	optimisme	lè guān zhǔ yì 乐观主义
op.ti.mist	(n.)	optimis	lè guān zhǔ yì zhě 乐观主义者, lè tiān pài 乐天派
op.ti.mum	(n.)	yang terbaik	zùi jiā dė 最佳的
		yang tertinggi	zùi gāo dė 最高的
op.tion	(n.)	pilihan	xuǎn zé 选择, xuǎn zé wù 选择物
or	(conj.)	atau	hùo 或, hùo zhě 或者
o.ral	(a.)	lisan	kǒu tóu dė 口头的
o.ral.ly	(adv.)	secara lisan	kǒu tóu shàng dė 口头上的
or.ange	(n.)	jeruk	gān 柑, jú zi 橘子
		warna jingga tua	chéng sè 橙色
or.ange.ade	(n.)	air jeruk	jú zi shǔi 橘子水
o.ra.tion	(n.)	pidato, orasi	yǎn shūo 演说
or.a.tor	(n.)	ahli pidato	yǎn shūo jiā 演说家
or.a.to.ry	(n.)	seni pidato	yǎn shūo shù 演说术
or.bit	(n.)	orbit	gǔi dào 轨道
or.chard	(n.)	kebun buah-buahan	gǔo shù yuán 果树園

or.ches.tra	(n.)	orkestra	yuè dùi 乐队, guǎn xián yùe dùi 管弦乐队
or.chid	(n.)	anggrek	lán huā 兰花
or.der	(n.)	perintah	mìng lìng 命令
		pesanan	dìng huò dān 订货单
		urutan, tata tertib	shùn xù 顺序, zhì xù 秩序
	(v.)	memerintahkan	mìng lìng 命令
		memesan	dìng 定, dìng hùo 订货
or.der.ly	(a.)	teratur	yǒu zhì xù 有秩序, zhěn qí 整齐
or.di.nal	(a.)	yang berurutan	shùn xù dė 顺序的
	(n.)	bilangan/nomor urutan	xù shù 序数
or.di.na.ry	(a.)	biasa	píng cháng 平常
or.gan	(n.)	alat tubuh	qì guān 器官
		alat pemerintahan, organ	jī guān 机关, fēng qín 风琴
or.gan.ist	(n.)	pemain organ	fēng qín yǎn zòu zhě 风琴演奏者
or.gan.i.za.tion	(n.)	organisasi hal mengatur	zǔ zhī 组织, jī gòu 机构, biān zhì 编制, gòu zào 构造, zǔ zhī shàng dė 组织上的, jī gòu shàng dė 机构上的
or.gan.ize	(v.)	mengorganisasi	zǔ zhī 组织, biān zǔ 编组
o.ri.ent	(n.)	timur	dōng fāng 东方
o.ri.en.tal	(a.)	yang berhubungan dengan timur	dōng fāng dė 东方的
	(n.)	orang timur	dōng fāng rén 东方人
or.i.gin	(n.)	asal, asal-usul	qǐ yuán 起源, yuán lái 原来
o.rig.i.nal	(a.)	asli, orisinil, semula	yuán lái dė 原来的
	(n.)	barang asli	yuán wù 原物
o.rig.i.nate	(v.)	berasal	qǐ yuán 起源
		timbul	fā shēng 发生
o.rig.i.na.tor	(n.)	pemula	chuàng shǐ rén 创始人, fā qǐ rén 发起人

or.na.ment	(n.)	perhiasaan, hiasan	zhuāng shì pǐn 装饰品, zhuāng shì 装饰
or.phan	(n.)	anak yatim	gū ér 孤儿
or.phan.age	(n.)	rumah panti asuhan	gū ér yuàn 孤儿院
or.tho.dox	(a.)	ortodoks	zhèng tóng dė 正 统 的, zhèng pài dė 正 派 的
oth.er	(a.)	yang lain	bié dė 别的, qí tā dė 其他的
	(pron.)	orang lain	bié rén 别人, tā rén 他人
		barang lain	bié dė dōng xī 别的东西
	(adv.)	yang lain, satu lagi	lìng wài 另外, bié dė 别的
oth.er.wise	(adv.)	selain itu, kalau tidak	lìng wài 另外, yào bù rán 要不然
	(conj.)	sebaliknya, kalau tidak	fǒu zé 否则, yào bù rán 要不然
ought	(aux. v.)	harus	yīng gài 应该, bì xū 必须
ounce	(n.)	ons	yīng liǎng 英两, àng sī 盎司
our	(pron.)	kita (kami) punya	wǒ mén dė 我们的
ours	(pron.)	kepunyaan kita (kami)	wǒ mén dė 我们 的
our.self	(pron.)	kami sendiri	wǒ mén zì jǐ 我 们 自 己
out	(adv.)	di luar, ke luar	zài wài 在 外, xiàng wài 向 外
		pergi	chū qù 出 去
out.break	(n.)	pecahnya, perjangkitan	bào fā 爆 发
out.burst	(n.)	semburan	pēn chū 喷 出
out.come	(n.)	hasil, akibat	jié gǔo 结 果
out.cry	(n.)	teriakan	hū hǎn 呼 喊, nà hǎn 呐 喊
out.do	(v.)	mengalahkan	shèng gùo 胜 过, chāo gùo 超 过
out.door	(a.)	di luar rumah	wū wài 屋 外, lù tiān 露 天
out.er	(a.)	sebelah luar	wài bù dė 外 部 的, wài miàn dė 外 面 的
out.er.most	(a.)	paling luar	zùi wài dė 最 外 的
out.er.wear	(n.)	baju luar	wài yī 外 衣
out.fit	(n.)	perlengkapan	chéng tào shè bèi 成 套 设 备
out.ing	(n.)	tamasya, pesiar	yóu lǎn 游 览, chū yóu 出 游
out.lay	(n.)	pengeluaran	zhī chū 支 出

out.let	(n.)	saluran keluar	pái shǔi kǒu 排水口
		jalan keluar	chū kǒu 出口
out.line	(n.)	garis besar	dà gāng 大纲, gài yào 概要
out.look	(n.)	pemandangan	fēng jǐng 风景, jǐng sè 景色
		harapan	zhǎn wàng 展望
out.num.ber	(v.)	lebih banyak dari, melebihi	dūo yú 多于
out-of-date	(a.)	ketinggalan zaman	gùo shí dė 过时的, lùo hòu dė 落后的
out.post	(n.)	pos terdepan	qián shào 前哨
out.put	(n.)	hasil, produksi	chū chǎn 出产, chǎn liàng 产量, chǎn pǐn 产品
out.rage	(n.)	kebiadaban	xiōng bào 凶暴, cán bào 残暴
out.set	(n.)	permulaan	kāi tóu 开头, zuì chū 最初
out.side	(n.)	sebelah luar	wài bù 外部, wài miàn 外面
out.si.der	(n.)	orang luar	páng guān zhě 旁观者, jú wài rén 局外人
out.size	(a.)	ukuran paling besar	tè dà hào 特大号
out.skirt	(n.)	daerah pinggiran kota	jiāo qū 郊区
out.spread	(a.)	terentang, terhampar	kùo zhāng 扩张, zhǎn kaī 展开
out.stand.ing	(a.)	terkemuka, terkenal	jié chū dė 杰出的, chū míng dė 出名的
out.ward	(a.)	bagian luar, keluar	wài miàn dė 外面的, xiàng wài dė 向外的
out.weigh	(v.)	lebih berat dari	zhòng yú 重于
o.val	(a.)	bujur telur	tǔo yuán xíng dė 椭园形的
		bentuk bujur telur	tǔo yuán xíng 椭园形
ov.en	(n.)	kompor, oven	lú 炉
o.ver	(adv.)	di atas, ke atas	zài shàng 在上, xiàng shàng 向上
		terbalik	fān dǎo 翻倒

		melebihi, lebih dari	chāo gùo 超过
		sisa	dūo yú 多余, shèng xià 剩下
		selesai, habis	jié shù 结束, wǎn lè 完了
	(prep.)	di atas	zài shàng miàn 在上面
		tentang, lewat	guān yú 关于, jīng gùo 经过
		di seberang, sekeliling	yuè gùo 越过, sì miàn 四面
o.ver.all	(a.)	keseluruhan	quán miàn dė 全面的, quán bù dė 全部的
o.ver.bear	(v.)	menindas	yā fú 压服
o.ver.coat	(n.)	mantel panjang/luar	wài yī 外衣
o.ver.come	(v.)	mengalahkan, mengatasi	zhēng fú 征服, kè fú 克服
o.ver.crowd	(v.)	membuat penuh sesak	jǐ mǎn 挤满
o.ver.do	(v.)	berbuat keterlaluan	zùo dė gùo hǔo 做得过火
o.ver.draft	(n.)	penarikan cek lebih dari uang simpanan	tòu zhī 透支
o.ver.draw	(v.)	menarik cek melebihi uang simpanan	tòu zhī 透支
		ditulis atau digambarkan secara berlebih-lebihan	kuā zhāng 夸张
o.ver.due	(a.)	melampaui batas waktu	guò qī dė 过期的
o.ver.ful.fill	(v.)	melaksanakan tugas lebih cepat dari target	chāo é wán chéng 超额完成
o.ver.hear	(v.)	mendengar secara kebetulan	ǒu rán tīng dào 偶然听到
o.ver.load	(n.)	beban yang terlalu berat	chāo zài 超载, guò zhòng 过重
o.ver.ly	(adv.)	sangat, terlalu	tài 太
o.ver.night	(adv.)	semalam	yī gè wǎn shàng 一个晚上
o.ver.seas	(adv.)	luar negeri, seberang laut	hǎi wài 海外
o.ver.sight	(n.)	kekhilafan	dà yì 大意
o.ver.size	(a.)	terlalu besar	tài dà dė 太大的

o.ver.sleep	(v.)	bangun kesiangan, tidur terlalu lama	shùi gùo tóu 睡过头
o.ver.state	(v.)	membesar-besarkan	kuā zhāng 夸张
o.ver.step	(v.)	melampaui, melewati	chāo yùe 超越, yùe gùo 越过
o.ver.stock	(v.)	menimbun terlalu banyak	cún huò guò duō 存货过多
o.vert	(a.)	jelas, terang	míng xiǎn dė 明显的
	(adj.)	lahir	wài biǎo dė 外表的
o.ver.take	(v.)	menyusul	gǎn shàng 赶上, zhùi shàng 追上
		menguasai	yā dǎo 压倒
o.ver.throw	(v.)	menggulingkan	tūi fān 推翻
	(n.)	keruntuhan	wǎ jiě 瓦解, kuǎ tái 垮台
o.ver.time	(n.)	lembur	jiā bān 加班
o.ver.top	(v.)	melampaui	chāo chū 超出, shèng gùo 胜过
o.ver.turn	(v.)	menjatuhkan, menggu-lingkan	tūi fān 推翻
o.ver.weight	(a.)	kelebihan berat	gùo zhòng dė 过重的, chāo zhòng dė 超重的
o.ver.whelm	(v.)	menjatuhkan	yā dǎo 压倒
		menghanyutkan	yān mò 淹没
o.ver.work	(v.)	bekerja melampaui batas	gōng zùo gùo dù 工作过度, gùo láo 过劳
owe	(v.)	berhutang	qiàn 欠, fù zhài 负债
owl	(n.)	burung hantu	māo tóu yīng 猫头鹰
own	(adj.)	kepunyaan sendiri	zì jǐ dė 自己的
	(v.)	memiliki, mengakui	yōng yǒu 拥有, chéng rèn 承认
own.er	(n.)	pemilik	yōng yǒu zhě 拥有者, yè zhǔ 业主
own.er.ship	(n.)	hak milik	sǔo yǒu quán 所有权
ox	(n.)	lembu jantan	gōng níu 公牛
ox.ida.tion	(n.)	oksidasi	yǎng huà 氧化
ox.y.gen	(n.)	oksigen	yǎng qì 氧气

o.zone	(n.)	ozon	chòu qì 臭气
		udara murni	xīn xiān kōng qì 新鲜空气

P

pace	(n.)	langkah	bù 步, bù fá 步伐
pa.cif.ic	(a.)	tenang	tài píng dė 太平的,
		damai	hé píng dė 和平的
pack	(n.)	pak	bāo 包, bāo gǔo 包裹
	(v.)	mengepak	bāo zhuāng 包装
pack.age	(n.)	bingkisan, bungkusan	bāo gǔo 包裹
	(v.)	membungkus	bāo 包, bāo zhuāng 包装
pack.er	(n.)	tukang bungkus	bāo zhuāng gōng rén 包装工人
pack.et	(n.)	pak, bungkusan kecil	bāo 包, xiǎo bāo 小包
pack.ing	(n.)	pengepakan, pembung-kusan	bāo zhuāng 包装
pack.ing-case	(n.)	peti barang	huò wù xiāng 货物箱
pad	(n.)	bloknot, bantalan, alas	pāi zhǐ bù 拍纸簿, diàn zi 垫子
pad.dle	(n.)	dayung	jiǎng 桨
	(v.)	mendayung	huà chuán 划船
pad.dy	(n.)	padi	dào 稻
pad.dy-field	(n.)	sawah	dào tián 稻田
page	(n.)	halaman buku	yè 页
pa.go.da	(n.)	pagoda	tā 塔
pail	(n.)	ember	tǐ tǒng 提桶
pail.ful	(n.)	seember penuh	mǎn tǒng 满桶
pain	(n.)	kesakitan, penderitaan	tòng kǔ 痛苦
	(v.)	sakit, menyakitkan	tòng 痛, shǐ rén tòng kǔ 使人痛苦
pain.ful	(a.)	menyakitkan	shǐ rén tòng kǔ dė 使人痛苦的

pain-kill.er	(n.)	penawar rasa sakit	zhǐ tòng yào 止痛药
pain.less	(a.)	tanpa rasa sakit	wú tòng dė 无痛的
paint	(n.)	cat	yóu qī 油漆
paint-brush	(n.)	kuas cat	yóu shūa 油刷
		kuas gambar	hùa bī 画笔
paint.er	(n.)	pelukis	hùa jiā 画家
		tukang cat	yóu qī gōng rén 油漆工人
paint.ing	(n.)	lukisan	huà 画, hùi huà 绘画
pair	(n.)	sepasang	yī dùi 一对, yī shuāng 一双
pa.ja.mas	(n.)	piyama	shùi yī 睡衣
pal.ace	(n.)	istana	gōng diàn 宫殿
palc	(a.)	pucat	cāng bǎi 苍白
palm	(n.)	telapak tangan	shǒu zhǎng 手掌
		pohon palem	zōng lú shù 棕榈树
pamph.let	(n.)	pamflet	xiǎo cè zi 小册子
pan	(n.)	panci	pán 盘, guō 锅
pan.da	(n.)	panda	xióng maō 熊猫
pane	(n.)	kaca jendela	chuāng bō lí 窗玻璃
pan.ic	(n.)	kepanikan	kǒng huāng 恐慌, huāng zhāng 慌张
pan.o.ra.ma	(n.)	pemandangan yang luas	quán jǐng 全景
pant	(v.)	terengah-engah	chuǎn qì 喘气
		mengharap-harapkan	kě wàng 渴望
	(n.)	napas pendek	chuǎn xī 喘息
pan.ther	(n.)	harimau kumbang	bào 豹
pants	(n.)	celana panjang	kù zi 裤子
pa.per	(n.)	kertas, surat kabar	zhǐ 纸, bào zhǐ 报纸
pa.per-mill	(n.)	pabrik kertas	zào zhǐ chǎng 造纸厂
pa.rade	(n.)	pawai, parade	yóu xíng 游行
pa.rad.er	(n.)	orang yang ikut pawai	yóu xíng zhě 游行者
par.a.dise	(n.)	surga	tiān táng 天堂

par.al.lel	(n.)	garis lintang sejajar	píng xíng xiàn 平行线
	(a.)	sejajar, paralel	píng xíng dė 平行的
par.a.site	(n.)	parasit	jì shēng dòng wù 寄生动物, jì shēng zhí wù 寄生植物
par.a.sit.ic	(a.)	yang bersifat parasit	jì shēng xìng dė 寄生性的
par.a.sol	(n.)	payung (matahari)	tài yáng sǎn 太阳伞
par.a.troops	(n.)	pasukan payung	sǎn bīng bù dùi 伞兵部队
par.cel	(n.)	bungkusan	bāo gùo 包裹
		paket pos	yóu baō 邮包
par.don	(n.)	maaf, ampun	yuán liàng 原谅
	(v.)	memaafkan	yuán liàng 原谅
par.ent	(n.)	ayah atau ibu	fù qīn 父亲, mǔ qīn 母亲
		orangtua	fù mǔ qīn 父母亲, jiā zhǎng 家长
park	(n.)	taman	gōng yuán 公园
		tempat parkir	tíng chē chǎng 停车场
park.ing	(n.)	parkir	tíng chē 停车
par.lia.ment	(n.)	parlemen	gúo hùi 国会
par.rot	(n.)	burung beo	yīng wǔ 鹦鹉
part	(n.)	bagian, peranan	bù fēn 部分, jiǎo sè 角色
par.take	(v.)	ikut serta, mengambil bagian	fēn dàn 分担
par.tial	(a.)	sebagian	yī bù fēn 一部分
par.tic.i.pant	(n.)	peserta, partisipan	cān jiā zhě 参加者
par.tic.i.pate	(v.)	ikut serta, ikut ambil bagian	cān jiā 参加
par.tic.i.pa.tion	(n.)	partisipasi	fēn xiǎng 分享, cān jiā 参加
par.ti.ci.ple	(n.)	partisip	fēn cí 分词
par.ti.cle	(n.)	partikel, butir	xū cí 虚词, kē lì 颗粒
par.tic.u.lar	(a.)	istimewa, khusus	tè shū 特殊, tè bié 特别
		teliti	xì zhì 细致, xiang xì 详细

	(n.)	keterangan-keterangan	xiàng mù 项目
		istimewa	tè sè 特色, tè diǎn 特点
par.tic.u.lar.ly	(adv.)	terutama	tè bié shì 特别是, yóu qí shì 尤其是
part.ing	(n.)	perpisahan	lí bié 离别
par.ti.san	(n.)	partisan	yóu jī dùi yuán 游击队员
		pengikut partai	dǎng rén 党人
part.ly	(adv.)	sebagian	yī bù fēn 一部分
part.ner	(n.)	rekan, partner	hǔo bàn 伙伴, hé zùo zhě 合作者
		jodoh	pèi ǒu 配偶
part-time	(a.)	sebagian waktu	bù fēn shí jiān 部分时间
		sambilan	jiān rèn dė 兼任的
par.ty	(n.)	partai, kelompok	dǎng 党, dǎng pài 党派, zǔ 组
		pesta	yàn hùi 宴会
pass	(v.)	lalu, lewat	gùo qù 过去, jīng gùo 经过
		lulus	tōng gùo 通过
		lulus ujian	jí gé 及格
	(n.)	surat jalan	tōng xíng zhèng 通行证
pass.a.ble	(a.)	dapat dilalui	kě tōng xíng dė 可通行的
pas.sage	(n.)	gang, jalan lintasan	zǒu láng 走廊, tōng lù 通路
		bagian dari buku	jié 节, duàn 段
pas.sen.ger	(n.)	penumpang	chéng kè 乘客
pass.er-by	(n.)	orang yang lewat	gùo lù rén 过路人
pass.ing	(n.)	meninggalnya, berlalu	qù shì 去世, tōng gùo 通过
	(a.)	lalu, lewat	jīng gùo dė 经过的
pas.sion	(n.)	antusiasme, kegairahan	rè qíng 热情, jī qíng 激情
pas.sive	(a.)	pasif, tidak giat	bèi dòng dė 被动的, xiāo jí dė 消极的
pass.port	(n.)	paspor	hù zhào 护照
past	(a.)	yang lalu	gùo qù dė 过去的
	(n.)	dulu, masa lalu	gùo qù 过去, wǎng shì 往事
	(adv.)	lewat	gùo 过

paste	(n.)	perekat, lem	jiāng hú 浆糊
	(v.)	menempelkan	tiē 贴
pas.tel	(n.)	pastel	yán sè là bǐ 颜色蜡笔
pas.time	(n.)	hiburan, rekreasi	xiāo qiǎn 消遣, yú lè 娱乐
pas.tor	(n.)	pendeta	mù shī 牧师
pas.try	(n.)	kue	gāo bǐng 糕饼, diǎn xīn 点心
pas.ture	(n.)	padang rumput	cǎo yuán 草原, mù chǎng 牧场
		rumput	mù cǎo 牧草
	(v.)	menggembalakan	fàng mù 放牧
		makan rumput	chī cǎo 吃草
pat	(v.)	menepuk	qīng pāi 轻拍
		mengetuk	qīng qiaō 轻敲
patch	(v.)	menambal	bǔ 补, féng bǔ 缝补
	(n.)	tambalan	bǔ dīng 补钉
pat.ent	(n.)	paten	zhuān lì 专利, zhuān lì quán 专利权
path	(n.)	jalan kecil	xiǎo lù 小路
path.way	(n.)	jalan kecil	xiǎo lù 小路
pa.tience	(n.)	kesabaran	rěn nài 忍耐
pa.tient	(a.)	sabar	rěn nài dė 忍耐的, nài xīn dė 耐心的
pa.tient.ly	(adv.)	dengan sabar	rěn nài di 忍耐地, nài xīn di 耐心地
pa.tri.ot	(n.)	patriot	ài guó zhě 爱国者
pa.tri.ot.ic	(a.)	patriotik	ài guó dė 爱国的
pa.tri.ot.ism	(n.)	patriotisme	ài guó zhǔ yì 爱国主义
pa.trol	(n.)	patroli	xún lúo 巡逻
	(v.)	berpatroli	xún lúo 巡逻
pa.tron	(n.)	pelindung, penyokong	bǎo hù rén 保护人, zàn zhù rén 赞助人
pa.tron.ess	(n.)	pelindung (wanita)	nǔ bǎo hù rén 女保护人
		penyokong (wanita)	nǔ zàn zhù yuán 女赞助员
pat.ron.ize	(v.)	melindungi, menyokong	bǎo hù 保护, zàn zhù 赞助
pat.tern	(n.)	pola	mo xíng 模型, yàng shì 样式

pause	(n.)	pause, istirahat	zàn tíng 暂停
pave	(v.)	mengaspal, meratakan	pū zù 铺路, pū píng 铺平
pave.ment	(n.)	trotoar, aspalan	rén xíng dào 人行道, lù miàn 路面
pa.vil.ion	(n.)	paviliun	tíng zi 亭子, xiāng fáng 厢房
paw	(n.)	cakar	zhǎo 爪
pawn	(n.)	bidak, pion	bīng 兵, zú 卒
		gadai	dàng 当, dǐ yā 抵押
	(v.)	menggadaikan	dàng 当
pawn.bro.ker	(n.)	pemilik rumah gadai	dàng pù lǎo bǎn 当铺老板
pawn.shop	(n.)	rumah gadai	dàng pù 当铺
pay	(v.)	membayar	fù 付, fù kuǎn 付款, huán qián 还钱
	(n.)	pembayaran, upah	gōng zī 工资, xīn jīn 薪金
pay.a.ble	(a.)	dapat dibayar	kě fù dė 可付的
pay-day	(n.)	hari bayaran/gajian	fā xīn rì 发薪日
pay.ee	(n.)	penerima uang	shōu kuǎn zhě 收款者, shōu qián rén 收钱人
pay.ment	(n.)	pembayaran	fù kuǎn 付款
pay-roll	(n.)	daftar gaji	gōng zī dàn 工资单
pea	(n.)	kacang polong	wān dòu 豌豆
peace	(n.)	perdamaian	hé píng 和平
		ketenteraman	tài píng 太平
peace.ful	(a.)	damai	hé píng dė 和平的
		tenteram	tài píng dė 太平的
peach	(n.)	buah persik	táo zi 桃子, táo shù 桃树
pea.cock	(n.)	burung merak	kǒng què 孔雀
peak	(n.)	puncak	shān dǐng 山顶, shān fēng 山峰
pea.nut	(n.)	kacang tanah	huā shēng 花生
pear	(n.)	buah pir	lí 梨, lí shù 梨树
pearl	(n.)	mutiara	zhēn zhū 珍珠
peas.ant	(n.)	petani	nóng mín 农民

peck	(n.)	paruh	zhuó 啄
	(v.)	memaruh, mematuk	zhuó 啄
pe.cul.iar	(a.)	aneh	gŭ guài dė 古怪的
		khas	tė shū dė 特殊
ped.al	(n.)	pedal, injak-injakan	tà băn 踏板
ped.dle	(v.)	berjualan keliling, menjajakan	tiāo mài 挑卖
ped.dler	(n.)	penjaja	xiăo fàn 小贩
peek	(v.)	mengintip	tōu kàn 偷看
peel	(n.)	kulit buah-buahan	gŭo pí 果皮
	(v.)	mengupas	bō 剥, bō pí 剥皮
peep	(v.)	mengintip, mengintai	tōu kàn 偷看, kūi shì 窥视
peer	(v.)	memandang dengan tajam	níng shì 凝视, zhù mù 注目
peg	(n.)	pasak	mù dīng 木钉
		pancang kecil	mù shuān 木栓
pen	(n.)	pena	gāng bĭ 钢笔
		kandang	lán 栏
pe.nal.ize	(v.)	menghukum	chŭ fá 处罚
pen.al.ty	(n.)	hukuman, pinalti	chéng fá 惩罚, fá qiú 罚球
pen.cil	(n.)	potlot, pensil	qiān bĭ 铅笔
pe.nin.su.la	(n.)	peninsula, semenanjung	bàn dăo 半岛
pen.knife	(n.)	pisau lipat, pisau kecil	zhé dāo 摺刀, xiăo dāo 小刀
pen.man	(n.)	ahli tulisan indah	shū fă jiā 书法家
		pengarang	zuò jiā 作家
pen-name	(n.)	nama samaran	bĭ míng 笔名
pen.ny	(n.)	mata uang	biàn shì 便士
pen.sion	(n.)	pensiun	yăng lăo jīn 养老金
		rumah penginapan	gōng yù 公寓
pen.ta.gon	(n.)	sisi lima, segi lima	wŭ biān xíng 五边形
peo.ple	(n.)	rakyat	rén mín 人民
pep.per	(n.)	merica	hú jiāo 胡椒

per	(prep.)	setiap	měi 每, měi yī 每一
per.ceive	(v.)	merasa	zhī jué 知觉, gǎn jué 感觉
per.cent	(n.)	persen	bǎi fēn zhī ... 百分之…
per.cen.ta.ge	(n.)	persentase	bǎi fēn lǜ 百分率
per.cept	(n.)	perasaan	zhī jué 知觉
per.cep.tion	(n.)	persepsi	zhī jué 知觉
perch	(v.)	hinggap	qī xī 栖息
per.fect	(a.)	sempurna	wán měi 完美, wán shàn 完善
per.form	(v.)	melakukan	shí xíng 实行, zhí xíng 执行
		mempertunjukkan	biǎo yǎn 表演, yǎn zoù 演奏
per.form.ance	(n.)	perbuatan, pertunjukan	biǎo xiàn 表现, biǎo yǎn 表演
per.form.er	(n.)	pemain sandiwara, pelaku	yǎn yuán 演员, zhí xíng zhě 执行者
per.fume	(n.)	minyak wangi, parfum	xiāng shǔi 香水
per.haps	(adv.)	barangkali	yě xǔ 也许, kǒng pà 恐怕
per.il	(n.)	bahaya	weī xiǎn 危险
pe.ri.od	(n.)	masa	shí qī 时期
		tanda titik	jù hào 句号
pe.ri.od.ic	(a.)	berkala	dìng shí dė 定时的
per.ish	(v.)	tewas, musnah	sǐ wáng 死亡, hǔi miè 毁灭
per.ma.nence	(n.)	ketetapan, keabadian	yǒng jiǔ xìng 永久性
per.ma.nent	(a.)	tetap, kekal, permanen	yǒng jiǔ dė 永久的
per.mis.sion	(n.)	izin	yǔn xǔ 允许, tóng yì 同意
per.mit	(v.)	mengizinkan	yǔn xǔ 允许
per.se.vere	(v.)	bertahan terus, gigih	jiān chí 坚持, bù qū bù náo 不屈不挠
per.sist	(v.)	mempertahankan	jiān chí 坚持
		bersikeras	wán gù 顽固
per.son	(n.)	orang, pribadi	rén 人, rén shēn 人身
per.so.na	(n.)	orang	rén 人
		orang yang disukai	shòu huān yíng dė rén 受欢迎的人
per.son.a.ble	(a.)	tampan, rupawan	piào liàng 漂亮
per.son.age	(n.)	orang yang terkemuka	míng rén 名人

per.son.al	(a.)	pribadi, perorangan	gè rén dė 个人的, sī rén dė 私人的
	(n.)	personal, kepegawaian	rén yuán 人员, rén shì 人事
per.son.al.i.ty	(n.)	kepribadian	gè xìng 个性, rén gé 人格
		tokoh	rén wù 人物
per.son.al.ly	(adv.)	sendiri	qīn zì 亲自
per.son.nel	(n.)	personil, personalia	quán tĭ rén yuán 全体人员
per.spec.tive	(n.)	perspektif	tòu shì huà 透视画
		pandangan	qián jĭng 前景
		prospek	qián tú 前途
per.suade	(v.)	meyakinkan	shūo fú 说服
pest	(n.)	hama	hài chóng 害虫
pet	(n.)	binatang kesayangan	wán shăng dòng wù 玩赏动物
		kesayangan	chŏng ài wù 宠爱物, chŏng ér 宠儿
pe.ti.tion	(n.)	petisi	qíng yuàn 请愿, qíng yuàn shū 请愿书
pe.ti.tion.er	(n.)	pemohon, orang yang menyampaikan petisi	qíng yuàn rén 请愿人 qíng qiú rén 请求人
pet.rol	(n.)	bensin	shí yóu 石油, qì yóu 汽油
pe.trol.eum	(n.)	minyak tanah	shí yóu 石油
pet.ty	(a.)	kecil, remeh, tak berarti	xì xiăo 细小, bù zhòng yào 不重要
phar.ma.cist	(n.)	ahli obat-obatan, apoteker	yào jì shī 药剂师
phar.ma.cy	(n.)	toko obat, apotek	xī yào fáng 西药房
phase	(n.)	tahap, bentuk	jiē duàn 阶段, xíng zhuàng 形状
phi.los.o.pher	(n.)	ahli filsafat, filsuf	zhé xué jiā 哲学家
phi.los.o.phy	(n.)	filsafat	zhé xué 哲学
phoe.nix	(n.)	burung ajaib usianya mencapai 500 atau 600 tahun (dalam cerita kuno dari Yunani dan Tiongkok)	fèng huáng 凤凰, bù sĭ niăo 不死鸟
phone	(n.)	telepon	diàn huà 电话

pho.net.ic	(a.)	menurut bunyi ucapan, fonetis	yǔ yīn dė 语音的
pho.ne.ti.cian	(n.)	ahli fonetik	yǔ yīn xué jiā 语音学家
pho.net.ics	(n.)	ilmu fonetik	yǔ yīn xué 语音学
pho.to	(n.)	foto, potret	zhào piàn 照片
pho.to.graph	(n.)	potret, foto	zhào piàn 照片
pho.tog.ra.pher	(n.)	juru potret	zhào xiàng shī 照相师
pho.tog.ra.phy	(n.)	fotografi	zhào xiàng shù 照相术, shè yǐng shī 摄影师
phrase	(n.)	frasa	duǎn yǔ 短语, piàn yǔ 片语
phys.ic	(n.)	obat	yī yào 医药
phys.i.cal	(a.)	fisik, badan, jasmani menurut alam	ròu tǐ dė 肉体的, shēn tǐ dė 身体的 zì rán dė 自然的
phy.si.cian	(n.)	dokter	yī shēng 医生, nèi kē yī shēng 内科医生
phys.i.cist	(n.)	ahli fisika	wù lǐ xué jiā 物理学家
phys.ics	(n.)	fisika	wù lǐ xué 物理学
pia.nist	(n.)	pemain piano, pianis	gāng qín jiā 钢琴家
pia.no	(n.)	piano	gāng qín 钢琴
pick	(v.)	memetik, memilih mencungkil mencopet mematuk	cái 采, tiāo xuǎn 挑选 tī 剔, wā 挖 pá 扒 zhúo 啄
pick.pock.et	(n.)	tukang copet	pá shǒu 扒手
pick.up	(v.)	mengambil	ná qǐ lái 拿起来, shí qǐ lái 拾起来
pic.nic	(n.)	piknik	jiāo yóu 郊游, yě cān 野餐
pic.nick.er	(n.)	peserta piknik	jiāo yóu zhě 郊游者, yě cān zhě 野餐者
pic.ture	(n.)	gambar	tú huà 图画

pie	(n.)	pastel, pai	xiàn bǐng 馅饼
piece	(n.)	sepotong	yī kuài 一块, yī jiàn 一件
		secuil	yī xiǎo piàn 一小片
pier	(n.)	dermaga	mǎ tóu 码头
pierce	(v.)	menusuk	cì 刺
pig	(n.)	babi	zhū 猪
pi.geon	(n.)	burung dara	gē zi 鸽子
pig.gy	(n.)	babi kecil	xiǎo zhū 小猪
pig.sty	(n.)	kandang babi	zhū lán 猪栏
pile	(n.)	tumpukan	duī 堆
	(v.)	menumpuk, menimbun	duī jī 堆积
pil.grim	(n.)	orang yang berziarah	xiāng kè 香客
		orang yang naik haji	cháo shèng zhě 朝圣者
pill	(n.)	tablet	yào wán 药丸
pil.lar	(n.)	tiang	zhù zi 柱子
pil.low	(n.)	bantal	zhěn tóu 枕头
pil.low-case	(n.)	sarung bantal	zhěn tóu tào 枕头套
pi.lot	(n.)	pilot, penerbang, pandu	feī xíng yuán 飞行员, lǐng háng yuán 领航员
pin	(n.)	penyemat, peniti, lencana	bié zhēn 别针
pin.cers	(n.)	penjepit	qián zi 钳子
pinch	(v.)	menjepit	jiá 挟
	(n.)	penjepit	jiá zi 挟子
pine	(n.)	pohon cemara	sōng shù 松树
	(v.)	merindukan, merana	kě wàng 渴望
pine.ap.ple	(n.)	nanas, nenas	fèng lí 凤梨
ping-pong	(n.)	tenis meja, pingpong	pīng pāng qiú 乒乓球
pink	(a.)	berwarna merah jambu	fěn hóng dė 粉红的
	(n.)	merah muda	fěn hóng sè 粉红色
pi.o.neer	(n.)	pelopor	xiān qū zhě 先驱者
		perintis jalan	kaī lù xiān fēng 开路先锋

pipe	(n.)	pipa	guǎn zi 管子, dǎo guǎn 导管, yān dǒu 烟斗
		seruling	dí zi 笛子
pip.er	(n.)	peniup suling	chuī dí rén 吹笛人
pi.rate	(n.)	bajak laut	hǎi dào 海盗
pis.tol	(n.)	pistol	shǒu qiāng 手枪
pit	(n.)	sumur, lubang tambang	kuàng jǐng 矿井, kuàng kēng 矿坑
pi.ti.ful	(a.)	menyedihkan	cí beī dė 慈悲的
pi.ti.less	(a.)	tidak berbelas kasihan	wú qíng dė 无情的
pit.man	(n.)	pekerja tambang batu bara	méi kuàng gōng rén 煤矿工人
pity	(n.)	belas kasihan	lián mǐn 怜悯
		sayang	wǎn xī 婉惜
	(v.)	mengasihi	kě lián 可怜
plac.ard	(n.)	plakat	zhāo tiē 招贴, gào shì 告示
place	(n.)	tempat	dì fāng 地方
	(v.)	menempatkan	fàng 放
plain	(a.)	tanah datar	píng yuán 平原
		jelas, terus terang	míng bǎi 明白, tǎn bǎi 坦白
plain.ly	(adv.)	dengan jelas	míng bǎi di 明白的
		dengan terus terang	tǎn bǎi di 坦白的
plan	(n.)	rencana	jì huà 计划
	(v.)	merencanakan	jì huà 计划, shè jì 设计
plane	(n.)	pesawat terbang	feī jī 飞机
		bidang datar	píng miàn 平面
		pengetam, serutan	bào 刨
plan.et	(n.)	planet	xíng xīng 行星
plank	(n.)	papan tebal	hòu bǎn 厚板
plant	(n.)	tumbuh-tumbuhan	zhí wù 植物
plant.er	(n.)	penanam	zhòng zhí zhě 种植者, zāi péi zhě 栽培者
plant.ing	(n.)	penanaman	zhòng zhí 种植, zāi péi 栽培

plate	(n.)	piring	pán zi 盘子
plate.ful	(n.)	sepiring penuh	măn pán 满盘
plat.form	(n.)	peron, panggung, mimbar	yuè tái 月台, jiăng tái 讲台
play	(v.)	bermain-main	wán shuă 玩耍
		berjudi	dŭ bó 赌博
		bertanding dengan	tóng ... bĭ sài 同…比赛
	(n.)	sandiwara, permainan	xì jù 戏剧, yóu xì 游戏
		judi	dŭ bó 赌博
play.er	(n.)	pemain (olahraga/ sandiwara/musik)	xuăn shŏu 选手, yăn yuán 演员, yăn zòu zhĕ 演奏者, qín shŏu 琴手
play.ground	(n.)	tempat bermain	yóu xì chăng 游戏场
		lapangan bermain atau olahraga	yùn dòng chăng 运动场
play.house	(n.)	gedung sandiwara	jù chăng 剧场
play.ing-card	(n.)	kartu permainan	zhĭ pái 纸牌
play.mate	(n.)	teman bermain	yóu bàn 游伴
play.wright	(n.)	dramawan, penulis nas-kah sandiwara	jù zùo jiā 剧作家
pla.za	(n.)	alun-alun, lapangan luas	guăng chăng 广场
plea	(n.)	pembelaan, dalih	biàn jiĕ 辩解, kŏu shí 口实
plead	(v.)	membela	biàn hù 辩护
		memohon dengan sangat	kĕn qiú 恳求
plead.er	(n.)	pembela	biàn hù rén 辩护人
plead.ing	(n.)	pembelaan	biàn hù 辩护
pleas.ant	(a.)	menyenangkan	yú kuài dė 愉快的, hăo wán dė 好玩的
pleas.ant.ly	(adv.)	dengan senang	yú kuài di 愉快地
please	(v.)	menyenangkan	shĭ rén xĭ huān 使人喜欢
		menggembirakan	shĭ rén gaō xìng 使人高兴
		silakan	qíng 请
pleased	(a.)	senang, puas	gāo xìng dė 高兴的, măn yì dė 满意的

pleas.ing	(a.)	menyenangkan	lìng rén xǐ huān dė 令人喜欢的
pleas.ure	(n.)	kesenangan	kuài lè 快乐
plen.ti.ful	(a.)	banyak, berlimpah-limpah	fēng fù 丰富
plen.ty	(n.)	banyak	duō 多, fēng fù 丰富
plot	(n.)	intrik, rencana jahat	yīn móu 阴谋
plough	(n.)	bajak	lí 犁
	(v.)	membajak	lí 犁, gēng 耕
pluck	(v.)	memetik, mencabut	cái 采, bá 拔
		menarik	lā 拉
	(n.)	keberanian	yǒng qì 勇气
pluck.y	(a.)	berani	yǒu yǒng qì dė 有勇气的
plug	(n.)	sumbat, steker	sè zí 塞子, diàn chā tóu 电插头
	(v.)	bekerja keras	kǔ gàn 苦干
		menyumbat	sè zhù 塞住
		memasang steker	chā shàng chā tóu 插上插头
plum.age	(n.)	bulu burung	yǔ máo 羽毛
plump	(a.)	montok	fēng mǎn dė 丰满的
plunge	(v.)	mencelupkan	jìn rù 浸入
		menyelam	tiào jìn shǔi zhōng 跳进水中, qián rù shǔi lǐ 潜入水里
plu.ral	(a.)	jamak	fù shù dė 复数的
		berjumlah banyak	duō shù dė 多数的
	(n.)	bentuk jamak	fù shù xíng shì 复数形式
plus	(a.)	plus, lebih	jiā dė 加的, zhèng dė 正的
	(prep.)	tambah	jiā 加
	(n.)	tanda tambah	jiā hào 加号, zhèng hào 正号
pock.et	(n.)	saku	yī dài 衣袋, kǒu dài 口袋
		uang	qián 钱
		dompet	qián baō 钱包
	(v.)	mengantongi	fàng jìn kǒu dai 放进口袋

pock.et-book	(n.)	buku catatan kecil	xiǎo bǐ jì bù 小笔记簿
		buku saku	xiù zhēn běn 袖珍本
pock.et-knife	(n.)	pisau saku	xiǎo daō 小刀
pock.et-money	(n.)	uang saku	líng yòng qián 零用钱
po.em	(n.)	syair, puisi	shī 诗
po.et	(n.)	penyair	shī rén 诗人
po.e.try	(n.)	puisi	shī gē 诗歌
point	(n.)	titik, ujung	diǎn 点, jiān duān 尖端
		angka	fēn shù 分数
		arti, pokok	yaò diǎn 要点
point.ed	(a.)	tajam	jiān rùi 尖锐, jiān lì 尖利
point.less	(a.)	tanpa angka	bù dé fēn 不得分, líng 零
		tiada arti	wú yì yì dė 无意义的
pois.on	(n.)	racun	dú yào 毒药
pois.on.ing	(n.)	racun	dú yào 毒药
pois.on.ous	(a.)	beracun	yǒu dú dė 有毒的
poke	(v.)	menusuk	cì 刺, chūo 戳
pok.er	(n.)	alat pengorek api	bō hǔo bàng 拨火棒
		permainan kartu remi	pū kè 扑克
pole	(n.)	tiang, tongkat	zhù zi 柱子, mù gàn 木竿
		kutub	jí 极
po.lem.ic	(a.)	polemik	zhēng lùn dė 争论的, biàn lùn dė 辩论的
	(n.)	polemik	zhēng lùn 争论, biàn lùn 辩论
pole-star	(n.)	bintang kutub	běi jí xīng 北极星
po.lice	(n.)	polisi	jǐng chá 警察
po.lice.man	(n.)	(petugas) polisi	jǐng chá 警察
pol.i.cy	(n.)	kebijakan, siasat	zhèng cè 政策, cè luè 策略
pol.i.cy.mak.er	(n.)	orang yang menentukan kebijakan	jué cè rén 决策人

pol.i.o	(n.)	penyakit lumpuh anak-anak	xiǎo ér má bì zhèng小儿麻痹症
pol.ish	(v.)	mengkilapkan, menyemir, memoles	cā liàng 擦亮, rùn shì 润饰
	(n.)	kilap	guāng zé 光泽, guāng huá 光滑
		semir	cā liàng jī 擦亮剂,
pol.ished	(a.)	yang dikilapkan, yang di-semir	cā liàng dė 擦亮的
po.lite	(a.)	sopan	yǒu lǐ mào dė 有礼貌的
po.lite.ness	(n.)	kesopanan	yǒu lǐ mào 有礼貌, sī wén 斯文
pol.i.tic	(a.)	bijaksana	xián míng 贤明
		diplomatis	zhèng cè xìng dė 政策性的
pol.it.i.cal	(a.)	bersifat politis	zhèng zhì dė 政治的, zhèng zhì shàng dė 政治上的
pol.i.ti.cian	(n.)	politikus	zhèng kè 政客, zhèng zhì jiā 政治家
pol.i.tics	(n.)	politik, ilmu politik	zhèn zhì 政治, zhèng zhì xué 政治学
pol.i.ty	(n.)	bentuk pemerintahan, bentuk negara	zhèng tǐ 政体
pol.lute	(v.)	mengotori	nòng zāng 弄脏
pol.lu.tion	(n.)	pengotoran, polusi	wū rán 污染
poly.clinic	(n.)	poliklinik	mén zhěn bù 门诊部 lián hé zhěn liáo suǒ 联合诊疗所
pol.y.tech.nic	(a.)	politeknik	duō zhǒng gōng yì dė 多种工艺的
po.made	(n.)	minyak rambut	tóu fà yóu 头发油
pomp	(n.)	kemegahan, kebesaran	zhuàng lì 壮丽
pond	(n.)	kolam	chí táng 池塘
po.ny	(n.)	kuda kecil	xiǎo mǎ 小马
pool	(n.)	kolam	chí 池, shǔi chí 水池

poor	(a.)	miskin, lemah	qióng 穷, kě lián 可怜, xū rùo 虚弱
pop	(a.)	umum, populer	tōng su dė 通俗的, dà zhòng dė 大众的, liú xíng dė 流行的
pop.u.lar	(a.)	populer, digemari	dà zhòng dė 大众的, liú xíng dė 流行的
pop.u.lar.ize	(v.)	mempopulerkan	dà zhòng huà 大众化, pŭ jí 普及
pop.u.late	(v.)	mendiami	jū zhù 居住
pop.u.la.tion	(n.)	jumlah penduduk	rén kŏu 人口, rén shù 人数
		penduduk	jū mín 居民
porce.lain	(n.)	porselen	cí qì 瓷器
pork	(n.)	daging babi	zhū ròu 猪肉
port	(n.)	pelabuhan	găng kŏu 港口
por.ta.ble	(a.)	yang mudah dibawa	qīng biàn dė 轻便的, shŏu tí dė 手提的
por.tage	(n.)	pengangkutan	bān yùn 搬运
		ongkos pengangkutan	yùn fèi 运费
por.tal	(n.)	pintu gerbang, portal, pintu masuk	rù kŏu 入口
por.ter	(n.)	penjaga pintu	shŏu mén yuán 守门员
		buruh pengangkut	bān yùn gōng rén 搬运工人
por.tion	(n.)	bagian	bù fēn 部分
		porsi	yī fēn 一分, yī kè 一客
por.trait	(n.)	potret, gambar orang	zhào xiàng照相, huà xiàng 画象
po.si.tion	(n.)	kedudukan, posisi	wèi zhì 位置, zhì wèi 职位, dì wèi 地位
		sikap	zī shì 姿势, tài dù 态度
		keadaan	xíng shì 形势
pos.i.tive	(a.)	tegas, pasti	míng què dė 明确的, kĕn dìng dė 肯定的
		positif	jī jí dė 积极的

pos.i.tive.ly	(adv.)	sungguh-sungguh	què shí di 确实地
		dengan pasti	kěn dìng di 肯定地,
		dengan aktif	jī jí di 积极地
pos.sess	(v.)	memiliki, mempunyai	yōng yǒu 拥有, jù yǒu 具有
pos.ses.sion	(n.)	barang milik	sǔo yǒu wù 所有物, cái chǎn 财产
		milik	zhàn yǒu 占有, yōng yǒu 拥有
pos.ses.sive	(a.)	mengenai kepunyaan	sǔo yǒu dė 所有的
	(n.)	kasus kepunyaan	sǔo yǒu gé 所有格
pos.sessor	(n.)	pemilik	sǔo yǒu rén 所有人,
			zhàn yǒu rén 占有人
pos.si.bil.i.ty	(n.)	kemungkinan	kě néng xìng 可能性
pos.si.ble	(a.)	mungkin	kě néng 可能
pos.si.bly	(adv.)	boleh jadi, barangkali	yě xǔ 也许, hùo zhě 或者
post	(n.)	tiang	zhī zhù 支柱
		pos jaga	shào zhàn 哨站, gǎng wèi 岗位
		jabatan	zhí wèi 职位
		pos	yóu zhèng 邮政
	(v.)	mengirim melalui pos, mengeposkan	yóu jì 邮寄
		menempatkan, memasang	pèi zhì 配置, zhāng tiē 张贴
post.age	(n.)	perangko	yóu fèi 邮费, yóu zi 邮资
		materai	yìn huā 印花
post.al	(a.)	mengenai (kantor) pos	yóu zhèng dė 邮政的
post.card	(n.)	kartu pos	míng xìn piàn 明信片
post.er	(n.)	poster, plakat	guǎng gào huà 广告画,
			xuān chuán huà 宣传画
post.man	(n.)	tukang pos	yóu chāi 邮差
post.mark	(n.)	cap pos, stempel pos	yóu chūo 邮戳
post-mas.ter	(n.)	kepala kantor pos	yóu zhèng jú zhǎng 邮政局长
post.of.fice	(n.)	kantor pos	yóu zhèng jú 邮政局

post.pone	(v.)	menangguhkan, menunda	yán chí 延迟, yán qī 延期
pos.ture	(n.)	sikap badan, postur	zī shì 姿势, zī tài 姿态
post-war	(a.)	sehabis perang	zhàn hòu 战后
pot	(n.)	pot bunga	huā pén 花盆
po.ta.to	(n.)	kentang	mǎ líng shǔ 马玲薯
po.ten.cy	(n.)	potensi, daya	lì liàng 力量, xiào lì 效力
po.tent	(a.)	kuat, manjur	yǒu lì dė 有力的, yòu xiào dė 有效的
po.ten.tial	(a.)	potensial, mungkin	qián zài dė 潜在的, kě néng dė 可能的
pot.ter.y	(n.)	barang tembikar	táo qì 陶器
poul.try	(n.)	unggas, ayam-itik	jiā qín 家禽, jī yā 鸡鸭
pounce	(n.)	menerkam	měng pū 猛扑
pound	(n.)	pon	bàng 镑
		tempat pengurungan binatang	shòu lán 兽栏, jiā chù lán 家畜栏
	(v.)	memukul-mukul	luàn dǎ 乱打, luàn qiāo 乱敲
		menumbuk	dǎo suì 捣碎
pour	(v.)	menyiram, menuangkan	guàn zhù 灌注, qīng dǎo 倾倒, dǎo chū 倒出
		mengalir	liú chū 流出
pov.er.ty	(n.)	miskin	pín qióng 贫穷
pow.der	(n.)	bedak	fěn 粉
		bubuk	fěn mò 粉末
		mesiu	hǔo yào 火药
pow.der-puff	(n.)	spons bedak	fěn pū 粉扑
pow.der-room	(n.)	kamar rias	huà zhuāng shì 化妆室
pow.er	(n.)	tenaga, kekuasaan	lì 力, lì liang 力量, shì lì 势力
pow.er.ful	(a.)	kuat, berkuasa	yǒu lì dė 有力的, yǒu shì lì dė 有势力的

pow.er.less	(a.)	tak berdaya, tak berkuasa	wú lì dė 无力的, wú néng lì dė 无能力的
prac.ti.ca.ble	(a.)	dapat dipraktekkan	xíng dé tòng dė 行得通的, kě xíng dė 可行的
prac.ti.cal	(a.)	praktis	shí jì dė 实际的
prac.ti.cal.ly	(adv.)	hampir-hampir	jī hū 几乎
		sebenarnya	shí jì shàng 实际上
prac.tice	(n.)	latihan, praktek	liàn xí 练习, shí jiàn 实践
		kebiasaan	xí guàn 习惯
prac.tise	(v.)	praktek	kai yè 开业
		mempraktekkan, menja- lankan	shí jiàn 实践, shí xíng 实行
prac.tised	(a.	berpengalaman	yǒu jīng yàn dė 有经验的
praise	(v.)	memuji	chēng zàn 称赞, biǎo yáng 表扬
pray	(v.)	berdoa, sembahyang	qí tǎo 祈祷
prayer	(n.)	orang yang berdoa	qí tǎo zhě 祈祷者
preach	(v.)	berkhotbah	chuán dào 传道, jiǎng dào 讲道
preach.er	(n.)	khatib, pendeta	chuán dào zhě 传道者, chuán jiàn shì 传教士, mù shī 牧师
pre.cede	(v.)	mendahului	yù xiān 预先
pre.ced.ence	(n.)	lebih didahulukan, lebih diutamakan	yōu xiān 优先
		hak lebih tinggi	yōu xiān quán 优先权
prec.e.dent	(n.)	yg dapat dijadikan contoh	xiān lì 先例
	(a.)	yang mendahului	lǐng xiān dė 领先的, xiān xíng dė 先行的
pre.ced.ing	(a.)	terdahulu	yǐ qián dė 以前的
		sebelumnya	qián 前
pre.cept	(n.)	ajaran	jiào xùn 教训

pre.cep.tor	(n.)	guru	lǎo shī 老师
pre.cious	(a.)	berharga	bǎo gùi dė 宝贵的
pre.cise	(a.)	tepat, persis	zhèng què 正确, jīng qùe 精确
pre.cise.ly	(adv.)	dengan tepat	zhèng què di 正确地
pre.ci.sion	(n.)	ketepatan, ketelitian	zhèng què 正确, jīng mì 精密
pre.dict	(v.)	meramalkan	yù yán 预言, yù gaò 预告
pre.dic.tion	(n.)	ramalan	yù yán 预言, yù gaò 预告
pre.dictor	(n.)	peramal	yù yán zhě 预言者, yù gaò zhě 预告者
pre.face	(n.)	kata pengantar, pendahu- luan	xù 序, xù yán 序言
pre.fer	(v.)	lebih menyukai	gèng xǐ huān 更喜欢, jiǎo xǐ huān 较喜欢
pre.fix	(n.)	awalan	qián zhui 前缀, cí tóu 词头
pre.mier	(n.)	perdana menteri	zǒng lǐ 总理, shǒu xiàng 首相
prem.iere	(n.)	pertunjukan perdana	shǒu cì yǎn chū 首次演出
prep.a.ra.tion	(n.)	persiapan	yù bèi 预备, zhǔn bèi 准备
pre.par.a.to.ry	(a.)	mengenai persiapan	yù bèi dė 预备的, zhǔn bèi dė 准备的
pre.pare	(v.)	menyiapkan	yù bèi 预备, zhǔn bèi 准备
pre.pay	(v.)	membayar lebih dahulu	yù fù 预付
prep.o.si.tion	(n.)	kata depan, preposisi	jiè cí 介词
prep.o.si.tion.al	(a.)	mengenai preposisi	jiè cí dė 介词的
pres.ence	(n.)	kehadiran	chū xí 出席
pres.ent	(a.)	hadir	chū xí 出席
		sekarang	xiàn zài 现在
	(n.)	hadiah	lǐ wù 礼物
		waktu sekarang	xiàn zài shí 现在时
	(v.)	menyajikan	tí chū 提出
		memperkenalkan	jiè shào 介绍
		menghadiahkan	zēng sòng 赠送, sòng lǐ 送礼

pres.ent.day	(a.)	masa kini	xiàn dài dė 现代的
pre.sent.ly	(adv.)	segera	bù jiǔ 不久, yī hùi ėr 一会儿
pre.serve	(v.)	mengawetkan	bǎo cún 保存
		melindungi	bǎo hù 保护
		mempertahankan	bǎo chí 保持
pre.serv.er	(n.)	pelindung	bǎo hù rén 保护人
pre.side	(v.)	mengetuai, memimpin	dàng zhǔ xí 当主席, zhǔ chí 主持
pres.i.den.cy	(n.)	jabatan presiden, kepresidenan	zǒng tǒng zhí 总统职
pres.i.dent	(n.)	presiden	zǒng tǒng 总统
		ketua	hùi zhǎng 会长
pres.i.den.tial	(a.)	mengenai presiden	zǒng tǒng dė 总统的
press	(v.)	menekan, memaksa	yā 压, qiáng qiú 强求
		mendesak	yōng jǐ 拥挤, cūi cù 催促
		memeras	yā zhà 压榨
	(n.)	pers	chū bǎn jiè 出版界, chū bǎn zhě 出版者
		mesin cetak	yìn shuā jī 印刷机
		alat memeras	yā zhà jī 压榨机
		tekanan	yā lì 压力
pres.sure	(n.)	tekanan, paksaan	yā lì 压力, qiáng pò 强迫
pres.tige	(n.)	wibawa	weī xìn 威信, shēng wàng 声望
pres.to	(adv.)	dengan cepat	jí shù di 急速地
pre.sume	(v.)	mengira, menganggap, mengandaikan	tuī cè 推测, jiǎ ding 假定
pre.tence	(n.)	pura-pura	jiǎ zhuāng 假装
pre.tend	(v.)	berpura-pura	jiǎ zhuāng 假装
		berdalih	jiè kǒu 借口
pre.tend.er	(n.)	orang yang berpura-pura	jiǎ zhuān zhě 假装者
pre.text	(n.)	dalih	jiè kǒu 借口
pret.ty	(a.)	cantik, manis	piào liàng 漂亮, měi lì 美丽

pre.vail	(v.)	menang	yōu shèng 优胜
		berlaku	tōng xíng 通行, liú xíng 流行
pre.vent	(v.)	mencegah	yù fáng 预防, fáng zhǐ 防止
pre.vent.a.ble	(a.)	yang dapat dicegah	ké yù fáng dė 可预防的, kě fáng zhǐ dė 可防止的
pre.ven.tion	(n.)	pencegahan	yù fáng 预防, fáng zhǐ 防止
pre.ven.tive	(a.)	bersifat pencegahan	yù fáng xìng dė 预防性的
pre.vious	(a.)	yang mendahului	xiān 先, qián 前
		yang lalu	yǐ qián 以前
previous.ly	(adv.)	sebelumnya	yǐ qián 以前, yù xiān 预先
pre-war	(a.)	sebelum perang	zhàn qián dė 战前的
prey	(n.)	mangsa, korban	bǔ shì wù 扑食物, xī shēng pǐn 牺牲品, bèi bǔ shì dė qín shòu 被扑食的禽兽
price	(n.)	harga	jià qián 价钱
price.less	(a.)	tak ternilai	wú jià dė 无价的, gùi zhòng dė 贵重的
prick	(v.)	menusuk	cì 刺
pride	(n.)	kesombongan	jiāo ào 骄傲
priest	(n.)	pendeta	jiào shì 教士, mù shī 牧师
pri.ma.cy	(n.)	kedudukan utama	shǒu wèi 首位
pri.mal	(a.)	yang pertama	zùi chū dė 最初的
		yang terpenting	zùi zhǔ yào dė 最主要的
pri.ma.ri.ly	(adv.)	pertama, mula-mula	dì yī 第一, yuán lái 原来
pri.ma.ry	(a.)	yang pertama	dì yī dė 第一的
		yang penting	zhǔ yào dė 主要的
prime	(a.)	utama, terbaik	zùi chū dė 最初的, dì yī dė 第一的, zùi yōu liáng dė 最优良的
prim.er	(n.)	buku bacaan permulaan	chū jí dú běn 初级读本, rù mén shū 入门书
prim.i.tive	(a.)	primitif	yuán shǐ dė 原始的, tài gǔ dė 太古的

prince	(n.)	putra raja, pangeran	wáng zi 王子, tài zì 太子
prin.cess	(n.)	putri raja	gōng zhǔ 公主
prin.ci.pal	(a.)	terutama	zhǔ yào dė 主要的,
			shǒu yào dė 首要的
prin.ci.ple	(n.)	asas, dasar	yuán lǐ 原理,
		prinsip	yuán zé 原则
print	(v.)	mencetak	yìn shuā 印刷
	(n.)	cetakan	yìn shuā pǐn 印刷品
print.er	(n.)	tukang cetak	yìn shuā gōng rén 印刷工人
print.ing	(n.)	pencetakan, percetakan	yìn shuā 印刷,
			yìn shuā shù 印刷术,
			yìn shuā yè 印刷业
pri.or	(a.)	lebih dahulu	xiān 先
	(adv.)	sebelumnya	zài xiān 在先,
			zài ... yǐ qián 在…以前
pri.or.i.ty	(n.)	prioritas	yōu xiān 优先
pris.on	(n.)	penjara	jiān láo 监牢
pris.on.er	(n.)	tahanan, pesakitan	qiǔ fàn 囚犯
pri.vate	(a.)	pribadi	sī rén dė 私人的
		rahasia	mì mì dė 秘密的
pri.vate.ly	(adv.)	sendirian	sī xià di 私下的
		secara diam-diam	mì mì di 秘密的
priv.i.lege	(n.)	hak istimewa	tè quán 特权
priv.i.ly	(adv.)	secara rahasia	mì mì di 秘密的
prize	(n.)	hadiah	jiǎng jīn 奖金, jiǎng pǐn 奖品
prize.man	(n.)	orang yang mendapat hadiah	dé jiǎng rén 得奖人
pro	(n.)	ahli, profesional	zhuān jiā 专家
	(prep.)	demi, untuk, menurut	wèi lė 为了, àn zhào 按照
	(adv.)	setuju	zàn chéng 赞成

pro-	(pref.)	memihak	qīn ... 亲···
pro-America	(n.)	pro-Amerika, memihak Amerika	qīn měi 亲美
prob.a.bil.i.ty	(n.)	kemungkinan	kě néng xìng 可能性
prob.a.ble	(a.)	mungkin	kě néng 可能, yě xǔ 也许
prob.a.bly	(adv.)	mungkin	hùo xǔ 或许, yě xǔ 也许
prob.lem	(n.)	soal, masalah	wèn tí 问题
pro.ce.dure	(n.)	prosedur	shǒu xù 手续, chéng xù 程序
pro.ceed	(v.)	maju, meneruskan	qián jìn 前进, jì xù 继续
pro.ceeds	(n.)	pendapatan, hasil	shōu rù 收入
pro.cess	(n.)	proses	gùo chéng 过程, jìn xíng 进行
		cara	fāng fǎ 方法, zhì fǎ 制法
pro.ces.sion	(n.)	pawai, prosesi	yóu xíng dùi wǔ 游行队伍
pro.claim	(v.)	mengumumkan	gōng bù 公布, xuān bù 宣布
proc.la.ma.tion	(n.)	pengumuman	gōng bù 公布, bù gào 布告, xuān bù 宣布
		proklamasi	xuān yán 宣言
pro.cure	(v.)	memperoleh	huò dé 获得
pro.duce	(v.)	membuat, menghasilkan	zhì zào 制造, shēng chǎn 生产
pro.duc.er	(n.)	produsen, penghasil	shēng chǎn zhě 生产者
prod.uct	(n.)	produk, hasil	chǎn wù 产物, wù chǎn 物产, chǎn pǐn 产品
pro.duc.tion	(n.)	produksi, pembuatan	shēng chǎn 生产, zhì zào pǐn 制造品
pro.duc.tive	(a.)	produktif	yǒu shēng chǎn lì dė 有生产力的, duō chǎn dė 多产的
pro.duc.tiv.i.ty	(n.)	produktivitas	shēng chǎn lì 生产力
		daya produksi	shēng chǎn néng lì 生产能力, dūo chǎn xìng 多产性
pro.fess	(v.)	menyatakan	biǎo shì 表示
pro.fes.sion	(n.)	pekerjaan, profesi	zhí yè 职业
		pernyataan	biǎo bǎi 表白

pro.fes.sion.al	(a.)	profesional	zhí yè dė 职业的
		ahli	zhuān mén dė 专门的
	(n.)	ahli	zhuān jiā 专家
pro.fes.sor	(n.)	guru besar, profesor	dà xué jiào shòu 大学教授
pro.fi.cien.cy	(n.)	keahlian, kecakapan	shú liàn 熟练, jīng tōng 精通
pro.fi.cient	(a.)	pandai, cakap	shú liàn dė 熟练的, jīng tōng dė 精通的
prof.it	(n.)	keuntungan, guna	lì yì 利益, yòng chǔ 用处
prof.it.a.ble	(a.)	menguntungkan	yǒu lì dė 有利的
prof.it.less	(a.)	tidak menguntungkan	wú lì dė 无利的, wú yì dė 无益的
pro.found	(a.)	dalam	shēn dė 深的, shēn ào dė深奥的
pro.gram	(n.)	acara	jié mù 节目
pro.gram.mer	(n.)	pembawa acara	jié mù bào gào yuán 节目报告员
pro.gress	(n.)	kemajuan	qián jìn 前进, jìn bù 进步, jìn xíng 进行
	(v.)	maju, berkembang	qián jìn 前进, fā zhǎn 发展
pro.gres.sive	(a.)	progresif	jìn bù dė 进步的, qián jìn dė 前进的
	(n.)	orang yang progresif	jìn bù fèn zi 进步份子
pro.hib.it	(v.)	melarang	jìn zhǐ 禁止
pro.hi.bi.tion	(n.)	larangan	jìn zhǐ 禁止, jìn lìng 禁令
pro.ject	(v.)	memproyeksikan	shè chū 射出, fā shè 发射
		merancangkan	jì huà 计划, shè jì 设计
		menonjol	tū chū 突出
proj.ect	(n.)	rencana	jì huà 计划
		proyek	gōng chéng 工程
pro.jcc.tor	(n.)	proyektor	jì huà zhě 计划者, fā qǐ rén 发起人, fàng yìng jī 放映机
pro.le.ta.ri.an	(n.)	proletar	wú chǎn jiē jí dė 无产阶级的
pro.le.ta.ri.at	(n.)	proletariat	wú chǎn jiē jí 无产阶级
pro.logue	(n.)	pendahuluan	xù yán 序言, kaī chǎng bái 开场白
pro.long	(v.)	memperpanjang	yán cháng 延长

prom.i.nence	(n.)	keunggulan	tū chū 突出, jié chū 杰出
prom.i.nent	(a.)	terkemuka, mencolok	jié chū dė 杰出的, tū chū dė 突出的
prom.ise	(v.)	berjanji, menjanjikan	yuè dìng 约定, dā yìng 答应
prom.is.ing	(a.)	berharapan, menjanjikan	yǒu xī wàng dė 有希望的, yǒu qián tú dė 有前途的
pro.mote	(v.)	menaikkan pangkat	tí shēng 提升
		mempromosikan	fā qǐ 发起, tí chàng 提倡
pro.mot.er	(n.)	promotor	fā qǐ rén 发起人, chuàng bàn rén 创办人
pro.mo.tion	(n.)	kenaikan pangkat	shēng jí 升级
		promosi	zēng jìn 增进
prompt	(a.)	cepat, segera	xùn sǔ 迅速, lì jí 立即
prompt.ly	(adv.)	dengan segera	xùn sù di 迅速的
pro.noun	(n.)	kata ganti	dài míng cí 代名词, daì cí 代词
pro.nounce	(v.)	mengucapkan	fā yīn 发音
		menyatakan	biǎo shì 表示, xuān gào 宣告
		menjatuhkan	pàn jué 判决
pro.nounce.ment	(n.)	pengumuman, pernyataan	shēng míng 声明, xuān gào宣告
pro.nun.ci.a.tion	(n.)	ucapan	fā yīn 发音
proof	(n.)	bukti	zhèng míng 证明, zhèng jù 证据
		cetakan percobaan	jiào yàng 校样
		percobaan	shí yàn 实验
	(a.)	tahan	nài 耐
prop.	(n.)	penyangga, penyokong	zhī zhù 支柱, zhī chí zhě 支持者
		baling-baling	lúo xuán jiǎng 螺旋桨
		perlengkapan di atas pentas	dǎo jù 道具
prop.a.gan.da	(n.)	propaganda	xuān chuán 宣传
pro.pa.gand.ist	(n.)	propagandis	xuān chuán yuán 宣传员
prop.a.gate	(v.)	menyebarkan	chuán bō 传播

pro.pel	(v.)	mendorong	tuī jìn 推进
prop.er	(a.)	pantas, wajar, cocok	zhèng dàng 正当, tuǒ dàng妥当, shì dàng 适当
prop.er.ly	(adv.)	dengan cara yang wajar	zhèng dàng di 正当地, shì dàng di 适当地, dāng rán 当然
prop.er.ty	(n.)	tanah milik, kekayaan	dì chǎn 地产, cái chǎn 财产
		sifat	xìng zhì 性质
		alat sandiwara	dào jù 道具
proph.e.cy	(n.)	ramalan	yù yán 预言
proph.e.sy	(v.)	meramalkan	yù yán 预言
proph.et	(n.)	peramal	yù yán jiā 预言家
		nabi	xiān zhī 先知
pro.por.tion	(n.)	bagian perbandingan	bù fēn 部分, bǐ lì 比例
pro.por.tion.al	(a.)	seimbang, sebanding	àn bǐ lì dė 按比例的, jūn héng dė 均衡的, xiāng chèn dė 相称的
pro.po.sal	(n.)	usul	tí yì 提议, jiàn yì 建议
		peminangan	qiú hūn 求婚
pro.pose	(v.)	mengusulkan	tí yì 提议, jiàn yì 建议,
		meminang	qiú hūn 求婚
		bermaksud	dǎ suàn 打算
prop.o.si.tion	(n.)	usul, rencana	tí yì 提议, jì huà 计划
		hal, soal	shì qíng 事情, wèn tí 问题
prose	(n.)	prosa	sǎn wén 散文
pros.e.cute	(v.)	melaksanakan, menuntut	zhí xíng 执行, kòng sù 控诉
pros.e.cu.tion	(n.)	penuntutan, pelaksanaan	kòng sù 控诉, zhí xíng 执行
pros.e.cu.tor	(n.)	penuntut	kòng sù rén 控诉人
pros.pect	(n.)	prospek, harapan	qián tú 前途
pros.pec.tive	(a.)	prospektif	yù qī dė 预期的

pros.per	(v.)	menjadi makmur	shǐ fán róng 使繁荣
pros.per.i.ty	(n.)	kemakmuran	fán róng 繁荣
pros.per.ous	(a.)	makmur	fán róng dė 繁荣的
pros.ti.tute	(n.)	pelacur	jì nǚ 妓女
pro.tect	(v.)	melindungi	bǎo hù 保护
pro.tec.tion	(n.)	perlindungan	bǎo hù 保护
pro.tec.tion.ism	(n.)	proteksionisme	bǎo hù mào yì zhèng cè 保护贸易政策
pro.tec.tive	(a.)	bersifat melindungi	bǎo hù xìng dė 保护性的
pro.tec.tor	(n.)	pelindung	bǎo hù rén 保护人
		alat pelindung	bǎo hù qì 保护器
pro.tein	(n.)	protein	dàn bǎi zhì 蛋白质
pro.test	(v.)	protes, sanggahan	kàng yì 抗议
pro.to.col	(n.)	protokol	wài jiāo lǐ jié 外交礼节, lǐ bīn 礼宾
pro.tract	(v.)	memperpanjang	yán cháng 延长
pro.trude	(v.)	menonjol keluar	shēn chū 伸出
proud	(a.)	bangga, angkuh	zì háo dė 自豪的, jiāo ào dė 骄傲的
proud.ly	(adv.)	dengan bangga	zì háo di 自豪地
		dengan sombong	jiāo ào di 骄傲地
prove	(v.)	membuktikan	zhèng míng 证明
prov.erb	(n.)	peribahasa	gé yán 格言
pro.vide	(v.)	menyediakan	gōng yìng 供应
		memberikan	gōng jǐ 供给
		menetapkan	guī dìng 规定
pro.vid.ing	(conj.)	asal saja, asalkan	zhǐ yào 只要
prov.ince	(n.)	propinsi	shěng 省
pro.vin.cial	(a.)	mengenai propinsi	shěng dė 省的
pro.vi.sion.al	(a.)	sementara	zàn shí dė 暂时的, lín shí dė 临时的
prov.o.ca.tion	(n.)	provokasi, penghasutan	tiǎo bō 挑拨
pro.voc.a.tive	(a.)	provokatif, bersifat meng-hasut	tiǎo bō xìng dė 挑拨性的

pro.voke	(v.)	menghasut	tiǎo bō 挑拨
pro.vok.ing	(a.)	menjengkelkan	lìng rén shēng qì 令人生气
prox.i.mate	(a.)	yang terdekat	zuì jìn dė 最近的
prox.im.i.ty	(n.)	dekatnya	jīe jìn 接近
pru.dence	(n.)	hati-hati, kebijaksanaan	jǐn shèn 谨慎, jīng míng 精明
pru.dent	(a.)	berhati-hati	jǐn shèn dė 谨慎的
		bijaksana	jīng míng dė 精明的
psy.chol.o.gy	(n.)	ilmu jiwa, psikologi	xīn lí xué 心理学
pub.lic	(a.)	umum	gōng gòng dė 公共的,
			gōng zhòng dė 公众的
	(n.)	khalayak ramai, umum	mín zhòng 民众, gōng zhòng 公众
pub.li.can	(n.)	pemilik losmen	kè diàn lǎo bǎn 客店老板
		pemilik rumah minum	jiǔ diàn lǎo bǎn 酒店老板
pub.li.ca.tion	(n.)	penerbitan, pengumuman	chū bǎn 出版, gōng bù 公布
pub.lic.house	(n.)	rumah minum	jiǔ diàn 酒店
		rumah makan kecil	yǐn shí diàn 饮食店
		losmen	kè diàn 客店
pub.lish	(v.)	menerbitkan	chū bǎn 出版
pub.lish.er	(n.)	penerbit	chū bǎn zhě 出版者
pud.ding	(n.)	puding	bù dīng 布丁
puff	(n.)	tiupan	chuī 吹
	(v.)	meniup	chuī 吹
pull	(v.)	menarik	lā 拉
		mencabut	bá 拔
pulse	(n.)	denyutan nadi	mài bó 脉膊
pump	(n.)	pompa	dǎ qì tǒng 打气筒
	(v.)	memompa	dǎ qì 打气, chōu shǔi 抽水
pump.kin	(n.)	labu kuning	nán guā 南瓜
punc.tu.al	(a.)	tepat pada waktunya	zhǔn shí dė 准时的
punc.tu.al.i.ty	(n.)	ketepatan waktu	zhǔn shí 准时

punc.tu.al.ly	(adv.)	dengan tepat waktu	zhǔn shí di 准时地
punc.tu.ate	(v.)	memberi tanda baca	biāo diǎn 标点, jiā biāo diǎn 加标点
punc.tu.a.tion	(n.)	pemberian tanda baca	biāo diǎn 标点, biāo diǎn fǎ 标点法
punc.ture	(n.)	kebocoran ban	lún taī lòu qì 轮胎漏气
	(v.)	menusuk, membocorkan	cì pò 刺破, shǐ lòu qì 使漏气
pun.ish	(v.)	menghukum	chǔ fá 处罚, chěng fá 惩罚
pun.ish.ment	(n.)	hukuman	chǔ fá 处罚, chěng fá 惩罚
pup	(n.)	anak anjing	xiāo gǒu 小狗
pu.pil	(n.)	murid	xúe shēng 学生
pup.pet	(n.)	golekan, boneka	mù ǒu 木偶, kǔi lěi 傀儡
pup.py	(n.)	anak anjing	xiǎo gǒu 小狗
pur.chase	(v.)	membeli	mǎi 买, gǒu mǎi 购买
pur.chas.er	(n.)	pembeli	gòu mǎi rén 购买人, mǎi zhǔ 买主
pure	(a.)	murni, bersih	chún 纯, chún cùi 纯粹
pu.ri.fy	(v.)	membersihkan	nòng qīng jié 弄清洁
pu.ri.ty	(n.)	kemurnian, kesucian	chún cùi 纯粹, chùn jié 纯洁
pur.ple	(n.)	warna ungu	zǐ sè 紫色
pur.pose	(n.)	tujuan, maksud	mù dì 目的, yì tú 意图
pur.pose.ful	(a.)	bertujuan	yǒu mù dė 有目的
		sengaja	gù yì dė 故意的
pur.pose.less	(a.)	tiada tujuan	wú mù dì dė 无目的的
		tiada arti	wú yì yì dė 无意义的
pur.pose.ly	(adv.)	dengan sengaja	gù yì di 故意地
purse	(n.)	dompet	qián dài 钱袋, qián baō 钱包
pur.sue	(v.)	mengejar	zhuī 追, zhuī gǎn 追赶, zhuī qíu 追求
pur.su.er	(n.)	pengejar	zhuī gǎn zhě 追赶者, zhuī qiú zhě 追求者
pur.suit	(n.)	pengejaran	zhuī gǎn 追赶, zhuī qiú 追求
push	(v.)	mendorong	tuī 推
		mendesak	bī pò 逼迫

puss	(n.)	kucing	xiǎo māo 小猫
pus.sy	(n.)	kucing	māo 猫
put	(v.)	meletakkan, menaruh	fàng 放
puz.zle	(n.)	teka-teki	mi 谜
		kebingungan	mí hùo 迷惑
		soal yang menyulitkan	nán tí 难题
	(v.)	membingungkan	shǐ rén mí huò 使人迷惑
py.ja.mas	(n.)	piyama	shùi yī 睡衣
pyr.a.mid	(n.)	piramida	jīn zì tā 金子塔

Q

quake	(v.)	berguncang	zhèn dòng 震动
	(n.)	gempa, gempa bumi	zhèn dòng 震动, dì zhèn 地震
qual.i.fi.ca.tion	(n.)	kualifikasi	zī gé 资格, tiáo jiàn 条件
qual.i.fied	(a.)	memenuhi syarat	yǒu zī gé dė 有资格的, hé gé dė 合格的
qual.i.fy	(v.)	memenuhi syarat	yǒu zī gé 有资格, hé gé 合格
		memberi sifat	xiū shì 修饰, xiàn dìng 限定
qual.i.ta.tive	(a.)	kualitatif	xìng zhì shàng dė 性质上的
		mengenai kualitas	zhì liàng shàng dė 质量上的
qual.i.ty	(n.)	mutu, kualitas	zhì liàng 质量, pǐn zhì 品质
quan.ti.ta.tive	(a.)	kuantitatif, mengenai kuantitas	shù liàng shàng dė 数量上的
quan.ti.ty	(n.)	kuantitas, jumlah	liàng 量, shù liàng 数量
quan.tum	(n.)	kuantum	dìng liang 定量, dìng é 定额
quar.rel	(n.)	pertengkaran	zhēng chǎo 争吵, chǎo jia 吵架
	(v.)	bertengkar	zhēng chǎo 争吵
quar.rel.some	(a.)	suka bertengkar	ài chǎo jià dė 爱吵架的, hào zhēng dė 好争的
quar.ter	(n.)	seperempat	sì fēn zhī yī 四分之一
		tiga bulan	jì 季
		setalen	èr jiǎo wǔ fēn 二角五分
quar.ter.ly	(a.)	triwulan	měi jì dė 每季的
	(n.)	majalah triwulan	jì kān 季刊
	(adv.)	tiap kuartal	měi jì 每季, yī jì yī cì一季一次

quar.to	(n.)	kuarto	sì kaī 四开, sì kaī běn 四开本
quay	(n.)	pelabuhan	mă tóu 码头
queen	(n.)	ratu, permaisuri	nŭ wáng 女王, wáng hòu 王后
queer	(a.)	aneh	gŭ guài 古怪
que.ry	(n.)	pertanyaan	yí wèn 疑问
quest	(n.)	penyelidikan	tàn sŭo 探索
ques.tion	(n.)	pertanyaan	wèn 问, wèn tí 问题
ques.tion.a.ble	(a.)	diragukan	lìng rén huái yí dė 令人怀疑的,
			kĕ yí dė 可疑的
ques.tion-mark	(n.)	tanda tanya	wèn hào 问号
queue	(n.)	antrean	pái cháng dùi 排长队, rén lóng 人龙
		kucir	biàn zi 辫子
quick	(a.)	cepat	kuài 快
quick.en	(v.)	mempercepat	jiā kuài 加快
quickly	(adv.)	dengan cepat	hĕn kuài di 很快地, xùn sù di 迅速地
qui.et	(a.)	tenang, diam	ān jìng dė 安静的, jì mò dė 寂寞的
qui.et.ly	(adv.)	dengan diam-diam	jìng jìng di 静静地
qui.et.ness	(n.)	kesunyian, ketenangan	ān jìng 安静, ān dìng 安定
quilt	(n.)	selimut kapas	mián bèi 棉被, bèi wō 被窝
qui.nine	(n.)	kina	kúi níng 奎宁,
			jīn jī nà shuāng 金鸡纳霜
quin.tal	(n.)	kuintal	gōng dàn 公担
quit	(v.)	meninggalkan, berhenti	lí kaī 离开, tíng zhĭ 停止
quite	(adv.)	sama sekali	wán quán 完全
		sungguh-sungguh	shí fēn 十分
quiz	(n.)	ujian, ulangan	cè yàn 测验
	(v.)	menguji	cè yàn 测验, kăo wèn 考问
quo.ta	(n.)	kuota	dìng é 定额
quo.ta.tion	(n.)	kutipan	yĭn yŭ 引语, yŭ lù 语录
quote	(v.)	mengutip	yĭn yòng 引用, yĭn lù 引录

R

rab.bit	(n.)	kelinci	tù zì 兔子
race	(n.)	ras, bangsa	zhǒng zú 种族, mín zú 民族
		perlombaan, pacuan	jìng sài 竞赛, sài mǎ 赛马
ra.cial	(a.)	rasial	zhǒng zú dė 种族的, rén zhǒng dė 人种的
ra.cial dis.crim.i.na.tion	(n.)	diskriminasi rasial	zhǒng zú qí shì 种族歧视
ra.cial.ism	(n.)	rasialisme	mín zú xìng 民族性, mín zú jīng shén 民族精神, zhǒng zú piàn jiàn 种族偏见
rack	(n.)	rak	jiā zi 架子
rack.et	(n.)	raket (tenis, badminton)	wǎng qiú pò 网球拍, yǔ qiú pò 羽球拍
ra.dar	(n.)	radar	léi dá 雷达
ra.diance	(n.)	sinar, cahaya	guāng 光, guāng huī 光辉
ra.diant	(a.)	bersinar	fā guāng dė 发光的, guāng huī dė 光辉的
ra.di.ate	(v.)	memancarkan, menyebar	fàng shè 放射, sàn fā 散发
ra.di.a.tion	(n.)	radiasi, pemancaran	fàng shè 放射, fú shè 辐射, fàng shè wù 放射物, fàng shè xiàn 放射线, fú shè xiàn 辐射线
ra.di.a.tor	(n.)	radiator	fú shè qì 辐射器, fú shè tǐ 辐射体

rad.i.cal	(a.)	radikal	jí duān dė 极端的,
			jí jìn dė 急进的
		akar, sampai akar-akarnya	gēn dė 根, gēn běn dė 根本的
ra.di.o	(n.)	radio	wú xiàn diàn 无线电,
			shōu yīn jī 收音机
ra.di.o-ac.tive	(a.)	radioaktif	fàng shè xìng dė 放射性的
ra.di.o.gram	(n.)	radiogram	wú xiàn diàn bào 无线电报
ra.di.o.set	(n.)	radio, pesawat radio	shōu yīn jī 收音机
rad.ish	(n.)	lobak	lúo bó 萝卜
ra.dius	(n.)	radius	bàn jìng 半径
raf.fi.a	(n.)	rafia	xiān wéi 纤维
raft	(n.)	rakit	mù fá 木筏
rag	(n.)	(kain) gombal	làn bù 烂布, pò bù 破布
		godaan	hú nào 胡闹
		gaduh	dǎo dàn 捣蛋
	(v.)	mengejek, menggoda	cháo xiào 嘲笑, qī fù 欺负
		menghina	wǔ rǔ 侮辱
rage	(n.)	kemarahan, kegusaran	dà nù 大怒, jī nù 激怒
	(v.)	mengamuk	fā nù 发怒, fen nù 愤怒, fā húo 发火
rag.ged	(a.)	compang-camping	pò làn 破烂, lán lǚ 褴露
rag.ging	(n.)	senda gurau	kāi wán xiāo 开玩笑
		gaduh	hú nào 胡闹
raid	(n.)	penyerbuan, serangan	xí jī 袭击, tū jī 突击
raid.er	(n.)	penyerbu, penyerang	xí jī zhé 袭击者
rail	(n.)	rel kereta api	tiě gǔi 铁轨
	(v.)	mencerca	zé mà 责骂
rail.road	(n.)	jalan kereta api	tiě lù 铁路, hǔo chē lù 火车路
rail.way	(n.)	jalan kereta api	tiě lù 铁路, hǔo chē lù 火车路
rail.way.man	(n.)	pekerja kereta api	tiě lù gōng rén 铁路工人
rai.ment	(n.)	pakaian	yī fú 衣服

rain	(n.)	hujan	yǔ 雨
rain.bow	(n.)	pelangi	hóng 虹, cái hóng 彩 虹
rain.coat	(n.)	jas hujan	yǔ yī 雨 衣
rain.drop	(n.)	tetesan hujan	yǔ dī 雨 滴
rain.fall	(n.)	hujan	xià yǔ 下 雨
rain.less	(a.)	tidak ada hujan	wú yǔ dė 无 雨 的
rain.proof	(a.)	tahan hujan	fáng yǔ dė 防 雨 的,
			bù tòu yǔ dė 不 透 雨 的
rain.y	(a.)	banyak hujan	duō yǔ dė 多 雨 的
raise	(v.)	mengangkat	jǔ qǐ 举 起, tí shēng 提 升
		menaikkan	tí gāo 提 高
		memelihara	fǔ yǎng 抚 养, sì yǎng 饲 养
rai.sin	(n.)	kismis	pú taó gān 葡 萄 干
rake	(n.)	penggaruk	pá 耙
	(v.)	menggaruk	pá 耙
		memberondong	sāo shè 扫 射
		mengumpulkan	shōu jí 收 集
ral.ly	(v.)	berkumpul, bersatu	jí hé 集 合, tuán jié 团 结
	(n.)	rapat, rapat umum	jí hùi 集 会, dà hùi 大 会
ram.ble	(v.)	jalan-jalan	sàn bù 散 步, liū dá 溜 达
ran.dom	(n.)	serampangan	hú luàn 胡 乱
		sembarangan	sǔi biàn 随 便
range	(n.)	deretan, barisan, jarak	pái liè 排 列, jù lí 距 离
rank	(n.)	barisan	háng liè 行 列
		tingkat	děng jí 等 级
		pangkat	dì wèi 地 位
rap.id	(a.)	cepat	kuài 快, xùn sù 迅 速
rap.id.ly	(adv.)	dengan cepat	xùn sù dì 迅 速 地
rare	(a.)	setengah masak	bàn shú dė 半 熟 的
		jarang terdapat, langka	shǎo yǒu dė 少 有 的

rare.ly	(adv.)	jarang terjadi	hěn shǎo 很少, bù cháng 不常
ras.cal	(n.)	bajingan	liú máng 流氓, wú lài 无赖
rash	(a.)	terburu-buru, gegabah	jí zào 急躁, lǔ mǎng 卤莽
rat	(n.)	tikus	lǎo shǔ 老鼠
rate	(n.)	perbandingan, kurs	bǐ lū 比率, huì duì lū 汇兑率
		kecepatan	sù dù 速度
		tarif, bea	jià gé 价格, shùi 税
	(v.)	menilai, mencerca	píng jià 评价, zé mà 责骂
rath.er	(adv.)	lebih suka	níng kě 宁可, níng yuàn 宁愿
		agak	shāo wēi 稍微, yǒu diǎn 有点
ra.tio	(n.)	perbandingan, rasio	bǐ 比, bǐ lū 比率
ra.tion	(n.)	ransum	kǒu liáng 口粮
		catuan	pèi jǐ liàng 配给量
	(v.)	meransum	gōng yìng liáng shì 供应粮食
		menjatahkan	pèi jǐ 配给
ra.tion.al	(a.)	rasional, masuk akal	yǒu lǐ xǐng dė 有理性的
		berakal	hé lǐ dė 合理的
rat.tle	(v.)	gemeretak	gā zhī dì xiǎng 嘎吱地响
		menjengkelkan	shǐ rén shēng qì 使人生气
raw	(a.)	mentah, kasar	shēng 生, cū 粗
ray	(n.)	sinar	guāng xiàn 光线
ray.on	(n.)	rayon	rén zào sī 人造丝
raze	(v.)	meruntuhkan, meratakan	hǔi huài 毁坏, chǎn píng 铲平
ra.zor	(n.)	pisau cukur	tì dāo 剃刀
reach	(v.)	mencapai	dào 到, dào dá 到达
		memberikan, menyampai-kan	dì 递, chuán di 传递
		menyentuh	chù dào 触到
re.act	(v.)	memberi reaksi	fǎn yìng 反应, qǐ zuò yòng 起作用
		bertindak ulang	chóng zùo 重作

re.ac.tion	(n.)	reaksi	fǎn dòng 反动,
			fǎn zùo yòng 反作用,
			fǎn yìng 反应
re.ac.tion.a.ry	(n.)	kaum reaksioner	fǎn dòng pài 反动派,
			fǎn dòng fèn zi 反动份子
re.act.or	(n.)	reaktor	fǎn yìng duī 反应堆
read	(v.)	membaca	dú 读, yuè dú 阅读
read.er	(n.)	pembaca	dú zhě 读者
read.i.ly	(adv.)	dengan mudah	róng yì di 容易地
		dengan cepat	xùn sù di 迅速地
		dengan rela	gān xīn di 甘心地
read.i.ness	(n.)	keadaan siap	zhǔn bèi zhuàng tài 准备状态
read.ing	(n.)	membaca	yuè dú 阅读, kàn shū 看书
		bacaan	dú wù 读物
read.ing-room	(n.)	kamar baca	yuè lǎn shì 阅览室
re.ad.just	(v.)	mengatur kembali	tiáo zhěng 调整
read.y	(a.)	siap, beres	yǒu zhǔn bèi dė 有准备的
read.y-made	(a.)	yang sudah jadi	xiàn chéng dė 现成的
real	(a.)	benar, nyata	zhēn 真, zhēn shí 真实, shí jì 实际
real.ism	(n.)	realisme	xiàn shí zhǔ yì 现实主义
real.ist	(n.)	realis	xiàn shí zhǔ yì zhě 现实主义者
real.is.tic	(a.)	realistis	xiàn shí zhǔ yì dė 现实主义的
re.al.i.ty	(n.)	realitas	zhēn shí xìng 真实性,
			xiàn shí xìng 现实性
real.iz.a.ble	(a.)	dapat diwujudkan	kě shí xiàn dė 可实现的
real.i.za.tion	(n.)	realisasi, perwujudan	shí xiàn 实现
		kesadaran	rèn shí 认识, lǐng hùi 领会
re.al.ize	(v.)	menyadari	rèn shí dào 认识到
		mewujudkan	shí xiàn 实现
real.ly	(adv.)	sebenarnya	zhēn shí di 真实地
		sungguh-sungguh	shí zài 实在

real.ty	(n.)	harta tidak bergerak	bù dòng chǎn 不动产
reap	(v.)	menyabit, memanen	shōu gē 收割, shōu hùo 收获
reap.er	(n.)	mesin pemanen/penuai	shōu gē jī 收割机
		pemanen, penuai	shōu gē zhě 收割者
re.ap.pear	(v.)	muncul kembali	zài xiàn 再现
rear	(v.)	menegakkan	shù lì 竖立, jiàn lì 建立
		memelihara	fǔ yǎng 抚养, sì yǎng 饲养
	(n.)	bagian belakang	hòu bù 后部
	(a.)	belakang	hoù bù dė 后部的, hoù fāng dė 后方的
rear.guard	(n.)	pasukan belakang	hòu wèi 后卫
re.arm	(v.)	mempersenjatai lagi	chóng xīn wǔ zhuāng 重新武装
re.ar.ma.ment	(n.)	persenjataan kembali	chóng xīn wǔ zhuāng 重新武装
rear.most	(a.)	paling belakang	zuì hòu dė 最后的
re.ar.range	(v.)	menyusun kembali	chóng xīn zhěng lǐ 重新整理, chóng xīn ān pái 重新安排
rear.ward	(n.)	bagian belakang	hòu fāng dė 后方的, hòu bù dė 后部的
		di belakang	zài hòu fāng 在后方
		ke belakang	xiàng hòu fāng 向后方
rea.son	(n.)	alasan, sebab	lǐ yoú 理由, yuán yīn 原因
reas.on.a.ble	(a.)	masuk akal	yǒu lǐ dė 有理的, hé lǐ dė 合理的
reb.el	(n.)	pemberontak	zào fǎn zhě 造反者, pàn luàn zhě 叛乱者
re.bel	(v.)	memberontak	zào fǎn 造反, pàn luàn 叛乱
		melawan	fǎn kàng 反抗
re.bel.lion	(n.)	pemberontakan	zào fǎn 造反, pàn luàn 叛乱
re.birth	(n.)	bangkit kembali	xīn shēng 新生

re.bound	(v.)	memantul kembali	tán húi 弹回
		sehat kembali	hūi fù jiàn kāng 恢复健康
re.build	(v.)	membangun kembali	chóng jiàn 重建, gǎi jiàn 改建
re.buke	(v.)	memarahi, mencela	zé mà 责骂, qiǎn zé 谴责
re.call	(v.)	memanggil kembali	zhào húi 召回
		menarik kembali	chè húi 撤回
		mengingat kembali	xiǎng qǐ 想起
	(n.)	penarikan kembali	zhào húi 召回, chè húi 撤回
		ingatan	húi yì 回忆, húi xiǎng 回想
re.ca.pit.u.late	(v.)	merangkum, meringkas	gài kùo 概括
re.cap.ture	(v.)	merebut kembali	duó húi 夺回
re.cast	(v.)	memperbaiki	xiū dìng 修订
		membentuk kembali	gǎi xiě 改写
re.ceipt	(n.)	kuitansi, tanda terima	shōu jù 收据, shōu tiáo 收条
		penerimaan	shōu dào 收到
re.ceive	(v.)	menerima	shōu dào 收到, jiē dào 接到
re.ceiv.er	(n.)	penerima	lǐng shōu zhě 领收者, jiē shōu zhě 接收者
re.cent	(a.)	baru-baru ini	zùi jìn dė 最近的, jìn lái dė 近来的
re.cent.ly	(adv.)	baru-baru ini	zùi jìn 最近, jìn lái 近来
re.cep.tion	(n.)	penerimaan, resepsi	jiē shōu 接收, jiē dài 接待, huān yíng hùi 欢迎会
re.cess	(n.)	istirahat	xiū xī 休息
		reses	xiū hùi 休会
re.ces.sion	(n.)	pengunduran	tùi 退, chè tùi 撤退
		resesi	jīng jì shuāi tùi 经济衰退
rec.i.pe	(n.)	resep makanan	shí pǔ 食谱
		resep obat	yào fāng 药方
re.cip.i.ent	(n.)	penerima	jiè shōu rén 接收人

re.cit.al	(n.)	deklamasi	lǎng sòng 朗 诵
		hafalan, resital	bèi sòng 背 诵
		cerita, pidato	xù shù 叙 述, yǎn shūo 演 说
		pertunjukan musik	yǎn zòu hùi 演 奏 会
re.cite	(v.)	menghafalkan	bèi sòng 背 诵
		mendeklamasikan	lǎng sòng 朗 诵
		menceritakan	jiǎng shù 讲 述
reck	(v.)	memperhatikan	zhù yì 注 意
		berhati-hati	liú xīn 留 心
reck.less	(a.)	sembrono	qīng shuài dė 轻 率 的
		nekat	mào xiǎn dė 冒 险 的
reck.on	(v.)	menghitung	suàn 算
		memperhitungkan	jì suàn 计 算
		berpendapat	rèn wéi 认 为
reck.on.ing	(n.)	perhitungan	suàn zhàng 算 账
		rekening	zhàng dān 帐 单
re.claim	(v.)	memperoleh kembali	shōu húi 收 回
		menggarap tanah rawa, menimbun laut menjadi tanah	kāi kěn 开 垦, tián zhù 填 筑
re.cline	(v.)	bersandar	kào 靠, yī kào 依 靠
rec.og.ni.tion	(n.)	pengenalan	biàn rèn 辨 认
		pengakuan	chéng rèn 承 认
re.cog.ni.zance	(n.)	surat jaminan	bǎo zhèng shū 保 证 书
		uang jaminan	bǎo zhèng jīn 保 证 金
rec.og.nize	(v.)	mengenali	rèn shí 认 识
		mengakui	chéng rèn 承 认
		menghargai	shǎng shí 赏 识
re.coil	(v.)	mundur	dào tùi 倒 退
		berkecut hati	wèi sù 畏 缩

rec.ol.lect	(v.)	mengingat kembali	húi yì 回忆
		berkumpul kembali	chóng xīn jí hé 重新集合, zài jí hé 再集合
rec.ol.lec.tion	(n.)	ingatan, pengenangan	jì yì 记忆, húi yì 回忆
re.com.mence	(v.)	memulai lagi	chóng xīn kāi shǐ 重新开始, zài kāi shǐ 再开始
rec.om.mend	(v.)	menganjurkan, memuji kebaikan	tuī jiàn 推荐
		menasihati	quàn gào 劝告
rec.om.men.da.tion	(n.)	rekomendasi	tūi jiàn 推荐, jìe shào 介绍
rec.om.pense	(v.)	memberi imbalan	chóu bào 酬报
		mengganti kerugian	péi cháng 赔偿
rec.on.cile	(v.)	mendamaikan, meng-akurkan	shǐ rén hé hǎo 使人和好
rec.on.ci.li.a.tion	(n.)	perukunan kembali	hé hǎo 和好, fù jiāo 复交
rec.on.dite	(a.)	sukar dimengerti	shēn ào dė 深奥的, gāo shēn dė 高深的
re.con.sider	(v.)	mempertimbangkan kembali	chóng xīn kǎo lù 重新考虑
re.con.struct	(v.)	merekonstruksi	chóng jiàn 重建, gāi jiàn 改建
rec.ord	(n.)	catatan, rekor	jì zai 记载, jì lù 记录
re.cord	(v.)	merekam	lù yīn 录音
re.cord.er	(n.)	pencatat	jì lù zhě 记录者
		perekam	lù yīn zhě 录音者
		alat merekam	lù yīn jī 录音机
re.count	(v.)	menghitung kembali	chóng suàn 重算
		menceritakan	xù shù 叙述
re.cov.er	(v.)	memperoleh kembali	shōu húi 收回
		sembuh	hūi fù jiàn kāng 恢复健康
		menebus	bǔ chǎng 补偿, bǔ jiù 补救

re.cov.er.able	(a.)	dapat dipulihkan	kě yī hǎo dė 可医好的,
			kě huī fù dė 可恢复的
		dapat diperoleh kembali	kě shōu húi dė 可收回的
re.cov.er.y	(n.)	kesembuhan	quán yù 痊愈
		didapatnya kembali	shōu húi 收回
re.cre.ate	(v.)	membuat lagi	chóng zùo 重作
		mencipta lagi	zài zào 再造
		menghibur diri	xiāo qiǎn 消遣, xīu yǎng 休养
rec.re.a.tion	(n.)	rekreasi, hiburan	yú lè 娱乐, xiāo qiǎn 消遣,
			xiū yǎng 休养
rec.tan.gle	(n.)	bujur sangkar	cháng fāng xíng 长方形
rec.ti.tude	(n.)	kelurusan, sikap adil	duān zhèng 端正, gōng zhèng 公正
rec.tor	(n.)	kepala perguruan tinggi,	dà xúe xiào zhǎng 大学校长,
		rektor	yuàn zhǎng 院长
red	(a.)	merah	hóng 红
	(n.)	warna merah	hóng sè 红色
re.dac.tion	(n.)	redaksi	biān jí 编辑
red.den	(v.)	menjadikan merah,	biàn hóng 变红
		memerah	
red.dish	(a.)	kemerah-merahan	dài hóng sè dė 带红色的
			dàn hóng 淡红
red-let.ter	(a.)	huruf merah	hóng zì dė 红字的
		hari besar	jié rì 节日, dà rì zi 大日子
red.ness	(n.)	merah, warna merah	hóng 红, hóng sè 红色
re.doub.le	(v.)	melipatgandakan	jiā bèi 加倍
		memperkuat	jiā qiáng 加强
re.dress	(v.)	memperbaiki	jiū zhèng 纠正, xiū zhèng 修正
red.skin	(n.)	orang Indian	hóng zhǒng rén 红种人
re.duce	(v.)	mengurangi, menurunkan	jiǎn shǎo 减少, jiǎn dī 减低
re.duc.tion	(n.)	pengurangan, penurunan	jiǎn shǎo 减少, jiǎn dī 减低

reed	(n.)	alang-alang	lú wěi 芦苇
reef	(n.)	batu karang	jiāo 礁
reek	(n.)	bau busuk	chòu qì 臭气, è chòu 恶臭
reel	(n.)	alat penggulung	juǎn tǒng 卷筒
	(v.)	menggulung	juǎn 卷
re-e.lect	(v.)	memilih kembali	chóng xuǎn 重选, gǎi xuǎn 改选
re-e.lec.tion	(n.)	pemilihan ulang	chóng xuǎn 重选, gǎi xuǎn 改选
re-en.ter	(v.)	masuk kembali	zài jìn 再进
		pendaftaran ulang	zài dēng jì 再登记
re.fec.tion	(n.)	pelengkap, penyegaran	bǔ chōng 补充, tí shén 提神
		makanan ringan	diǎn xīn 点心
re.fec.to.ry	(n.)	kantin	shì táng 食堂, xiǎo chī bù 小吃部
re.fer	(v.)	menyerahkan	wěi tūo 委托, jiāo gěi 交给
		menunjuk, menunjuk pada	zhǐ 指, cān kǎo 参考
		mengenai	tán dào 谈到, tí jí 提及
ref.er.ee	(n.)	wasit	caí pàn yuán 裁判员
ref.er.ence	(n.)	referensi, surat keterangan	cān kǎo 参考, cān kǎo shū 参考书
		surat rekomendasi	tūi jiàn shū 推荐书, zhèng míng shū 证明书
ref.er.en.dum	(n.)	referendum, pemungutan suara umum	guó mín tóu piào 国民投票
ref.er.ent	(n.)	sasaran	dùi xiàng 对象
		tujuan pembicaraan	tǎo lùn mù biāo 讨论目标
re.fill	(v.)	mengisi kembali	zài zhuāng 再装, zài tián 再填
	(n.)	pengisian kembali	bǔ chōng 补充
		pengisi	bǔ chōng wù 补充物
re.fine	(v.)	memurnikan, menyuling	jīng liàn 精练
re.fit	(v.)	memperbaiki	xiū lǐ 修理
re.flect	(v.)	memantulkan	fǎn shè 反射
		mencerminkan	fǎn yìng 反映
		merenungkan	fǎn shěng 反省

re.flec.tion	(n.)	perenungan, pemikiran	fǎn shěng 反省, kǎo lǜ 考虑
		pantulan, refleksi	fǎn shè 反射
		pencerminan	fǎn yìng 反映
re.flex	(a.)	refleks	fǎn shè dė 反射的
re.form	(v.)	memperbaiki	gǎi gé 改革, gǎi liáng 改良
ref.or.ma.tion	(n.)	reformasi	gǎi gé 改革, gǎi liáng 改良
re.form.a.to.ry	(n.)	panti asuhan	jiào yǎng sǔo 教养所
		panti rehabilitasi	gǎn hùa yuàn 感化院
re.form.er	(n.)	pembaharu	gǎi gé zhě 改革者,
			gǎi liáng zhě 改良者
re.form.ism	(n.)	paham pembaharuan	gǎi liáng zhǔ yì 改良主义
re.frain	(v.)	menahan diri	yì zhì 抑制, rěn zhù 忍住
re.fresh	(v.)	menyegarkan kembali	tí shén 提神, zhèn zùo 振作,
			shǐ qīng xǐng 使清醒
re.fresh.er	(n.)	penyegar	léng yǐn pǐn 冷饮品
re.fresh.ing	(a.)	menyegarkan	tí shén dė 提神的,
			liáng shuǎng dė 凉爽的
re.fresh.ment	(n.)	penyegaran	shuǎng kuài 爽快
		minuman segar	chá diǎn 茶点
		makanan ringan	diǎn xīn 点心
re.frig.er.a.tor	(n.)	lemari es	bīng xiāng 冰箱
re.fu.el	(v.)	mengisi bahan bakar	jiā rán liào 加燃料
		mengisi bensin	jiā yóu 加油
ref.uge	(n.)	perlindungan	bì nàn 避难, bì hù 庇护
		tempat perlindungan	bì nàn sǔo 避难所,
			yǐn cáng chù 隐藏处
ref.u.gee	(n.)	pengungsi	nàn mín 难民
re.fund	(v.)	membayar kembali	fù huán 付还, chāng huán 偿还
re.fus.al	(n.)	penolakan	jù jué 拒绝
re.fuse	(v.)	menolak	jù jué 拒绝
ref.u.ta.tion	(n.)	sangkalan	fǎn bó 反驳, bó chì 驳斥

re.fute	(v.)	menyangkal	fǎn bó 反驳, bó chì 驳斥
re.gain	(v.)	mendapat kembali	shōu húi 收回
re.gard	(v.)	menganggap	rèn wéi 认为
		mengindahkan	zhòng shì 重视
re.gard.ful	(a.)	penuh perhatian	zhù yì dė 注意的,
			liú xīn dė 留心的
re.gard.ing	(prep.)	mengenai	guān yú 关于
re.gard.less	(a.)	tidak memperhatikan	bù zhù yì dė 不注意的
		tidak menghiraukan	bù zhòng shì dė 不重视的,
			hū shì 忽视
re.gen.cy	(n.)	perwalian kerajaan	shè zhèng 摄政
re.gen.er.ate	(v.)	memperbaharui	gēng xīn 更新
		menghidupkan kembali	zài shēng 再生
		memperbaiki	gǎi zào 改造
re.gen.er.a.tion	(n.)	pembaruan	gēng xīn 更新
		regenerasi	zài shēng 再生
		perbaikan	gǎi zào 改造
re.gent	(n.)	wali raja	shè zhèng zhě 摄政者
re.gime	(n.)	rezim	zhèng tǐ 政体, tǒng zhì 统治
reg.i.ment	(n.)	resimen	tuán 团
re.gion	(n.)	daerah, wilayah	dì qū 地区, dì dài 地带
re.gion.al	(a.)	regional	dì qū dė 地区的
		kedaerahan	jú bù dė 局部的
reg.is.ter	(n.)	daftar, buku daftar	dēng jì 登记, dēng jì bù 登记簿,
			zhù cè 注册, zhù cè bù 注册簿,
			guà hào 挂号
	(v.)	mendaftarkan	dēng jì 登记, zhù cè 注册
reg.is.trar	(n.)	pencatat, pendaftar	dēng jì yuán 登记员
reg.is.tra.tion	(n.)	pendaftaran	dēng jì 登记
reg.is.try	(n.)	tempat pendaftaran	dēng jì chù 登记处

re.gress	(n.)	kemunduran	tùi bù 退 步, tùi húi 退 回
	(v.)	mundur	tùi húi 退 回, dào tùi 倒 退
re.gres.sion	(n.)	kemunduran	dào tùi 倒 退,
		regresi	jīng jì shuāi tùi 经 济 衰 退
re.gret	(v.)	menyesal	ào hǔi 懊 悔, bào qiàn 抱 歉,
			yí hàn 遗 憾
re.gret.ful	(a.)	sangat menyesalkan	ào hǔi dė 懊 悔 的,
			yí hàn dė 遗 憾 的
re.gret.ta.ble	(a.)	pantas disesalkan	shǐ rén yí hàn dė 使 人 遗 憾 的
reg.u.lar	(a.)	teratur	yǒu guī zé dė 有 规 则 的,
			yǒu guī lù dė 有 规 律 的
reg.u.lar.i.ty	(n.)	sifat beraturan	guī lù xìng 规 律 性
reg.u.lar.ly	(adv.)	secara teratur	yǒu guī zé di 有 规 则 的
reg.u.late	(v.)	mengatur, menyetel	tiáo zhěng 调 整, tiáo jié 调 节
reg.u.la.tion	(n.)	regulasi, peraturan	guī zé 规 则, tiáo lì 条 例
reg.u.la.tor	(n.)	alat pengatur	tiáo jié qì 调 节 器,
			tiáo zhěng qì 调 整 器
re.ha.bil.i.tate	(v.)	merehabilitasikan	shǐ hūi fù 使 恢 复,
			shǐ fù zhí 使 复 职
re.ha.bil.i.ta.tion	(n.)	rehabilitasi	fù zhí 复 职, hūi fù 恢 复,
			fù xing 复 兴
re.hash	(v.)	pengolahan dalam bentuk baru	gǎi zuò 改 作, gǎi xǐe 改 写
re.hears.al	(n.)	latihan	pái yǎn 排 演, pǎi liàn 排 练
reign	(v.)	memerintah	tǒng zhì 统 治
	(n.)	pemerintahan	tǒng zhì 统 治
rein	(n.)	tali kekang	jiāng 缰
	(v.)	mengekang	yì zhì 抑 制, zhī pèi 支 配
re.in.force	(v.)	memperkuat	jiā qiáng 加 强
		menambah bantuan	bǔ chōng 补 充

re.in.state	(v.)	mengembalikan	huī fù 恢复
		mendudukkan kembali	fù yuán 复原
re.is.sue	(v.)	menerbitkan kembali	chóng yìn 重印
re.ject	(v.)	menolak	jù jué 拒绝, tuì diào 退掉
		mengapkir	pái chú 排除
	(n.)	apkiran	fèi pǐn 废品
re.jec.tion	(n.)	penolakan	jù jué 拒绝
		pengapkiran	pái chì 排斥, pái chú 排除
re.joice	(v.)	gembira	xǐ yùe 喜悦, gāo xìng 高兴
re.join	(v.)	menjawab	dá biàn 答辩, húi dá 回答
		menggabungkan lagi	zài cān jiā 再参加, guī dùi 归队
re.late	(v.)	menceritakan	xù shù 叙述
		menghubungkan	lián xì 联系
		berhubungan dengan	yǒu guān 有关, shè jí 涉及
re.la.tion	(n.)	hubungan, famili	guān xì 关系, qīn qī 亲戚
rel.a.tive	(a.)	nisbi	yǒu guān zì dė 有关系的
		relatif	bǐ jiào dė 比较的
	(n.)	sanak, famili	qīn qī 亲戚
		kata ganti hubung	lián xì dài cí 联系代词
rel.a.tive.ly	(adv.)	secara relatif	xiāng dùi di 相对的, bǐ jiào di 比较的
re.lax	(v.)	beristirahat	xiū xī 休息, sōng xiè 松懈
		mengendurkan	sōng jìn 松劲
re.lax.a.tion	(n.)	istirahat	xiū xī 休息
re.lay	(n.)	lari beranting	jiē lì sài pǎo 接力赛跑
		pengganti	huàn bān 换班, jiē tì rén yuán 接替人员
	(v.)	meletakkan lagi	chóng fàng 重放
		memancarkan/menyampaikan lagi	zhuǎn bō 转播, chóng bō 重播

re.lease	(v.)	membebaskan	shì fàng 释放
		melepaskan	fàng sōng 放松
rel.e.vance	(n.)	hubungan, pertalian	guān lián 关联
rel.e.vant	(a.)	bersangkut paut, relevan	guān lián dė 关联的,
			zhòng kěn dė 中肯的
re.li.a.bil.i.ty	(n.)	hal dapat dipercaya	kě kào xìng 可靠性
re.li.a.ble	(a.)	dapat dipercaya	kě kào dė 可靠的
re.li.ance	(n.)	kepercayaan	xìn lài 信赖, xìn tūo 信托
re.li.ant	(a.)	percaya	xìn lài dė 信赖的
rel.ic	(n.)	barang peninggalan	yí wù 遗物, gǔ jī 古迹
re.lief	(n.)	gambar timbul, relief	fú xiàng 浮象, fú diāo 浮雕
		pertolongan	jiù jì 救济
		keringanan	qīng sōng 轻松
		pembebasan	jiě chú 解除
re.lieve	(v.)	menyokong, mengurangi	jiù jì 救济, jiǎn qīng 减轻
		membebaskan, mengganti	jiě chú 解除, dài tì 代替
re.li.gion	(n.)	agama	zōng jiào 宗教
re.li.gious	(a.)	mengenai agama	zōng jiào dė 宗教的
rel.ish	(n.)	rasa, rasa sedap	wèi 味, měi wèi 美味
re.ly	(v.)	menyandarkan	yī lài 依赖
		percaya pada	xìn lài 信赖
re.main	(v.)	tinggal, tertinggal	dòu liú 逗留, yì liú 遗留
		tetap	zhào jiù 照旧
re.main.der	(n.)	sisa	cán yú 残余
		orang yang tersisa	shèng xià dė rén 剩下的人
re.make	(v.)	membuat sekali lagi	chóng zùo 重做, gǎi zào 改造
re.mand	(v.)	mengirim kembali	jì húi 寄回, sòng húi 送回
re.mark	(v.)	memperhatikan	zhù yì 注意, biǎo shì 表示
		menyatakan	shūo 说

re.mark.a.ble	(a.)	menarik perhatian	zhí dé zhù yì dė值得注意的
		menakjubkan	xī qí dė希奇的
rem.e.dy	(n.)	obat	yào pǐn药品
	(v.)	mengobati	zhì liáo治疗, yī liáo医疗
re.mem.ber	(v.)	mengingat	jì dé记得
		menghadiahkan	sòng lǐ gěi送礼给
		menyampaikan salam	wèn hòu问候, wèn hǎo问好
re.mem.brance	(n.)	ingatan, kenangan	jì yì记忆, húi yì回忆
re.mind	(v.)	mengingatkan, memper-hatikan	tí xǐng提醒
re.miss	(a.)	lalai, lengah	shū hū疏忽
re.mis.sion	(n.)	pengampunan, permaafan	shè miǎn赦免, huō miǎn豁免
re.mod.el	(v.)	mengubah model, membangun kembali	gǎi xíng改型, gǎi biān改编
re.morse	(n.)	penyesalan yang men-dalam	tòng huǐ痛悔, huǐ hèn悔恨
re.mote	(a.)	jauh	yáo yuǎn遥远
re.mov.al	(a.)	pemindahan	bān qiān搬迁, bān jiā搬家
		pemecatan	miǎn zhí免职
re.move	(v.)	memindahkan	bān dòng搬动, bān jiā搬家
		pindah rumah	chú qù除去, tūo diào脱掉
		melepaskan, memecat	gé zhí革职
re.new	(v.)	memperbarui	fù xīng复兴
		mengulangi	chóng xīn kaī shǐ重新开始
re.nounce	(v.)	meninggalkan	fàng qì放弃
		tidak mengakui	fǒu rèn否认
ren.o.vate	(v.)	memperbaharui	gé xīn革新
re.nown	(n.)	kemasyhuran	míng wàng名望, shēng wàng声望
re.nowned	(a.)	terkenal	yòu míng dė有名的

rent	(v.)	menyewa, menyewakan	zū 租, chū zū 出 租
	(n.)	uang sewa	zū jīn 租 金, zū fèi 租 费
rent.al	(n.)	uang sewa	zū jīn 租 金
rent.er	(n.)	penyewa	zū dė rén 租 的 人
rent-free	(a.)	tanpa uang sewa	miǎn fèi jū zhù 免 费 居 住,
			bǎi zhù 白 住
re.o.pen	(v.)	membuka kembali	chóng kāi 重 开, zài kāi 再 开
re.or.gan.iza.tion	(n.)	reorganisasi	gǎi zǔ 改 组
re.or.gan.ize	(v.)	mereorganisasi	gǎi zǔ 改 组
re.pair	(v.)	memperbaiki	xiū lǐ 修 理
re.pair.a.ble	(a.)	dapat diperbaiki	kě xiū lǐ dė 可 修 理 的
rep.a.ra.tion	(n.)	pemberian ganti rugi	péi chăng 赔 偿
re.pay	(v.)	membayar kembali	chàng huán 偿 还
		membalas	bào dá 报 达
re.peal	(v.)	mencabut, meniadakan	chè xiāo 撤 销, fèi zhǐ 废 止
re.peat	(v.)	mengulangi	chóng fù 重 复, fǎn fù 反 复
re.pel	(v.)	memukul mundur	jī tùi 击 退, dǎ tùi 打 退
re.pent	(v.)	menyesal	hòu hŭi 后 悔, ào hŭi 懊 悔
rep.e.ti.tion	(n.)	pengulangan	chóng fù 重 复, fǎn fù 反 复
re.pine	(v.)	menggerutu	mán yuàn 埋 怨
re.place	(v.)	menempatkan kembali	fàng húi 放 回
		mengganti	dài tì 代 替
re.plete	(a.)	penuh	chōng mǎn 充 满
re.ply	(v.)	menjawab	húi dá 回 答, dá fù 答 复
re.port	(v.)	melaporkan	bào gào 报 告
	(n.)	laporan	bào gào 报 告
re.port.er	(n.)	pelapor	bào gào rén 报 告 人
		wartawan	tōng xùn yuán 通 讯 员, jì zhě 记 者
re.pose	(v.)	istirahat	xiū xī 休 息
		menitipkan	jì tuō 寄 托

rep.re.sent	(v.)	mewakili	dài biǎo 代表
		menggambarkan	miáo xiě 描写
		memainkan peran	bàn yǎn 扮演
		menjelaskan	shūo míng 说明
rep.re.sen.ta.tion	(n.)	perwakilan	dài biǎo 代表
		gambaran	huà xiàng 画象
		penjelasan	shūo míng 说明
rep.re.sent.a.tive	(a.)	bersifat mewakili	dài biǎo dė 代表的, dài lǐ dė 代理的
	(n.)	wakil	dài biǎo 代表, dài biǎo rén 代表人, dài lǐ rén 代理人
re.press	(v.)	menindas, menahan	yā pò 压迫, zhèn yā 镇压, yā zhì 压制
re.pres.sion	(n.)	penindasan, penahanan	zhèn yā 镇压, yā zhì 压制
re.pres.sive	(a.)	bersifat menekan	zhèn yā dė 镇压的
		bersifat menindas	yā zhì dė 压制的
re.print	(v.)	mencetak ulang	chóng yìn 重印
re.proach	(v.)	mencela, menyalahkan	zé bèi 责备, zhǐ zé 指责
re.pro.cess	(v.)	diproses lagi	zài jiā gōng 再加工, gǎi zào 改造
re.pro.duce	(v.)	membiak	fán zhí 繁殖
		reproduksi	zài shēng chǎn 再生产
re.proof	(n.)	teguran, celaan	zé bèi 责备, xùn chì 训斥
re.prove	(v.)	menegur, mencela	zé bèi 责备, xùn chì 训斥
rep.tile	(n.)	binatang melata	pá xíng dòng wù 爬行动物
re.pub.lic	(n.)	republik	gòng hé gúo 共和国
re.pulse	(v.)	memukul mundur	dǎ tùi 打退, jī tùi 击退
rep.u.ta.tion	(n.)	reputasi	míng shēng 名声, míng yù 名誉
re.pute	(n.)	nama baik, reputasi	míng shēng 名声, míng yù 名誉
re.quest	(v.)	meminta, memohon	qíng qíu 请求, kěn qiú 恳求
re.quire	(v.)	menghendaki	yào qiǔ 要求

re.quite	(v.)	membalas budi	bào dá 报答
re.scind	(v.)	menarik kembali	fèi zhǐ 废止
		menghapuskan	qǔ xiāo 取消
res.cue	(v.)	menyelamatkan	yíng jiù 营救, wǎn jiù 挽救
res.cu.er	(n.)	penyelamat	jiù xīng 救星, yíng jiù zhě 营救者
re.search	(n.)	riset, penelitian	diào chá 调查, yán jiū 研究
re.sem.blance	(n.)	kemiripan, kesamaan	lèi sì 类似
re.sem.ble	(v.)	menyerupai, mirip	xiāng sì 相似, xiāng xiàng 相象
re.sent	(v.)	benci akan	yuàn hèn 怨恨
re.serve	(v.)	menyimpan	bǎo cún 保存
		mencadangkan	chǔ bèi 储备
		memesan	yù dìng 预订, dìng 定
	(n.)	cadangan	chǔ bèi wù 储备物, chǔ bèi jīn 储备金
re.serv.ist	(n.)	pasukan cadangan	hòu bèi jūn 后备军
res.er.voir	(n.)	waduk	shǔi kù 水库
re.set	(v.)	memasang kembali	chóng fàng 重放, chóng pái 重排
re.side	(v.)	tinggal	jū zhù 居住
res.i.dence	(n.)	tempat tinggal	zhù zhài 住宅, zhù sǔo 住所
res.i.dent	(n.)	penduduk	jū mín 居民
re.sign	(v.)	meletakkan jabatan	cí zhì 辞职
res.ig.na.tion	(n.)	peletakan jabatan	cí zhì 辞职
re.sist	(v.)	menentang	dǐ kàng 抵抗
re.sist.ance	(n.)	perlawanan, pertentangan	dǐ kàng 抵抗, fǎn kàng 反抗
re.sist.ant	(a.)	bersifat menentang	fǎn kàng dė 反抗的, dǐ kàng dė 抵抗的
	(n.)	orang yang melawan	fǎn kàng zhě 反抗者, dǐ kàng zhě 抵抗者
res.o.lute	(a.)	tegas, pasti	jiān jué dė 坚决的, gǔo duàn dė 果断的
res.o.lu.tion	(n.)	ketetapan hati, resolusi	jué xīn 决心, jué yì 决议

re.solve	(v.)	memutuskan	jué xīn 决心, jué yì 决议
		memecahkan	jiě jué 解决
		menguraikan	fēn jiě 分解
re.sort	(n.)	tempat peristirahatan	shèng dì 胜地, xiū yǎng dì 休养地
re.sound	(v.)	bergema, menggema	fǎn xiǎng 反响, húi yīn 回音
re.source	(n.)	sumber	zī yuán 资源
		akal	zhì móu 智谋
re.spect	(v.)	menghormati	zūn jìng 尊敬
re.spect.ing	(prep.)	mengenai	guān yú 关于
re.spec.tive	(a.)	masing-masing	gè zì dė 各自的
res.pi.ra.tion	(n.)	pernapasan, respirasi	gè gè dė 各个的
res.pi.ra.tor	(n.)	alat pernapasan	hū xī qì 呼吸器
re.spond	(v.)	menjawab	húi dá 回答, xiǎng yìng 响应
		menanggapi	fǎn yìng 反应
re.sponse	(n.)	jawaban	dá fù 答复, xiǎng yìng 响应
		tanggapan	fǎn yìng 反应
re.spon.si.bil.i.ty	(n.)	tanggung jawab	zé rèn 责任
re.spon.si.ble	(a.)	bertanggung jawab	fù zé dė 负责的, yǒu zé rèn gǎn dė 有责任感的
rest	(n.)	istirahat, tidur	xiū xī 休息, shùi jiào 睡觉
		sisa	shèng yú bù fēn 剩余部分
		lain-lainnya	qí tā 其他
	(v.)	beristirahat, tidur	xiū xī 休息, shùi jiào 睡觉
		berhenti	tíng dùn 停顿
re.state	(v.)	mengemukakan kembali	chóng shēn 重申
		mengulangi	chóng jiǎng 重讲
res.tau.rant	(n.)	restoran, rumah makan	cái guǎn 菜馆, fàn diàn 饭店
rest.ful	(a.)	penuh ketenangan, tenteram	ān jìng 安静, ān dìng 安定
rest.less	(a.)	resah, gelisah	bù ān dė 不安的

res.to.ra.tion	(n.)	pemulihan, restorasi	huī fù 恢复
re.store	(v.)	memulihkan	huī fù 恢复
		mengembalikan	guī huán 归还
		memperbaiki	xiū jiàn 修建, xiū hǎo 修好
re.strain	(v.)	menahan	kè zhì 克制, kòng zhì 控制
re.strict	(v.)	membatasi, mengikat	xiàn zhì 限制, yuè shù 约束
re.stric.tion	(n.)	pembatasan	xiàn zhì 限制, xiàn dìng 限定
re.sult	(n.)	akibat	jié gǔo 结果
		hasil	chéng gǔo 成果, chéng jī 成绩
re.su.me	(n.)	ikhtisar, ringkasan	zhāi yào 摘要, gài yào 概要
re.sume	(v.)	mendapat kembali	shōu húi 收回
		meneruskan	jì xù 继续
re.take	(v.)	pemotretan kembali	chóng pāi 重拍, chóng shè 重摄
		merebut kembali	duó húi 夺回
re.tail	(n.)	eceran	líng mài 零卖, líng shòu 零售
	(v.)	menjual eceran	líng mài 零卖, líng shòu 零售
re.tail.er	(n.)	pedagang eceran	líng shòu shàng 零售商
re.tain	(v.)	mempertahankan	bǎo chí 保持
		menyimpan, mengingat	bǎo liú 保留, jì yì 记忆
re.tard	(v.)	memperlambat	yán chí 延迟
re.tell	(v.)	menceritakan kembali	zài jiǎng 再讲, chóng shù 重述
re.ten.tion	(n.)	penyimpanan, ingatan	bǎo liú 保留, jì yì lì 记忆力
re.tire	(v.)	mengundurkan diri, pensiun	yǐn tùi 引退, tùi xiū 退休
re.touch	(v.)	memperbaiki, memperhalus, memoles	rùn sè 润色
re.treat	(v.)	mundur	tùi què 退却, chè tùi 撤退
re.trench	(v.)	menghemat	jié yuē 节约
ret.ro.spect	(n.)	pandangan ke masa lalu	huí gù 回顾
ret.ro.spec.tion	(n.)	pandangan ke masa lalu, kenangan masa lampau	huí gù 回顾

re.turn	(v.)	kembali, mengembalikan	húi lái 回来, gūi huán 归还
		menjawab	húi dá 回答
re.un.i.on	(n.)	reuni, bersatu kembali	zài jié hé 再结合
		berkumpul kembali	chǒng jù 重聚
re.u.nite	(v.)	menyatukan kembali	zài jié hé 再结合, hé jiě 和解
re.veal	(v.)	membuka rahasia	jiē lù 揭露
rev.el	(v.)	berpesta pora, bersukaria	kuáng huān 狂欢, kuáng xǐ 狂喜
rev.el.er	(n.)	orang yang berpesta pora, orang yang bersukaria	kuáng huān zhě 狂欢者
re.venge	(v.)	membalas dendam	bào chóu 报仇
re.verse	(v.)	membalikkan	diān dǎo 颠倒
		memutarbalikkan	dào zhuǎn 倒转
re.view	(v.)	meninjau kembali	húi gù 回顾, fù xí 复习
		memeriksa	jiǎn chá 检查, jiǎn yùe 检阅
		menimbang	píng lùn 评论
	(n.)	tinjauan, pertimbangan	fù xí 复习, píng lùn 评论
		pemeriksaan	jiǎn chá 检查, jiǎn yuè 检阅
re.view.er	(n.)	peninjau buku, penulis resensi buku	píng lùn zhě 评论者
		pemeriksa	jiǎn yuè zhě 检阅者
re.vile	(v.)	mencaci maki	rǔ mà 辱骂
re.vise	(v.)	memperbaiki, merevisi	xiū dìng 修订, xiū zhèng 修正
re.vis.er	(n.)	orang yang merevisi	jiào dìng zhě 校订者, xiū dìng zhě 修订者
re.vi.sion	(n.)	revisi, perbaikan	xiū dìng 修订, xiū dìng bǎn 修订版
re.vi.sion.ism	(n.)	revisionisme	xiū zhèng zhǔ yì 修正主义
re.vi.sion.ist	(n.)	revisionis	xiū zhèng zhǔ yì zhě 修正主义者
re.vis.it	(v.)	mengunjungi lagi	zài fáng 再访, chóng yóu 重遊
re.viv.al	(n.)	kebangkitan kembali	fù xīng 复兴
re.vive	(v.)	menyadarkan	shǐ sū xǐng 使苏醒
		menghidupkan kembali	fù xīng 复兴

re.voke	(v.)	mencabut, meniadakan	chè xiāo 撤销, qǔ xiāo 取消
re.volt	(v.)	memberontak, berevolusi	qǐ yì 起义, nào gé mìng 闹革命
rev.o.lu.tion	(n.)	revolusi	gé mìng 革命
		perputaran	xuán zhuǎn 旋转, xún huàn 循环
rev.o.lu.tion.a.ry	(a.)	revolusioner	gé mìng dė 革命的
		putar	xuán zhuǎn dė 旋转的
	(n.)	orang yang revolusioner	gé mìng jiā 革命家
rev.o.lu.tion.ist	(n.)	orang yang revolusioner	gé mìng jiā 革命家
re.volve	(v.)	berputar	xuán zhuān 旋转
		memutarkan	shǐ xuán zhuǎn 使旋转
re.volv.er	(n.)	pistol	shǒu qiāng 手枪
re.ward	(n.)	hadiah	jiǎng shǎng 奖赏
		upah	chóu láo jīn 酬劳金
		ganjaran	bào chóu 报酬
	(v.)	membalas jasa	bào dá 报答
		menghadiahi	jiǎng lǐ 奖励
re.word	(v.)	mengucapkan lagi	chóng shuō 重说
re.write	(v.)	menulis kembali	chóng xiě 重写, gǎi xǐe 改写
rheu.mat.ic	(a.)	rematik	fēng shī dė 风湿的
	(n.)	penderita rematik	huàn fēng shī bìng dė rén 患风湿病的人
rheu.ma.tism	(n.)	penyakit rematik	fēng shī bìng 风湿病
rhyme	(n.)	sajak	shī 诗
rhythm	(n.)	irama	yùn lù 韵律
rib	(n.)	tulang rusuk, iga	lèi gǔ 肋骨
rib.bon	(n.)	pita	sī dài 丝带
rice	(n.)	beras, nasi	mǐ 米, fàn 饭
rich	(a.)	kaya	fù 富, fù yǒu 富有
		subur	fēng fù 丰富, fù ráo 富饶
rich.es	(n.)	kekayaan	cái fù 财富
rid	(v.)	melepaskan diri dari	shǐ bǎi tuō 使摆脱

ride	(v.)	naik, menunggang	chéng 乘, dā 搭, qí 骑
ri.fle	(n.)	senapan	bù qiāng 步枪
right	(a.)	benar, kanan	duì 对, zhèng què 正确, yòu 右
	(n.)	hak, keadilan	quán lì 权利, gōng zhèng 公正
		ketepatan	zhèng qùe 正确
		kanan, golongan kanan	yòu biān 右边, yòu pài 右派
	(adv.)	tepat	zhèng qùe dì 正确地
right.eous	(a.)	lurus, adil	zhèng zhí 正值, gōng zhèng 公正
right.ist	(n.)	golongan kanan	yòu pài fèn zi 右派分子, yòu qīng fèn zi 右倾分子
right.ly	(adv.)	dengan tepat	zhèng qùe di 正确地, zhèng dàng di 正当地
rig.id	(a.)	kaku, keras	jiāng yìng 僵硬, yán gé 严格
rim	(n.)	pinggir	biān yuán 边缘
ring	(n.)	cincin, lingkaran	jiè zhǐ 戒指, huán 环
		gelanggang	bǐ sài chǎng 比赛场, quán jī chǎng 拳击场
	(v.)	berdering	líng xiǎng 铃响
		membunyikan bel	àn líng 按玲, yáo líng 摇铃
		menelepon	dǎ diàn huà 打电话
ri.ot	(n.)	kerusuhan	sāo dòng 骚动, nào shì 闹事
ri.ot.er	(n.)	pengacau, perusuh	bào tú 暴徒
rip	(v.)	menyobek	sī liè 撕裂, chě pò 扯破
ripe	(a.)	masak, matang	shú 熟
rip.en	(v.)	memasakkan	shǐ chéng shú 使成熟
ripe.ness	(n.)	kematangan	chéng shú 成熟
rise	(v.)	naik	zēng zhǎng 增长, shàng zhǎng 上涨
		bangun, bangkit	zhàn qǐ lái 站起来, qǐ lì 起立
		terbit	shàng shēng 上升, shēng qǐ 升起
risk	(n.)	bahaya, risiko	wēi xiǎn 危险, mào xiǎn 冒险
	(v.)	mengambil risiko	mào xiǎn 冒险

risk.y	(a.)	berbahaya	wēi xiǎn dė 危险的
		mengandung risiko	mào xiǎn dė 冒险的
rite	(n.)	upacara	yí shí 仪式, diǎn lǐ 典礼
ri.val	(n.)	lawan	duì shǒu 对手
		pesaing, konkuren	jìng zhēng zhě 竞争者
riv.er	(n.)	sungai	hě 河
road	(n.)	jalan	lù 路, dào lù 道路
road-block	(n.)	penghadang jalan	lù zhàng 路障
	(v.)	menghalang-halangi, merintangi	zǔ ài 阻碍, fáng ài 妨碍
road-side	(n.)	pinggir jalan	lù páng 路旁, lù biān 路边
road.way	(n.)	jalan kendaraan	chē lù 车路, chē dào 车道, chē xíng dào 车行道
roar	(v.)	mengaung, meraung	hǒu 吼, páo xiāo 咆哮
roast	(v.)	memanggang	kǎo 烤
rob	(v.)	merampok	qiǎng 抢, qiǎng jié 抢劫
rob.ber	(n.)	perampok	qiǎng dào 强盗, dào zéi 盗贼
rob.ber.y	(n.)	perampokan	qiǎng jié shì jiàn 抢劫事件
robe	(n.)	jubah	cháng páo 长袍
rob.ot	(n.)	robot	jī qì rén 机器人
rock	(n.)	batu, batu karang	shí tóu 石头, yán shí 岩石
	(v.)	mengayun-ayun, meng-goyang	yáo 摇, yáo dòng 摇动
rock.er	(n.)	kursi goyang	yáo yi 摇椅
rock.et	(n.)	roket	hǔo jiàn 火箭
rock.et.ry	(n.)	ilmu peroketan	hǔo jiàn xué 火箭学, hǔo jiàn jì shù 火箭技术
rock.y	(a.)	banyak batu	dūo shí tóu dė 多石头的, dūo yán shí dė 多岩石的
		goyang	yáo dòng dė 摇动的
rod	(n.)	cambuk, tangkai, batang	biān zi 鞭子, gàn 竿

rogue	(n.)	bajingan	liú máng 流氓
rois.ter	(v.)	gembar-gembor	dà chuī dà lèi 大吹大擂
rois.ter.er	(n.)	orang yang gembar-gembor	dà chūi dà lèi dė rén 大吹大擂的人
role	(n.)	peran, tugas	jiǎo sè 角色, rèn wù 任务
roll	(v.)	berguling-guling	gǔn 滚, gǔn dòng 滚动
		menggulung	juǎn 卷
		oleng	yáo bǎi 摇摆
	(n.)	gulung, rol, gulungan	yī juǎn 一卷
		daftar nama	míng ce 名册
		buku absen	diǎn míng bù 点名簿
roll-back	(n.)	penurunan harga barang	yā dī wù jià 压低物价
roll-call	(n.)	apel	diǎn míng 点名
rol.lick	(v.)	bersuka-ria	xǐ xì 喜戏
ro.mance	(n.)	roman	làng màn xiǎo shuō 浪漫小说
ro.man.tic	(a.)	romantis	làng màn zhǔ yǐ dė 浪漫主义的
ro.man.ti.cism	(n.)	romantisme	làng màn zhǔ yì 浪漫主义
roof	(n.)	atap	wū dǐng 屋顶
roof.ing	(n.)	pemasangan atap	gài wū dǐng 盖屋顶
room	(n.)	ruang, kamar	kōng jiān 空间, fáng jiān 房间
		kesempatan	jī hùi 机会
room.er	(n.)	penyewa rumah	fáng kè 房客
		penumpang rumah	jì sù zhě 寄宿者
room.ful	(n.)	sekamar penuh	mǎn fáng jiān 满房间
room.y	(a.)	luas, lapang	kuān chǎng 宽敞, kuān dà 宽大
roost.er	(n.)	ayam jantan	gōng jī 公鸡
root	(n.)	akar	gēn 根
rooted	(a.)	berakar	yǒu gēn dė 有根的, shēng lė gēn dė 生了根的
rope	(n.)	tali	shéng zi 绳子

rose	(n.)	bunga mawar	méi guī huā 玫瑰花
ro.se.ate	(a.)	berwarna seperti mawar	méi guī sè dė 玫瑰色的
ros.y	(a.)	berwarna merah	méi guī sè dė 玫瑰色的
rot	(v.)	membusuk	fŭ làn 腐烂
ro.ta.ry	(a.)	berputar	xuán zhuăn dė 旋转的, zhuàn dòng dė 转动的
ro.tate	(v.)	berputar	zhuàn dòng 转动, xuán zhuăn 旋转
ro.ta.tion	(n.)	putaran, perputaran, rotasi	zhuàn dòng 转动, xuán zhuăn 旋转
rot.ten	(a.)	busuk	fŭ làn dė 腐烂的
rouge	(n.)	gincu pipi, pemerah/perona muka	yān zhī 胭脂
rough	(a.)	kasar	cū 粗
roughen	(v.)	menjadikan kasar	nòng cū 弄粗, biàn cū 变粗
rough.ly	(adv.)	secara kasar	cū 粗, cū bào di 粗暴地, cū liè di 粗劣地
round	(a.)	bundar	yuán 园, yuán xíng dė 园形的
		bulat	wán zhěng dė 完整的
	(n.)	ronda	xún húi 巡回, xún luó 巡逻
		ronde	húi hé 回合
		bentuk bulat	yuán tĭ 园体, qiú xíng wù 球形物
		sekitar	zhōu wéi 周围, fàn wéi 范围
round.ly	(adv.)	dengan gesit, dengan aktif	húo pō di 活泼地, nŭ lì di 努力地
rouse	(v.)	membangkitkan	huàn xĭng 唤醒, shĭ zhèn zùo 使振作
route	(n.)	rute	lù xiàn 路线
rou.tine	(n.)	rutin	cháng wù 常务, lì xíng gōng shì 例行公事
		kebiasaan sehari-hari	cháng guī 常规
rove	(v.)	mengembara	liú làng 流浪

rov.er	(n.)	pengembara	liú làng zhě 流浪者
row	(n.)	barisan, deretan	pái 排, háng 行
row	(v.)	mendayung	hùa 划, hùa chuán 划船
row	(n.)	percekcokan, keributan	chǎo jià 吵架, sāo luàn 骚乱
roy.al	(a.)	keluarga raja	wáng shì dė 王室的
		mengenai raja	guó wáng dė 国王的
roy.al.ty	(n.)	honorarium, royalti	(gěi zuò zhě dė) gǎo fèi (给作者的) 稿费
		kedudukan/kekuasaan raja	wáng wèi 王位, wáng quán 王权
rub	(v.)	menggosok	cā 擦, mó cā 摩擦
rub.ber	(n.)	karet	xiàng pí 橡皮
		penghapus	xiàng pí cā 橡皮擦
rub.bish	(n.)	sampah, omong kosong	lā jī 垃圾, fèi huà 废话
rude	(a.)	kasar	cū lǔ dė 粗鲁的, wú lǐ 无礼
rude.ly	(adv.)	secara kasar	cū lǔ di 粗鲁地, wú lǐ di 无礼地
rude.ness	(n.)	kekasaran	cū lǔ 粗鲁, wú lǐ 无礼
rug	(n.)	permadani kecil, babut	xiǎo dì zhān 小地毡
ru.in	(n.)	kehancuran, reruntuhan	hǔi miè 毁灭, fèi xū 废墟
rule	(n.)	peraturan	guī zé 规则
		kebiasaan	guàn lì 惯例
		kekuasaan	tǒng zhì quán 统治权
rul.er	(n.)	yang memerintah	tǒng zhì zhě 统治者
		mistar	zhí chě 直尺
ru.mour	(n.)	desas-desus, kabar angin	yáo yán 谣言, fēng shēng 风声
rump	(n.)	pantat	pì gǔ 屁股
run	(v.)	lari	pǎo 跑
		mengurus, menjalankan	guǎn lǐ 管理, jīng yíng 经营
		menghidupkan	kaī dòng 开动
		mengalir	liú 流, liú dòng 流动

run.a.way	(v.)	melarikan diri	táo wáng 逃亡, táo mìng 逃命
run.ner	(n.)	pelari	sài pǎo yùn dòng yuán 赛跑运动员
run.ner-up	(n.)	nomor dua	yà jūn 亚军
run.way	(n.)	landasan kapal terbang	fēi jī pǎo dào 飞机跑道
ru.ral	(a.)	pedusunan, pedesaan	xiāng cūn dė 乡村的,
			nóng cūn dė 农村的
rush	(v.)	buru-buru, cepat-cepat	gǎn kuài 赶快
		menyerbu	chōng 冲, tū jìn 突进
		mendesak	cuī cù 催促
	(n.)	kesibukan	fán máng 繁忙
		gerakan maju yang cepat	tū jìn 突进, jí jìn 急进
		desakan, berebut maju	qiǎng xiān 抢先,
			zhēng xiān kǒng hòu 争先恐后
		berebut membeli	qiǎng goù 抢购
rusk	(n.)	roti kering	mián bāo gān 面包干
rust	(n.)	karat, tahi besi	xiù 锈
	(v.)	berkarat	shēng xiù 生锈
rus.tic	(a.)	bersuasana pedusunan	xiāng cūn dė 乡村的
		kasar	cū yě dė 粗野的
		kedusun-dusunan	xiāng xià qì 乡下气, tǔ qì 土气
rust.less	(a.)	anti karat	bù xiù dė 不锈的
rust.y	(a.)	berkarat	shēng xiù dė 生锈的

S

sab.o.tage	(n.)	sabotase	pò huài 破 坏, dǎo luàn 捣 乱
sa.bot.eur	(n.)	penyabot, perusak	pò hùai fèn zì 破 坏 分 子
sack	(n.)	karung	dài 袋
sack.ful	(n.)	sekarung penuh	mǎn 满 袋
sac.ra.ment	(n.)	sakramen	shèng lǐ 圣 礼
sa.cred	(a.)	keramat, suci	shén shèng dė 神 圣 的
sac.ri.fice	(n.)	pengorbanan, korban	xī shèng 牺 牲, jì pǐn 祭 品
sad	(a.)	sedih	bēi aī dė 悲 哀 的,
			bēi shāng dė 悲 伤 的
sad.den	(v.)	menyedihkan	fā chóu 发 愁
		membuat sedih	shǐ rén shāng xīn 使 人 伤 心
sad.dle	(n.)	pelana	ān zi 鞍 子, mǎ ān 马 鞍
sad.ness	(n.)	kesedihan	yòu chóu 忧 愁, shāng xīn 伤 心
sa.fa.ri	(n.)	safari, ekspedisi berburu	lú xíng 旅 行, chū liė 出 猎
safe	(a.)	aman	ān quán 安 全
	(n.)	peti besi	bǎo xiǎn xiāng 保 险 箱
safe.ly	(adv.)	dengan selamat	píng ān di 平 安 地
		dengan aman	ān quán di 安 全 地
safe.ty	(n.)	keselamatan, keamanan	ān quán 安 全, zhì ān 治 安
sa.ga	(n.)	saga, kisah kepahlawanan	yīng xióng gù shì 英 雄 故 事
sail	(n.)	layar, perahu layar	fān 帆, fān chuán 帆 船
	(v.)	berlayar	háng xíng 航 行
sail.boat	(n.)	perahu layar	fān chuán 帆 船
sail.cloth	(n.)	kain layar	fān bù 帆 布

sail.ing	(n.)	berlayar	háng xíng 航行, háng hǎi航海
sail.or	(n.)	pelaut	shǔi shǒu 水手, hǎi yuán 海员
saint	(n.)	orang suci	shèng rén 圣人
sake	(n.)	demi, untuk kepentingan	wèi lė 为了, qǐ jiàn 起见
sal.a.ry	(n.)	gaji	xīn jīn 薪金, xīn shǔi 薪水
sale	(n.)	penjualan	chū shòu 出售, chū mài 出卖
sales.man	(n.)	salesman,	xiāo hùo yuán 销货员,
		penjual barang-barang	tuī xiāo yuán 推销员
sa.li.va	(n.)	air liur	kǒu shǔi 口水
salm.on	(n.)	ikan salem	guī yǔ 鲑鱼
sal.on	(n.)	salon, ruangan tamu	huì kè tíng 会客厅
sa.loon	(n.)	tempat hiburan	yú lè chǎng 娱乐场
		tempat cukur	lǐ fà diàn 理发店
		tempat minum	jiǔ guǎn 酒馆
salt	(n.)	garam	yán 盐
salt.y	(a.)	asin	xián 咸
		cerdik	jī zhì dė 机智的
sa.lute	(n.)	salut, pemberian hormat	xíng lǐ 行礼, jíng lǐ 敬礼
salve	(n.)	obat salep	yào gāo 药膏
		obat penawar sakit	zhǐ tòng yào 止痛药
sal.vo	(n.)	salvo, tembakan serentak	qí shè 齐射, qí fàng 齐放
same	(a.)	sama	yī yàng dė 一样的,
			tóng yàng dė 同样的
	(pron.)	sesuatu yang sama	tóng yàng dė rén 同样的人,
			tóng yàng dė shì 同样的事
sam.ple	(n.)	contoh	yàng pǐn 样品, yàng běn 样本
san.a.tor.i.um	(n.)	sanatorium, peristirahatan	liáo yǎng yuàn 疗养院
sand	(n.)	pasir	shā 沙
sand.pa.per	(n.)	ampelas	shā zhǐ 砂纸
sar.dine	(n.)	ikan sarden	shā dīng yú 沙丁鱼

satch.el	(n.)	tas sekolah	shū bāo 书包
sat.el.lite	(n.)	satelit	wèi xīng 卫星
sat.in	(n.)	kain satin	duàn zi 缎子
sat.is.fac.tion	(n.)	kepuasan	mǎn zú 满足, mǎn yì 满意
sat.is.fy	(v.)	memuaskan	lìng rén mǎn yì 令人满意
Sat.ur.day	(n.)	hari Sabtu	xīng qī liù 星期六
sauce	(n.)	saus	jiàng yóu 酱油, diáo wèi pǐn 调味品
sau.cer	(n.)	lepek	dié zi 碟子
sau.sage	(n.)	sosis	là cháng 腊肠
sav.age	(n.)	orang biadab	yě mán rén 野蛮人
	(a.)	ganas, buas	yě mán 野蛮, xiòng è 凶恶
sav.age.ry	(n.)	kekejaman, kebuasan	cán rěn 残忍, yě mán 野蛮
sav.ant	(n.)	orang yang terpelajar,	yǒu xué wèn dė rén 有学问的人,
		cendekiawan	xúe zhě 学者, míng jiā 名家
save	(v.)	menyelamatkan	jiù 救, yíng jiù 营救
		menghemat	jié shěng 节省, jié yuè 节约
		menabung	chǔ xù 储蓄
sav.er	(n.)	penyelamat	yíng jiù zhě 营救者, jiù xīng 救星
		penghemat	jié yuè zhě 节约者
sav.ing	(n.)	pertolongan	jiù jì 救济, jiù zhù 救助
		tabungan	chǔ xù 储蓄
		penghematan	jié shěng 节省, jié yuè 节约
		uang tabungan	chǔ xù jīn 储蓄金
sa.vour	(n.)	rasa	wèi 味, wèi dào 味道
		kekhasan	fēng wèi 风味
saw	(n.)	gergaji	jù zi 锯子
	(v.)	menggergaji	jù 锯
saw-mill	(n.)	penggergajian	jù mù chǎng 锯木厂
saw.yer	(n.)	tukang gergaji	jù mù gōng rén 锯木工人
say	(v.)	mengatakan	shūo 说

say.ing	(n.)	pembicaraan, peribahasa	shūo huà 说话, yán lùn 言论
		pepatah	gé yán 格言, yàn yǔ 谚语
scale	(n.)	piring timbangan	chèng pán 秤盘
		skala	chǐ dù 尺度, bǐ lì chǐ 比例尺
		derajat	děng jí 等级, jiē jí 阶级
		sisik	lín 鳞
scan.dal	(n.)	perbuatan memalukan	chǒu shì 丑事
		skandal	chǒu wén 丑闻
scar	(n.)	bekas luka	bā 疤, shāng bā 伤疤, shāng hén 伤痕
scarce	(a.)	tidak cukup	quē fá 缺乏, bù gòu 不够
		jarang, langka	shǎo jiàn dė 少见的
		sukar didapat	nán dé dė 难得的
scarce.ly	(adv.)	hampir tidak	jī hū méi yǒu 几乎没有, jiǎn zhí bù 简直不
scarce.ness	(n.)	kelangkaan	xī shǎo 稀少
scare	(n.)	ketakutan	jīng huāng 惊慌
	(v.)	menakuti	kǒng hè 恐吓
scare.crow	(n.)	orang-orangan sawah	dào cǎo rén 稻草人
scarf	(n.)	selendang , syal	wéi jīn 围巾
scar.let	(n.)	warna merah tua	xiān hóng sė 鲜红色
scat.ter	(v.)	menaburkan	sàn bō 散播
		menghamburkan	shǐ fēn sàn 使分散
scav.en.ger	(n.)	tukang sapu jalan	qīng dào fū 清道夫
sce.na.ri.o	(n.)	skenario	diàn yǐng jù běn 电影剧本
sce.nar.ist	(n.)	penulis skenario	diàn yǐng jù zùo jiā 电影剧作家
scene	(n.)	pemandangan, dekor	fèng jǐng 风景, bù jǐng 布景
		adegan	chǎng miàn 场面
		tempat	dì diǎn 地点, xiàn chǎng 现场
scen.er.y	(n.)	pemandangan, dekor	fèng jǐng 风景, bù jǐng 布景
scent	(n.)	bau, harum	qì wèi 气味, xiāng wèi 香味
		minyak wangi	xiāng shǔi 香水

scent.less	(a.)	tak berbau	méi yōu qì wèi dė 没有气味的
sched.ule	(n.)	daftar isi	mù lù 目录
		daftar nama	míng dān 名单
		daftar rencana	jì huà biǎo 计划表
scheme	(n.)	rencana, bagan	jì huà 计划, tú biǎo 图表
		rencana kotor	yīn móu 阴谋
schem.er	(n.)	perencana, penyusun	guī huà zhě 规划者
		komplot	yīn moú jiā 阴谋家
schol.ar	(n.)	sarjana, pelajar	xué zhě 学者, xué shēng 学生
schol.ar.ship	(n.)	ilmu pengetahuan	xúe wèn 学问
		beasiswa	jiǎng xué jīn 奖学金
school	(n.)	kawanan, kelompok	qún 群
		sekolah, fakultas, akademi	xüe xiào 学校, xué yuàn 学院
school.bag	(n.)	tas sekolah	shū bāo 书包
school-book	(n.)	buku pelajaran	kè běn 课本, jiào kē shū 教科书
school.boy	(n.)	anak sekolah dasar	xiǎo xué shēng 小学生
school.fel.low	(n.)	teman sekolah	tóng xué 同学
school.house	(n.)	gedung sekolah	xiào shè 校舍
school.ing	(n.)	pendidikan	jiào yù 教育
school-leav.er	(n.)	anak lulusan sekolah	bì yè shēng 毕业生
school.mas.ter	(n.)	kepala sekolah	lǎo shī 老师, xiào zhǎng 校长
school.mate	(n.)	teman sekolah	tóng xué 同学
school.mis.tress	(n.)	guru wanita	nǚ lǎo shī 女老师
		kepala sekolah (wanita)	nǚ xiào zhǎng 女校长
school.room	(n.)	ruangan kelas	jiào shì 教室, kè táng 课堂
sci.ence	(n.)	ilmu pengetahuan	kē xué 科学
sci.en.tist	(n.)	ahli sains	kē xué jiā 科学家
scis.sor	(v.)	menggunting	jiǎn 剪
scis.sors	(n.)	gunting	jiǎn daō 剪刀
scoff	(v.)	mengejek	cháo xiào 嘲笑

scold	(v.)	mencaci maki, memarahi	mà 骂, zé mā 责骂
scoop	(n.)	sekop, ceduk	chǎn 铲, sháo zi 勺子
scoot.er	(n.)	sekuter	jī qì zì xíng chē 机器自行车
scope	(n.)	lapangan, jangkauan	chǎng suǒ 场所, yǎn jiè 眼界
		kesempatan	jī hùi 机会
		ruang lingkup	fàn wéi 范围
score	(n.)	skor	dé fēn 得分, bǐ fēn 比分
		bekas goresan, bekas luka	kè hěn 刻痕, shāng hěn 伤痕
score-book	(n.)	buku skor	jì fēn cè 积分册
scor.er	(n.)	pencatat skor	jī fēn yuán 记分员, dé fēn zhě 得分者
scorn	(n.)	cemoohan, hinaan	miǎo shì 藐视, qīng mie 轻蔑
	(v.)	memandang rendah, mencemoohkan	miǎo shì 藐视, qīng mie 轻蔑
scor.pion	(n.)	kalajengking	xiē zi 蝎子
scout	(n.)	pengintai	zhěn chá yuán 侦察员
		pandu, pramuka	tóng zi jūn 童子军
	(v.)	mengintai, menolak	zhēn chá 侦察, pái chì 排斥
		mengejek	jī xiào 讥笑
scrab.ble	(v.)	menggaruk, mencakar	zhuā 抓
		mencorat-coret	luàn tú 乱涂
scrap	(n.)	carik	sùi piàn 碎片
	(v.)	membatalkan	fèi chú 废除
scrape	(v.)	mengerik, menggores	gua 刮, xue 削
		menggosok	cā 擦
		mengumpulkan	còu 凑, còu jī 凑积
	(n.)	goresan	cā hěn 擦痕, cā shāng 擦伤
scrap.er	(n.)	alat pengerik	guā dāo 刮刀
scratch	(v.)	menggaruk, mencakar	zhuā 抓
		mencorat-coret	luàn tú 乱涂, luàn xiě 乱写

scream	(v.)	berteriak	hū hǎn 呼喊, jiào hǎn 叫喊
		menjerit	jiān jiào 尖叫
screen	(n.)	layar	mù 幕, yín mù 银幕
		tirai, gorden	bǐng fēng 屏风, lián 帘
	(v.)	melindungi	bǎo bì 保庇, bǎo hù 保护
		menyaring	zhēn bié 甄别, shěn chá 审查
screen.play	(n.)	cerita untuk film, skenario	diàn yǐng jù běn 电影剧本
screw	(n.)	sekrup	luó sī 螺丝, luó sī dīng 螺丝钉
screw-driv.er	(n.)	obeng	xuán záo 旋凿
script	(n.)	penulisan, tulisan tangan	shū xiě 书写, shǒu xiě tǐ 手写体
		naskah siaran	guǎng bō gǎo 广播稿
scrip.ture	(n.)	buku suci	shèng shū 圣书
		kitab Injil	shèng jīng 圣经
sculpt	(v.)	memahat, mengukir	diāo kè 雕刻
sculp.tor	(n.)	pemahat, ahli patung	diāo kè jiā 雕刻家
sculp.ture	(n.)	pengukiran	diāo kè 雕刻
		barang ukiran	diāo kè pǐn 雕刻品
sea	(n.)	laut	hǎi 海, hǎi yáng 海洋
sea.board	(n.)	daerah pesisir	yán hǎi dì qū 沿海地区, hǎi àn xiàn 海岸线
sea-breeze	(n.)	angin laut	hǎi fēng 海风
sea.coast	(n.)	pantai	hǎi àn 海岸, hǎi bīn 海滨
sea.far.er	(n.)	pelaut	shǔi shǒu 水手, háng hǎi zhě 航海者
sea-gull	(n.)	burung camar	hǎi ōu 海鸥
sea-horse	(n.)	kuda laut	hǎi mǎ 海马
seal	(n.)	cap	tú zhāng 图章
		segel	fēng kǒu 封口, fēng yìn 封印
		anjing laut	hǎi bào 海豹
	(v.)	mencap, menyegel	gài yìn 盖印, fēng 封, fēng bì 封闭
sea.man	(n.)	pelaut	shǔi shǒu 水手

sea.man.ship	(n.)	ilmu pelayaran	háng hǎi shù 航海术
sea.plane	(n.)	pesawat terbang laut	hǎi shàng fēi jī 海上飞机
sea.port	(n.)	bandar, pelabuhan	hǎi gǎng 海港
search	(v)	mencari, mencarikan, menggeledah	xún zhǎo 寻找, sōu chá 搜查
search.light	(n.)	lampu sorot	tàn zhào dēng 探照灯
sea.shore	(n.)	pantai	hǎi ān 海岸
sea.sick	(a.)	mabuk laut	yùn chuán 晕船
sea.side	(n.)	tepi laut	hǎi biān 海边
sea.son	(n.)	musim	jì jié 季节
sea.son.a.ble	(a.)	sesuai dengan musimnya	yìng shí dė 应时的, jí shí dė 及时的
sea.son.al	(a.)	musiman	jì jié xìng dė 季节性的
sea.son.ing	(n.)	bumbu	tiáo wèi pǐn 调味品
seat	(n.)	tempat duduk	zuò wèi 座位
	(v.)	menyediakan tempat duduk	gōng gěi zuò wèi 供给座位
sea-water	(n.)	air laut	hǎi shǔi 海水
sea.weed	(n.)	rumput laut	hǎi cǎo 海草
se.cede	(v.)	menarik diri, mengundurkan diri	tùi chū 退出
se.ced.er	(n.)	orang yang menarik diri	tùi chū zhě 退出者
sec.ond	(n.)	detik	miǎo 秒
		sebentar	piān kè 片刻
		kedua	dì èr 第二
		tanggal dua	èr hào 二号
sec.on.da.ry	(a.)	kedua	dì èr dė 第二的, cì yaò dė 次要的, fù dė 副的
sec.ond-class	(n.)	kelas dua	èr děng dė 二等的, dì èr liú dė 第二流的
sec.ond-hand	(a.)	tangan kedua	dì èr shǒu dė 第二手的, jiān jiē dė 间接的
		bekas pakai	jiù dė 旧的, yòng gùo dė 用过的

sec.ond.ly	(adv.)	yang kedua	dì èr 第二, qí cì 其次
sec.ond-rate	(a.)	yang kelas dua	èr děng dė 二等的
		rendah mutunya	dì èr liú dė 第二流的
se.cre.cy	(n.)	kerahasiaan	mì mì 秘密
se.cret	(a.)	rahasia	mì mì 秘密
sec.re.ta.ri.al	(a.)	mengenai pekerjaan sekretaris	mì shū dė 秘书的
sec.re.ta.ri.at(e)	(n.)	sekretariat, kepaniteraan	mì shū chū 秘书处, shū jì chù 书记处
sec.re.tary	(n.)	sekretaris	mì shū 秘书, shū jì 书记
se.crete	(v.)	menyembunyikan	yǐn cáng 隐藏
se.cret.ly	(adv.)	secara rahasia	mì mì dė 秘密的
sec.tion	(n.)	bagian	bù fēn 部分
sec.tor	(n.)	sektor, kawasan	fāng miàn 方面, dì qū 地区
se.cure	(a.)	aman, kukuh	ān quán dė 安全的, láo gù 牢固
	(v.)	mengamankan, menjamin	bǎo hù 保护, bǎo zhèng 保证
		mendapatkan	hùo dė 获得
se.cu.ri.ty	(n.)	keamanan	ān quán 安全
se.dan	(n.)	sedan, tandu	jiào chē 轿车, jiào zi 轿子
see	(v.)	melihat	kàn 看, kàn jiàn 看见
		mengerti, menemui	míng bǎi 明白, hùi jiàn 会见
seed	(n.)	benih	zhǒng zi 种子
seed.er	(n.)	orang yang menabur benih	bō zhǒng zhě 播种者
		alat penabur benih	bō zhǒng jī 播种机
seek	(v.)	mencari	zhǎo 找, xún zhǎo 寻找
seem	(v.)	tampaknya, rupa-rupanya	hǎo xiàng 好象, sì hū 似乎
seem.ly	(a.)	pantas, patut	qià dàng di 恰当地, shì dàng di 适当地
see.saw	(n.)	papan jungkat-jungkit	qiāo qiāo bǎn 跷跷板
seg.ment	(n.)	bagian	bù fēn 部分
seize	(v.)	menangkap, merebut	zhūo 捉, duó qǔ 夺取

sel.dom	(adv.)	jarang	hěn shǎo 很少, bù cháng 不常
se.lect	(v.)	memilih	xuǎn zé 选择
	(a.)	yang terpilih, pilihan	jīng gùo xuǎn zé dė 经过选择的, jīng xuǎn dė 精选的
se.lec.tion	(n.)	pilihan, seleksi	xuǎn zé 选择
se.lec.tive	(a.)	bersifat memilih, selektif	xuǎn zé dė 选择的
		berdasarkan pilihan	xuǎn zé xìng dė 选择性的
self	(n.)	diri, sendiri	běn shēn 本身, zì jǐ 自己, zì wǒ 自我
self-con.trol	(n.)	pengendalian diri	zì wǒ kòng zhì 自我控制
self-cul.ture	(n.)	belajar sendiri, otodidak	zì xiū 自修
self-de.fence	(n.)	pembelaan diri	zì wèi 自卫
self.ish	(a.)	egois	zì sī zì lì 自私自利
self-help	(n.)	pertolongan terhadap diri sendiri	zì zhù 自助
		berdikari	zì lì gēng shēng 自力更生
self.less	(a.)	tidak mementingkan diri sendiri	wú sī dė 无私的
self-sat.is.fied	(a.)	puas diri	zì mǎn dė 自满的
self-will	(n.)	keras kepala	rèn xìng 任性, gù zhí 固执
sell	(v.)	menjual	mài 卖
sell.er	(n.)	penjual	mài zhě 卖者
sell.out	(v.)	menjual habis	mài wán 卖完
sem.blance	(n.)	kesamaan, kemiripan	lèi sì 类似
		penampilan	wài biǎo 外表
se.men	(n.)	air mani	jīng yì 精液
se.mes.ter	(n.)	semester	xué qī 学期, bàn xué nián 半学年
sem.i-co.lon	(n.)	titik-koma	fēn hào 分号
sem.i.col.on.y	(n.)	semikoloni	bàn zhí mín dì 半殖民地
sem.i-fi.nal	(n.)	semifinal	bàn jué sài 半决赛
sem.i-fi.nal.ist	(n.)	semifinalis	bàn jué sài xuǎn shǒu 半决赛选手

sem.i.nar	(n.)	seminar	tǎo lùn hùi 讨论会
sen.ate	(n.)	senat	cān yì yuán 参议院, shàng yuàn 上院
sen.ator	(n.)	senator	cān yì yuán 参议员
send	(v.)	mengirim	jì 寄, pài 派
send.er	(n.)	pengirim	jì sòng zhě 寄送者
send-off	(n.)	mengantarkan orang yang akan bepergian	sòng xíng 送行, huān sòng 欢送
se.nior	(n.)	orang yang lebih tua, senior	nián zhǎng dė 年长的, qián bèi dė 前辈的
	(a.)	lebih tinggi tingkatnya	shàng jí dė 上级的
sen.sa.tion	(n.)	sensasi, kegemparan	hōng dòng shì jiàn 轰动事件, sǒng rén tīng wén 耸人听闻
sen.sa.tion.al	(a.)	yang menggemparkan	hōng dòng dė 轰动的
		sensasional	sǒng rén tīng wén dė 耸人听闻的
sense	(n.)	perasaan, pengertian	gǎn jué 感觉, gài niàn 概念
		panca indra	wǔ guān gǎn jué 五官感觉
sense.less	(a.)	pingsan	hūn dǎo 昏倒
		bodoh	yú bèn dė 愚笨的
		tidak berperasaan	wú gǎn júe dė 无感觉的
sen.si.bil.i.ty	(n.)	kepekaan	mǐn gǎn xìng 敏感性
		perasaan	gǎn jué 感觉
sen.si.ble	(a.)	berakal sehat	míng zhì dė 明智的
		yang dapat dirasakan	kě gǎn jué dė 可感觉的
sen.si.tive	(a.)	sensitif, peka	gùo mǐn dė 过敏的
sen.tence	(n.)	kalimat, hukuman	jù zi 句子, pàn jué 判决
sen.ti.ment	(n.)	perasaan	gǎn qíng 感情
		sentimen	gǎn qíng yòng shì 感情用事
sen.ti.men.tal	(a.)	sentimental, mengenai perasaan	gǎn qíng dė 感情的
sen.ti.nel	(n.)	pengawal	wèi bīng 卫兵

sen.try	(n.)	pengawal	wèi bīng 卫兵
sep.a.ra.ble	(a.)	yang dapat dipisahkan	kě fēn lí dė 可分离的
sep.a.rate	(v.)	memisahkan	fēn lí 分离
	(a.)	terpisah	fēn lí dė 分离的
sep.a.rate.ly	(adv.)	secara terpisah	fēn bié dė 分别的, gè bié dė 个别的
sep.a.ra.tion	(n.)	pemisahan	fēn lí 分离, fēn gé 分隔
sep.a.ra.tor	(n.)	orang yang memisahkan	fēn lí zhě 分离者
		alat pemisah	fēn lí qì 分离器
Sep.tem.ber	(n.)	September	jiǔ yuè 九月
se.quence	(n.)	rentetan	lián xù 连续
		urutan	cì xù 次序
		akibat	jié guǒ 结果
se.quent	(a.)	berikutnya	jì xù dė 继续的
		sebagai akibat	jié guǒ dė 结果的
serge	(n.)	kain kepar dari wol	bì jī 哔叽
ser.geant	(n.)	sersan	jūn shì 军士, zhōng shì 中士
se.ri.al	(a.)	serial	lián xù dė 连续的
		yang bersambung	lián zài dė 连载的
	(n.)	cerita bersambung	lián zài xiǎo shúo 连载小说
ser.ies	(n.)	seri, rentetan,	lián xù 连续, xì liè 系列,
		rangkaian	lián chuàn 连串
se.ri.ous	(a.)	serius, sungguh-sungguh	yán sù 严肃, rèn zhēn 认真
se.ri.ous.ly	(adv.)	secara serius	yán sù di 严肃地
		secara sungguh-sungguh	rèn zhēn di 认真地
se.ri.ous.ness	(n.)	kesungguhan	yán sù 严肃, rèn zhēn 认真
ser.mon	(v.)	berkhotbah	chuán dào 传道, shuō jiào 说教
	(n.)	khotbah	chuán dào 传道, shuō jiào 说教
ser.pent	(n.)	ular besar	dà shé 大蛇
ser.vant	(n.)	pelayan, bujang	yòng rén 佣人, pú rén 仆人
ser.vant.maid	(n.)	pelayan (wanita)	nǔ pú rén 女仆人

serve	(v.)	melayani, mengabdi	zhāo dài 招待, fú wù 服务
		menyediakan	gōng yìng 供应
		mulai memukul bola	kāi qiú 开球, fā qiú 发球
serv.er	(n.)	pemukul bola pertama	kāi qiú zhě 开球者, fā qiú zhě 发球者
		pelayan	fú wù yuán 服务员
		wadah makanan	shí qì 食器, cài pán 菜盘
serv.ice	(n.)	pelayanan	zhāo dài 招待, fú wù 服务
		dinas	fú yì 服役
		pukulan bola pertama	kāi qiú 开球, fā qiú 发球
		peralatan makan	shí qì 食器, cān jú 餐具
	(v.)	memperbaiki	xiū lǐ 修理
serv.ice.a.ble	(a.)	berguna	yǒu yòng dė 有用的
serv.ice.man	(n.)	angkatan bersenjata	jūn rén 军人, wǔ zhuāng rén yuán 武装人员
		tukang reparasi	xiū lǐ yuán 修理员
ses.sion	(n.)	sidang	huì yì 会议, kāi tíng 开庭
set	(v.)	meletakkan, menempatkan	fàng 放
		memasang	zhuāng zhì 装置
		terbenam	lùo 落, chén lùo 沉落
	(n.)	setelan, kumpulan	tào 套, zǔ 组
		perlengkapan	yòng jù 用具
set-back	(n.)	kemunduran	tùi bù 退步
		mengalami kegagalan	cuò zhé 挫折
set.tle	(v.)	menetap	dìng jū 定居
		menyelesaikan	jiě jué 解决, tiáo tíng 调停
		membereskan	zhěng dùn 整顿, ān pái 安排
		turun, menurun	chén 沈, chén xià 沈下
set.tle.ment	(n.)	penyelesaian	jiě jué 解决
		perkampungan	zhù jiā qū 住家区
sev.en	(n.)	tujuh	qī 七

sev.en.teen	(n.)	tujuh belas	shí qī 十七
sev.enth	(n.)	ketujuh	dì qī 第十七
		tanggal tujuh	qī hào 七号
sev.en.ti.eth	(n.)	ketujuh puluh	dì qī shí 第七十
		sepertujuh puluh	qī shí fēn zhī yī 七十分之一
sev.en.ty	(n.)	tujuh puluh	qī shí 七十
sev.er.al	(a.)	beberapa	jǐ gè 几个, ruò gān 若干
sev.er.al.ly	(adv.)	sendiri-sendiri	gè zì 各自
		secara terpisah	fēn bié di 分别地
se.vere	(a.)	keras	yán lì 严厉, yán zhòng 严重
		sederhana	pǔ sù 朴素
se.vere.ly	(adv.)	dengan keras	yán lì dı 严厉的, yán zhòng di 严重的, yán sù di 严肃的, yán gé di 严格的
sew	(v.)	menjahit	féng 缝, féng rèn 缝纫
sew.er	(n.)	tukang jahit	féng yī gōng rén 缝衣工人, féng yi jiàng 缝衣匠
sew.ing	(n.)	jahit-menjahit	féng rèn 缝纫, zhēn xiàn húo 针线活
sex	(n.)	kelamin, jenis kelamin	xìng 性, xìng bié 性别
sex.u.al	(a.)	seksual	xìng 性, liàng xìng dė 两性的
shab.by	(a.)	jorok, jembel	lán lǚ dė 褴褛的, pò làn dė 破烂的
		hina	bēi bǐ 卑鄙
shack	(n.)	gubuk	péng fáng 棚房
shack.le	(n.)	belenggu	liào kào 镣铐
shade	(n.)	tempat teduh, naungan	yìn 荫, yìn liáng chù 阴凉处
		tirai	màn 幔, péng 蓬
	(v.)	menaungi, melindungi	zhē bì 遮蔽
shad.ow	(n.)	bayangan	yǐng zi 影子
		(jumlah) sedikit	yī diǎn 一点
	(v.)	menaungi	zhē bì 遮蔽
		membayangi, membuntuti	gēn sǔi 跟随

shad.ow.y	(a.)	rindang	yīn sēn sēn dė 阴森森的,
			dūo yǐng dė 多影的
shad.y	(a.)	teduh, rindang	yìn liáng dė 荫凉的
		curang	bù lǎo shí dė 不老实的
shake	(v.)	bergoyang, menggoyang	yáo 摇, yáo dòng 摇动
		mengocok	jiǎo dòng 搅动
		gemetar	fā dǒu 发抖
shak.er	(n.)	orang yang mengocok	yáo dòng zhě 摇动者
		alat pengocok	yáo dòng qì 摇动器
shall	(v.)	akan, dapat	jiāng 将, hùi 会
shal.low	(a.)	dangkal	qiǎn 浅
shame	(n.)	malu	xiū chí 羞耻, cán kùi 惭愧
shame.ful	(a.)	memalukan	kě chí dė 可耻的, diū liǎn dė 丢脸的
shame.less	(a.)	tak tahu malu	wú chí dė 无耻的, bù yào liǎn 不要脸
sham.poo	(n.)	shampo	xǐ fà shǔi 洗发水
	(v.)	mencuci rambut	xǐ fà 洗发, xǐ tóu fà 洗头发
shape	(n.)	bentuk	yàng zi 样子, xíng zhuàng 形状
		keadaan	qíng kuàng 情况, zhuàng tài 状态
	(v.)	membentuk	zào xíng 造形, sù zào 塑造
shape.less	(a.)	tak berbentuk	wú xíng dė 无形的,
			bù chéng yàng zi 不成样子
shape.ly	(a.)	berbentuk indah	yàng zi hǎo dė 样子好的,
			xiàng yàng dė 象样的
share	(n.)	bagian, andil, saham	fèn èr 份儿, gǔ fèn 股份
	(v.)	membagi	fēn pèi 分配
		sama-sama menanggung	fēn dàn 分担
		sama-sama memakai	fēn xiǎng 分享
share.hold.er	(n.)	pemegang saham	gǔ dōng 股东
shark	(n.)	ikan hiu	shā yú 鲨鱼
		penipu	piàn zi 骗子

sharp	(a.)	tajam, runcing	jiān rùi 尖锐, rùi lì 锐利
		cerdik	líng mǐn 灵敏, mǐn rùi 敏锐
		cekatan, gesit	mǐn jiè 敏捷, húo pō 活泼
		jelas	míng xiǎn 明显, xiǎn míng 显明
		pedas	kè pó 刻薄, jiān suān 尖酸
		hebat, seru	qiáng liè 强烈, jù liè 剧烈
	(adv.)	tepat	zhèng 正, zhǔn shí di 准时地
		cepat, segera	gǎn kuài 赶快
		mendadak	tū rán 突然
sharp.en	(v.)	meruncingkan, mengasah	xuē jiān 削尖, shǐ jiān rùi 使尖锐, mó lì 磨利
sharp.en.er	(n.)	alat pengasah	xūe dāo 削刀, mò chuáng 磨床
sharp.ly	(adv.)	dengan tajam	jiān rùi di 尖锐地, kè bó di 刻薄地
sharp.ness	(n.)	ketajaman	jiān rùi 尖锐
sharp.shoot.er	(n.)	jago tembak	shén qiāng shǒu 神枪手
shat.ter	(v.)	menghancurkan	zá suì 砸碎
shave	(n.)	mencukur	tì 剃, guā 刮
shav.ing	(n.)	cukur (kumis)	tì xū 剃须
she	(pron.)	ia, dia (untuk perempuan)	tā 她
shear	(v.)	mencukur (bulu domba)	jiǎn (yáng máo) 剪 (羊毛)
		memotong (bulu)	jiǎn ... máo 剪…毛
shears	(n.)	gunting besar	dà jiǎn dāo 大剪刀
shed	(n.)	bangsal	péng 棚
	(v.)	bercucuran	liú 流, liú chū 流出
		mencucurkan	shǐ liú chū 使流出
		memancarkan	fàng shè 放射, sàn fā 散发
		melepaskan, terlepas	tūo lùo 脱落
sheep	(n.)	domba	yáng 羊, mián yáng 绵羊
sheep.cote	(n.)	kandang domba	yáng shè 羊舍, yáng péng 羊棚
sheep.skin	(n.)	kulit domba	yáng pí 羊皮

sheet	(n.)	seprei, alas tilam	bèi dān 被单
		helai, lembar	zhāng 张
shelf	(n.)	rak	jià zi 架子
shell	(n.)	kulit keras, kulit kerang	ké 壳, bèi ké 贝壳
shell.fish	(n.)	kerang-kerangan	bèi 贝
shel.ter	(n.)	tempat perlindungan	dǔo bì chù 躲避处, bì nàn sǔo 避难所
	(v.)	bersembunyi	dǔo bì 躲避
shep.herd	(n.)	gembala	mù mín 牧民, mù yáng zhě 牧羊者
shield	(n.)	perisai	dùn pái 盾牌
shil.ling	(n.)	mata uang Inggris	xiān lìng 先令
shine	(v.)	bersinar, memancarkan sinar	fā guāng 发光, fàng guāng 放光
		menyemir	cā liàng 擦亮
	(n.)	kilauan	guāng zé 光泽
shin.ing	(a.)	bersinar	fā guāng dė 发光的
		terkemuka	zuō yuè dė 卓越的, jié chū dė 杰出的
ship	(n.)	kapal	chuán 船
ship.ment	(n.)	kapal barang	hùo chuán 货船
		pengangkutan barang	zhuāng hùo 装货, zhuāng yùn 装运
ship.own.er	(n.)	pemilik kapal	chuán zhǔ 船主
ship.per	(n.)	pengirim, pengangkut	yùn hùo rén 运货人
ship.ping	(n.)	perkapalan	chuán bó 船舶, hǎi yùn 海运
ship.wreck	(n.)	kecelakaan kapal	chuán zhī shī shī 船只失事
ship.wright	(n.)	pekerja pembuatan kapal	zào chuán gōng rén 造船工人
ship.yard	(n.)	galangan kapal	zào chuán cháng 造船厂, chuán wù 船坞
shirt	(n.)	kemeja	chèn shān 衬衫
shiv.er	(n.)	kepingan	sùi piàn 碎片, sùi kuài 碎快
		getaran, gigil	fā dǒu 发抖
	(v.)	menghancurkan	dǎ sùi 打碎
		menggigil, gemetar	fā dǒu 发抖

shock	(n.)	syok, goncangan	dǎ jī 打击, zhèn dòng 震动
	(v.)	mengejutkan	shǐ zhèn dòng 使震动
		menggoncangkan	shǐ zhèn jīng 使震惊,
			shòu dǎ jī 受打击
shoe	(n.)	sepatu	xié zi 鞋子
shoe.black	(n.)	tukang semir sepatu	cā xié gōng rén 擦鞋工人
shoe.black.ing	(n.)	semir sepatu	pí xié yóu 皮鞋油
shoe-lace	(n.)	tali sepatu	xié dài 鞋带
shoe-string	(n.)	tali sepatu	xié dài 鞋带
shoot	(v.)	menembak, melepaskan	shè jī 射击, fā shè 发射
		bertunas	fā yá 发芽
		membuat film	pò shè diàn yǐng 拍摄电影
		(harga barang) melonjak	(wù jià) bào zhǎng (物价)暴涨
	(n.)	tunas, pucuk	yá 芽, miáo 苗, nèn zhi 嫩枝
shoot.er	(n.)	penembak	shè shǒu 射手
shoot.ing	(n.)	penembakan	shè jǐ 射击
		berburu	shòu liè 狩猎, dǎ liè 打猎
		pembuatan film	pò shè diǎn yǐng 拍摄电影
		tempat berburu	shòu liè chǎng 狩猎场
		tempat latihan menembak	shè jī chǎng 射击场
		penembakan bola ke gawang	shè mén 射门
		penembakan bola basket ke keranjang	tóu lán 投蓝
shop	(n.)	toko	diàn 店, shāng diàn 商店
		bengkel	chē jiān 车间, gōng chǎng 工场
		perusahaan	yíng yè 营业
shop-girl	(n.)	wanita pelayan toko	nǔ diàn yuán 女店员
		pramuniaga	nǔ yíng yè yuán 女营业员
shop.keep.er	(n.)	pemilik toko	diàn zhǔ 店主
shop-lift.er	(n.)	pencopet toko	diàn pù pá shǒu 店铺扒手

shop.per	(n.)	pembeli di toko	shāng diàn gù kè 商店顾客
shop.ping	(n.)	berbelanja	gòu wù 购物, mǎi dōng zī 买东西
shop-win.dow	(n.)	etalase toko	chú chuāng 橱窗
shore	(n.)	pantai	hǎi bīn 海滨, hǎi biān 海边
short	(a.)	pendek	duǎn 短, ǎi 矮
		singkat	jiǎn duǎn 简短, jiǎn luè 简略
		tidak cukup	bù gòu dė 不够的
	(n.)	bunyi pendek	duǎn yīn 短音
		singkatan	jiǎn luè 简略
short.age	(n.)	kekurangan	quē shǎo 缺少, bù gòu 不够
short.com.ing	(n.)	kekurangan, kelemahan	quē diǎn 缺点, rùo diǎn 弱点
short.en	(v.)	memendekkan, memper-pendek	nòng duǎn 弄短, sù duǎn 缩短
short.hand	(n.)	tulisan cepat, steno	sù xiě 速写
short.hand.ed	(a.)	kekurangan tenaga, keku-rangan pembantu	quē shǎo rén shǒu 缺少人手
short-lived	(a.)	berumur pendek	duǎn mìng dė 短命的
		tidak lama	zàn shí dė 暂时的, bù jiǔ dė 不久的
short.ly	(adv.)	segera, tak lama	lì kè 立刻, bù jiǔ 不久
short.ness	(n.)	kependekan	duǎn 短, ǎi 矮
		kekurangan	duǎn shǎo 短少
		kesingkatan	jiǎn duǎn 简短
shorts	(n.)	celana pendek	duǎn kù 短裤
short-sight.ed	(a.)	mata dekat	jìn shì yǎn dė 近视眼的
		yang berpandangan dangkal	yǎn guāng qiǎn dė 眼光浅的
short-term	(n.)	jangka pendek	duǎn qī 短期
shot	(n.)	tembakan	shè jī 射击, kaī qiāng 开枪
		penembak	qiāng shǒu 枪手
		lemparan bola basket ke keranjang	tóu lán 投蓝
		pemotretan	shè yǐng 摄影, paī shè 拍摄

shot.gun	(n.)	senapan berburu	liè qiāng 猎枪
should	(v.)	harus	yīng gài 应该
shoul.der	(n.)	bahu, pundak	jiān 肩
	(v.)	memikul	fù dàn 负担
shout	(v.)	meneriakkan, berteriak	hū hǎn 呼喊, hǎn jiào 喊叫
	(n.)	teriak, teriakan	hū hǎn 呼喊, jiào shēng 叫声
shove	(v.)	mendorong	tuī 推
shov.el	(n.)	sekop	chǎn 铲
show	(v.)	memperlihatkan	zhǎn shì 展示, xiǎn shì 显示
		mempertunjukkan	zhǎn chū 展出, yǎn chū 演出
		menuntun	yǐn dǎo 引导, dài lǐng 带领
		muncul	lù miàn 露面, chū xiàn 出现
		menunjukkan	zhǐ chū 指出, zhǐ shì 指示
	(n.)	pameran	zhǎn lǎn 展览, zhǎn lǎn hùi 展览会
		pertunjukan	biǎo yǎn 表演, yǎn chū 演出
		bioskop	diàn yǐng 电影
show-case	(n.)	lemari kaca, etalase	chú chuāng 橱窗, chén liè chú 陈列橱
show.er	(n.)	hujan lebat, hujan sebentar	bào yǔ 暴雨, zhèn yǔ 阵雨
		orang yang memberi pe-tunjuk	zhǐ shì yuán 指示员
		alat penunjuk	zhǐ shì qì 指示器
show-room	(n.)	ruang pameran	chén liè shì 陈列室, zhǎn lǎn shì 展览室
show-win.dow	(n.)	etalase	chú chuāng 橱窗
shriek	(v.)	menjerit, memekik	jiān jiào 尖叫
shrink	(v.)	mengerut, takut akan	shōu sù 收缩, wèi sù 畏缩
shut	(v.)	menutup	guān 关
shut-down	(n.)	penutupan pabrik	gōng chǎng tíng gōng 工厂停工, guān bì 关闭
shut.ter	(n.)	daun jendela	bǎi yè chuāng 百叶窗
shut.tle-cock	(n.)	bola bulu tangkis, kok	yǔ máo qiú 羽毛球

shy	(a.)	malu	hài xiǔ 害羞, pà xiū 怕羞
shy.ly	(adv.)	dengan malu-malu	hài xiū dė 害羞的
shy.ness	(n.)	perasaan malu	hài xiū 害羞
sick	(a.)	sakit	shēng bìng 生病
		memuakkan	yào ǒu 要呕, xiǎng ǒu 想呕
		rindu	kě wàng dė 渴望的, xiǎng niàn dė 想念的
		jemu, bosan	yàn juàn 厌倦, yàn wù 厌恶
sick.en	(v.)	jatuh sakit	shēng bìng 生病
		memualkan	lìng rén zùo ǒu 令人作呕
		membosankan	lìng rén yàn juàn 令人厌倦
sick.le	(n.)	arit	lián dāo 镰刀
sick-list	(n.)	daftar orang sakit	bìng rén míng dān 病人名单
sick.ly	(a.)	sakit-sakitan	duō bìng dė 多病的
sick.ness	(n.)	penyakit	jí bìng 疾病
		mual, mabuk udara	oǔ tù 呕吐
side	(n.)	sisi, samping	biān 边, páng biān 旁边, shēn páng 身旁
		pihak	fāng miàn 方面
side-board	(n.)	bufet	shí qì guì 食器柜
side.walk	(n.)	trotoar	rén xíng dào 人行道
siege	(n.)	pengepungan	bāo wéi 包围
si.es.ta	(n.)	tidur siang	wǔ shùi 午睡
sieve	(n.)	ayakan	shaī zi 筛子
sift	(v.)	mengayak	shaī 筛
		menyelidiki, menyaring	xì chá 细查
sigh	(n.)	keluh, napas panjang	tàn shēng 叹声, tàn xī 叹息
	(v.)	menarik napas panjang, mengeluh	tàn qì 叹气, tàn xī 叹息
sight	(n.)	penglihatan	shì lì 视力, shì jué 视觉
		pemandangan	jǐng sè 景色, fēng jǐng 风景

sight.less	(a.)	buta	máng mù dė 盲目的
sight.seeing	(n.)	bertamasya, cuci mata	yóu lǎn 游览, guān guāng 观光
sight.seer	(n.)	pelancong	yóu kè 游客
sign	(n.)	tanda	jì hào 记号, fú hào 符号
		pertanda	yù zhào 预兆, zhēng zhào 征兆
		gelagat	jī xiàng 迹象
	(v.)	menandatangani	qiān zi 签字
		memberi isyarat	dǎ xìn hào 打信号, zùo shǒu shì 作手势
sig.nal	(n.)	tanda, sinyal	xìn hào 信号
	(v.)	memberi tanda	fā xìn hào 发信号
		memberi isyarat	dǎ xìn hào 打信号
sig.nal.ize	(v.)	menonjolkan	shǐ xiǎn zhù 使显著, shǐ tū chū 使突出
sig.nal.ly	(adv.)	secara menonjol, secara mencolok	xiǎn zhù di 显著地
sig.nal.man	(n.)	orang yang memberikan tanda	xìn hào yuán 信号员
sig.na.to.ry	(n.)	orang yang menanda-tangani	qiān zì rén 签字人
sig.na.ture	(n.)	tanda tangan	qiān zì 签字, qiān míng 签名
sign.board	(n.)	papan nama usaha, papan iklan	zhāo pái 招牌
sig.net	(n.)	cap, stempel	tú zhāng 图章
sig.nif.i.cance	(n.)	arti	yì yì 意义, hán yì 含义
		arti penting	yì yì zhòng dà 意义重大
sig.nif.i.cant	(a.)	berarti	yǒu yì yì dė 有意义的
		berarti penting	yì yì zhòng dà dė 意义重大的
sig.ni.fi.ca.tion	(n.)	arti, arti kata	yì sī 意思, cí yì 词意
		pengertian	tōng yì 通义
sig.ni.fy	(v.)	menandakan, berarti	biǎo shì 表示, yǒu yì yì 有意义

sign.post	(n.)	papan penunjuk jalan	lù biāo 路标
si.lence	(n.)	kesunyian	jì jíng 寂静, sù jìng 肃静
		keadaan hening, diam	chén mò 沈默, ān jìng 安静
	(v.)	mendiamkan	shǐ ān jìng 使安静, shǐ chén mò 使沈默
si.lent	(a.)	diam, sunyi	chén mò dė 沈默的, wú shēng dė 无声的, jì jìng dė 寂静的
si.lent.ly	(adv.)	dengan diam	jìng jìng di 静静地, chén mò di 沈默地
silk	(n.)	sutra	sī 丝, chóu duàn 绸缎
silk.worm	(n.)	ulat sutra	cán 蚕
sil.ly	(a.)	tolol, pandir	shă 傻, hú tú 胡涂
sil.ver	(n.)	perak, uang perak	yín 银, yín bì 银币
		barang-barang yang dibuat dari perak	yín qì 银器
sil.ver.smith	(n.)	pembuat barang-barang perak	yín qì gōng rén 银器工人
sil.ver.ware	(n.)	barang-barang perak	yín qì 银器
		alat-alat makan	cān jù 餐具
sim.i.lar	(a.)	serupa, mirip, sama	lèi sì 类似, xiāng xiāng 相像, tóng yàng dė 同样的
sim.i.lar.i.ty	(n.)	kesamaan, kemiripan	tóng yàng 同样, lèi sì 类似
sim.i.lar.ly	(adv.)	demikian pula, sama	tóng yàng di 同样地, tóng yàng 同样
sim.ple	(a.)	sederhana, mudah	jiăn dān 简单, jiăn yì 简易
sim.plic.i.ty	(n.)	kesederhanaan	jiăn dān 简单, jiăn yì 简易
sim.pli.fi.ca.tion	(n.)	penyederhanaan	jiăn dān huà 简单化
sim.pli.fy	(v.)	menyederhanakan	shǐ jiăn dān huà 使简单化
sim.ply	(adv.)	dengan sederhana	jiăn dān di 简单地
		dengan mudah	jiăn yì di 简易地

sim.u.late	(v.)	pura-pura, meniru	jiǎ zhuāng 假装, mó fǎng 模仿
sin	(n.)	dosa	zùi è 罪恶, zùi gùo 罪过
	(v.)	berdosa	fàn zùi 犯罪
since	(prep.)	sejak, semenjak	zì cóng 自从
	(adv.)	sejak itu	hòu lái 后来, yǐ hòu 以后
	(conj.)	sejak	... yǐ lái … 以来, zì ... yǐ lái 自…以来, zì ... yǐ hòu 自…以后
		karena	yīn wèi 因为
sin.cere	(a.)	jujur, tulus	zhēn chéng 真诚, chéng kěn 诚恳
sin.cere.ly	(adv.)	dengan jujur	zhēn chéng di 真诚地
		dengan tulus	chéng kěn di 诚恳地
sin.ful	(a.)	penuh dosa	zùi è shēn zhòng dė 罪恶深重的
sing	(v.)	bernyanyi	chàng gé 唱歌
singe	(v.)	membakar, menghangus-kan, menggosongkan	shāo 烧, shāo jiāo 烧焦
sing.er	(n.)	penyanyi	gē shǒu 歌手, gē chàng jiā 歌唱家
sing.ing	(n.)	nyanyian	chàng gē 唱歌
sin.gle	(a.)	satu, satu-satu	dān yī 单一, gè bié dė 个别的
		bujangan, lajang	dān shēn dė 单身的
	(n.)	pertandingan tunggal	dān dǎ bǐ sài 单打比赛
sin.glet	(n.)	kaus dalam, baju dalam	bèi xīn 背心, chèn yī 衬衣
sin.gly	(adv.)	satu demi satu	dān dú di 单独地, gė zi di 各自地
sing.song	(n.)	lagu dan irama yang sama, suara datar	dān diào 单调
	(a.)	menjemukan	dān diào dė 单调的, bù jīng cái dė 不精采的
sin.gu.lar	(a.)	aneh, ajaib	qí miào dė 奇妙的
		tunggal	dān shù dė 单数的
	(n.)	bentuk tunggal	dān shù xíng shì 单数形式

sin.is.ter	(a.)	pertanda buruk	bù jí lì 不吉利
		jahat	yīn xiǎn 阴险, xié è 邪恶
sink	(v.)	tenggelam	chén 沈, chén mò 沈没
		menenggelamkan	shǐ chén mò 使沈没, dǎ chén 打沈
		merosot	xià jiàng 下降, jiàng dī 降低
		menghilang	xiāo chén 消沈
sir	(n.)	tuan, gelar bangsawan	xiān shēng 先生, jué shì 爵士
sis.ter	(n.)	saudara perempuan	jiě mèi 姐妹
elder sister	(n.)	kakak perempuan	jiě jiè 姐姐
younger sister	(n.)	adik perempuan	mèi mėi 妹妹
sis.ter.hood	(n.)	persaudaraan	jiě mèi guān xì 姐妹关系
sister-in-law	(n.)	kakak/adik ipar perempuan	xiǎo gū 小姑, xiǎo yí 小姨, sǎo sǎo 嫂嫂, dì xí 弟媳
sit	(v.)	duduk	zùo 坐
site	(n.)	tempat, situs	chǎng sǔo 场所
sit.u.a.tion	(n.)	letak, kedudukan, keadaan	wèi zhì 位置, xíng shì 形势
six	(n.)	enam	liù 六
six.fold	(a.)	enam kali lipat	liù bèi 六倍
six.teen	(n.)	enam belas	shí liù 十六
six.teenth	(n.)	keenam belas	dì shí liù 第十六
sixth	(n.)	keenam, tanggal enam	dì liù 第六, liù hào 六号
six.ti.eth	(n.)	keenam puluh	dì liù shí 第六十
		seperenam puluh	liù shí fēn zhī yī 六十分之一
six.ty	(n.)	enam puluh	liù shí 六十
siz.a.ble	(a.)	cukup besar	xiāng dàng dà 相当大
size	(n.)	ukuran, besarnya	chǐ cùn 尺寸, dà xiǎo 大小
skate	(v.)	bermain sepatu luncur	huá bīng 滑冰
	(n.)	sepatu luncur	bīng xié 冰鞋
skat.er	(n.)	pemain sepatu luncur	huá bīng zhě 滑冰者
skat.ing	(n.)	permainan sepatu luncur	huá bīng 滑冰, liū bīng 溜冰

skel.e.ton	(n.)	kerangka	gǔ gé 骨骼
sketch	(n.)	sketsa	sù xiě 速写, sù miaó 素描, cǎo tú 草图
		uraian singkat	gai yào 概要
	(v.)	membuat sketsa	sù xiě 速写, cǎo nǐ 草拟,
			shè jì tú àn 设计图案
ski	(n.)	ski	xuě qiào 雪橇, huá xuě jī 滑雪屐
	(v.)	main ski	huá xuě 滑雪
skill	(n.)	kecakapan, keterampilan	jì néng 技能, jì qiǎo 技巧
skill.ful	(a.)	mahir, ahli	shú liàn dė 熟练的
skin	(n.)	kulit	pí 皮, pí fū 皮肤
	(v.)	menguliti, mengupas kulit	bō 剥, bō pí 剥皮
skin-deep	(a.)	dangkal	fū qiǎn 肤浅
skin.ny	(a.)	kurus sekali	hěn shòu 很瘦
		tinggal kulit pembalut tu-lang	pí bāo gǔ 皮包骨
skip	(v.)	melompat	tiào yùe 跳跃, bèng tiào 蹦跳
skirt	(n.)	rok	qún zi 裙子
skull	(n.)	tengkorak	tóu gài gǔ 头盖骨
sky	(n.)	langit	tiān 天, tiān kōng 天空
sky-blue	(a.)	biru langit	tiān lán sè 天蓝色
sky.lark	(n.)	sejenis burung	yún què 云雀
sky.light	(n.)	atap kaca	tiān chuāng 天窗
sky.scrap.er	(n.)	pencakar langit	mó tiān lóu 摩天楼
slack	(a.)	kendur	sōng xiè 松懈
		lamban	lǎn sàn 懒散, huǎn màn 缓慢
	(v.)	mengendurkan	fàng sōng 放松
		memperlambat	fàng màn 放慢
		bermalas-malas	tōu lǎn 偷懒
	(n.)	bagian yang kendur	sōng xiè bù fēn 松懈部分
slack.er	(n.)	pemalas	lǎn hàn 懒汉

slan.der	(n.)	fitnah	fěi bàng 诽谤, wū mie 诬蔑
	(v.)	memfitnah	fěi bàng 诽谤, wū mie 诬蔑
slang	(n.)	ucapan populer	lǐ yǔ 俚语
slap	(v.)	menampar	guāi 掴, dǎ ěr guāng 打耳光
slate	(n.)	batu tulis	shí bǎn 石板
slate-pencil	(n.)	gerip	shí bi 石笔
slaugh.ter	(n.)	penyembelihan	tú zǎi 屠宰
		pembantaian	tú shā 屠杀
	(v.)	menyembelih	tú zǎi 屠宰
		membantai	tú shā 屠杀
slaugh.ter-house	(n.)	rumah pemotongan hewan, penjagalan	tú zǎi chǎng 屠宰场, tú chǎng 屠场
slave	(n.)	budak	nú lì 努力
slay	(v.)	membunuh	shā hài 杀害, shā sǐ 杀死
slay.er	(n.)	pembunuh	sā rén zhě 杀人者, xiōng shǒu 凶手
sleep	(n.)	tidur	shùi mián 睡眠, shùi jiào 睡觉
	(v.)	tidur	shùi jiào 睡觉
sleep.er	(n.)	orang yang tidur	shùi mián zhě 睡眠者
		gerbong tidur	qǐn chē 寝车, wò chē 卧车
		bantalan rel	zhěn mù 枕木
sleep.ing	(n.)	tidur	shùi jiào 睡觉
sleep.less	(a.)	tak dapat tidur	shī mián 失眠
sleep.y	(a.)	mengantuk	dǎ kē shùi 打瞌睡
sleeve	(n.)	lengan baju	xiù zi 袖子
sleeve.less	(a.)	tidak berlengan	wú xìu dė 无袖的
sleigh	(n.)	pengeretan, kereta salju	xǔe qiào 雪橇, xǔe chē 雪车
slen.der	(a.)	langsing, ramping	xì cháng 细长, miáo tiáo 苗条
slice	(n.)	kerat, potong, iris	piàn 片, bó piàn 薄片, qiē piàn 切片
		bagian	fèn 份, bù fēn 部份
slick	(a.)	licin	guāng huá 光滑
		licik, curang	yuán huá 园滑, bù chéng kěn 不诚恳

		cerdik	cóng míng 聪明
		cekatan	líng húo 灵活
slide	(v.)	meluncur, meluncurkan	huá 滑, huá dòng 滑动
		menyelipkan	shǐ huá jìn 使滑进, shǐ liū jìn 使溜进
	(n.)	film slide	húo dòng piàn 活动片, huàn dēng piàn 幻灯片
		kaca mikroskop	xiǎn wēi jìng bō lí piàn 显微镜玻璃片
		tempat meluncur	huá bǎn 滑板, huá lù 滑路
slide-rule	(n.)	mistar hitung	jì suàn chǐ 计算尺
slight	(a.)	enteng	qīng weī 轻微
		sedikit	yī diǎn 一点, xì weī 细微
		kurus kecil	shòu rùo 瘦弱, shòu xiǎo 瘦小
	(v.)	mengabaikan	hū shì 忽视, miǎo shì 藐视
		menganggap enteng	qīng miè 轻蔑
	(n.)	sikap yang meremehkan	qīng miè 轻蔑
slight.ly	(adv.)	sedikit	qīng weī di 轻微地
		agak	shāo weī 稍微
slim	(a.)	ramping, langsing	xì cháng 细长, miáo tiáo 苗条
		lemah	shuāi ruò 衰弱
		sedikit sekali	xī shǎo 稀少
		tipis	weī bó 微薄
		licin, licik	jiǎo húa 狡猾
slip	(v.)	tergelincir, terpeleset	huáo jiāo 滑跤, huá dǎo 滑倒
		keliru	gǎo cùo 搞错
		melorot	huá tuō 滑脱
		menyelinap pergi	liū zǒu 溜走, liū chū qù 溜出去
		melepaskan	fàng zòu 放走, fàng gùo 放过
		memasukkan	sè rù 塞入, fàng jìn 放进
	(n.)	jatuh tergelincir	huá jiāo 滑跤, huá dǎo 滑倒
		kekhilafan, kekeliruan	cùo wù 错误
		secarik kertas	zhǐ tiáo 纸条

		rok dalam	dǐ qún 底裙, nǔ chèn yī 女衬衣, nèi qún 内裙
		sarung, sarung bantal	taò 套, zhěn tóu taò 枕头套
		cangkokan	chā zhī 插枝, jiē zhī 接枝
slip.per	(n.)	sandal	tuō xié 拖鞋
slo.gan	(n.)	semboyan, slogan	kǒu hào 口号
slope	(n.)	lereng	xié pō 斜坡
	(v.)	melereng	qīng xié 倾斜
		memiringkan	shǐ qīng xié 使倾斜
slow	(a.)	pelan, lambat	màn 慢
		lamban, tumpul	chí dùn 迟钝
	(adv.)	lambat, pelan-pelan	màn 慢, màn màn di 慢慢地
	(v.)	memperlambat	fàng màn 放慢, jiǎn sù 减速
slow.ly	(adv.)	pelan-pelan	màn 慢, màn màn di 慢慢地
sly	(a.)	licik	jiǎo huá 狡猾
small	(a.)	kecil	xiǎo 小
small.pox	(n.)	cacar	tiān huā 天花
smart	(a.)	hebat, lihai	lì hài 厉害
		seru	jù liè 剧烈
		cerdas, cerdik	líng lī 伶利, mǐn jié 敏捷
		tampan, cantik	piào liàng 漂亮
	(v.)	merasa sakit sekali	jù tòng 剧痛
		merasa sedih sekali	beī tòng 悲痛
	(n.)	sangat kesakitan	jù tòng 剧痛
		sangat sedih	beī tòng 悲痛
smash	(v.)	menghancurkan	dǎ sùi 打碎
		menabrak dengan keras	měng zhuàng 猛撞
		smes	měng kòu 猛扣
		remuk redam, hancur	wǎ jiě 瓦解, fěn sùi 粉碎
smash.er	(n.)	pemecah, penghancur	dǎ suì zhé 打碎者

smear	(n.)	noda, fitnah	wū diǎn 污点, fěi bàng 诽谤
	(v.)	menodai, mengotori	diàn wū 玷污, nòng zāng 弄脏
		memfitnah	fěi bàng 诽谤
smell	(n.)	bau, indra penciuman	qì wèi 气味, xiù jué 嗅觉
	(v.)	mencium, berbau	xiù 嗅, fā chū qì wèi 发出气味, fā chòu 发臭
smile	(v.)	tersenyum	weī xiào 微笑
	(n.)	senyuman	weī xiào 微笑, xiào róng 笑容
smith	(n.)	tukang besi	tiě gōng 铁工, tiě jiàng 铁匠
smog	(n.)	kabut campur asap	yān wù 烟雾
smoke	(n.)	asap	yān 烟
	(v.)	berasap	mào yān 冒烟
		merokok	chōu yān 抽烟, xī yān 吸烟
smok.er	(n,)	perokok	xī yān zhě 吸烟者
smok.ing	(n.)	merokok, berasap	xī yān 吸烟, mào yān 冒烟
smooth	(a.)	halus, licin	guāng huá 光滑, píng huá 平滑
		lancar	shùn lì 顺利, píng wěn 平稳
		tenang	píng jìng 平静
	(v.)	melicinkan	lòng guāng huá 弄光滑
		meratakan	lòng píng 弄平
		menghilangkan	xiāo chú 消除
		mereda	píng jìng xià lái 平静下来
smug	(a.)	puas dengan diri sendiri	zì mǎn dė 自满的
smug.gle	(v.)	menyelundupkan	zǒu sī 走私
	(n.)	penyelundupan	zǒu sī 走私
snack	(n.)	makanan kecil	diǎn xīn 点心
snail	(n.)	siput	guā niú 蜗牛
snake	(n.)	ular	shé 蛇
snap	(v.)	menggigit, mematahkan	yǎo zhù 咬住, zhé duàn 折断
		bercepat-cepat	jí máng 急忙
		menjepret dengan kamera	kuài pò 快拍, kuài zhào 快照

	(n.)	menggigit	yǎo 咬
		kancing	kòu zi 扣子
		bunyi yang keras	pǐ pò shēng 劈拍声
snatch	(v.)	merenggut	dúo qǔ 夺取, qiǎng duó 抢夺
	(n.)	renggutan	qiǎng dúo 抢夺
		bagian	piàn duàn 片断
sneer	(v.)	mengejek	jī xiào 讥笑
sneeze	(n.)	bersin	pēn tì 喷嚏
	(v.)	bersin	dǎ pēn tì 打喷嚏
sniff	(v.)	menghirup, mengendus	xī 吸
snip	(v.)	menggunting	jiǎn 剪
snipe	(v.)	menembak dengan sembunyi-sembunyi	jū jī 狙击
snip.er	(n.)	penembak tersembunyi	jū jī shǒu 狙击手
snore	(v.)	mendengkur, mengorok	dǎ hān 打鼾
snow	(n.)	salju	xuě 雪
	(v.)	turun salju	xià xuě 下雪
snow.fall	(n.)	hujan salju	xià xuě 下雪
snow.flake	(n.)	kepingan salju	xuě piàn 雪片
snow.man	(n.)	orang-orangan salju	xuě rén 雪人
snow-shoe	(n.)	sepatu salju	xuě xié 雪鞋
snow.storm	(n.)	badai salju	bào fēng xuě 暴风雪
snow-white	(a.)	putih seperti salju	xuě bǎi 雪白
snow.y	(a.)	penuh salju	duō xuě dė 多雪的
		putih seperti salju	xuě bǎi dė 雪白的
snub	(v.)	mencerca	zé mà 责骂
		mengejek, mencemooh	xī luò 奚落
so	(adv.)	demikian, begitu	nà mė 那么, rú cǐ 如此
		juga, sama	yě yī yàng 也一样, yě nà yàng 也那样
		amat	feī cháng 非常
	(conj.)	oleh sebab itu	yīn cǐ 因此

soak	(v.)	merendam, membasahi	jìn shī 浸湿, nòng shī 弄湿
so-and-so	(n.)	si anu	móu móu 某某
soap	(n.)	sabun	féi zào 肥皂
soar	(v.)	membubung tinggi	gāo fēi 高飞
sob	(v.)	menangis, tersedu-sedu, terisak-isak	kū qì 哭泣
so.ber	(a.)	sadar	qīng xǐng dė 清醒的
		tenang	léng jìng dė 冷静的
so-called	(a.)	apa yang dinamakan	sŭo wèi 所谓
so.cial	(a.)	mengenai masyarakat, sosial	shè hùi dė 社会的, shè jiāo dė 社交的
so.cial.ism	(n.)	sosialisme	shè hùi zhŭ yì 社会主义
so.cial.ist	(n.)	sosialis	shè hùi zhŭ yì zhě 社会主义者
so.cial.ite	(n.)	tokoh terkemuka di masyarakat	shè huì huó dòng jiā 社会活动家 shè huì zhī míng rén shì 社会知名人士
so.cial.i.za.tion	(n.)	sosialisasi	shè huì huà 社会化, shè huì zhŭ yì huà 社会主义化
so.cial.ize	(v.)	mensosialisasikan	shĭ shè huì huà 使社会化
so.ci.al.i.ty	(n.)	masyarakat	shè hùi 社会
so.ci.e.ty	(n.)	masyarakat	shè hùi 社会
so.ci.ol.o.gy	(n.)	sosiologi	shè hùi xué 社会学
sock	(n.)	kaus kaki	wà zi 袜子
so.da	(n.)	soda	sū dă shŭi 苏打水
so.fa	(n.)	sofa	shā fā 沙发
soft	(a.)	lunak, lembek	ruăn 软, róu ruăn 柔软
soft.ball	(n.)	sofbol	léi qiú 垒球
soft.en	(v.)	melunakkan	ruăn huà 软化
soft.ly	(adv.)	pelan-pelan	qīng qīng di 轻轻地
soil	(n.)	tanah	tŭ 土, tŭ răng 土壤
	(v.)	mengotori	nòng zāng 弄脏

so.lar	(a.)	mengenai matahari	tài yáng dė 太阳的
sol.dier	(n.)	prajurit	bīng 兵, shì bīng 士兵
sole	(n.)	tapak kaki	jiǎo dǐ 脚底
	(a.)	tunggal	dān dú dė 单独的
sol.emn	(a.)	khidmat	yán sù 严肃, zhuāng yán 庄严
sol.id	(a.)	padat, kuat	jié shí 结实
	(n.)	benda padat	gù tǐ 固体
sol.i.dar.i.ty	(n.)	solidaritas	tuán jié 团结
		kesetiakawanan	yī zhì 一致
so.lid.i.fy	(v.)	memperkuat	gǒng gù 巩固
		mempersatukan	tuán jié 团结
so.lo	(n.)	nyanyian tunggal	dú chàng 独唱
	(a.)	tunggal	dān dú dė 单独的
so.lo.ist	(n.)	penyanyi tunggal	dú chàng zhě 独唱者
sol.u.ble	(a.)	yang dapat dilarutkan	kě róng jiě dė 可溶解的
		dapat diselesaikan	kě jiě jué dė 可解决的
so.lute	(n.)	benda larut, larutan	róng jiě wù 溶解物
so.lu.tion	(n.)	penyelesaian, pemecahan	jiě jué 解决
		cara penyelesaian	jiě jué fǎ 解决法
		larutan, pelarutan	róng yì 溶液, róng jiě 溶解
solve	(v.)	memecahkan, menjawab	jiě jué 解决, jiě dá 解答
some	(a.)	beberapa, sedikit	jǐ gè 几个, rùo gān 若干, yī xiē 一些
		sesuatu	móu yī 某一
	(pron.)	beberapa orang	yī xiē rén 一些人
		suatu barang	yī xiē wù 一些物
some.bod.y	(pron.)	seseorang	móu rén 某人, yǒu rén 有人
some.how	(adv.)	entah bagaimana	bù zhī zěn yàng 不知怎样, mò míng qí miaò 莫名其妙
		bagaimanapun	wú lùn rú hé 无论如何
some.one	(pron.)	seseorang, ada orang	móu rén 某人, yǒu rén 有人

some.thing	(n.)	sesuatu	móu shì 某事, móu wù 某物
some.time	(adv.)	suatu waktu, kapan-kapan	móu shí hòu 某时候, rì hòu 日后
		pernah	céng jīng 曾经
some.times	(adv.)	kadang-kadang	yǒu shí 有时
some.what	(adv.)	agak	shāo weī 稍微, yǒu diǎn 有点
some.where	(adv.)	di suatu tempat, di mana	móu dì 某地, shén mè dì fāng 什么地方
son	(n.)	putra, anak laki-laki	ér zi 儿子
son.ic	(a.)	sonik	shēng bō dė 声波的
son-in-law	(n.)	menantu laki-laki	nǔ xù 女婿
song	(n.)	nyanyian	gē 歌, gē qǔ 歌曲
song.ster	(n.)	penyanyi, biduan	gē shǒu 歌手
song.stress	(n.)	penyanyi wanita	nü ge shöu 女歌手
soon	(adv.)	segera	lì kè 立刻, bù jiǔ 不久
sop	(v.)	mencelupkan	jìn 浸
	(n.)	suapan	hùi lù lǐ wù 贿赂礼物
sop.py	(a.)	basah	cháo shī dė 潮湿的
so.pra.no	(n.)	penyanyi sopran	nǔ gaō yīn gē shǒu 女高音歌手
		suara sopran	nǔ gaō yīn 女高音
sore	(a.)	sakit	tòng 痛
		marah	shēng qì 生气
sor.row	(n.)	kesedihan	shāng xīn 伤心, beī shāng 悲伤
sor.ry	(a.)	menyesal	yí hàn dė 遗憾的, aò hǔi dė 懊悔的
		menyedihkan	nán guò dė 难过的, shāng xīn dė 伤心的
		maaf	dùi bù qǐ 对不起
sort	(n.)	jenis, macam	zhǒng lèi 种类
	(v.)	memisah-misahkan	fēn lèi 分类
		menyortir	tiāo xuǎn 挑选

so-so	(a.)	biasa saja	pǔ pǔ tōng tōng 普普通通,
			píng píng cháng cháng平平常常
soul	(n.)	jiwa, arwah	líng hún 灵魂, xīn líng 心灵
		orang	rén 人
sound	(a.)	sehat, sempurna	jiàn quán 健全, wán zhěng 完整
		keras	jiān gù 坚固
		dapat dipercaya	wěn dāng 稳当
	(n.)	bunyi, suara	shēng yīn 声音
	(v.)	membunyikan	nòng xiáng 弄响
		berbunyi	fā chū shēng yīn 发出声音
sound.ly	(adv.)	secara sehat	jiàn quán di 健全地
		dengan keras	jiān gù di 坚固地
		dengan sempurna	wán shàn di 完善地
soup	(n.)	sop	tāng 汤
sour	(a.)	masam	suān 酸
source	(n.)	sumber, mata air	yuán 源, yuǎn quán 源泉
souse	(v.)	menceburkan, mence-	jìn 浸, pào 泡
		lupkan, merendam	
south	(n.)	selatan	nán 南, nán fāng 南方
	(a.)	selatan	nán fàng dė 南方的
	(adv.)	ke selatan	xiàng nán 向南
south-east	(n.)	tenggara	dōng nán 东南,
			dōng nán bù 东南部
	(a.)	tenggara	dōng nán dė 东南的
	(adv.)	ke tenggara	xiàng dōng nán 向东南
south-east.er	(n.)	angin tenggara	dōng nán fēng 东南风
south-east.ern	(a.)	tenggara	dōng nán dė 东南的
south.er.ly	(a.)	arah selatan	xiàng nán dė 向南的,
			piān nán dė 偏南的
south.ern	(a.)	selatan, sebelah selatan	nán 南, nán fāng dė 南方的
south.ern.er	(n.)	orang selatan	nán fāng rén 南方人

south.ern.most	(a.)	bagian paling selatan	zùi nán duān dė 最南端的, jí nán dė 极南的
south.ward	(adv.)	arah selatan	xiàng nán 向南
		ke arah selatan	xiàng nán fāng dė 向南方的
south-west	(n.)	bagian barat daya	xī nán 西南, xī nán bù 西南部
south-west.er	(n.)	barat daya	xī nán fāng 西南方
south-west.ern	(a.)	barat daya	xī nán dė 西南的
sou.ve.nir	(n.)	tanda mata	jì niàn pǐn 纪念品
sov.er.eign	(n.)	orang yang berkuasa	tǒng zhì zhě 统治者
		raja	wáng 王
sov.er.eign.ty	(n.)	kedaulatan	zhǔ quán 主权, tǒng zhì quán 统治权
sow	(n.)	babi betina	mǔ zhū 母猪
	(v.)	menaburkan benih	bō zhòng 播种
sow.er	(n.)	penabur	bō zhòng zhě 播种者
sow.ing-ma.chine	(n.)	mesin penabur benih	bō zhǒng jī 播种机
soy	(n.)	kedelai	dà dòu 大豆
soy.bean	(n.)	kedelai	dà dòu 大豆
soy.sauce	(n.)	kecap	jiàng yóu 酱油
space	(n.)	ruang	kōng jiān 空间, kōng dì 空地
		angkasa	tài kōng 太空
space.man	(n.)	angkasawan, antariksawan	tài kōng rén 太空人
spade	(n.)	alat penggali, sekop	tiě qiāo 铁锹
spare	(a.)	sisa	duō yú dė 多余的
		cadangan	bèi yòng dė 备用的
		hemat	jié yuè 节约, jié shěng 节省
		kurus	shòu 瘦
	(v.)	meluangkan	chōu kōng 抽空
		menghemat	jié shěng 节省
		memberi	ràng gěi 让给
	(n.)	suku cadang	bèi jiàn 备件, bèi yòng dė líng jiàn 备用的零件

spare-rib	(n.)	tulang iga babi	pái gǔ 排骨
spark	(n.)	percikan, bunga api	hǔo huā 火花
	(v.)	mengeluarkan bunga api	fā hǔo huā 发火花
spark.le	(v.)	mengeluarkan bunga api	fā huǒ huā 发火花
		berkilau-kilauan	shǎn yào 闪耀
	(n.)	kilauan, cahaya berkelip	shǎn guāng 闪光, shǎn yào 闪耀
spar.row	(n.)	burung gereja	má què 麻雀
sparse	(a.)	jarang	xī shǎo 稀少, xī shū 稀疏
speak	(v.)	bicara	shuō hùa 说话, jiǎng hùa 讲话
speak.er	(n.)	pembicara	jiǎng hùa zhě 讲话者, fā yán rén 发言人
spear	(n.)	tombak	máo 矛
spe.cial	(a.)	istimewa, khusus	tè bié dė 特别的, tè shū dė 特殊的
spe.cial.ist	(n.)	spesialis, ahli	zhuān jiā 专家, zhuān kē yī shēng 专科医生
spe.ci.al.i.ty	(n.)	keistimewaan, keahlian	tè xìng 特性, zhuān cái 专才, zhuān yè 专业
spe.cial.i.za.tion	(n.)	spesialisasi	zhuān mén huà 专门化, zhuān yè huà 专业化
spe.cial.ize	(v.)	menspesialisasikan	zhuān yè huà 专业化
		mengkhususkan	tè shū huà 特殊化
spe.cial.ly	(adv.)	khususnya	tè bié 特别
spe.cies	(n.)	jenis	zhǒng 种
spe.cif.ic	(a.)	spesifik, khusus	zhǒng dė 种的, tè shū dė 特殊的, tè xiào dė 特效的
	(n.)	obat spesifik	tè xiào yào 特效药
spe.cif.i.cal.ly	(adv.)	tegasnya, khususnya	míng què di 明确地, tè shū di 特殊地, fēn mén bié lèi 分门别类

spec.i.fi.ca.tion	(n.)	spesifikasi, perincian	xiáng xì shūo míng 详细说明
spec.i.fy	(v.)	menetapkan	zhǐ dìng 指定
		memberi perincian	xiáng xì shūo míng 详细说明
spec.i.men	(n.)	contoh	biaō běn 标本, yàng běn 样本
spe.cious	(a.)	kelihatannya benar tetapi sebenarnya salah	sì shì ér fēi 似是而非
speck	(n.)	noda, bintik	bān diǎn 斑点, weī lì 微粒
speck.le	(n.)	bintik kecil	xiǎo bān diǎn 小斑点
spec.ta.cle	(n.)	pertunjukan besar	qí guān 奇观
		pemandangan	jǐng xiàng 景象
		kacamata	yǎn jìng 眼镜
spec.ta.tor	(n.)	penonton	cān guān zhě 参观者, páng guān zhě 旁观者
spec.u.late	(v.)	memikirkan, berspekulasi	sī sǔo 思索, tóu jī 投机
spec.u.la.tion	(n.)	pemikiran, spekulasi	sī sǔo 思索, tuī cè 推测, tóu jī 投机
spec.u.la.tor	(n.)	spekulan, perenung	sī sǔo zhě 思索者
		pengadu untung	kōng lùn jiā 空论家, tóu jī zhě 投机者
speech	(n.)	bahasa	yú yán 语言
		pidato	yǎn shūo 演说, jiǎng hùa 讲话
speed	(n.)	kecepatan	sù dù 速度
	(v.)	mempercepat	jiā kuài 加快, jiā sù 加速
speed.way	(n.)	jalan raya lintas cepat	gāo sù gōng lù 高速公路
speed.y	(a.)	cepat	xǔn sù dė 迅速的, lì kè dė 立刻的
spell	(v.)	mengeja	pīn yīn 拼音
	(n.)	aplusan, giliran bekerja	lún bān 轮班
		mantra, pesona	zhòu yǔ 咒语, mó lì 魔力
spell.bound	(a.)	terpesona	rù mí dė 入迷的
spell.ing	(n.)	ejaan	pīn yīn 拼音
spend	(v.)	menghabiskan	huā fèi 花费
		membelanjakan	xiāo fèi 消费
		melewatkan	xiāo mó 消磨

spend.thrift	(n.)	pemboros	làng fèi zhě 浪费者
sphere	(n.)	bola, bulatan	qiú 球, yuán tǐ 园体
		bidang, lingkungan	fàn wéi 范围
spice	(n.)	rempah-rempah, bumbu	xiāng liào 香料, tiáo wèi pǐn 调味品
	(v.)	membumbui	jiā xiāng liào 加香料
spi.der	(n.)	labah-labah	zhī zhū 蜘蛛
spill	(v.)	tumpah, menumpahkan	yì chū 溢出, liú chū 流出, shǐ yì chū 使溢出, shǐ liú chū 使流出
spin	(v.)	memintal, memutar	fǎng 纺, xuán zhuǎn 旋转
		memusingkan	tóu yūn 头晕
spi.nal	(adj.)	mengenai tulang punggung	jǐ gǔ dė 脊骨的, jǐ zhuī dė 脊椎的
spine	(n.)	tulang punggung	jǐ gǔ 脊骨
spin.ner	(n.)	pemintal	fǎng shā zhě 纺纱者, fǎng shā gōng rén 纺纱工人
spin.ning	(n.)	pemintalan	fǎng 纺, fǎng shā 纺纱
spin.ning-mill	(n.)	pabrik pemintalan	fǎng shā chǎng 纺纱厂
spi.ral	(a.)	pilin, berbentuk spiral	luó xuán xíng dė 螺旋形的
spir.it	(n.)	semangat, roh, jiwa	jīng shén 精神, xīn líng 心灵, líng hún 灵魂
		jin, hantu	yāo guài 妖怪, gǔi 鬼
		minuman keras	liè jiǔ 烈酒
		spiritus	jiǔ jīng 酒精
	(v.)	menyemangatkan	gǔ wǔ 鼓舞
spir.it-lamp	(n.)	lampu spiritus	jiǔ jīng dēng 酒精灯
spir.it.less	(a.)	tidak bersemangat	méi yǒu jīng shén dė 没有精神的
spir.it.u.al	(a.)	berkenaan dengan roh, spiritual	xīn líng shàng dė 心灵上的
spit	(v.)	meludah	tǔ tán 吐痰
spite	(n.)	dengki, dendam	è yì 恶意, yuàn hèn 怨恨

spite.ful	(a.)	penuh dendam	huái hèn dė 怀恨的
splash	(v.)	berpercikan, memercikkan	jiàn 溅, feī jiàn 飞溅,
			jiàn shī 溅湿, pō shī 泼湿
splen.did	(a.)	bagus sekali, indah sekali	měi miào 美妙, tài měi lė 太美了
split	(v.)	membelah, belah, retak	gē liè 割裂, fēn liè 分裂
	(a.)	retak, belah	fēn liè dė 分裂的
	(n.)	keretakan, sobekan	fēn liè 分裂, liè kǒu 裂口, liè féng 裂缝
spoil	(v.)	merusak, membusuk	sǔn huài 损坏, fǔ làn 腐烂
	(n.)	barang curian	zāng wù 脏物
		barang rampasan	luè duó wù 掠夺物, zhàn lì pǐn 战利品
spoil.er	(n.)	perampok, perampas	lùe duó zhě 掠夺者
spoken	(a.)	yang diucapkan	kǒu shūo dė 口说的
		ucapan sehari-hari	kǒu tóu dė 口头的
spokes.man	(n.)	juru bicara	fā yán rén 发言人
sponge	(n.)	spons, bunga karang	hǎi mián 海绵
	(v.)	menghapus dengan spons	yòng hǎi mián cā 用海绵擦
sponge-cake	(n.)	bolu	dàn gāo 蛋糕
spong.er	(n.)	orang yang hidup me-numpang pada orang lain	shí kè 食客
spon.sor	(n.)	sponsor	fā qǐ rén 发起人, bǎo zhèng rén 保证人
	(v.)	mensponsori	fā qǐ 发起, bǎo zhèng 保证
spon.ta.ne.i.ty	(n.)	spontanitas	zì fā xìng 自发性
spon.ta.neous	(a.)	spontan	zì fā dė 自发的
spoof	(v.)	menipu, membohongi	mán piàn 瞒骗
spoon	(n.)	sendok	tāng chí 汤匙, tiáo gēng 调羹
spoon.ful	(a.)	sesendok penuh	mǎn chí 满匙
sport	(n.)	permainan, olahraga	yóu xì 游戏, yùn dòng 运动
	(v.)	bermain-main	yóu xì 游戏, wán shǔa 玩耍
		berolahraga	yùn dòng 运动
sports.man	(n.)	olahragawan	yùn dòng yuán 运动员

sports.man.ship	(n.)	sikap sportif	yùn dòng yuán jīng shén 运动员精神, tǐ yù dào dé 体育道德
spot	(n.)	bintik, noda	bān diǎn 斑点, wū diǎn 污点
		tempat	chǎng sǔo 场所, dì diǎn 地点
		sedikit	yī diǎn 一点
	(v.)	menodai	diǎn wū 玷污, nòng zāng 弄脏
		membuat titik	dǎ diǎn 打点, diǎn zhùi 点缀
spray	(n.)	buih, percikan air	làng huā 浪花, shǔi huā 水花
	(v.)	menyemprot	pēn 喷
spray.er	(n.)	alat penyemprot	pēn shè qì 喷射器, pēn tǒng 喷筒
spread	(v.)	menyebarkan	sàn bù 散布
		mengembangkan	zhǎn kaī 展开, shēn zhǎng 伸展
		membentangkan	pū kaī 铺开, dǎ kaī 打开
		mengoleskan, mengolesi	fū 敷, tú 涂
spring	(v.)	melompat	tiào 跳, tiào yuè 跳跃
	(n.)	musim semi	chūn tiān 春天
		mata air, sumber	quán 泉, yuán quán 源泉
		per, pegas	tán huáng 弹簧, fā tiáo 发条
spring.time	(n.)	musim semi	chūn jì 春季, chūn tiān 春天
spring.y	(a.)	elastis, lentur	yǒu tán xìng dė 有弹性的
sprin.kle	(v.)	menyebarkan	sàn bù 散布
		menghamburkan	sā 洒
sprint	(n.)	lari jarak pendek	duǎn pǎo 短跑
sprint.er	(n.)	pelari jarak pendek	duǎn pǎo xuǎn shǒu 短跑选手
sprout	(v.)	bertunas	fā yá 发芽
		tumbuh	shēng zhǎng 生长
	(n.)	tunas	yá 芽
spry	(a.)	lincah, gesit	huó pō 活泼, mǐn jié 敏捷
spume	(n.)	buih	pào mò 泡沫
spunk	(n.)	keberanian, semangat	yǒng qì 勇气, shēng qì 生气

spur	(n.)	taji, pacu	jī jù 鸡距, tī mǎ cì 踢马刺
	(v.)	mendorong	dū cù 督促
		berlari kencang	bēn chí 奔驰
		memacu	yòng mǎ cì tī 用马刺踢
spu.ri.ous	(a.)	palsu	jiǎ dė 假的
spy	(n.)	mata-mata	jiàn dié 间谍
	(v.)	memata-matai	zhēn chá 侦察, zhēn tàn 侦探
squab.ble	(n.)	pertengkaran	chǎo jià 吵架
squall	(n.)	badai	kuáng fēng 狂风
	(v.)	menangis sambil berteriak	tí kū 啼哭
square	(n.)	persegi empat	zhèng fāng xíng 正方形
		lapangan	guǎng chǎng 广场
	(a.)	persegi	zhèng fāng xíng dė 正方形的
		jujur	zhèng zhí 正直
		cocok	fú hé 符合
	(v.)	mengkuadratkan	nòng fāng 弄方, nòng zhèng弄正
		menyelesaikan, melunaskan	suàn qīng 算请, qīng zhang清帐
		mencocokkan	shǐ fú hé 使符合
square.ly	(adv.)	secara jujur	zhèng zhí di 正直地
		tepat	zhèng zhōng 正中
squash	(n.)	labu	nán guā 南瓜
	(v.)	meremas	yā suì压碎
squeeze	(v.)	memeras	jǐ 挤, yā zhà 压榨
squir.rel	(n.)	bajing, tupai	sōng shǔ 松鼠
stab	(v.)	menikam, menusuk	cì 刺
sta.bil.i.ty	(n.)	stabilitas	wěn dìng 稳定
sta.bi.li.za.tion	(n.)	stabilisasi	wěn dìng 稳定
sta.bi.lize	(v.)	menstabilkan	shǐ wěn dìng 使稳定, shǐ ān dìng 使安定
sta.bi.liz.er	(n.)	alat penstabil, stabilisator	wěn dìng qì 稳定器

sta.ble	(n.)	kandang kuda	mǎ jiù 马厩, mǎ péng 马棚
	(a.)	stabil	wěn dìng dė 稳定的,
			ān dìng dė 安定的
stack	(n.)	tumpukan kayu	mù caí duī 木材堆
		tumpukan	duī 堆
		timbunan rumput, gabah	cǎo dǔo 草垛, gǔ duī 谷堆
	(v.)	menumpuk, menimbun	duī jī 堆积
sta.dium	(n.)	stadion	tǐ yù chǎng 体育场
staff	(n.)	staf	gōng zùo rén yuán 工作人员,
			zhí yuán 职员
		tongkat	zhàng 杖, gàn 竿
		bahan pokok	shēng húo bì xù pǐn生活必需品
stag	(n.)	rusa jantan	mǔ lù 牡鹿, xióng lù 雄鹿
stage	(n.)	panggung, pentas	wǔ tái 舞台
		taraf	chéng dù 程度, jiē duàn 阶段
	(v.)	mementaskan	shàng yǎn 上演,
			bān shàng wǔ tái 搬上舞台
stag.ger	(v.)	sempoyongan	yáo bǎi 摇摆
		mengejutkan, menggem-parkan	shǐ zhèn jīng 使震惊
stag.nant	(a.)	mandek, berhenti	tíng zhì 停滞, bù liú dòng 不流动
stag.nate	(v.)	berhenti	tíng zhì 停滞, bù liú dòng 不流动
stag.na.tion	(n.)	mandek, tidak mengalir	tíng zhì 停滞, bù liú dòng 不流动
stain	(n.)	kotoran, noda	wū diǎn 污点
		mengotorkan, menodai	zhān wū 沾污, nòng zāng 弄脏
stain.less	(a.)	tak bernoda	méi yǒu wū diǎn 没有污点
		tak berkarat	bù xiù dė 不锈的
stair	(n.)	tangga	tī 梯, jiē tī 阶梯, lóu tī 楼梯
stair.case	(n.)	tangga	lóu tī 楼梯

stake	(n.)	tonggak, pancang	zhuāng 桩, biāo zhuāng 标桩
	(v.)	memancangkan	lì zhuāng 立桩, chā zhuāng插桩
		mempertaruhkan	dǎ dǔ 打赌
stale	(a.)	usang, basi	chén jiù 陈旧, chén fǔ 陈腐
stalk	(n.)	batang, tangkai	yè bǐng 叶柄, huā gěng 花梗
stall	(n.)	kandang sapi	niú lán 牛栏
		kedai kecil	xiǎo wū 小屋
stam.i.na	(n.)	daya tahan, stamina	chí jiǔ lì 持久力, gàn jìn 干劲
stamp	(n.)	cap, segel materai	tú zhāng 图章, yìn huā 印花
		prangko	yóu piào 邮票
	(v.)	mencap	gài yìn 盖印
		menempelkan prangko	tie yóu piào 贴邮票
		menumbuk, menginjak	chúi dǎ 捶打, tà 踏, jiàn tà 践踏
stand	(v.)	berdiri	zhàn 站, lì 立
		berada	zùo lùo 座落, zài 在
		bertahan, berlaku	bǎo chí 保持, yǒu xiào 有效
		menempatkan	ān zhì 安置, shǐ zhàn lì 使站立
		menahan	rěn shòu 忍受, dǐng zhù 顶住
		mempertahankan	jiān chǐ 坚持
		mentraktir	qíng 请, qíng kè 清客
	(n.)	berdiri	zhàn lì 站立
		pendirian	lì chǎng 立场
		tribun	kàn tái 看台, guān tái 观台
		kios, stan	tān zi 摊子
		perhentian	tíng liú chù 停留处, zhàn 站
		cantelan	jià 架
stand.ard	(n.)	standar	biāo zhǔn 标准, shǔi zhǔn 水准
stand-point	(n.)	sudut pandang, pendirian	guān diǎn 观点, lì chǎng 立场
stand.still	(n.)	macet, berhenti	tíng zhǐ 停止, tíng dùn 停顿
star	(n.)	bintang	xīng 星

star.let	(n.)	bintang kecil	xiǎo xīng xīng 小星星
		pemain kecil (muda)	xiǎo míng xīng 小明星
star.light	(n.)	cahaya bintang	xīng guāng 星光
star.lit	(a.)	bercahaya bintang	yǒu xīng guāng dė 有星光的
stare	(v.)	memandang, menatap	zhù shì 注视, níng shì 凝视
start	(v.)	mulai	kaī shǐ 开始
		berangkat	dòng shēn 动身, chū fā 出发
		mengejutkan	jīng dòng 惊动
		menyebabkan	yin qǐ 引起
start.er	(n.)	orang yang berangkat	chū fā zhě 出发者
		stater	qǐ dòng jī 起动机
star.tle	(v.)	mengejutkan	jīng dòng 惊动
		mengagetkan	shǐ rén chī jīng 使人吃惊
star.va.tion	(n.)	penderitaan kelaparan	jī huāng 饥荒
		mati kelaparan	è sǐ 饿死
starve	(v.)	menderita kelaparan	jī è 饥饿
		mati kelaparan	è sǐ 饿死
state	(n.)	negara	gúo jiā 国家
		keadaan	qíng xíng 情形
	(v.)	menyatakan	shēng míng 声明
		menerangkan	chén shù 陈述
state.ly	(a.)	agung, megah	zhuāng yán 庄严, táng huáng 堂皇
state.ment	(n.)	pernyataan	shēng míng 声明, shēng míng shū 声明书
state-owned	(a.)	milik negara	gúo yǒu dė 国有的
states.man	(n.)	negarawan	zhèng zhì jiā 政治家
stat.ic	(a.)	tidak bergerak, statis	jìng zhǐ 静止
sta.tion	(n.)	stasiun	chē zhàn 车站
		kantor, pos	jú 局, gǎng wèi 岗位

sta.tion.a.ry	(a.)	tetap, tidak berubah	gù dìng dė 固定的,
			wěn dìng dė 稳定的
sta.tion.er	(n.)	pedagang alat-alat tulis	wén jù shāng 文具商
sta.tion.er.y	(n.)	alat-alat tulis	wén jù 文具
		kertas surat	xìn zhǐ 信纸
stat.ist	(n.)	ahli statistik	tǒng jì jiā 统计家
sta.tis.ti.cal	(a.)	mengenai statistik	tǒng jì dė 统计的,
			tǒng jì xué dė 统计学的
stat.is.ti.cian	(n.)	ahli statistik	tǒng jì xué jiā 统计学家,
			tǒng jì jiā 统计家,
			tǒng jì yuán 统计员
sta.tis.tics	(n.)	statistik	tǒng jì 统计
stat.ue	(n.)	patung	ǒu xiàng 偶象
stat.ure	(n.)	tinggi badan	shēn gaō 身高
		perawakan, sosok tubuh	shēn cái 身材
sta.tus	(n.)	keadaan, status	qíng shì 情势, dì wèi 地位,
			shēn fèn 身份
stat.ute	(n.)	undang-undang	fǎ lìng 法令
stay	(v.)	tinggal	dòu liú 逗留, zàn zhù 暂住
		berhenti	zhàn zhù 站住, tíng zhǐ 停止
		menunda	yán chí 延迟
		menghentikan	zhǐ zhù 止住, zhì zhǐ 制止
		menahan, menopang	zhī cheng 支撑, zhī chí 支持
	(n.)	topang	zhī zhù 支柱
		tinggal	dòu liú 逗留
stead.fast	(a.)	tetap	jiān dìng 坚定, jiān jué 坚决
stead.i.ly	(adv.)	dengan tetap	wěn gù di 稳固地,
			wěn dìng di 稳定地
stead.i.ness	(n.)	ketetapan, keteguhan	wěn gù xìng 稳固性,
			jiān dìng xìng 坚定性

stead.y	(a.)	tetap, mantap	wěn gù 稳固, píng wěn 平稳
steak	(n.)	potongan daging	ròu piàn 肉片
		bistik	pá 扒, niú pá 牛扒
steal	(v.)	mencuri	tōu 偷
stealth	(n.)	tindakan yang dilakukan secara diam-diam	mì mì xíng dòng 秘密行动
steam	(n.)	uap air	shǔi zhēng qì 水蒸汽
	(v.)	menguap	zhēng fā 蒸发
		mengukus	zhēng 蒸
steam.er	(n.)	kapal uap	qì chuán 汽船
		alat untuk mengukus	zhēng lóng 蒸笼
steel	(n.)	baja	gāng 钢
steel-works	(n.)	pabrik baja	liàn gāng chǎng 炼钢厂
steep	(a.)	curam	dǒu xié 陡斜
	(v.)	merendam	jìn shī 浸湿
		mendalami	shēn rù 深入
steep.le	(n.)	menara	jiān tǎ 尖塔
steer	(v.)	mengemudikan	jià shǐ 驾驶
stem	(n.)	tangkai, gagang	jīng 茎, gěng 梗
		akar kata	cí gàn 词干
		haluan	chuán tóu 船头
	(v.)	membendung	dǔ zhù 堵住, dǎng zhù 挡住
stench	(n.)	bau busuk	chòu qì 臭气
sten.cil	(n.)	stensil	yóu yìn 油印
ste.no.graph	(n.)	tulisan steno	sù jì wén zì 速记文字
	(v.)	menulis steno	sù jì 速记
ste.no.grapher	(n.)	juru tulis steno	sù jì yuán 速记员
ste.no.graphy	(n.)	stenografi, tulisan cepat	sù jì 速记, sù jì fǎ 速记法
step	(n.)	langkah	jiǎo bù 脚步
		tindakan	bù zòu 步骤

		anak tangga	tī jí 梯级, tái jiē 台阶
	(v.)	melangkah	jǔ bù 举步, zǒu 走
		menginjakkan	tà 踏
step.broth.er	(n.)	saudara tiri laki-laki	yì fù xiōng dì 异父兄弟, yì mǔ xiōng dì 异母兄弟
step.child	(n.)	anak tiri	jì zǐ nū 继子女
step.daugh.ter	(n.)	anak tiri perempuan	jì nū 继女
step.fa.ther	(n.)	ayah tiri	jì fù 继父
step.moth.er	(n.)	ibu tiri	jì mǔ 继母
step.sis.ter	(n.)	saudara tiri perempuan	yì fù jiě mèi 异父姐妹, yì mǔ jiě mèi 异母姐妹
step.son	(n.)	anak tiri laki-laki	jì zi 继子
ste.reo	(n.)	stereo	tǐ shí jìng 体实镜
ste.reo.gram	(n.)	gambar tiga dimensi	lì tǐ tú 立体图
		potret tiga dimensi	lì tǐ zhào xiàng 立体照相
ster.ile	(a.)	steril	bù yù dė 不育的
		mandul	pín jǐ dė 贫瘠的
		bebas dari kuman	wú xì jūn dė 无细菌的
ste.ril.i.ty	(n.)	kemandulan	bù yù 不育
		bebas dari kuman	wú jūn zhuàng tài 无菌状态
ster.il.i.za.tion	(n.)	sterilisasi	xiāo dú 消毒
ster.il.ize	(v.)	mensterilkan	xiāo dú 消毒
stern	(n.)	buritan	chuán wěi 船尾, wěi bù 尾巴
	(a.)	keras	yán lì 严历
stew	(v.)	mengukus, merebus pelan-pelan	zhēng 蒸
stew.ard	(n.)	pelayan (laki-laki)	fú wù yuán 服务员
		pramugara	chéng wù yuán 乘务员
stew.ard.ess	(n.)	pramugari	nǔ chéng wù yuán 女乘务员
		pelayan (perempuan)	nǔ fú wù yuán 女服务员

stick	(n.)	tongkat, batang	shǒu zhàng 手杖, zhī tiáo 枝条
	(v.)	melekat, melekatkan	nián zhù 粘住, nián tie 粘贴
		menusuk	chuō 戳, chì 刺
stick.y	(a.)	lengket	nián xìng dė 粘性的
stiff	(a.)	keras, kaku	yìng 硬, jiāng yìng 僵硬, shēng yìng 生硬
		bersikeras, gigih	wán qiáng 顽强, jué qiáng 倔强
		sukar, sulit	jiān nán dė 艰难的, fèi jīn dė 费劲的
	(n.)	mayat	jiāng shī 僵尸
stiff.en	(v.)	mengeras, menjadi kaku	yìng huà 硬化, jiāng huà 僵化
		memperkuat	jiā qiáng 加强
still	(n.)	penyuling	zhēng liú qì 蒸馏器
		kesunyian	jì jìng 寂静
	(a.)	diam	jìng 静, jìng zhǐ 静止
		sunyi	jì jìng dė 寂静的
		tenang	píng jìng dė 平静的
	(v.)	menenangkan	shǐ jìng zhǐ 使静止, shǐ píng jìng 使平静
		menyuling	zhēng liú 蒸馏
	(adv.)	masih	hái shì 还是, rén jiù 仍旧
		bahkan	hé kuàng 何况
		tetapi ... masih	kě shì ... hái 可是…还
still-born	(a.)	lahir mati	sǐ chǎn dė 死产的
stim.u.lant	(a.)	stimulan	cì jī xìng dė 刺激性的
		yang merangsang	shǐ xīng fèn dė 使兴奋的
	(n.)	obat perangsang	xīng fèn jì 兴奋剂
stim.u.late	(v.)	merangsang	cì jī 刺激
		menggairahkan	shǐ xīng fèn 使兴奋
stim.u.la.tion	(n.)	perangsangan	cì jī zùo yòng 刺激作用, xīng fèn zùo yòng 兴奋作用

sting	(v.)	menyengat	dīng 叮, cì 刺
	(n.)	sengatan, tusukan	dīng 叮, ci 刺
stin.gy	(a.)	kikir, pelit	lìn sè 吝啬, xiǎo qì 小气
		terlalu sedikit, tak cukup	guò xiǎo 过小, bù zú 不足
stink	(v.)	bau busuk	è chòu 恶臭
stip.u.late	(v.)	menetapkan	guī dìng 规定
stir	(v.)	mengocok, mengaduk	jiǎo dòng 搅动,
		menggerakkan	yí dòng 移动, yáo dòng 摇动
		menghasut	shān dòng 煽动
	(n.)	adukan	jiǎo bàn 搅拌
		keributan, kekacauan	sāo dòng 骚动, dòng dàng 动荡
stir.ring	(a.)	yang menggemparkan	jī dòng rén xīn dė 激动人心的
stitch	(v.)	menjahit	féng 缝, féng bǔ 缝补
		stik, jahitan	yī zhēn 一针, yī féng 一缝
stock	(n.)	batang	gàn 干
		persediaan	cún hùo 存货, cún liào 存料
		ternak	jiā chù 家畜
		saham	gǔ fèn 股份, gǔ piào 股票
	(v.)	menyimpan	chǔ cún 储存, chǔ cáng 储藏
		menyediakan	gōng yìng 供应
stock.ade	(n.)	pagar	zhà lán 栅栏, wéi lán 围栏
	(v.)	memagari	wéi zhù 围住, lán zhù 拦住
stock.ing	(n.)	kaus kaki panjang	cháng wà zi 长袜子
stom.ach	(n.)	perut	wéi 胃, dǔ zi 肚子
stone	(n.)	batu	shí 石, shí tóu 石头, shí kuài 石块
		batu nisan	beī shí 碑石
		batu permata	bǎo shí 宝石
		biji	guǒ hé 果核
stone.less	(a.)	tak berbiji	wú hé dė 无核的

stone.ma.son	(n.)	tukang batu	shí gōng 石工
ston.y	(a.)	penuh batu	duō shí toú dė 多石头的
stool	(n.)	bangku	dèng zi 凳子
stoop	(v.)	membungkuk	qū shēn 屈身, wān yāo 弯腰
stop	(v.)	berhenti, menghentikan	tíng zhǐ 停止, zhi zhù 止住
		macet	dǔ sè 堵塞
		menginap	dòu liú 逗留, gùo yè 过夜
	(n.)	perhentian	tíng chē 停车, chē zhàn 车站
		penghentian	tíng zhǐ 停止, zhōng zhǐ 中止
stor.age	(n.)	penyimpanan	chǔ cáng 储藏
		tempat penyimpanan	chǔ cáng shì 储藏室
store	(n.)	toko	shāng diàn 商店, diàn pù 店铺
		persediaan	chǔ cáng 储藏
	(v.)	menumpuk, menyimpan	duī jī 堆积, chǔ cáng 储藏
		menyediakan	gōng yìng 供应
store.house	(n.)	gudang	cāng kù 仓库
store.keeper	(n.)	pemilik toko	diàn zhǔ 店主
sto.rey	(n.)	tingkat	céng 层
storm	(n.)	badai	bào fēng yǔ 暴风雨
		amukan	bào nù 暴怒
		serangan gencar	měng gōng 猛攻
	(v.)	datang angin ribut	qǐ fēng bào 起风暴
		mengamuk	bào nù 暴怒, nù mà 怒骂
		menggempur	měng gōng 猛攻
storm.y	(a.)	penuh badai	duō fēng bào dė 多风暴的
sto.ry	(n.)	tingkat, loteng	céng 层, lóu 楼
		cerita	gù shì 故事
		riwayat	zhuàn jì 传记
		bohong	huǎng hùa 谎话

stout	(a.)	gemuk, kuat	féi pàng 肥胖, jié shí 结实
	(n.)	bir hitam	hèi mài jiǔ 黑麦酒
stove	(n.)	tungku, kompor	hǔo lú 火炉
	(v.)	memanggang, membakar	hōng gān 烘干, kǎo gān 烤干
stow	(v.)	memuat	zhuāng 装
straight	(a.)	lurus, jujur	zhí 直, zhèng zhí 正直, lǎo shí 老实
	(n.)	garis lurus	zhí xiàn 直线
	(adv.)	lurus	zhí 直
		langsung	zhí jiē 直接
		dengan jujur	lǎo shí di 老实地
straight.en	(v.)	meluruskan	lòng zhí 弄直
		membetulkan	jiū zhèng 纠正
		membatasi	xiàn zhì 限制
strange	(a.)	aneh, ganjil	qí guài 奇怪, lí qí 离奇
		asing	mò shēng dė 陌生的, shēng shū dė 生疏的
strange.ly	(adv.)	dengan aneh	qí guài di 奇怪地, qí miào di 奇妙的
stran.ger	(n.)	orang asing	mò shēng rén 陌生人
		orang yang tak dikenal	shēng kè 生客
stran.gle	(v.)	mencekik	è sǐ 扼死
strap	(n.)	sabuk, tali	pí daì 皮带, daì 带
stra.te.gi.cal	(a.)	berhubungan dng strategi	zhàn luè shàng dė 战略上的
stra.te.gi.cal.ly	(adv.)	secara strategis, menurut siasat	zhàn luè shàng 战略上
stra.te.gics	(n.)	strategis	bīng fǎ 兵法
strat.e.gist	(n.)	ahli siasat perang	zhàn luè jiā 战略家
strat.e.gy	(n.)	strategi, siasat	zhàn luè 战略
straw	(n.)	jerami	dào cǎo 稻草
straw.ber.ry	(n.)	buah arbei, stroberi	cǎo měi 草梅
straw.board	(n.)	karton	cǎo zhǐ bǎn 草纸板

stray	(v.)	tersesat	mí lù 迷路
		menyimpang	lí tí 离题, zǒu rù qí tú 走入歧途
	(a.)	sesat	mí lù dė 迷路的
	(n.)	orang yang tersesat	mí lù zhě 迷路者
		hewan yang tersesat	mí lù jiā chù 迷路家畜
stream	(n.)	aliran, arus	liú 流
		sungai kecil	xiǎo hé 小河
	(v.)	mengalir	liú 流
		melambai-lambai	piaō yáng 飘扬
street	(n.)	jalan	jiē 街, jiē dào 街道, mǎ lù 马路
street.car	(n.)	trem	diàn chē 电车
strength	(n.)	tenaga, kekuatan	lì 力, lì qì 力气, lì liáng 力量
strength.en	(v.)	memperkuat	jiā qiáng 加强
stress	(n.)	tekanan	yā lì 压力, qiáng diào 强调
		tekanan bunyi	zhòng yīn 重音
	(v.)	menekankan, menitik-beratkan	qiáng diào 强调, zhòng dú 重读
stretch	(v.)	membentang, membentangkan	shēn zhǎng 伸展
		mengulurkan	shēn cháng 伸长
strict	(a.)	keras, ketat, teliti	yán gé 严格, yán mì 严密, jīng mì 精密
strict.ly	(adv.)	dengan keras	yán gé di 严格地
		dengan teliti	jīng mì di 精密地
stride	(v.)	melangkah	kuà 跨
		melangkah maju	mài jìn 迈进
	(n.)	langkah	bù 步
strife	(n.)	perselisihan, pertengkaran	chōng tū 冲突
strike	(v.)	memukul	dǎ 打
		menyerang	xí jī 袭击, tū jī 突击
		mogok	bà gōng 罢工
		membunyikan, berbunyi	qiaō xiǎng 敲响, xiǎng 响

		menikam, menusuk	cì 刺, chuō 戳
		menembus ke dalam	shēn rù 深入, shǐ shēn rù使深入
	(n.)	serangan	xí jī 袭击, tū jī 突击
		pemogokan	bà gōng 罢工
strik.er	(n.)	penyerang	gōng jī zhě 攻击者
		pemogok	bà gōng zhě 罢工者
strik.ing	(a.)	yang mencolok	xiǎn zhù dė 显著的
		yang mengejutkan	jīng rén dė 惊人的
string	(n.)	tali	xì shéng 细绳, dài zi 带子
		senar	xián 弦
strip	(v.)	menguliti	bō 剥, bō pí 剥皮
		menanggalkan baju	tūo yī fú 脱衣服
		mengambil dengan paksa	bō duó 剥夺, duó qǔ 夺取
stripe	(n.)	garis, strip	xiàn tiáo 线条, tiáo wén 条纹
strive	(v.)	berusaha, berjuang	nǔ lì 努力, fèn dòu 奋斗
stroke	(n.)	pukulan	dǎ jī 打击
		serangan otak	zhòng fēng 中风
		bunyi lonceng	zhōng shēng 钟声, zhōng míng 钟鸣
	(v.)	mengusap, membelai	fǔ mó 抚摩
stroll	(v.)	berjalan-jalan	liū dā 溜达, sàn bù 散步, guàng jiē 逛街
strong	(a.)	kuat	qiáng zhuàng 强壮, qiáng dà 强大
		keras	qiáng liè 强烈, nóng hoù 浓烈
		kokoh	jiān gù 坚固, wěn gù 稳固
		teguh	jiān qiáng 坚强 jiān dìng 坚定
	(adv.)	dengan kuat	yǒu lì dì 有力地
		dengan keras	qiáng liè dì 强烈地
strong.hold	(n.)	benteng, kubu	bǎo lěi 堡垒, yào sài 要塞
strong.ly	(adv.)	dengan kuat, dengan keras	yǒu lì di 有力地, qiáng liè di 强烈地
struc.tur.al	(a.)	struktural	jié gòu shàng dė 结构上的
		mengenai susunan	gòu zào shàng dė 构造上的, zǔ zhī shang dė 组织上的

struc.ture	(n.)	struktur, susunan	jié gòu 结构, gòu zào 构造, zǔ zhǐ 组织
strug.gle	(v.)	berjuang	dòu zhēng 斗争, fèn dòu 奋斗
		meronta-ronta	zhěng zha 挣扎
	(n.)	perjuangan	dòu zhēng 斗争, fèn dòu 奋斗
strut	(v.)	berjalan dengan sombong	dà yaō dà bǎi di zǒu 大摇大摆地走
	(n.)	penopang	zhī zhù 支柱
stub.born	(a.)	keras kepala	wán gù 顽固
stu.dent	(n.)	pelajar, mahasiswa	xué shēng 学生, dà xué shēng 大学生
studied	(a.)	yang direncanakan	yǒu jì huà dė 有计划的
		yang disengaja	gù yì dė 故意的
stu.dio	(n.)	studio	huà shì 画室, zhì piàn chǎng 制片厂, bō yīn shì 播音室
stu.di.ous	(a.)	rajin belajar	yòng gōng dė 用功的
		sangat berhati-hati	shèn zhòng dė 慎重的
stud.y	(n.)	pelajaran	xué xí 学习
		penelitian	yán jiū 研究
		mata pelajaran	xué kē 学科
		bidang studi	yán jiū kē mù 研究科目
		kamar belajar	shū fáng 书房, yán jiū shì 研究室
	(v.)	belajar, meneliti	xué xí 学习, yán jiū 研究
stuff	(n.)	barang	dōng xī 东西
		bahan	cái liào 材料
		barang tenunan	fǎng zhī pǐn 纺织品
	(v.)	menyumbat	sè 塞
		menyumbat sepenuhnya	sè mǎn 塞满
		mengisi	tián 填
		mengisi sepenuhnya	tián mǎn 填满
		memasukkan	zhuāng 装
		memasukkan sepenuh-penuhnya	zhuāng mǎn 装满

		makan sekenyang-ke-nyangnya	bǎo shì 饱食, chi dé bǎo bǎo dė 吃得饱饱的
stuff.ing	(n.)	isian	tián liào 填料
stuff.y	(a.)	pengap	mèn 闷, bù tòu qì 不透气
stum.ble	(v.)	tersandung jatuh	bàn dǎo 绊倒
		tersandung	bàn 绊
stu.pid	(a.)	bodoh	yú bèn 愚笨, yú chǔn 愚蠢
	(n.)	orang bodoh	shǎ guā 傻瓜, hú tú chóng 胡涂虫
stur.dy	(a.)	kokoh, kuat	jiān dìng 坚定, jiān qiáng 坚强
		kekar	zhuó zhuàng 茁壮
stut.ter	(n.)	hal bicara menggagap	kǒu chī 口吃
	(v.)	menggagap	kǒu chī 口吃
sty	(n.)	kandang babi	zhū quán 猪圈
style	(n.)	gaya	zuò fēng 作风, fēng gé 风格
		corak mode	yàng shì 样式
styl.ist	(n.)	perancang gaya	shè jì shī 设计师
sub.class	(n.)	cabang jenis	xiǎo lèi 小类
sub.di.vide	(v.)	membagi lagi	zài fēn 再分
sub.due	(v.)	menundukkan	zhēng fú 征服
sub.group	(n.)	grup kecil	xiǎo zǔ 小组
sub.head.ing	(n.)	anak judul	xiǎo biāo tí 小标题, fù biāo tí 副标题
sub.ject	(n.)	warga negara	guó mín 国民
		pokok pembicaraan	zhǔ tí 主题
		pokok kalimat	zhǔ yǔ 主语
		mata pelajaran	xué kē 学科, kē mù 科目
		pokok	zhǔ tǐ 主体
	(a.)	yang dipengaruhi, yang dikendalikan	shòu zhī pè dė 受支配的
	(v.)	menaklukkan, menunduk-kan	zhēng fú 征服
sub.jec.tive	(a.)	subjektif	zhǔ guān dė 主观的

sub.join	(v.)	menambahkan	fù jiā 附加, tiān bǔ 添补
sub.ju.gate	(v.)	menaklukkan	zhēng fú 征服
sub.junc.tive	(a.)	pengandaian	xū nǐ dė 虚拟的
		bentuk pengandaian	xū nǐ yú qì 虚拟语气
sub.ma.rine	(a.)	mengenai dasar laut	hǎi dǐ dė 海底的
	(n.)	kapal selam	qián shǔi tǐng 潜水艇
sub.merge	(v.)	menyelam ke dalam air	qián shǔi 潜水
		tenggelam	chén mò 沉没
sub.mis.sion	(n.)	penyerahan	qū fú 屈服
		kepatuhan	fú cóng 服从
sub.mit	(v.)	tunduk, menyerah	fú cóng 服从, qū fú 屈服
		mengajukan	chéng sòng 呈送,
		menyampaikan	tí jiaō 提交
sub.or.di.nate	(a.)	bawahan	xià jí dė 下级的
	(v.)	menundukkan	shǐ fú cóng 使服从
sub.scribe	(v.)	menandatangani	qiān shǔ 签署, qiān míng 签名
		menyumbang	juān zhù 捐助
		berlangganan koran atau majalah	dìng yuè 订阅
sub.scrib.er	(n.)	orang yg menandatangani	qiān míng rén 签名人
		orang yang berlangganan	dìng yuè zhě 定阅者
		orang yang menyumbang	juān zhù rén 捐助人
sub.scrip.tion	(n.)	tanda tangan	shǔ míng 署名, qiān míng 签名
sub.se.quent	(a.)	yang berikut	yǐ hoù dė 以后的
sub.se.quent.ly	(adv.)	kemudian	hòu lái 后来
sub.si.dize	(v.)	memberi subsidi	jīn tiē 津贴
sub.si.dy	(n.)	subsidi, tunjangan	bǔ zú jīn 补足金, jīn tiē jīn 津贴金
sub.sist	(v.)	hidup	shēng cún 生存
sub.sist.ence	(n.)	nafkah	shēng jì 生计
		hidup, biaya hidup	shēng cún 生存, shēng húo fèi 生活费

sub.stance	(n.)	zat, bahan	zhì 质, wù zhì 物质
		isi pokok	jī běn nèi róng 基本内容
sub.stan.tial	(a.)	yang pokok, penting	běn zhì dė 本质的,
			jī běn shàng dė 基本上的
sub.sta.tion	(n.)	stasiun cabang	fēn zhàn 分站
		(kantor) cabang	fēn jú 分局
sub.sti.tute	(n.)	pengganti	dài tì zhě 代替者, dài tì pǐn 代替品
	(v.)	mengganti, menggantikan	tì daì 替代, daì tì 代替
sub.sti.tu.tion	(n.)	penggantian	tì daì 替代, daì tì 代替
sub.ti.tle	(n.)	anak judul	xiǎo biāo tí 小标题, fù biāo tí 副标题
sub.tle	(a.)	lembut, halus	jīng xì 精细
sub.tract	(v.)	mengurangi	jiǎn 减, jiǎn qù 减去
sub.trac.tion	(n.)	pengurangan	jiǎn fǎ 减法
sub.urb	(n.)	pinggiran kota	jiaō wài 郊外
sub.ver.sion	(n.)	subversi	diān fù 颠复
sub.ver.sive	(a.)	subversif	diān fù dė 颠复的
sub.vert	(v.)	menumbangkan (pemerintahan)	diān fù 颠复
sub.way	(n.)	(jalan) kereta api bawah tanah	dì xià tiě dào 地下铁道
suc.ceed	(v.)	berhasil	chéng gōng 成功
		menggantikan	jì chéng 继承
suc.cess	(n.)	sukses, keberhasilan	chéng gōng 成功
		kemenangan	shèng lì 胜利
suc.cess.ful	(a.)	berhasil baik	chéng gōng dė 成功的
suc.ces.sion	(n.)	suksesi	jì chéng 继承, jiē bān 接班
		penggantian generasi	lián xù xìng 连续性
suc.ces.sive	(a.)	berturut-turut	lián xù dė 连续的
suc.ces.sor	(n.)	penerus	jì chéng rén 继承人,
			jiē bān rén 接班人

such	(a.)	seperti itu	nà yàng dė 那样的
		seperti ini	zhè yàng dė 这样的
		sedemikian, yg demikian	zhè zhǒng 这种, nà zhǒng 那种
	(pron.)	orang serupa ini	zhè yàng dė rén 这样的人
		hal serupa ini	zhè yàng dė shì 这样的事
		barang serupa ini	zhè yàng dė dōng xī 这样的东西
		demikian	rú cǐ 如此
such.like	(a.)	semacam itu	tóng yàng dė 同样的, xiàng nà yàng dė 象那样的
suck	(v.)	menghisap	xī 吸, xī shōu 吸收
sud.den	(a.)	tiba-tiba, mendadak	tū rán dė 突然的
sud.den.ly	(adv.)	dengan tiba-tiba	tū rán 突然, hū rán 忽然
suf.fer	(v.)	mengalami	zāo shòu 遭受
		menderita	zāo nàn 遭难, shòu kǔ 受苦
suf.fer.er	(n.)	penderita	shòu nàn zhě 受难者, shòu hài zhě 受害者
suf.fer.ing	(n.)	penderitaan	zaī nàn 灾难, kǔ nàn 苦难, shòu nàn 受难
suf.fice	(v.)	mencukupi	zú gòu 足够, mǎn zú 满足
suf.fi.cien.cy	(n.)	kecukupan	chōng zú 充足
suf.fi.cient	(a.)	cukup	chōng zú dė 充足的, zú gòu dė 足够的
suf.fix	(n.)	akhiran	hòu zhuì 后缀, cí wěi 词尾
	(v.)	membubuhi akhiran	tián cí wěi 填词尾
suf.fo.cate	(v.)	menyebabkan mati lemas	mēn sǐ 闷死
sug.ar	(n.)	gula	táng 糖
	(v.)	memberi gula	jiā táng 加糖
sug.ar-beet	(n.)	lobak gula, bit	tián cài 甜菜
sug.ar-cane	(n.)	tebu	gān zhè 甘蔗
sug.ar.y	(a.)	mengandung gula	hán táng dė 含糖的

sug.gest	(v.)	menyarankan	tí yì 提议, jiàn yì 建议
sug.ges.tion	(n.)	saran, usul	yì jiàn 意见, jiàn yì 建议
su.i.cide	(n.)	bunuh diri	zì shā 自杀
		orang yang bunuh diri	zì shā zhě 自杀者
		perbuatan bunuh diri	zì shā xíng wéi 自杀行为
suit	(n.)	gugatan	kòng sù 控诉
		setelan	yī tào 一套
		setelan jas (pakaian)	yī tào xí zhuāng 一套西装
		peminangan	qiú hūn 求婚
	(v.)	cocok, sesuai	hé shì 合适, shí yìng 适应
suit.a.ble	(a.)	pantas, cocok	shì dàng dė 适当的, hé shì dė 合适的
suit.case	(n.)	kopor	pí xiāng 皮箱
suit.or	(n.)	penggugat	kòng sù zhě 控诉者
		peminang	qiú hūn zhě 求婚者
sum	(n.)	jumlah	zòng shù 总数
		soal hitungan	suàn shù wèn tì 算术问题
		ringkasan	gài yào 概要
		sejumlah uang	jīn é 金额
	(v.)	menjumlahkan	hé jì 合计
		menyimpulkan	zǒng jié 总结
		meringkas	gài guā 概括
sum.ma.rize	(v.)	meringkas	gài guā 概括
sum.ma.ry	(a.)	ringkas	gài guā dė 概括的, gài yào dė 概要的
	(n.)	ringkasan	gài yào 概要, tí yào 提要
sum.mer	(n.)	musim panas	xià tiān 夏天
sum.mer.time	(n.)	musim panas	xià jì 夏季, xià tiān 夏天
sum.mit	(n.)	puncak	dǐng diǎn 顶点, zùi gāo feng 最高峰
sum.mon	(v.)	memanggil	zhào huàn 召唤, hū huàn 呼唤
		mengumpulkan	zhào jí 召集

sum.mons	(n.)	panggilan	zhào huàn 召唤, chuán huàn 传唤
		surat panggilan	chuán piào 传票
	(v.)	memanggil	chuán huàn 传唤
sun	(n.)	matahari	tài yáng 太阳, rì 日
sun-bath	(n.)	mandi cahaya matahari	rì guāng yù 日光浴
Sun.day	(n.)	hari Minggu	xīng qī rì 星期日, lǐ bài tiān 礼拜天
sun.down	(n.)	matahari terbenam	rì lùo 日落
sun.flow.er	(n.)	bunga matahari	xiàng rì kuí 向日葵
sun.glass.es	(n.)	kacamata hitam	tài yáng yǎn jìng 太阳眼镜, hèi yǎn jìng 黑眼镜
sun.light	(n.)	sinar matahari	rì guāng 日光, yáng guāng 阳光
	(a.)	riang	kuài húo 快活
sun.ny	(a.)	panas, terang	duō yáng guāng dė 多阳光的
sun.rise	(n.)	matahari terbit	rì chū 日出
sun.set	(n.)	matahari terbenam	tài yáng xià shān 太阳下山, rì luò 日落
sun.shade	(n.)	payung penahan sinar matahari	yáng sǎn 阳伞
		kerai penahan sinar matahari	tiān péng 天棚
sun.shine	(n.)	sinar matahari	rì guāng 日光
su.per	(a.)	super	tè jí dė 特级的, chāo jí dė 超级的
su.per.hu.man	(a.)	melebihi manusia biasa	chāo rén dė 超人的
su.per.i.or	(a.)	terbaik, unggul	zùi yōu xiù dė 最优秀的,
		pimpinan, atasan	shàng jí 上级,
		sombong	gaō aò dė 高傲的, jiaō aò dė 骄傲的
		superior	chaō jí dė 超级的, chaō yuè dė 超越的
	(n.)	pembesar, orang atasan	zhǎng guān 长官, shàng jí 上级
		orang yang lebih tua	zhǎng bèi 长辈
		unggulan	yōu shèng zhě 优胜者, yōu xiù zhě 优秀者

su.per.i.or.i.ty	(n.)	keunggulan	yōu yuè xìng 优越性, yōu shì 优势
su.per.la.tive	(a.)	yang teratas	zuì shàng dė 最上的
		yang tertinggi	zuì gaō dė 最高的
	(n.)	bentuk superlatif	zuì gaō jí 最高级,
			zuì gaō jí dān cí 最高级单词
su.per.man	(n.)	manusia super	chāo rén 超人
su.per.mar.ket	(n.)	supermarket	chāo jí shì chăng 超级市场
su.per.sede	(v.)	menggantikan	dài tì 代替
su.per.son.ic	(a.)	supersonik	chāo yīn sù dė 超音速的
su.per.sti.tion	(n.)	ketakhayulan, takhayul	mí xìn 迷信
su.per.struc.ture	(n.)	bangunan bagian atas	shàng céng jiān zhù 上层建筑
su.per.vise	(v.)	mengawasi	jiān shì 监视
su.per.vi.sor	(n.)	supervisor, pengawas	jiān dū rén 监督人
sup.per	(n.)	makan malam	wăn cān 晚餐, wăn fàn 晚饭
sup.ple.ment	(n.)	tambahan	bŭ chōng 补充, bŭ chōng wù 补充物
sup.pli.cate	(v.)	memohon, meminta	āi qiú 哀求, qí qiú 祈求
sup.pli.ca.tion	(n.)	permohonan, permintaan	āi qiú 哀求, qí qiú 祈求
sup.ply	(v.)	menyediakan, memberikan	gōng yìng 供应, gōng jĭ 供给
	(n.)	persediaan	gōng yìng 供应,
			gōng yìng pĭn 供应品
		perbekalan	shēng húo yòng pĭn 生活用品
sup.port	(v.)	mendukung, menyokong	zhī chí 支持, zhī yuán 支援
		membiayai	zī zhù 资助
		memelihara	fŭ yăng 抚养
		menyangga	zhī chēng 支撑, zhī jià 支架
	(n.)	sokongan, dukungan	zhī chí 支持, zhī yuán 支援
		pemeliharaan	fŭ yăng 抚养
		penyangga	zhī zhù 支柱
		pendukung, penyokong	zhī chí zhĕ 支持者,
			zhī yuán zhĕ 支援者

sup.port.er	(n.)	penyokong	zhī chí zhě 支持者
		pendukung	yōng hù zhě 拥护者
		suporter	lā lā dùi 啦啦队
sup.pose	(v.)	menduga	caī xiǎng 猜想, liào xiǎng 料想
		mengandaikan	jiǎ dìng 假定, jiǎ shǐ 假使
sup.po.si.tion	(n.)	perkiraan	tuī cè 推测
		pengandaian	jiǎ dìng 假定
sup.press	(v.)	menindas	zhèn yā 镇压, yā pò 压迫
		menahan	rěn zhù 忍住
		membredel	jìn zhǐ chū bǎn 禁止出版
		menyembunyikan	yǐn cáng 隐藏, yǐn mán 隐瞒
sup.pres.sion	(n.)	penindasan	zhèn yā 镇压
		penyembunyian	yǐn cáng 隐藏
		pembredelan	jìn zhǐ fā xíng 禁止发行
su.prem.a.cy	(n.)	supremasi, keunggulan	zuì gaō quán lì 最高权力, bà quán 霸权, yōu shì 优势
su.preme	(a.)	tertinggi, paling unggul	zùi gaō 最高
sure	(a.)	tentu, pasti, yakin	yī dìng 一定, bì rán 必然, què xìn 确信, què shí 确实
	(adv.)	benar-benar, sungguh	dì què 的确
		tentu saja	dāng rán 当然
sure.ly	(adv.)	tentu saja	dāng rán 当然
		dengan pasti	què shí 确实, yī dìng 一定, bì dìng 必定
sure.ty	(n.)	kebenaran	què shí xìng 确实性
		jaminan, tanggungan	bǎo zhèng wù 保证物, dàn bǎo wù 担保物
		penanggung	bǎo zhèng rén 保证人
sur.face	(n.)	permukaan	biǎo miàn 表面
sur.geon	(n.)	ahli bedah	wài kē yī shēng 外科医生

sur.ger.y	(n.)	pembedahan	wài kē 外科
		ilmu bedah	wài kē xué 外科学
		kamar bedah	wài kē shì 外科室
sur.gi.cal	(a.)	mengenai pembedahan	wài kē dė 外科的
sur.mount	(v.)	mengatasi	kè fú 克服
sur.mount.a.ble	(a.)	yang dapat diatasi	kě kè fú dė 可克服的
sur.name	(n.)	nama keluarga	xìng 姓
		alias	bié hào 别号, bié míng 别名
sur.pass	(v.)	melebihi, mengungguli	shèng gùo 胜过, chaō guò 超过
sur.plus	(n.)	kelebihan	shèng yú 剩余, yíng yú 盈余
sur.prise	(n.)	keheranan, kejutan	jīng qí 惊奇
		surprais	yì wài shì 意外事
	(v.)	mengejutkan	shǐ rén jīng qí 使人惊奇, shǐ rén zhèn jīng 使人震惊
sur.pris.ing	(a.)	yang mengherankan	jīng rén dė 惊人的
		yang mengejutkan	yì wài dė 意外的
sur.rend.er	(v.)	menyerah	tóu xiáng 投降
		melepaskan, meninggalkan	fàng qì 放弃
	(n.)	penyerahan	tóu xiáng 投降
sur.round	(v.)	mengelilingi, mengepung	wéi rǎo 围绕, huán rǎo 环绕
sur.round.ing	(a.)	sekeliling	zhōu wéi dė 周围的, sì zhōu dė 四周的
sur.round.ings	(n.)	lingkungan	huán jìng 环境, zhōu wéi 周围
		keadaan sekitar	zhōu wéi shì wù 周围事物, zhōu wéi qíng xíng 周围情形
sur.vey	(v.)	survei, peninjauan	shì chá 视察, guān chá 观察
		mengukur	cè liáng 测量
		memeriksa	diào chá 调查, jiǎn chá 检查
	(n.)	peninjauan, pemeriksaan	shì chá 视察, diào chá 调查
		pengukuran	cè liáng 测量

sur.vey.ing	(n.)	pengukuran tanah	cè liáng 测量
		ilmu pengukuran	cè liáng xué 测量学
sur.vey.or	(n.)	pengukur	cè liáng yuán 测量员
sur.viv.al	(n.)	hal hidup terus	shēng cún 生存
		kelangsungan hidup	bǎo quán shēng mìng 保全生命
sur.vive	(v.)	hidup lebih lama	gèng cháng mìng 更长命
		masih hidup	hái huó zhė 还活着
		menyelamatkan nyawa	bǎo quán shēng mìng 保全生命, táo shēng 逃生
sur.vi.vor	(n.)	orang yang selamat	táo shēng zhě 逃生者, tūo xiǎn zhě 脱险者
sus.pect	(v.)	mencurigai	huái yí 怀疑
	(n.)	tersangka	xián yí fàn 嫌疑犯
	(a.)	yang dicurigai	kě yí dė 可疑的
sus.pend	(v.)	menggantungkan	diào 吊, xuán guà 悬挂
		menunda	yán chí 延迟
		menghentikan	shǐ tíng zhǐ 使停止
		menskors	lè lìng tíng zhí 勒令停职, lè lìng tíng xué 勒令停学
sus.pen.der	(n.)	tali selempangan	bèi dài 背带, diào dài 吊带
sus.pense	(n.)	kebimbangan	dān xīn 担心
sus.pic.ion	(n.)	kecurigaan	huái yí 怀疑
sus.pi.cious	(a.)	mencurigakan	lìng rén huái yí dė 令人怀疑的
sus.tain	(v.)	menopang	zhī chēng 支撑
		meneruskan	wéi chí 维持
		menderita	shòu hài 受害, shòu nàn 受难
sus.te.nance	(n.)	makanan	liáng shì 粮食
swal.low	(v.)	menelan	tūn 吞
	(n.)	burung layang-layang	yàn zi 燕子
swamp	(n.)	rawa	zhǎo zé 沼泽
	(v.)	membanjiri	yān mò 淹没

swan	(n.)	angsa	tiān é 天鹅
swear	(v.)	bersumpah	fā shì 发誓
sweat	(n.)	keringat	hàn 汗
	(v.)	berkeringat	liú hàn 流汗, chū hàn 出汗
sweat.er	(n.)	kemeja dari wol	máo yī 毛衣
sweep	(v.)	menyapu	sǎo 扫, dǎ sǎo 打扫
sweep.er	(n.)	penyapu	dǎ sǎo zhě 打扫者
sweet	(a.)	manis	tián 甜, tián mì 甜蜜
		harum	fēn fāng 芬芳
		cantik	měi lì 美丽, měi miào 美妙
	(n.)	manisan	tián diǎn xīn 甜点心
		permen	táng guǒ 糖果
		kekasih, yang tercinta	qīn ài dė 亲爱的
sweet.en	(v.)	membubuhi gula	jiā táng 加糖
		membuat lebih manis	shǐ gēng tián mì 使更甜蜜
		membuat lebih manis	shǐ gēng kě ài 使更可爱
sweet-heart	(n.)	kekasih	ài rén 爱人, qíng rén 情人
sweet.meat	(n.)	manisan	tián guǒ 甜果
swell	(v.)	membengkak	zhǒng zhàng 肿胀
		membengkakkan	shǐ zhǒng zhàng 使肿胀
		mengembang	péng zhàng 膨胀
swift	(a.)	cepat	kuài 快, xùn sù 迅速
swim	(v.)	berenang	yóu yǒng 游泳
swim.mer	(n.)	perenang	yóu yǒng zhě 游泳者
swin.dle	(v.)	menipu	qī piàn 欺骗
swin.dler	(n.)	penipu	piàn zi 骗子
swine	(n.)	babi	zhū 猪
swing	(v.)	menggoyangkan	bǎi dòng 摆动, yáo dòng 摇动
		memutar	xuán zhuǎn 旋转
		mengayunkan	yáo huàng 摇晃
	(n.)	ayunan	qiū qiān 秋千

switch	(n.)	saklar	diàn zhá 电闸, diàn mén 电门
		tombol, kenop	kaī guān 开关
		ranting	zhī tiáo 枝条, biān zi 鞭子
		rotan	téng tiáo 藤条
	(v.)	berubah, mengubah	zhuǎn biàn 转变 , gǎi biàn 改变
		mengganti, berganti	zhuǎn huàn 转换
		memutar	níng zhuǎn 拧转, niǔ zhuǎn扭转
sword	(n.)	pedang	jiàn 剑
syl.la.ble	(n.)	suku kata	yīn jié 音节
syl.la.bus	(n.)	silabus, ikhtisar rencana	jiào xué dà gāng 教学大钢
		pelajaran	jiào àn 教案
sym.bol	(n.)	lambang	xiàng zhēng 象征
		simbol	jì hào 记号, fú hào 符号
sym.bol.ic	(a.)	simbolis	xiàng zhēng xìng dė 象征性的
sym.bol.ism	(n.)	simbolisme	xiàng zhēng zhǔ yì 象征主义
sym.bol.ize	(v.)	melambangkan	xiàng zhēng 象征
		menandakan	dǎ fú hào 打符号, dǎ jì hào 打记号
sym.met.ry	(n.)	simetri	dùi chèng 对称
sym.pa.thet.ic	(a.)	simpatik	tóng qíng dė 同情的
sym.pa.thize	(v.)	bersimpati	tóng qíng 同情
		ikut berduka cita	diào sāng 吊丧
sym.pa.thiz.er	(n.)	simpatisan	tóng qíng zhě 同情者
sym.pa.thy	(n.)	simpati	tóng qíng 同情, tóng qíng xīn 同情心
sym.pho.ny	(n.)	orkes simfoni	jiāo xiǎng yuè 交响乐
sym.po.sium	(n.)	simposium	zùo tán hùi 座谈会
symp.tom	(n.)	simtom	zhèng hòu 症候, zhèng zhuàng 症状
		gejala	zhēng zhào 征兆
syn.o.nym	(n.)	sinonim	tóng yì cí 同义词
syn.op.sis	(n.)	sinopsis, ikhtisar	tí yào 提要, gāng yào 纲要
syn.tax	(n.)	sintaksis, ilmu tata kalimat	jù fǎ 句法

syn.the.sis	(n.)	sintesis, perpaduan	zōng hé 综合, hé chéng 合成
sy.rup	(n.)	sirup	táng jiàng 糖酱, táng shǔi 糖水
sys.tem	(n.)	sistem	zhì dù 制度, xì tǒng 系统, tǐ xì 体系
		susunan	zǔ zhī xìng 组织性
		cara	fāng fǎ 方法
sys.tem.at.ic	(a.)	sistematis	yǒu xì tǒng dė 有系统的
		secara teratur	yǒu zǔ zhī dė 有组织的
sys.tem.at.i.cal.ly	(adv.)	secara sistematis	yǒu xì tǒng di 有系统地
		menurut susunan	yǒu zǔ zhī di 有组织地
sys.tem.a.tize	(v.)	mengatur rapi, menyusun rapi	xì tǒng huà 系统化

T

ta.ble	(n.)	meja	zhuō zi 桌子
		tabel	biǎo 表, xiàng mù biǎo 项目表
ta.ble-cloth	(n.)	taplak meja	zhuō bù 桌布
tab.let	(n.)	tablet	yào piàn 药片
ta.ble-ten.nis	(n.)	tenis meja, pingpong	pīng pāng qiú 乒乓球
ta.ble-ware	(n.)	alat-alat makan	cān jù 餐具
tab.loid	(n.)	tabloid, surat kabar kecil	xiǎo bào 小报
ta.boo	(n.)	larangan, tabu	jìn jì 禁忌
	(v.)	melarang, menabukan	jìn jì 禁忌
tab.u.late	(v.)	membuat/menyusun tabel	zhì biǎo 制表, liè biǎo 列表
tab.u.la.tor	(n.)	pembuat tabel	zhì biǎo rén 制表人
		alat untuk membuat tabel	zhi biǎo jī 制表机
tac.tics	(n.)	taktik, siasat	zhàn shù 战术, cè luè 策略
tail	(n.)	ekor	wěi 尾, wěi bā 尾巴
tail.or	(n.)	tailor, tukang jahit	féng yī jiàng 缝衣匠, cái féng 裁缝
take	(v.)	mengambil	nǎ 拿, nǎ zǒu 拿走
		membawa pergi	dài zǒu 带走
		makan, minum	chī 吃, hē 喝
		menyewa	zū 租, zū lìn 租赁
		memakan waktu	huā fèi shí jiān 花费时间
		menerima	jiē shòu 接受
		memperoleh	huò dé 获得
		mencatat	jì lù 记录
		naik	chéng 乘

take-off	(n.)	lepas landas	qǐ feī 起飞
tale	(n.)	kisah, cerita	gù shì 故事
tal.ent	(n.)	bakat	tiān cái 天才
		kecakapan	cái néng 才能
talk	(v.)	berbicara	shūo huà 说话, tán huà 谈话
	(n.)	pembicaraan	tán huà 谈话, hùi tán 会谈
talk.at.ive	(a.)	suka bicara	ài shūo huà dė 爱说话的, dūo zǔi 多咀
tall	(a.)	tinggi	gāo 高
tame	(a.)	jinak	xún 驯, xún fú 驯服
tang	(n.)	bau tajam	chòu qì 臭气, chòu wèi 臭味
tan.gle	(n.)	kekusutan, kekacauan	jiū chán 纠缠, jiū fēn 纠纷
	(v.)	mengusutkan	chán jié 缠结, jiū chán 纠缠
tank	(n.)	tank	tǎn kè chē 坦克车
		tempat air, tangki	shǔi tǒng 水桶, yóu tǒng 油桶
tank.er	(n.)	kapal tangki, truk tangki	yóu chuán 油船, yóu chē 油车
tap	(n.)	keran	lóng tóu 龙头, shǔi zǔi 水咀
		ketuk	qīng qiaō 轻敲, qīng pò 轻拍
	(v.)	membuka keran	kaī shǔi lóng tóu 开水龙头
		membuka sumbat	fàng shǔi 放水
		mengetuk	qīng qiāo 轻敲, qīng pò 轻拍
tape	(n.)	pita	cí dài 磁带
tape-re.cord.er	(n.)	alat perekam	cí dài lù yīn jī 磁带录音机
tape worm	(n.)	cacing pita	tiáo chóng 条虫
tap.i.o.ca	(n.)	pati, kanji, tapioka	mù shǔ diàn fěn 木薯淀粉
tar.get	(n.)	bulan-bulanan, sasaran	bǎ 靶, mù biāo 目标
		target	zhǐ biāo 指标
tar.iff	(n.)	tarif	jià mù biǎo 价目表
		bea, cukai	guān shùi 关税
task	(n.)	tugas	gōng zùo 工作
		kewajiban	rèn wù 任务

taste	(v.)	mencicipi	cháng 尝
	(n.)	rasa	zī wèi 滋味
		selera	qù wèi 趣味, kǒu wèi 口味
taste.ful	(a.)	enak, sedap	měi wèi dė 美味的
taste.less	(a.)	hambar, tawar	wú wèi dė 无味的
tat.tle	(v.)	mengobrol	xián tán 闲谈
tat.too	(n.)	gambar tato	wén shēn 文身
tax	(n.)	pajak	shùi 税, shùi wù 税务
	(v.)	mengenakan pajak	zhēng shùi 征税
tax.a.tion	(n.)	perpajakan	fù shuì 赋税, shuì shōu 税收
tax.i	(n.)	taksi	chū zū qì chē 出租汽车
tax.is	(n.)	urutan	shùn xù 顺序, paí liè 排列
tax.pay.er	(n.)	pembayar pajak	nà shùi rén 纳税人
tea	(n.)	teh	chá 茶
		minuman teh	chá diǎn 茶点
tea-cake	(n.)	kue untuk hidangan minum teh	chá diǎn 茶点
teach	(v.)	mengajar	jiào 教, jiào dǎo 教导, jiào shū 教书
teach.er	(n.)	guru	lǎo shī 老师, jiào shī 教师
teach.ing	(n.)	pengajaran	jiào xué 教学, jiào xun 教训
tea.cup	(n.)	cangkir teh	chá bēi 茶杯
tea-ket.tle	(n.)	teko teh	chá hú 茶壶
tea-leaf	(n.)	daun teh	chá yè 茶叶
team	(n.)	regu, rombongan	xiǎo duì 小队, qiú dùi 球队
tea.pot	(n.)	teko teh	chá hú 茶壶
tear	(n.)	air mata	yǎn lèi 眼泪
		sobekan	sī liè 撕裂, liè féng 裂缝
	(v.)	menyobek	sī 撕, chě 扯
tease	(v.)	menggoda	xì nòng 戏弄
		meminta dengan paksa	qiáng qiú 强求

tea-spoon	(n.)	sendok teh	chá chí 茶匙
tech.nic	(n.)	teknis	jì shù shàng dė技术上的
tech.ni.cal	(a.)	teknis	jì shù shàng dė技术上的
tech.ni.cian	(n.)	teknisi	jì shī技师, jì gōng技工, jì shù rén yuán技术人员
tech.nique	(n.)	teknik	jì shù技术
tech.nol.o.gist	(n.)	ahli teknologi	jì shù zhuān jiā技术专家
tech.nol.o.gy	(n.)	teknologi	gōng yì xué 工艺学, gōng yè jì shù 工业技术
teem	(v.)	penuh dengan	chōng mǎn 充满, fù yú 富于
teen	(n.)	gadis cilik	miào líng shǎo nǔ 妙龄少女
teen-ager	(n.)	anak tanggung, anak be- lasan tahun	shí dūo sùi qīng nián 十多岁青年
teens	(n.)	umur belasan tahun	shí dūo sùi 十多岁
teeth	(n.)	gigi	yá chǐ 牙齿
teethe	(v.)	tumbuh gigi	chū yá 出牙
tel.e.cast	(n.)	siaran televisi	diàn shì guǎng bō 电视广播
	(v.)	menyiarkan melalui televisi	diàn shì zhuǎn bō 电视转播
tel.e.com.mu.ni.ca.tion	(n.)	telekomunikasi	diàn xìn 电信
tel.e.film	(n.)	film televisi	diàn shì yǐng piàn 电视影片
tel.e.gram	(n.)	telegram	diàn bào 电报
tel.e.graph	(n.)	telegraf, telegram	diàn bào 电报, diàn bào jī 电报机
	(v.)	mengirim telegram	dǎ diàn bào 打电报
tel.e.graph.er	(n.)	pengirim telegram	bào wù yuán 报务员
tel.e.graph.ic	(a.)	mengenai telegram	diàn bào dė 电报的, diàn xìn dė 电信的
tel.e.graph.y	(n.)	ilmu telegram	diàn bào xué 电报学
tel.e.phone	(n.)	telepon	diàn huà 电话
	(v.)	menelepon	dǎ diàn huà 打电话
tel.e.pho.to	(n.)	potret jarak jauh	chuán zhēn diàn bào传真电报

tel.e.pho.to.graph	(n.)	potret yang dikirimkan melalui kawat atau radio	chuán zhēn diàn bào 传真电报
tel.e.scope	(n.)	teleskop	wàng yuǎn jìng 望远镜
tel.e.view	(v.)	menonton televisi	kàn diàn shì 看电视
	(n.)	gambar televisi	diàn shì xiàng 电视象
		acara televisi	diàn shì jié mù 电视节目
tel.e.vise	(v.)	menyiarkan melalui televisi	diàn shì bō sòng 电视播送
tel.e.vi.sion	(n.)	televisi	diàn shì 电视
tell	(v.)	menceritakan, mengatakan	jiǎng 讲, jiǎng shù 讲述, shuō说
		memberitahukan	gào sù 告诉
		menyuruh	fēn fù 吩咐, jiào 叫
		menghitung	jì 计
		menyebutkan angka	shù 数
tell.er	(n.)	kasir	chū nà yuán 出纳员
		pembicara	jiǎng huà rén 讲话人
tell.tale	(n.)	pengadu	bān nòng shì feī dė rén 搬弄是非的人
		pembuka rahasia	gào mì zhě 告密者
tem.per	(n.)	tabiat	xìng qíng 性情
tem.per.a.ture	(n.)	temperatur	wēn dù 温度, tǐ wēn 体温
tem.pest	(n.)	prahara, badai	bào fēng yǔ 暴风雨
tem.ple	(n.)	kelenteng, kuil	miào yǔ 庙宇, sì miào 寺庙
		pelipis	tài yáng xué 太阳穴
tem.po.ra.ry	(a.)	sementara	zàn shí dė 暂时的
tempt	(v.)	menggoda	yǐn yòu 引诱, yòu hùo 诱惑
ten	(n.)	sepuluh	shí 十
ten.ant	(n.)	penyewa tanah	diàn hù 佃户
		penyewa rumah	fáng kè 房客
tend	(v.)	merawat	zhào guǎn 照管, kàn hù 看护
		mengurus	guǎn lǐ 管理
		cenderung	qū xiàng 趋向, qīng xiàng 倾向

tend.en.cy	(n.)	kecenderungan	qū shì 趋势, qīng xiàng 倾向
ten.der	(n.)	perawat	kàn hù rén 看护人
		penjaga	kàn shǒu rén 看守人
		penawaran, tender	bào jià 报价, tóu biaō 投标
	(v.)	mengajukan	tí chū 提出, tí gōng 提供
		mengikuti tender	tóu biaō 投标
	(a.)	empuk	nèn 嫩
		lemah, lembut	róu rùo 柔弱, ruǎn rùo 软弱
ten.fold	(adv.)	sepuluh kali lipat	shí bèi 十倍
ten.nis	(n.)	tenis	wǎng qiú 网球
tense	(n.)	waktu	shí taì 时态
	(a.)	tegang	jǐn zhāng dė 紧张的
ten.sion	(n.)	tegangan, ketegangan	zhāng lì 张力, lā lì 拉力
tent	(n.)	tenda	zhàng péng 帐篷
	(v.)	berkemah	zhá yíng 扎营
tenth	(n.)	kesepuluh	dì shí 第十
		sepersepuluh	shí fēn zhī yī 十分之一
term	(n.)	jangka waktu	qí xiàn 期限
		semester	xué qí 学期
		istilah	shù yú 术语
	(pl.)	syarat-syarat	tiáo jiàn 条件
ter.mi.nal	(n.)	batas akhir	zhōng diǎn 终点
		terminal, penghentian	chē zhàn 车站
ter.mi.nate	(v.)	berakhir, mengakhiri	zhōng zhǐ 终止, jié shù 结束
ter.mi.na.tion	(n.)	kesudahan, penghentian	jié shù 结束, zhōng zhǐ 终止
ter.race	(n.)	teras	lù tái 露台
ter.ri.ble	(a.)	mengerikan	kě pà dė 可怕的
		hebat	lì hài 厉害
ter.ri.fy	(v.)	menakuti	kǒng xià 恐吓
ter.ri.to.ry	(n.)	daerah kekuasaan, teritori	líng tǔ 领土

ter.ror	(n.)	teror	kǒng bù 恐怖
ter.ror.ism	(n.)	terorisme	kǒng bù zhèng cè 恐怖政策,
			kǒng bù zhèng zhì 恐怖政治
ter.ror.ist	(n.)	teroris	kǒng bù fèn zì 恐怖份子
test	(n.)	ujian, percobaan	cè yàn 测验, shì yàn 试验
	(v.)	menguji, mencoba	cè yàn 测验, shì yàn 试验, jiǎn yàn 检验
tes.ta.ment	(n.)	surat wasiat	yí shū 遗书, yí zhǔ 遗嘱
		Injil	shèng yùe shū 圣约书
test.ator	(n.)	orang yang meninggalkan surat wasiat	yí zhǔ rén 遗嘱人
test.ee	(n.)	orang yang diuji	shòu cè yàn zhě 受测验者
test.er	(n.)	orang yang menguji	cè yàn zhě 测验者,
			jiǎn yàn zhě 检验者
tes.ti.mo.nial	(n.)	tanda penghargaan	jiǎng zhuàng 奖状
		surat keterangan	zhèng míng shū 证明书
tes.ti.mo.ny	(n.)	kesaksian	zhèng yán 证言, zhèng míng 证明
test-tube	(n.)	tabung percobaan	shì yàn guǎn 试验管, shì guǎn 试管
tes.ty	(a.)	mudah marah	yì nù dė 易怒的
		tidak sabar	xìng jǐ dė 性急的
tet.a.nus	(n.)	tetanus	pò shàng fēng 破伤风
text	(n.)	teks, naskah	yuán wén 原文, běn wén 本文
		buku pelajaran	kè běn 课本, jiào kē shū 教科书
text.book	(n.)	buku pelajaran	kè běn 课本, jiào kē shū 教科书
tex.tile	(a.)	mengenai tekstil	fǎng zhī dė 纺织的
	(n.)	tekstil, barang tekstil	fǎng zhī pǐn 纺织品
than	(conj.)	daripada	bǐ 比, bǐ qǐ 比起
thank	(v.)	berterima kasih	gǎn xiè 感谢, xiè xiè 谢谢
thank.ful	(a.)	berterima kasih	gǎn xiè dė 感谢的, gǎn jī dė 感激的
thank.less	(a.)	tidak berterima kasih	bù gǎn jī dė 不感激的,
			bù lǐng qíng 不领情

thanks	(n.)	terima kasih	gǎn jī 感激, gǎn xiè 感谢, xiè xiè 谢谢
thanks.giv.ing	(n.)	rasa syukur	xiè ēn 谢恩, gǎn ēn 感恩
		hari pernyataan terima kasih	gǎn ēn jié 感恩节
that	(a.)	itu	nà 那, nà gè 那个
	(pron.)	itu	nà gè 那个
	(adv.)	begitu	nà mè 那么, nà yàng 那样
	(conj.)	bahwa, agar, supaya	nà shì 那是, yǐ biàn 以便, wèi zhě 为着
		sebab itu	yīn wèi 因为
the	(art.)	ini, itu	zhè 这, nà 那
the.a.tre	(n.)	teater, gedung bioskop	diàn yǐng yuàn 电影院
		gedung sandiwara	xì yuàn 戏院, jù yuàn 剧院
theft	(n.)	pencurian	tōu qiè 偷窃
their	(pron.)	kepunyaan mereka	tā mēn dė 他们的
theirs	(pron.)	kepunyaan mereka	tā mēn dė 他们的
		barang mereka	tā mèn dė dōng xī 他们的东西
the.ism	(n.)	aliran ketuhanan	yǒu shén lùn 有神论
them	(pron.)	mereka	tā mèn 他们
theme	(n.)	tema, pokok	tí mù 题目, zhǔ tí 主题
them.selves	(pron.)	mereka sendiri	tā mèn zì jǐ 他们自己
then	(adv.)	pada waktu itu	dāng shí 当时
		sesudah itu	rán hòu 然后
		maka	nà mė 那么
thence	(adv.)	dari sana	cóng nà lǐ 从那里
		oleh karena, jadi	yīn cǐ 因此
thence.forth	(adv.)	sejak saat itu	cóng nà shí qǐ 从那时起
the.o.lo.gian	(n.)	ahli teologi	shén xúe jiā 神学家
the.ol.o.gy	(n.)	ilmu ketuhanan	shén xúe 神学
the.o.rem	(n.)	dalil, rumus	dìng lǐ 定理, yuán lǐ 原理
the.o.rist	(n.)	ahli teori	lǐ lùn jiā 理论家

the.o.rize	(v.)	membuat teori	jiàn lì lǐ lùn 建立理论,
			zuò chū lǐ lùn 作出理论
the.o.ry	(n.)	teori	lǐ lùn 理论
there	(adv.)	di sana, di situ	zài nà lǐ 在那里, zài nà biān 在那边
		ke sana, ke situ	dào nà lǐ 到那里, dào nà biān 到那边
		sana, situ	nà lǐ 那里, nà biān 那边
there.a.bout(s)	(adv.)	di dekat sana	zài nà fu jìn 在那附近
		kira-kira	dà yuè 大约
there.af.ter	(adv.)	sesudah itu, kemudian	cǐ hòu 此后, yǐ hòu 以后
there.at	(adv.)	pada waktu itu	dāng shí 当时
		pada tempat itu	dāng dì 当地
there.by	(adv.)	karena itu	yīn cǐ 因此
there.for	(adv.)	karena itu	yīn cǐ 因此
there.fore	(adv.)	karena itu	yīn cǐ 因此
there.from	(adv.)	dari sana	cóng nà lǐ 从那里
there.in	(adv.)	di sana	zài nà lǐ 在那里
		di antaranya	qí zhōng 其中
		dalam tempat itu	zaì nà dì táng 在那地方
there.of	(adv.)	dari itu	yóu cǐ 由此
there.on	(adv.)	di atas itu	zài qí shàng 在其上
there.to	(adv.)	ke sana	dào nà lǐ 到那里
		tambahan pula	cǐ wài 此外
there.up.on	(adv.)	di atas itu	zài qí shàng 在其上
		lalu, setelah itu	yú shì 于是
		segera	lì kè 立刻
there.with	(adv.)	dengan itu	yǔ cǐ 与此
		bersama dengan itu	yǔ cǐ tóng shí 与此同时
		dengan segera	súi jí 随即, lì kè 立刻
there.with.al	(adv.)	di samping itu	cǐ wài 此外
		bersamaan dengan itu	yǔ cǐ tóng shí 与此同时
		kemudian	jiē zhė 接着

ther.mom.e.ter	(n.)	termometer, alat peng-ukur suhu/panas	wēn dù ji 温度计, wēn dù biǎo 温度表
ther.mos	(n.)	termos	rè shǔi píng 热水瓶
these	(a.)	ini (jamak)	zhè xiē 这些
the.sis	(n.)	tesis	mìng tí 命题, lùn tí 论题
they	(pron.)	mereka	tā mėn 他们
thick	(a.)	tebal, kental	hòu 厚, nóng 浓, nóng hòu 浓厚
thick.en	(v.)	mempertebal	jiā hòu 加厚
		mengentalkan	jiā nóng 加浓
thief	(n.)	maling, pencuri	zeí 贼, xiǎo tōu 小偷
thieve	(v.)	mencuri	tōu qiè 偷窃
thiev.er.y	(n.)	pencurian	tōu qiè xíng wėi 偷窃行为, tōu qiè shì jiàn 偷窃事件
thigh	(n.)	paha	dà tǔi 大腿
thin	(a.)	tipis, kurus	bó 薄, shòu 瘦
thine	(pron.)	kepunyaanmu	nǐ dė 你的
thing	(n.)	benda, barang	dōng xī 东西
		hal	shì 事
think	(v.)	berpikir, memikirkan	xiǎng 想, kǎo lù 考虑
think.a.ble	(a.)	dapat dipikirkan	kě xiǎng xiàng dė 可想象的
think.er	(n.)	ahli pikir	sī xiǎng jiā 思想家
third	(n.)	ketiga	dì sān 第三
		tanggal tiga	sān hào 三号
third.class	(a.)	kelas tiga	sān děng 三等
third.ly	(adv.)	yang ketiga	dì sān 第三
thirst	(n.)	haus	kě 渴, kǒu kě 口渴
	(v.)	haus akan, ingin sekali	kě wàng 渴望, hěn xiǎng 很想
thir.teen	(n.)	tiga belas	shí sān 十三
thir.teenth	(n.)	ketiga belas	dì shí sān 第十三
		tanggal tiga belas	shí sān hào 十三号
		sepertiga belas	shí sān fēn zhī yī 十三分之一

thir.ti.eth	(n.)	ketiga puluh	dì sān shí 第三十
		tanggal tiga puluh	sān hào 三号
		sepertiga puluh	sān shí fēn zhī yī 三十分之一
thir.ty	(n.)	tiga puluh	sān shí 三十
this	(a.)	ini	zhè 这, zhè gè 这个
thith.er	(adv.)	ke sana, ke situ	xiàng nà biān 向那边
thorn	(n.)	duri	cì 刺, jīng jí 荆棘
thorn.y	(a.)	berduri	yǒu cì dė 有刺的
		sulit, rumit	kùn nàn 困难, jí shǒu 棘手
thor.ough	(a.)	sama sekali	chōng fēn dė 充分的, chè dǐ dė 彻底的
thor.ough.bred	(n.)	keturunan murni	liáng zhǒng dė 良种的
thor.ough.fare	(n.)	jalan besar	dà dào 大道
thor.ough.ly	(adv.)	sepenuhnya, sama sekali	chōng fēn di 充分地, chè dǐ di 彻底地
those	(a.)	itu	nà xiē 那些
thou	(pron.)	anda	nǐ 你
though	(conj.)	meskipun	suī rán 虽然
thought	(n.)	pikiran	sī kǎo 思考, sī xiǎng 思想
thought.ful	(a.)	penuh perhatian	yǒu sī xiǎng dė 有思想的, guān xīn dė 关心的
thought.less	(a.)	tidak memikirkan	bù kǎo lǜ dė 不考虑的, wú sī xiǎng dė 无思想的
		lalai, alpa	qīng shùai 轻率, cū xīn dė 粗心的
thou.sand	(n.)	ribu	qiān 千
thou.sandth	(n.)	keseribu	dì yī qiān 第一千
		seperseribu	qiān fēn zhī yī 千分之一
thrash	(v.)	mencambuk	biān dǎ 鞭打
thread	(n.)	benang	xiàn 线
threat	(n.)	ancaman	kǒng xià 恐吓, weī xié 威胁
threat.en	(v.)	mengancam	kǒng xià 恐吓, weī xié 威胁
three	(n.)	tiga	sān 三

three.fold	(a.)	lipat tiga	sān bèi 三倍
three.score	(n.)	enam puluh	liù shí 六十
		umur enam puluh tahun	liù shí sùi 六十岁
thresh	(v.)	menumbuk padi	dă gŭ 打谷
thresh.old	(n.)	ambang pintu	mén kăn 门槛
thrice	(adv.)	tiga kali	sān cì 三次
thrift	(n.)	penghematan	jié jiăn 节俭
thrift.less	(a.)	boros	làng fèi 浪费
thrill	(v.)	menggetarkan	zhèn dòng 震动
		menggairahkan	shĭ rén xīng fèn 使人兴奋
thrive	(v.)	tumbuh dengan subur	xīng wàng 兴旺, fán róng 繁荣
throat	(n.)	kerongkongan, tenggo-rokan	hóu lóng 喉咙
throne	(n.)	mahkota, takhta	wáng wèi 王位, băo zuò 宝座
throng	(n.)	khalayak ramai, gerom-bolan orang	rén qún 人群
	(v.)	berdesak-desakan, ber-kerumun	jĭ măn 挤满
through	(prep.)	melalui	jīng gùo 经过, tōng gùo 通过
		karena	yīn wèi 因为
through.out	(prep.)	di seluruh, sepanjang	biàn jí 遍及, guān chuān 贯穿
	(adv.)	seluruh, di mana-mana	quán bù 全部, dào chù 到处
throw	(v.)	melempar, membuang	pāo 抛, diū 丢
thrust	(v.)	menusuk, menikam	chuō 戳, cì 刺
		mendorong	tuī 推, tuī jìn 推进
thumb	(n.)	jempol, ibu jari	mŭ zhĭ 拇指
thun.der	(n.)	petir, guntur	léi 雷
	(v.)	mengguntur, mengge-muruh	dă léi 打雷, hōng lōng 轰隆
thun.der-bolt	(n.)	halilintar, petir	léi diàn 雷电

thun.der-storm	(n.)	hujan petir	léi yǔ 雷雨
Thurs.day	(n.)	hari Kamis	xīng qī sì 星期四
thus	(adv.)	demikian	zhè yàng 这样, rú cǐ 如此
		sebab itu	yīn ér 因而
thy	(a.)	kepunyaanmu	nǐ dė 你的
thy.self	(pron.)	anda sendiri	nǐ zì jǐ 你自己
ti.ar.a	(n.)	mahkota bersusun tiga yang dikenakan oleh Paus	jiào huáng sān chóng guān 教皇三重冠
tick.et	(n.)	tiket, karcis	piào 票
tide	(n.)	air pasang	cháo shǔi 潮水
ti.di.ness	(n.)	kerapian	zhěng qí 整齐, zhěng jié 整洁
ti.dy	(a.)	rapi, teratur	zhěng jié 整洁, zhěng qí 整齐
tie	(n.)	dasi	lǐng dài 领带
		pertalian, hubungan	lián xì 联系, guān xì 关系
	(v.)	mengikat	xì 系, kǔn 捆, bǎng 绑
ti.ger	(n.)	harimau	lǎo hǔ 老虎
tight	(a.)	ketat, kencang	jǐng 紧
tight.en	(v.)	mengetatkan	nòng jǐng 弄紧
		mengencangkan	lā jǐng 拉紧
tight.ly	(adv.)	kencang, dengan kencang	jǐng 紧, jǐng jǐng di 紧紧地
		dengan ketat	jǐng mì di 紧密的
ti.gress	(n.)	harimau betina	cí lǎo hǔ 雌老虎
tile	(n.)	genting	wǎ piàn 瓦片
till	(prep.)	sampai, hingga	dào ... wéi zhǐ 到…为止, zhí dào 直到
	(v.)	mengerjakan tanah, membajak	gēng tián 耕田, gēng 耕
till.er	(n.)	petani	nóng fū 农夫
tim.ber	(n.)	kayu, kayu bangunan	shù mù 树木, mù cái 木材, mù liào 木料
time	(n.)	waktu	shí jiān 时间
		jam, pukul	shí kè 时刻, diǎn zhōng 点钟
		zaman	shí dài 时代

		kali	cì 次, húi 回
		musim	jì jié 季节
		kesempatan	shí jī 时机, jī hùi 机会
time.less	(a.)	tak habis-habisnya, abadi	yǒng yuǎn 永远, yǒng jiǔ 永久
time.ly	(a.)	tepat pada waktunya	jí shí dė 及时的, hé shí dė 合时的
time-ta.ble	(n.)	jadwal	shí jiān biǎo 时间表
tim.id	(a.)	takut-takut, malu	dǎn xiǎo dė 胆小的
tim.ing	(n.)	perhitungan waktu	jì shí 计时
		penentuan waktu	dìng shí 定时
		ketepatan waktu	yìng shí 应时
tin	(n.)	timah, kaleng	xī 锡, mǎ kǒu tiě 马口铁, guàn tóu 罐头
tin.ny	(a.)	yang berhubungan dengan timah	xī dė 锡的
		yang mengandung timah	hán xī dė 含锡的
ti.ny	(a.)	kecil sekali	weī xiǎo 微小, xì xiǎo 细小
tip	(v.)	miring	qīng xié 倾斜
		memiringkan	shǐ qīng xié 使倾斜
		mengetuk	qīng qiáo 轻敲, qīng pò 轻拍
		memberi persen	gěi xiǎo fèi 给小费, gě shǎng qián 给偿钱
	(n.)	ujung	jiān duān 尖端
		persen	xiǎo feì 小费, shǎng qián 偿钱
		petunjuk, nasihat	zhǐ shì 指示, zhōng gào 忠告
tip.toe	(n.)	ujung jari kaki	jiǎo jiān 脚尖
tip-top	(a.)	paling tinggi	jué dǐng 绝顶, zùi gāo fēng 最高峰
		paling baik	zùi hǎo dė 最好的
tire	(n.)	ban	lún tāi 轮胎
	(v.)	melelahkan	shǐ rén pí láo 使人疲劳
		menjemukan	shǐ rén yàn juàn 使人厌倦
		menjadi lelah	pí láo 疲劳
		menjadi bosan	yàn juàn 厌倦

tired	(a.)	lelah, letih	pí láo 疲劳, pí juàn 疲倦, yàn juàn 厌倦
tire.less	(a.)	tak mengenal lelah	bù juàn dė 不倦的, bù yàn dė 不厌的
tire.some	(a.)	membosankan	shĭ rén yàn juàn 使人厌倦
		menjemukan	shĭ rén tăo yàn 使人讨厌
		mengesalkan, meletihkan	shĭ rén pí láo 使人疲劳, shĭ rén pí juàn 使人疲倦
tis.sue	(n.)	tisu, tenunan, jaringan	zhī wù 织物, zŭ zhī 组织
tis.sue-pa.per	(n.)	kertas tisu	shā zhĭ 砂纸, bó zhĭ 薄纸
ti.tle	(n.)	judul	biaō tí 标题, tí mù 题目, shū míng 书名
		gelar	xián tóu 衔头, guān xián 官衔, xué wèi 学位
to	(prep.)	ke	xiàng 向, wăng 往
		kepada	dùi 对, zhēn dùi 针对
		sampai, untuk, terhadap	dào 到, gĕi 给, dùi yú 对于
toad	(n.)	semacam katak	lài há má 癞蛤蟆
toast	(n.)	roti panggang	kăo miàn baō 烤面包
		minum untuk memberi selamat, sulang	zhù jiŭ 祝酒
	(v.)	memanggang	kăo 烤, hōng 烘
		minum untuk memberi selamat, bersulang	zhù jiŭ 祝酒, wèi ... ér gān bèi 为…而干杯
		menghangatkan badan	qŭ nŭan 取暖, hōng nuăn 烘暖
toast.er	(n.)	alat pemanggang roti	hōng lú 烘炉
to.bac.co	(n.)	tembakau	yān căo 烟草, yān yè 烟叶
to-day	(n., adv.)	hari ini	jīn tiān 今天
toe	(n.)	jari kaki	jiăo zhĭ 脚趾
to.ga	(n.)	jubah	yuán jiăo dà guà 园角大褂

to.geth.er	(adv.)	bersama-sama	yī qǐ 一起, yī tóng 一同
toil	(v.)	kerja keras	kǔ gàn 苦干
toil.et	(n.)	hal berdandan	hùa zhuāng 化桩, dǎ bàn 打扮
		meja toilet	shū zhuāng taí 梳桩台
		kamar kecil	guàn xǐ shì 盥洗室, cè sǔo 厕所
toil.et-paper	(n.)	kertas kloset	wèi shēng zhǐ 卫生纸
toil.some	(a.)	melelahkan	xīn kǔ dė 辛苦的
tol.e.rance	(n.)	toleransi, kelapangan dada	kuān róng 宽容
		kesabaran	rĕn nài 忍耐
tol.er.ant	(a.)	bersikap toleran, sabar	kuān dà dė 宽大的,
			kuān róng dė 宽容的,
			rĕn nài dė 忍耐的
tol.er.ate	(v.)	menyabarkan diri	róng rĕn 容忍
		melapangkan dada	kuǎn róng 宽容
tol.er.a.tion	(n.)	toleransi	kuān róng 宽容, róng rĕn 容忍
toll	(n.)	bea, bea jalan	fèi 费, tōng xíng fèi 通行费,
			tōng gùo shùi 通过税
		bunyi lonceng	zhōng shēng 钟声
	(v.)	bunyi, berbunyi	xiǎng 响, qiáo xiǎng 敲响
toll-gate	(n.)	pintu tol	shōu fèi mén 收费门
to.ma.to	(n.)	tomat	fán qié 番茄
tomb	(n.)	kuburan, makam	fén mù 坟墓
tomb-stone	(n.)	batu nisan	mù bēi 墓碑
tom.cat	(n.)	kucing jantan	xióng māo 雄猫
tom.fool	(n.)	orang yang bodoh sekali	dà shǎ guā 大傻瓜
to.mor.row	(n.)	besok	míng tiān 明天
ton	(n.)	ton	yīng dūn 英吨
tone	(n.)	bunyi	shēng yīn 声音
		nada	diào zi 调子, yīn diào 音调
		kesehatan	jiàn kāng 健康

tongs	(n.)	jepitan	qián 钳, hǔo qián 火钳
tongue	(n.)	lidah	shé 舌, shé tóu 舌头
ton.ic	(n.)	obat kuat	bǔ yào 补药
to.night	(n.)	malam ini	jīn wǎn 今晚
too	(adv.)	juga	yě 也
		terlalu	tài 太
tool	(n.)	alat	gōng jù 工具
		kaki tangan	zhǎo yá 爪牙, zǒu gǒu 走狗
tooth	(n.)	gigi	yá chǐ 牙齿
tooth.ache	(n.)	sakit gigi	yá chǐ tòng 牙齿痛
tooth.brush	(n.)	sikat gigi	yá shuā 牙刷
tooth-paste	(n.)	odol, pasta gigi	yá gaō 牙膏
tooth.pick	(n.)	tusuk gigi	yá qiān 牙签
tooth.some	(a.)	enak, lezat	měi wèi dė 美味的, kě kǒu dė 可口的
top	(n.)	puncak	dǐng 顶
		daun	yè zi 叶子
		tutup	gài zi 盖子
		gasing	tuó luó 陀螺
	(v.)	menutup, mengatapi	gài 盖, jiā dǐng 加顶
		mengalahkan, melebihi	shèng gùo 胜过, sài gùo 赛过, gāo yú 高于
top.er	(n.)	peminum berat	jiǔ gǔi 酒鬼
top.ic	(n.)	topik, pokok pembicaraan	lùn tí 论题, tí mù 题目
top.most	(a.)	paling atas	zùi gāo dė 最高的
torch	(n.)	obor	hǔo bǎ 火把
tor.ment	(n.)	kesengsaraan	tòng kǔ 痛苦
	(v.)	menyengsarakan	shǐ tòng kǔ 使痛苦
		menyiksa	zhé mó 折磨
tor.ment.or	(n.)	penyiksa	zhé mó zhě 折磨者
tor.na.do	(n.)	tornado	dà xuán fēng 大旋风
tor.pe.do	(n.)	torpedo	yǔ léi 鱼雷

tor.toise	(n.)	kura-kura	wū guī 乌龟
tor.tu.ous	(a.)	berliku-liku	qū zhé 曲折, wān wān qū qū 弯弯曲曲
tor.ture	(n.)	penyiksaan, penganiayaan	kǎo dǎ 拷打, nuè dài 虐待, zhé mó 折磨
	(v.)	menyiksa, menganiaya	kǎo dǎ 拷打, nuè dài 虐待
toss	(v.)	melemparkan ke atas	xiàng shàng diū 向上丢
		mengayunkan ke atas	xiàng shàng yáng 向上扬
		mengombang-ambingkan	shǐ dòng dàng 使动荡, shǐ yáo pǎi 使摇摆
	(n.)	lemparan ke atas	diū shàng qù 丢上去
to.tal	(a.)	sama sekali	zǒng 总, quán 全
		mutlak	júc dùi dė 绝对的, wán quán dė 完全的
	(n.)	jumlah	zǒng shù 总数, zǒng hé 总和
	(v.)	menjumlahkan	hé jì 合计, zǒng jì 总计
to.tal.i.ty	(n.)	keseluruhan, totalitas	quán bù 全部, zǒng shù 总数
to.tal.ly	(adv.)	semua, sama sekali	tǒng tǒng 统统, wán quán 完全
tot.ter	(v.)	berjalan terhuyung-huyung	mán shān 蹒跚, liàng qiàng 踉跄
touch	(v.)	menyentuh	jiē chù 接触, mō 摸
		mengharukan	chù dòng 触动, gǎn dòng 感动
	(n.)	sentuhan	jiē chù 接触
touch.ing	(a.)	mengharukan	shǐ rén gǎn dòng 使人感动
touch.y	(a.)	mudah tersinggung, cepat marah	yì nù dė 易怒的
		tidak sabar	xìng jí dė 性急的
tough	(a.)	liat, alot	rèn 韧, jiān rèn 坚韧
		kuat	qiáng zhuàng 强壮
		kasar	cū lǔ 粗鲁
		keras	wán qiáng 顽强, wán gù 顽固
	(n.)	penjahat	è gùn 恶棍, wú lài 无赖

tough.en	(v.)	menguatkan	shǐ jiān rèn 使坚韧
		menjadi kuat	biàn rèn 编韧
tour	(n.)	tur, perjalanan keliling	zhōu yóu 周游, lǚ xíng 旅行
	(v.)	berkeliling, bertamasya	zhōu yóu 周游, lǚ xíng 旅行
tour.ism	(n.)	kepariwisataan, turisme	guān guāng tuán 观光团, lǚ xíng shì yè 旅行事业
tour.ist	(n.)	turis, wisatawan	yóu kè 游客, lǚ kè 旅客
tour.na.ment	(n.)	turnamen, pertandingan	bǐ sài 比赛, jǐn biaō sài 锦标赛
tout	(v.)	menarik pembeli	zhāo lái 招徕
tow	(v.)	menyeret, menarik dengan tali/rantai	tuō yǐn 拖引
to.ward(s)	(prep.)	ke, terhadap	xiàng 向, duì yú 对于
tow.el	(n.)	handuk	máo jīn 毛巾
tow.el-horse	(n.)	gantungan handuk, rak handuk	máo jīn jià 毛巾架
tow.er	(n.)	menara	tā 塔
town	(n.)	kota	chéng shì 城市
towns.folk	(n.)	penduduk kota	shì mín 市民
towns.man	(n.)	orang kota	shì mín 市民
toy	(n.)	mainan	wán jù 玩具
	(v.)	bermain-main	wán shuā 玩耍
		mempermainkan	wán nòng 玩弄
trace	(v.)	mengikuti jejak	gēn zōng 跟踪
		menjiplak	lín mó 临摹, miáo hùi 描绘
	(n.)	bekas, jejak	hén jī 痕迹, zú jī 足迹, jiǎo yìn 脚印
track	(n.)	bekas, jejak	zú jī 足迹
		jalan kecil	xiǎo lù 小路
		rel, jalan kereta api	guǐ dào 轨道
	(v.)	mengikuti jejak	gēn zōng 跟踪
trac.tor	(n.)	traktor	tuō lā jī 拖拉机

trade	(n.)	perniagaan, perdagangan	mào yì 贸易, shāng yè 商业
	(v.)	berdagang	zùo shēng yì 做生意,
			zùo mǎi mài 做买卖
trade-mark	(n.)	merek dagang	shāng biaō 商标
trad.er	(n.)	pedagang	shāng rén 商人
trades.man	(n.)	pedagang kecil	xiǎo shāng rén 小商人,
			líng shòu shāng 零售商
tra.di.tion	(n.)	tradisi	chuán tǒng 传统, guàn lì 惯例
tra.di.tion.al	(a.)	tradisional	chuán tǒng dė 传统的
traf.fic	(n.)	lalu lintas	jiaō tōng 交通
		perdagangan	mào yì 贸易, mǎi mài 买卖
	(v.)	berdagang, berjual beli	zuò shēng yì 做生意,
			zùo mǎi mài 做买卖
trag.e.dy	(n.)	tragedi, lakon sedih	beī jù 悲剧
		kejadian yg menyedihkan	cǎn jù 惨剧, cǎn àn 惨案
trag.ic	(a.)	lakon yang menyedihkan	beī jù dė 悲剧的
		menyedihkan, tragis	beī cán dė 悲惨的, beī tòng dė 悲痛的
trail	(n.)	jejak, bekas	zú jī 足迹, hén jī 痕迹
		jalan kecil	xiǎo lù 小路
	(v.)	mengikuti jejak	gēn zōng 跟踪, zhuī zōng 追踪
train	(n.)	kereta api	hǔo chē 火车
		deretan	liè 列, háng liè 行列
		rombongan	sǔi xíng rén yuán 随行人员
	(v.)	berlatih, melatih	xùn liàn 训练, duàn liàn 锻炼
train.ee	(n.)	pengikut latihan	shòu xùn rén yuán 受训人员
train.er	(n.)	pelatih	jiào liàn 教练
train.ing	(n.)	latihan	xùn liàn 训练
trait	(n.)	sifat, ciri	pǐn zhì 品质, tè xìng 特性
trai.tor	(n.)	pengkhianat	mài gúo zéi 卖国贼, pàn tú 叛徒
tram	(n.)	trem	diàn chē 电车

tram.car	(n.)	trem	diàn chē 电车
tram.stop	(n.)	tempat perhentian trem	diàn chē zhàn 电车站
tram.way	(n.)	jalan trem	diàn chē dào 电车道
tramp	(v.)	berjalan kaki	bù xíng 步行
	(n.)	petualang	liú làng zhě 流浪者
		gelandangan	liú làng qǐ gaì 流浪乞丐
		perjalanan kaki	tú bù lǚ xíng 徒步旅行
tram.ple	(v.)	menginjak	tà 踏
		menginjak-injak	jiàn tà 践踏, róu lìn 蹂躏
trans.act	(v.)	melakukan, melaksanakan	bàn lǐ 办理, chǔ lǐ 处理
trans.ac.tion	(n.)	transaksi	jiaō yì 交易
		notulen	hùi bào 会报
tran.scribe	(v.)	menyalin	chǎo xiě 抄写, téng xiě 誊写
		merekam	jì lù 记录, lù zhì 录制
tran.script	(n.)	catatan	bǐ jì 笔记
trans.fer	(v.)	transfer, memindahkan	zhuǎn yí 转移, zhuǎn yùn 转运
		menyerahterimakan	yí jiaō 移交
		ganti kereta api	huàn chē 换车
		ganti kapal	huàn chuán 换船
	(n.)	pemindahan	zhuǎn yí 转移
		pemindahan rekening	zhuǎn zhàng 转帐
		pemindahan tangan	zhuǎn ràng 转让
		penukaran tiket	huàn chē piào 换车票
trans.fix	(v.)	menusuk	cì chuān 刺穿, chuō chuān 戳穿
trans.form	(v.)	berubah, berganti	zhuǎn biàn 转变, zhuǎn huàn 转换
		berubah bentuk	biàn xíng 变形
		mengubah bentuk	gǎi zào 改造
trans.fuse	(v.)	memindahkan	zhuǎn yí 转移
		memindahkan darah	shù xuè 输血
tran.sis.tor	(n.)	transistor	bàn dǎo tǐ 半导体

tran.sit	(n.)	transit	gùo jìng yùn shù 过境运输
		terusan, jalan terus	tōng gùo 通过
tran.si.tion	(n.)	transisi, peralihan	zhuǎn biàn 转变, gùo dù 过渡
tran.si.tive	(a.)	transitif	jí wù dė 及物的
trans.late	(v.)	menerjemahkan	fān yì 翻译
trans.la.tion	(n.)	penerjemahan	fān yì 翻译
		terjemahan	yì wén 译文, fān yì běn 翻译本
trans.la.tor	(n.)	penerjemah	fān yì jiā 翻译家, fān yì zhě 翻译者
			fān yì yuán 翻译员
trans.mit	(v.)	memancarkan	chuán bō 传播
trans.mit.ter	(n.)	pemancar	chuán bō zhě 传播者
			chuán bō jī 传播机
trans.par.ent	(a.)	transparan	tòu míng dė 透明的
trans.port	(n.)	pengangkutan	yùn shù 运输
		kapal pengangkut	yùn shù chuán 运输船
		pesawat pengangkut	yùn shù feī jī 运输飞机
	(v.)	mengangkut	yùn shù 运输
trans.por.ta.tion	(n.)	pengangkutan, transportasi	yùn shù 运输
trap	(n.)	perangkap, jerat	xiàn jǐng 陷阱, quán tào 圈套
	(v.)	menangkap dengan	yòu bǔ 诱捕,
		perangkap, menjerat	xiàn hài 陷害
trau.ma	(n.)	luka berat	chuāng shāng 创伤
trav.el	(v.)	mengadakan perjalanan, bepergian	lǚ xíng 旅行
	(n.)	perjalanan	lǚ xíng 旅行, lǚ chéng 旅程,
			háng chéng 行程
trav.el.ler	(n.)	pelancong, wisatawan	lǚ xíng zhě 旅行者, lǚ kè 旅客
trav.el.ling	(n.)	hal perjalanan	lǚ xíng 旅行
trav.e.logue	(n.)	catatan perjalanan	yóu jì 遊记
		film pemandangan perjalanan	fēng jǐng piàn 风景片

tray	(n.)	baki, nampan	tuō bán 托盘
tread	(v.)	memijak, menginjak	tà 踏, jiàn tà 践踏
treas.ure	(n.)	harta, barang berharga	cái bǎo 财宝
	(v.)	menyimpan secara rahasia	mì cáng 密藏
		menghargai	zhēn zhòng 珍重
		sangat menyayangi	zhēn xī 珍惜
treas.ur.er	(n.)	bendaharawan	cái kù 财库
		pemegang buku	kuài jì 会计
treas.ur.y	(n.)	perbendaharaan	gúo kù 国库
		tempat menyimpan barang berharga	bǎo kù 宝库
treat	(v.)	memperlakukan	dùi dài 对待
		mengobati	yī zhì 医治
		membicarakan	tán pàn 谈判
		menjamu, mentraktir	kuǎn dài 款待, qíng kè 请客
treat.ise	(n.)	risalah khusus	zhuān tí lùn wén 专题论文
treat.ment	(n.)	perlakuan	dài yù 待遇
		pengobatan	yī liào 医疗
		pembahasan	lùn shù 论述
treat.y	(n.)	perjanjian	tiáo yùe 条约
tre.ble	(a.)	berlipat tiga	sān bèi 三倍
tree	(n.)	pohon	shù 树
trem.ble	(v.)	gemetar	fā dǒu 发抖
tre.men.dous	(a.)	hebat, mengejutkan	jīng rén dė 惊人的
		menakutkan	kě pà dė 可怕的
		besar sekali	jù dà dė 巨大的
		amat sangat	feī cháng 非常
trench	(n.)	parit	gòu 沟
trend	(n.)	kecenderungan, arah	qīng xiàng 倾向, qū xiàng 趋向, fāng xiàng 方向

tri.ad	(n.)	tritunggal, tiga serangkai	sān jié hé 三结合, sān rén yī zǔ 三人一组, sān jiàn yī tào 三件一套
tri.al	(n.)	percobaan	cháng shì 尝试, shì yàn 试验
		pemeriksaan pengadilan	shěn xùn 审讯
tri.an.gle	(n.)	segitiga	sān jiǎo 三角
tribe	(n.)	suku bangsa	zhǒng zú 种族, bù lùo 部落
trib.une	(n.)	tribune, mimbar	jiǎng tái 讲台
trick	(n.)	tipu daya	guǐ jì 诡计
		permainan	bǎ xì 把戏
	(v.)	memperdayakan, menipu	hōng piàn 哄骗
trick.er.y	(n.)	penipuan	qī piàn 欺骗
trick.y	(a.)	penuh tipu daya	gǔi jì duō duān 诡计多端
tri.fle	(n.)	barang sepele, tetek bengek	xiǎo shì 小事
	(v.)	menyia-nyiakan, membuang-buang	làng fèi 浪费
		mempermainkan	wán nòng 玩弄
tril.lion	(n.)	trilyun	wàn yì 万亿
trip	(n.)	perjalanan pendek	dǔan tú lǚ xíng 短途旅行
tri.ple	(a.)	rangkap tiga, lipat tiga	sān chóng dė 三重的, sān bèi dė 三倍的
trip.lex	(a.)	berlapis tiga	sān chóng dė 三重的
tri.umph	(n.)	kemenangan besar	dà shèng lì 大胜利
	(v.)	mendapat kemenangan	qǔ dé shèng lì 取得胜利
troop	(n.)	pasukan	jūn dùi 军队
		kelompok	qún 群, dùi 队
troop.er	(n.)	pasukan berkuda	qí bīng 骑兵
trop.ic	(n.)	daerah tropis	rè dài 热带
trop.i.cal	(a.)	mengenai daerah tropis	rè dài dė 热带的

trou.ble	(n.)	kesulitan	kùn nàn 困难
		kesusahan	kǔ nǎo 苦恼
		penyakit	máo bìng 毛病, jí bìng 疾病
		keributan	fēng bō 风波, jiū fēn 纠纷
		susah payah	xīn kǔ 辛苦, láo kǔ 劳苦
	(v.)	menyusahkan	shǐ rén kǔ nǎo 使人苦恼
		merepotkan	shǐ rén fèi xīn 使人费心, shǐ rén fèi shén 使人费神, shǐ rén má fán 使人麻烦
trou.ble.some	(a.)	menyusahkan	shǐ rén má fán dė 使人麻烦的, lìng rén tǎo yàn dė 令人讨厌的
trou.ser	(n.)	celana, celana panjang	kù zi 裤子, cháng kù 长裤
tru.ant	(n.)	pemalas	tōu lǎn zhě 偷懒者
		pembolos	táo xué zhě 逃学者
truck	(n.)	truk	zài huò chē 载货车
trudge	(v.)	berjalan dengan susah payah	bá shè 跋涉
true	(a.)	benar	zhēn dė 真的, zhēn shí 真实
		setia	zhōng shí 忠实
		sejati	zhēn zhèng dė 真正的
trum.pet	(n.)	terompet	lǎ bā 喇叭
trunk	(n.)	batang pohon	shù gàn 树干
		kopor	pí xiāng 皮箱
		tubuh	qū gàn 躯干, shēn tǐ 身体
		belalai	xiàng bí 象鼻
		jalan utama	gàn xiàn 干线, gàn lù 干路
trust	(n.)	kepercayaan	xìn rèn 信任, xìn yòng 信用
	(v.)	mempercayai	xìn rèn 信任
		mempercayakan	xìn tuō 信托, wěi tuō 委托
truth	(n.)	kebenaran	zhēn lǐ 真理, zhēn shí xìng 真实性

try	(v.)	mencoba	shì 试, chăng shì 尝试, shì yàn 试验
		berusaha	nŭ lĭ 努力
		menguji	kăo yàn 考验
		pemeriksaan dalam peng-adilan	shĕn xùn 审讯
tub	(n.)	pasu, tempayan	shŭi tŏng 水桶, shŭi pén 水盆
		bak mandi	xĭ zăo 洗澡, mù yù 沐浴
tube	(n.)	pipa, pembuluh	gŭan 管
Tues.day	(n.)	hari Selasa	xīng qī èr 星期二
tug	(v.)	menarik, menyeret	tuō lā 拖拉
tum.ble	(v.)	jatuh	diē dăo 跌倒
		berguling-guling	fān gŭn 翻滚, dă gŭn 打滚
tu.mour	(n.)	tumor	liú 瘤, zhŏng liú 肿瘤
tune	(n.)	lagu	diào 调, diào zi 调子
		serasi	hé xié 和谐
	(v.)	menala	tiáo xié 调谐, tiáo hé 调和
tun.nel	(n.)	terowongan	suì dào 隧道
tur.ban	(n.)	sorban, ikat kepala	tóu jīn 头巾
tur.key	(n.)	kalkun	huŏ jī 火鸡
turn	(v.)	berputar, memutar	zhŭan 转, xuán zhŭan 旋转
		berpaling	fān zhŭan 翻转, zhŭan xiàng 转向, huí tóu 回头
		mengubah	găi biàn 改变
		berbelok, membelok	zhŭan wān 转弯
	(n.)	putaran	zhuăn dòng 转动, xuán zhŭan 旋转
		belokan	zhŭan wān chù 转弯处
		giliran	lún liú 轮流, lún bān 轮班
turn.coat	(n.)	pembelot, pengkhianat	pàn nì 叛逆, biàn jié zhĕ 变节者
turn.ing	(n.)	titik balik	zhuăn zhè diăn 转折点
turn.over	(v.)	mempertumbangkan	diān fù 颠复

tur.tle	(n.)	penyu	hǎi guī 海龟
tusk	(n.)	gading gajah	xiàng yá 象牙
tu.tor	(n.)	guru pribadi	jiā tíng jiào shī 家庭教师, sī rèn jiào shī 私人教师
tweak	(v.)	menjewer	jiū 揪, níng 拧
twelfth	(n.)	kedua belas	dì shí èr 第十二
		tanggal dua belas	shí èr hào 十二号
		seperdua belas	shì èr fēn zhī yī 十二分之一
twelve	(n.)	dua belas	shí èr 十二
twen.ti.eth	(n.)	kedua puluh	dì èr shí 第二十
		tanggal dua puluh	èr shí hào 二十号
		seperdua puluh	èr shí fēn zhī yī 二十分之一
twen.ty	(n.)	dua puluh	èr shí 二十
twice	(adv.)	dua kali	liǎng cì 两次
		dua kali lipat	liǎng bèi 两倍
twig	(n.)	dahan kecil	yā zhī 桠枝
twi.light	(n.)	senjakala	huáng hūn 黄昏
twin	(n.)	kembar	shuāng taī 双胎, shuāng shēng zi 双生子
twin.kle	(v.)	berkelip-kelip	shǎn shùo 闪烁
twist	(v.)	membengkokkan	niǔ wān 扭弯
		berbelok-belok	pán xuán 盘旋, chán rǎo 缠绕
two	(n.)	dua	èr 二
two.fold	(a.)	dua kali lipat	liǎng bèi dė 两倍的
		dua ganda	shuāng chóng dė 双重的
	(adv.)	melipatgandakan	jiā bèi 加倍
		berlipat ganda	shuāng chóng 双重
type	(n.)	tipe, macam, jenis	xíng 型, lèi xíng 类型
		contoh	bǎng yàng 榜样, mó fǎng 模仿
		huruf cetak	qiān zì 铅字

	(v.)	mengetik	dǎ zì 打字
type-set.ter	(n.)	tukang set	pái zì gōng rén 排字工人
type.writ.er	(n.)	mesin tulis, mesin tik	dǎ zì jī 打字机
ty.phoid	(n.)	penyakit tifus	shāng hán 伤寒
ty.phoon	(n.)	topan, taifun	tái fēng 台风
ty.phus	(n.)	penyakit tifus	bān zhěn shāng hán 斑疹伤寒
typ.i.cal	(a.)	khas	diǎn xíng dė 典型的
typ.i.fy	(v.)	melambangkan	xiàng zhēng 象征
ty.pist	(n.)	pengetik, juru tik	dǎ zì yuán 打字员
tyr.an.ny	(n.)	kekejaman, kelaliman	bào nuè 暴虐
		pemerintahan lalim	bào zhèng 暴政
ty.rant	(n.)	raja lalim	bào jūn 暴君
tyre	(n.)	ban	lún taī 轮胎

U

ug.li.ness	(n.)	kejelekan, keburukan	chǒu 丑, chǒu lòu 丑陋, chǒu è 丑恶
ug.ly	(a.)	jelek	chǒu 丑, chǒu lǒu 丑陋
		buruk	chǒu è 丑恶
		berbahaya	xiǎn è 险恶
ul.ti.mate	(a.)	terakhir	zùi hòu dė 最后的
		penghabisan	jié jú 结局
		pokok, asal	jī běn dė 基本的, gēn běn dė 根本的
ul.ti.mate.ly	(adv.)	akhirnya	zùi hòu 最后, zhōng jiū 终究
ul.ti.ma.tum	(n.)	ultimatum	aī dì měi dùn shū 哀的美顿书, zùi hòu tōng dié 最后通谍
ul.tra	(a.)	ultra, teramat sangat	jí duān dė 极端的
	(n.)	kaum radikal	jí jìn fèn zi 急进份子
ul.tra-	(pref.)	teramat sangat, terlalu	jí duān 极端, chaō 超
ul.tra.son.ic	(a.)	ultrasonik	chaō yīn sù dė 超音速的, chaō shēng dė 超声的
ul.tra.son.ics	(n.)	ilmu ultrasonik	chaō shēng xúe 超声学
ul.tra.vi.o.let	(a.)	ultraviolet	zǐ wài xiàn 紫外线
um.brel.la	(n.)	payung	sǎn 伞, yǔ sǎn 雨伞
um.pire	(n.)	wasit	gōng zhèng rén 公证人, cái pàn yuán 裁判员
un-	(pref.)	tidak	bù 不
un.a.bashed	(a.)	tidak tahu malu	bù hài xiū dė 不害羞的
un.a.ble	(a.)	tidak dapat, tidak sanggup	bù hùi dė 不会的, bù néng dė 不能的
un.ac.cept.a.ble	(a.)	tidak dapat diterima	bù néng jiē shòu dė 不能接受的

un.ac.com.pa.nied	(a.)	tidak dengan teman, sen-dirian	méi yǒu bàn lǚ dė 没有伴侣的, wú sǔi cóng dė 无随员的
un.ac.com.plished	(a.)	yang tidak selesai	wèi wán chéng dė 未完成的
		yang tidak berbakat	wú cái néng dė 无才能的
un.ac.count.a.ble	(a.)	tidak dapat dimintai per-tanggungjawaban	wú zé rèn dė 无责任的
		tidak dapat dimengerti	bù kě lǐ jiě dė 不可理解的
un.ac.cus.tomed	(a.)	tidak biasa	bù píng cháng dė 不平常的
un.ac.quaint.ed	(a.)	tidak kenal	bù rèn shí dė 不认识的
un.ad.vised	(a.)	gegabah	qīng shǔai dė 轻率的
un.af.fect.ed	(a.)	tidak dipengaruhi	bù shòu yǐng xiǎng dė 不受影响的
		tidak dibuat-buat	zì rán dė 自然的
		sederhana	pǔ sù dė 朴素的
un.aid.ed	(a.)	tanpa bantuan	wú zhù dė 无助的
un.al.ter.a.ble	(a.)	tak dapat diubah	bù biàn dė 不变的
un.arm	(v.)	meletakkan senjata	fàng xià wǔ qì 放下武器
		melucutkan senjata	jiě chú wǔ zhùang 解除武装
un.armed	(a.)	tak bersenjata	bù dài wǔ qì dė 不带武器的
un.a.void.a.ble	(a.)	tak dapat dihindarkan	bù kě bì miàn dė 不可避免的
un.a.ware	(a.)	tidak tahu	bù zhī dào dė 不知道的
		tidak sadar	bù zì jué dė 不自觉的
un.bal.ance	(v.)	tidak seimbang	bù píng héng 不平衡
un.bear.a.ble	(a.)	tidak dapat menahan	shòu bù liǎo dė 受不了的
un.be.com.ing	(a.)	tidak pantas	bù hé shì dė 不合适的
un.be.lief	(n.)	tidak beragama	wú zōng jiào xìn yǎng dė 无宗教信仰的
un.be.liev.er	(n.)	orang yg tidak beragama	bù xìn yǎng zōng jiào dė rén 不信仰宗教的人
un.bend	(v.)	meluruskan	nòng zhí 弄直
un.bend.ing	(a.)	keras kepala	wán gù dė 顽固的

un.bind	(v.)	melepaskan	jiě kaī 解开, shì fàng 释放
un.blessed	(a.)	tidak beruntung, malang	bù xìng 不幸
un.blush.ing	(a.)	tidak tahu malu	wú chǐ dė 无耻的
un.bolt	(v.)	membuka	dă kaī 打开
un.bound.ed	(a.)	tidak terbatas	wú xiàn dė 无限的
un.break.a.ble	(a.)	tidak dapat dipecahkan	bù kě pò dė 不可破的
un.bro.ken	(a.)	utuh	wán zhěng 完整
		tidak terputus-putus	bù duàn dė 不断的
un.bur.den	(v.)	meringankan beban	jiǎn qīng fù dān 减轻负担
		mencurahkan isi hati	biǎo bǎi 表白
un.but.ton	(v.)	membuka kancing	jiě niǔ kòu 解纽扣
un.can.ny	(a.)	aneh	lí qí dė 离奇的
		gaib	shén mì dė 神秘的
un.ceas.ing	(a.)	tidak henti-hentinya	bù tíng dė 不停的
un.cer.tain	(a.)	tidak pasti	bù yī dìng dė 不一定的
		ragu-ragu	yóu yù bù jué 犹豫不决
un.chain	(v.)	melepaskan	shì fàng 释放
un.change.a.ble	(a.)	tidak dapat berubah	bù kě gǎi biàn dė 不可改变的
un.changed	(a.)	tidak berubah	bù biàn dė 不变的
un.civ.il	(a.)	kurang ajar, tidak beradab	méi yǒu lǐ mào dė 没有礼貌的, cū yě dė 粗野的
un.cle	(n.)	paman	bó fù 伯父, shū fù 叔父, jiù fù 舅父, gū zhàng 姑丈, yī zhàng 姨丈
un.clean	(a.)	tidak bersih	bù jié dė 不洁, bù gān jìng 不干净, bù qíng jié dė 不清洁的
un.close	(v.)	membuka, terlihat	dă kaī 打开, lù chū 露出
un.clothed	(a.)	tidak berpakaian, telanjang	lǔo tǐ 裸体, yī sī bù guà 一丝不挂
un.coil	(v.)	menguraikan	jiě kāi 解开
un.com.fort.a.ble	(a.)	merasa tidak enak	bù shū fú 不舒服
un.com.mon	(a.)	tidak biasa, luar biasa	feī cháng dė 非常的

un.con.cerned	(a.)	tidak ambil pusing	mò bù guān xīn 漠不关心
un.con.di.tion.al	(a.)	tidak bersyarat	wú tiáo jiàn dė 无条件的
un.con.di.tion.al.ly	(adv.)	tanpa syarat	wú tiáo jiàn di 无条件地
un.con.di.tioned	(a.)	tidak bersyarat	wú tiáo jiàn dė 无条件的
un.con.nect.ed	(a.)	tidak bertalian	bù lián jié dė 不连结的, wú guān xì dė 无关系的
un.con.quer.a.ble	(a.)	tidak dapat ditundukkan	bù kě zhēng fú dė 不可征服的
un.con.scious	(n.)	bawah sadar	wú yì shí dė 无意识的
	(a.)	tidak sadar	bù shěng rén shì 不省人事
un.con.sti.tu.tion.al	(a.)	tidak konstitusional	fǎn xiàn fǎ dė 反宪法的
un.con.trolled	(a.)	tidak terkendali	bù shòu kòng zhì dė不受控制的
un.con.ven.tion.al	(a.)	tidak konvensional	pò lì dė 破例的, feī cháng gūi dė 非常规的
un.cork	(v.)	membuka sumbat	kaī sè zi 开塞子
un.count.a.ble	(a.)	tidak dapat dihitung	bù kě shù dė 不可数的
un.count.ed	(a.)	.tidak dapat dihitung	wú shù dė 无数的
un.coup.le	(v.)	melepaskan	chè sàn 拆散
un.cov.er	(v.)	membuka membuka kedok	dǎ kaī 打开, jiē kaī 揭开 jiē lù 揭露, bào lù 暴露
un.cracked	(a.)	tidak ada retaknya	wú liè féng dė 无裂缝的
un.curl	(v.)	meluruskan	nòng zhí 弄直
un.de.cid.ed	(a.)	belum memutuskan bimbang	wèi jué dìng dė 未决定的 yóu yù bù jué 犹豫不决
un.de.filed	(a.)	bersih, murni	chún jié dė 纯洁的
un.de.ni.a.ble	(a.)	tak dapat disangkal	bù kě fou rèn dė 不可否认的
un.der	(prep.)	di bawah di bawahnya	zài xià miàn 在下面 zài ... yǐ xià 在…以下, zài ... zhi xià 在…之下
un.der-	(pref.)	di bawah kurang dari	zài ... xià 在…下, bù zú 不足, shǎo yú 少于

un.der.clothes	(n.)	pakaian dalam	nèi yī 内衣
un.der.cov.er	(a.)	secara rahasia	mì mì jìn xíng dė 秘密进行的
un.der.done	(a.)	setengah masak	bàn shú 半熟
un.der.es.ti.mate	(v.)	menaksir terlalu rendah	guò dī gū jì 过低估计
		memandang rendah	dī gū 低估
un.der.gar.ment	(n.)	pakaian dalam	nèi yī 内衣
un.der.go	(v.)	mengalami	zaō shòu 遭受, jīng lì 经历
un.der.ground	(adv.)	di bawah tanah	zaì dì xià 在地下,
		secara rahasia	mì mì di 秘密地
un.der.hand	(a.)	dengan licik	bēi bǐ dė 卑鄙的
un.der.line	(v.)	menggarisbawahi	zài ... huà xiàn 在…划线
		menekankan	qiáng diào 强调
un.der.most	(a.)	paling bawah	zùi di dė 最低的, zùi xià dė 最下的
un.der.neath	(adv.)	di bawah	zài dì xià 在地下
un.der.stand	(v.)	mengerti	míng bǎi 明白, dǒng dé 懂得
un.der.stand.ing	(n.)	pengertian	míng bǎi 明白, liǎo jiě 了解
un.der.take	(v.)	menjalankan, melakukan	dān rèn 担任
un.der.tak.ing	(n.)	perusahaan	qǐ yè 企业
un.der.tone	(n.)	suara rendah	xiǎo shēng 小声
un.der.val.ue	(v.)	merendahkan	xiǎo kàn 小看
un.der.wear	(n.)	pakaian dalam	nèi yī 内衣
un.der.world	(n.)	neraka	dì yù 地狱
un.do	(v.)	membuka	dǎ kaī 打开
		menghapus	qǔ xiāo 取消
		melepaskan	jiě kaī 解开
		merusak	hǔi huài 毁坏, nòng huài 弄坏
un.de.vel.oped	(a.)	belum maju	bù fā zhǎn dė 不发展的
un.dis.ci.plined	(a.)	tak berdisiplin	wú jì lù dė 无纪律的
un.do.ing	(n.)	buka, lepas	dǎ kaī 打开, jiě kaī 解开
		kehancuran	miè wáng 灭亡

un.done	(a.)	yang belum terselesaikan	wèi wán chéng dė 未完成的,
			wèi zùo hǎo dė 未做好的
		terlepas	jiě kaī dė 解开的, tuō kaī dė 脱开的
un.doubt.ed	(a.)	tidak ragu-ragu	wú yí dė 无疑的, què shí dė 确实的
un.draw	(v.)	menarik supaya terbuka	lā kāi 拉开
un.dreamed-of	(a.)	tak dimimpi-mimpikan	mèng xiǎng bù dào 梦想不到
un.dress	(v.)	menanggalkan pakaian	tuō yī fú 脱衣服
un.due	(a.)	tidak pantas	bù dàng dė 不当的
		tidak sah	feī fǎ dė 非法的
un.dy.ing	(a.)	abadi	bù xiǔ dė 不朽的, bù miè dė 不灭的,
			yǒng yuǎn dė 永远的
un.earned	(a.)	yang diterima tanpa kerja	bù láo ér huò 不劳而获
un.earth	(v.)	menemukan	fā xiàn 发现
un.eas.i.ly	(adv.)	dengan gelisah	bù ān di 不安地
un.eas.y	(a.)	gelisah	bù ān 不安
un.em.ployed	(a.)	menganggur, tuna karya	xián zhé 闲着, shī yè 失业
un.em.ploy.ment	(n.)	pengangguran	shī yè 失业
un.en.dur.a.ble	(a.)	tak dapat menahan	nán rěn dė 难忍的,
			bù kě rěn dė 不可忍的
un.eq.ual	(a.)	tidak sama	bù tóng dė 不同的
		tidak adil	bù píng děng 不平等
un.e.ven	(a.)	tidak rata	bù píng 不平, bù qí 不齐
		tidak seimbang	bù píng héng 不平衡
un.ex.am.pled	(a.)	tiada bandingannya	wú bǐ dė 无比的
un.ex.pect.ed	(a.)	tak terduga, tak tersangka	xiǎng bù dào dė 想不到的
un.fair	(a.)	tidak adil	bù gōng píng 不公平
un.faith.ful	(a.)	tidak setia	bù zhōng shí 不忠实
un.fa.mil.iar	(a.)	tidak kenal	bù shú xī dė 不熟悉的
		tidak biasa	bù xí guàn dė 不习惯的
un.fast.en	(v.)	menanggalkan, membuka	jiě kaī 解开, sōng kaī 松开

un.fa.vour.a.ble	(a.)	tidak bermaksud baik	méi yǒu hǎo yì dė 没有好意的,
		tidak menguntungkan	bù lì dė 不利的
un.feel.ing	(a.)	tidak berperasaan	méi yǒu gǎn jué dė没有感觉的,
			wú qíng dė 无情的
un.feigned	(a.)	yang benar	zhēn shí 真实
		yang tidak palsu	bù xū wěi 不虚伪
un.fet.tered	(a.)	tak terkekang, bebas	wú jū shù dė 无拘束的,
			zì yóu zì zài dė 自由自在的
un.fin.ished	(a.)	yang belum selesai	wèi zùo hǎo dė 未做好的,
			wèi wán chéng dė 未完成的
un.fit	(a.)	tidak cocok	bù hé shì dė 不合适的
un.fold	(v.)	membuka	dǎ kaī 打开, kaī fàng 开放
un.fore.seen	(a.)	tak terduga	yì wài dė 意外的
un.for.tu.nate	(a.)	sial, tidak beruntung	bù xìng 不幸
un.found.ed	(a.)	tidak berdasar	méi yǒu jī chǔ dė 没有基础的
un.freeze	(v.)	mencair	jiě dòng 解冻
un.friend.ly	(a.)	tidak bersahabat	bù yǒu hǎo dė 不友好的
un.furl	(v.)	membentangkan	jiě kāi 解开, dǎ kāi 打开
un.gain.ly	(a.)	kaku dan canggung	bèn zhuō 笨拙, cū bèn 粗笨
un.god.ly	(a.)	tak beriman	bù xìn shén dė 不信神的
un.gov.ern.a.ble	(a.)	tak dapat dikendalikan	nán kòng zhì dė 难控制的
un.gra.cious	(a.)	kurang ajar	bù lǐ mǎo 不礼貌, cū yě dė 粗野的
un.gram.mat.i.cal	(a.)	tak sesuai dengan tata bahasa	bù hě yǔ fǎ dė 不合语法的
un.grate.ful	(a.)	tidak berterima kasih	wàng ēn fù yì 忘恩负义
un.ground.ed	(a.)	tak berdasar	méi yǒu gēn jù dė 没有根据的
un.guard.ed	(a.)	lengah	dà yì 大意
		tidak dijaga	méi yǒu fáng bèi 没有防备
un.hand	(v.)	melepaskan, lepas tangan	fàng shǒu 放手
un.hand.y	(a.)	tidak terampil	bù líng qiǎo dė 不灵巧的,
			bèn zhuō dė 笨拙的

un.hap.py	(a.)	tidak senang	bù kuài lè 不快乐
		tidak bahagia	bù xìng fú 不幸福
un.health.y	(a.)	tidak sehat	bù jiàn kāng dė 不健康的,
			bù wèi shēng dė 不卫生的
un.heard	(a.)	belum pernah dengar	méi yǒu tīng gùo 没有听过
		belum pernah terjadi	kōng qián dė 空前的
un.heed.ed	(a.)	tidak mendapat perhatian	bù shòu zhù yì dė 不受注意的
un.ho.ly	(a.)	tidak suci	bù shén shèng dė 不神圣的
un.hurt	(a.)	tanpa luka, selamat	bù shòu shāng dė 不受伤的
uni-	(pref.)	satu, bersatu	yī 一, yī zhì 一致
u.ni.form	(a.)	sama, seragam	yī zhì dė 一致的, yī lū dė 一律的
	(n.)	pakaian seragam	zhì fú 制服
u.ni.fy	(v.)	mempersatukan	tǒng yī 统一
u.ni.lat.er.al	(n.)	secara sepihak	yī fāng dė 一方的, dān fāng dė 单方的
un.im.por.tant	(a.)	tidak penting	bù zhòng yào dė 不重要的
un.in.hab.it.ed	(a.)	tidak ada penghuninya	wú rén jū zhù 无人居住
un.in.jured	(a.)	tidak terluka	wèi shòu shāng dė 未受伤的
un.in.ter.est.ed	(a.)	tidak tertarik	wú dòng yú zhōng dė 无动于衷的
un.in.ter.rupt.ed	(a.)	tak henti-hentinya	bù tíng dė 不停的, bù duàn dė 不断的
u.nion	(n.)	perserikatan, perkumpulan	lián hé huì 联合会, xié huì 协会
		perkawinan	hūn yīn 婚姻
		penyatuan, perpaduan	lián hé 联合, jié hé 结合
u.nion.ist	(n.)	anggota serikat buruh	gōng huì huì yuán 工会会员
u.nique	(a.)	unik	wú bǐ dė 无比的
u.ni.son	(n.)	persesuaian	yì zhì 一致
u.nit	(n.)	kesatuan, satu	dān wèi 单位, gè tǐ 个体
u.nite	(v.)	bersatu, mempersatukan	lián hé 联合, tuán jié 团结
u.ni.ty	(n.)	persatuan	tǒng yī 统一, tuán jié 团结
u.ni.ver.sal	(a.)	umum	pǔ biàn dė 普遍的
		sedunia	quán shì jiè dė 全世界的
		semesta	yǔ zhòu dė 宇宙的

u.ni.verse	(n.)	alam semesta	yǔ zhòu 宇宙
		seluruh dunia	quán shì jiè 全世界
		seluruh bidang	zōng hé xìng 综合性
u.ni.ver.si.ty	(n.)	universitas	dà xué 大学
un.just	(a.)	tidak adil	bù gōng píng dė 不公平的
un.kind	(a.)	tidak ramah	bù hé shàn dė 不和善的,
			bù qīn qiè dė 不亲切的
un.known	(a.)	tak dikenal	wú míng dė 无名的
un.lace	(v.)	melepas tali	jiě kaī 解开
un.law.ful	(a.)	tidak sah	feī fǎ dė 非法的
un.learned	(a.)	tidak berpendidikan	wú wén huà dė 无文化的,
			wú zhī shí dė 无知识的
un.leash	(v.)	membuka tali	jiě kaī 解开
		mengendorkan	sōng kaī 松开
un.less	(conj.)	jika tidak	rú guǒ bù 如果不
		kecuali kalau	chú feī 除非
un.let.tered	(a.)	buta huruf	wén máng 文盲,
			bù shí zì dė 不识字的
un.like	(a.)	tidak sama, berlainan	bù tóng dė 不同的
un.like.ly	(a.)	tak mungkin	wèi bì dė 未必的
		tak dapat dipercaya	bù kě kaò dė 不可靠的
un.lim.it.ed	(a.)	tak terbatas	wú xiàn dė 无限的
un.load	(v.)	membongkar muatan	xiè huò 卸货
un.lock	(v.)	membuka kunci	kaī suō 开锁
un.luck.y	(a.)	malang, sial	bù xìng dė 不幸的, dǎo méi dė 倒霉的
un.man.ly	(a.)	pengecut	nùo rùo dė 懦弱的
un.man.ner.ly	(a.)	tidak sopan, kasar	bù lǐ mào 不礼貌, cū yě 粗野
un.mask	(v.)	membuka kedok	bào lù 暴露, jiē fā 揭发
un.match.a.ble	(a.)	tiada bandingannya	wú bǐ dė 无比的
un.mean.ing	(a.)	tidak ada artinya	wú yì yì dė 无意义的

un.mer.ci.ful	(a.)	kejam	cán rěn 残忍
un.mind.ful	(a.)	tidak menghiraukan	bù zhù yì dė 不注意的
un.mixed	(a.)	tidak bercampur, murni	chún cùi dė 纯粹的
un.mor.al	(a.)	tidak berhubungan dengan moral	wú guān dào dé dė 无关道德的
un.moved	(a.)	tidak terharu	wú dòng yú zhōng dė 无动于衷的
		teguh	bù dòng yáo dė 不动摇的
un.nat.u.ral	(a.)	melawan kodrat, melawan tabiat	bù hé rén qíng dė 不合人情的
		tidak wajar	fàn chàng dė 反常的
		tidak alami	bù zì rán dė 不自然的
		buatan	rén zào dė 人造的
un.ne.ces.sary	(a.)	tidak perlu	bù bì yào dė 不必要的
un.nerve	(v.)	mematahkan semangat	shǐ qì něi 使气馁
un.not.iced	(a.)	tidak diperhatikan	bù bèi zhù yì dė 不被注意的
un.num.bered	(a.)	tak terhitung	wú shù dė 无数的
un.oc.cu.pied	(a.)	tidak didiami	méi rén zhù dė 没人住的
		kosong	kōng dė 空的
		sedang tidak bekerja	kòng xián 空闲
un.pack	(v.)	membongkar, membuka	dǎ kaī 打开, jiě kaī 解开
un.paid	(a.)	belum dibayar	wèi huán dė 未还的
		tidak dibayar	wú bào chóu dė 无报酬的
un.par.al.leled	(a.)	tidak ada bandingannya	wú bǐ dė 无比的, wú shuang dė 无双的
un.pleas.ant	(a.)	tidak menyenangkan	bù yú kuài dė 不愉快的
un.pop.u.lar	(a.)	tidak disukai, tidak populer	bù shòu huān yíng dė 不受欢迎的
un.prac.ti.cal	(a.)	tidak praktis	bù shí jì dė 不实际的
un.prec.e.dent.ed	(a.)	tidak pernah terjadi sebelumnya	kōng qián dė 空前的

un.pre.ju.diced	(a.)	tidak berpihak tidak berprasangka	méi yǒu piān jiàn dė 没有偏见的 méi yǒu chéng jiàn dė 没有成见的
un.pre.pared	(a.)	tidak ada persiapan	méi yǒu zhǔn bèi dė 没有准备的
un.pre.tend.ing	(a.)	tidak sombong	bù jiāo ào dė 不骄傲的
un.pro.duc.tive	(a.)	tidak menghasilkan, tidak produktif	bù shēng chǎn dė 不生产的, feī shēng chǎn xìng dė 非生产性的
un.prof.it.a.ble	(a.)	tidak menguntungkan	méi yǒu lì yì dė 没有利益的, méi yǒu yòng dė 没有用的
un.prom.is.ing	(a.)	tidak berharapan	méi yǒu xī wàng dė 没有希望的
un.qual.i.fied	(a.)	tidak bermutu tidak memenuhi syarat	bù hé gé dė 不合格的 bù hé tiáo jiàn dė 不合条件的
un.ques.tion.a.ble	(a.)	tidak dapat disangkal tidak diragukan lagi	wú yí dė 无疑的 háo wú yí wèn dė 毫无疑问的
un.qui.et	(a.)	tidak tenang	bù ān jìng dė 不安静的
un.real	(a.)	tidak menurut kenyataan khayal	bù zhēn shí dė 不真实的 huàn xiǎng dė 幻想的
un.rea.son.a.ble	(a.)	tidak masuk akal	bù hé lǐ dė 不合理的, wú lǐ dė 无理的
un.re.li.a.ble	(a.)	tak dapat dipercaya, tak dapat diandalkan	bù kě kào dė 不可靠的
un.re.quit.ed	(a.)	tidak dapat balasan tidak dapat imbalan	wú bào dá dė 无报达的 wú shāng dė 无偿的
un.re.served	(a.)	tidak menyembunyikan berterus-terang	bù yǐn mán dė 不隐瞒的 tǎn bái dė 坦白的
un.rest	(n.)	kegelisahan	bù ān 不安
un.ri.valled	(a.)	tiada tandingannya	wú bǐ dė 无比的, wú dí dė 无敌的
un.roll	(v.)	membuka gulungan	dǎ kaī 打开, tān kaī 摊开
un.ruf.fled	(a.)	tenang	píng jìng 平静
un.ru.ly	(a.)	tak dapat dikendalikan	bù néng kòng zhì dė 不能控制的
un.safe	(a.)	tidak aman	bù ān quán 不安全
un.sat.is.fac.to.ry	(a.)	tidak memuaskan	bù lìng rén mǎn yì dė 不令人满意的

un.sat.is.fied	(a.)	tidak puas	bù mǎn zú dė 不满足的
un.say	(v.)	membatalkan, menarik kembali	qǔ xiāo 取消, chè húi 撤回
un.screw	(v.)	melepaskan dengan cara memutar	nǐu sōng 扭松, níng sōng 拧松
un.seal	(v.)	membuka segel	kaī qǐ 开启, chāi kaī 拆开
un.sea.son.a.ble	(a.)	tidak menurut musimnya	bù hé shí lìng dė 不合时令的
un.seen	(a.)	tidak kelihatan	kàn bù jiàn dė 看不见的
un.self.ish	(a.)	tidak mementingkan diri sendiri	wú sī dė 无私的
un.set.tle	(v.)	mengganggu	dǎo luàn 捣乱
un.shak(e).a.ble	(a.)	tak tergoncangkan, teguh	bù dòng yáo 不动摇, jiān dìng bù yí 坚定不移
un.sight.ly	(a.)	jelek, tidak sedap dipan-dang	nán kàn dė 难看的
un.skill.ful	(a.)	tidak terampil	bù líng qiǎo dė 不灵巧的, bèn zhūo dė 笨拙的
un.sound	(a.)	tidak waras	bù jiàn quán dė 不健全的, yǒu bìng dė 有病的
un.spar.ing	(a.)	royal	bù lìn sè 不吝啬, kāng kǎi 慷慨
un.speak.a.ble	(a.)	tak terkatakan	shuō bù chū dė 说不出的
un.sta.ble	(a.)	tidak stabil	bù wěn dìng dė 不稳定的
un.stead.y	(a.)	goyah, tidak kokoh	dòng yaó dė 动摇的, bù jiān dìng dė 不坚定的
un.stressed	(a.)	tanpa tekanan	bù qiáng diào dė 不强调的, bù zhòng dú dė 不重读的
un.stud.ied	(a.)	tidak sengaja	bù gù yì dė 不故意的
un.suit.a.ble	(a.)	tidak cocok	bù shì hé 不适合, bù shì dàng 不适当

un.think.a.ble	(a.)	tak dapat dibayangkan	bù kě xiǎng xiàng dė 不可想象的
un.think.ing	(a.)	tidak memakai otak	bù dòng nǎo jīn dė 不动脑筋的
un.ti.dy	(a.)	tidak rapi	bù zhěng qí 不整齐,
			bù zhěng jié 不整洁
un.tie	(v.)	membuka, melepaskan	jiě kaī 解开, jiě fàng 解放
un.til	(prep.)	hingga, sampai	dào 到
	(conj.)	hingga	dào ... wéi zhǐ 到…为止
un.to	(prep.)	sampai	dào 到
un.true	(a.)	tidak betul	bù zhēn shí dė 不真实的
		tidak setia	bù zhōng 不忠
un.truth	(n.)	kebohongan	huǎng yán 谎言
		kepalsuan	xū jiǎ 虚假
un.used	(a.)	tidak terpakai	bù yòng dė 不用的
		tak biasa	bù guàn dė 不惯的
un.u.su.al	(a.)	luar biasa	feī cháng 非常,
			bù píng cháng dė 不平常的
un.wary	(a.)	tidak hati-hati	bù xiǎo xīn 不小心
		tidak awas	bù jǐn shèn 不谨慎
un.wea.ried	(a.)	tak mengenal lelah	bù pí juàn dė 不疲倦的,
			bù qú bù náo dė 不屈不挠的
un.wel.comed	(a.)	tidak disukai	bù shòu huān yíng dė 不受欢迎的
un.well	(a.)	tak enak badan,	bù shū fú 不舒服,
		kurang sehat, sakit	yǒu bìng dė 有病的
un.will.ing	(a.)	segan, enggan, tidak mau	bù yuàn yì dė 不原意的
un.wind	(v.)	memutarlepaskan	zhuǎn kaī 转开,
		membongkar, membuka	chāi kaī 拆开, jiě kaī 解开
un.wise	(a.)	tidak bijaksana , bodoh	bù gāo míng dė 不高明的,
			yú bèn dė 愚笨的
un.wished-for	(a.)	tidak mengharapkan	bù xī wàng 不希望
un.wit.ting	(a.)	tanpa disadari	bù zhī bù jué dė 不知不觉的

un.wont.ed	(a.)	tidak biasa, jarang	bù xì guàn dė 不习惯的, shǎo jiàn dė 少见的
un.worth.y	(a.)	tidak layak, tidak penting	bù pèi 不配, bù zhí dė 不值得, bù zhòng yào 不重要
un.writ.ten	(a.)	tidak tertulis	feī shū miàn dė 非书面的
		tidak ditulis menurut tata bahasa	bù chéng wén dė 不成文的
un.yield.ing	(a.)	keras hati	wán qiáng dė 顽强的
		pantang menyerah	bù qū dė 不屈的
up	(adv.)	ke atas, di atas	xiàng shàng 向上, zài shàng 在上
up.hill	(a.)	sulit	jiān nán 艰难, jiān kǔ 艰苦
		menanjak	shàng pō dė 上坡的
	(adv.)	ke atas	xiàng shàng 向上
up.hold	(v.)	mendukung, menjunjung	zhī chí 支持, jǔ qǐ 举起
up.keep	(n.)	pemeliharaan, perawatan	tiáo yǎng 调养, bǎo yǎng 保养
up.land	(n.)	pegunungan	gaō dì 高地, shān dì 山地
up.lift	(v.)	mengangkat	jǔ qǐ 举起
		memajukan	chù jìn 促进
		meningkatkan semangat	zhèn zùo 振作, dǎ qǐ jīng shén 打起精神
up.on	(prep.)	di atas	zài shàng miàn 在上面
up.per	(a.)	atas, tinggi	shàng 上, gaō 高
	(n.)	bagian atas	shàng bù 上部
up.per.most	(a.)	paling atas	zùi shàng dė 最上的
		paling tinggi	zùi gāo dė 最高的
	(adv.)	paling tinggi, paling atas	zùi gāo 最高, zùi shàng 最上
up.raised	(a.)	terangkat	jǔ qǐ 举起
up.right	(a.)	tegak lurus	zhí lì dė 直立的
		jujur	zhèng zhí dė 正直的
	(adv.)	tegak lurus	bǐ zhí 笔直

up.rise	(v.)	melambung ke atas	shēng qǐ 升起
		memberontak	qǐ yì 起义
up.ris.ing	(n.)	pemberontakan	qǐ yì 起义
up.roar	(n.)	kegaduhan	chǎo chǎo rǎng rǎng 吵吵嚷嚷
up.root	(v.)	membantun, menumbangkan	lián gēn bá diào 连根拔掉
		memusnahkan sampai akar-akarnya	gēn chú 根除, jué miè 绝灭
up.set	(v.)	menggulingkan, menumbangkan	tuī fān 推翻, diān fù 颠复
	(n.)	penggulingan	tuī fān 推翻, diān fù 颠复
		kerusuhan, gangguan	rǎo luàn 扰乱, kǔ nǎo 苦恼
up.shot	(n.)	kesudahan	jié guǒ 结果, jié jú 结局
up.side	(n.)	bagian atas	shàng biān 上边, shàng miàn 上面, shàng bù 上部
		keadaan kacau balau	luàn qī bā zāo 乱七八糟
up.side-down	(a.)	terbalik, kacau balau	diān dǎo dė 颠倒的, luàn qī bā zāo dė 乱七八糟的
up.stair(s)	(a.)	tingkat atas	lóu shàng 楼上
	(adv.)	di atas loteng	zài lóu shàng 在楼上
		ke atas loteng	xiàng lóu shàng 向楼上
up.start	(n.)	orang yang kaya mendadak	bào fā hù 暴发户
up.stream	(a.)	ke hulu, ke udik	wǎng shàng yóu 往上游, nì liú 逆流
up.surge	(n.)	kenaikan, peningkatan	gāo zhǎng 高涨
up.swing	(v.)	menaikkan	tí gāo 提高, xiàng shàng 向上
up-to-date	(a.)	paling baru, terbaru	zùi zīn shì dė 最新式的, shí máo dė 时髦的
up.town	(n.)	pusat perumahan dalam kota	zhù zhái qū 住宅区

up.turn	(v.)	memutar balik	fǎn zhuàn 反转
	(n.)	kenaikan harga	wù jià shàng zhǎng 物价上涨
		keadaan pasar membaik	shì kuàng hǎo zhuǎn 市况好转
up.ward	(a.)	ke atas	xiàng shàng dė 向上的
ur.ban	(a.)	mengenai kota	chéng shì dė 城市的
ur.bane	(a.)	sopan	yǒu lǐ mào dė 有礼貌的
urge	(v.)	mendorong	tuī dòng 推动
		mendesak	cuī cù 催促
		meminta	yào qiú 要求
ur.gen.cy	(n.)	urgensi, keadaan yang mendesak	jǐn jí 紧急, pò qiè 迫切
ur.gent	(a.)	urgen, mendesak, penting	jǐn jí dė 紧急的, pò qiè dė 迫切的
u.ri.nate	(v.)	kencing, buang air kecil	xiǎo biàn 小便
u.rine	(n.)	air kencing	niào 尿, niào shǔi 尿水
us	(pron.)	kita, kami	wǒ mėn 我们
us.able	(a.)	dapat dipakai	kě yòng dė 可用的, hé yòng dė 合用的
us.age	(n.)	penggunaan, pemakaian	shǐ yòng 使用, yùn yòng 运用
use	(v.)	menggunakan, memakai	yòng 用, shǐ yòng 使用, lì yòng 利用
	(n.)	penggunaan, kegunaan	shǐ yòng 使用, lì yòng 利用 yòng tú 用途, xiào yòng 效用
used	(a.)	bekas	yòng gùo dė 用过的, bàn jiù dė 半旧的
use.ful	(a.)	yang berguna, bermanfaat	yòu yòng dė 有用的, yǒu yì dė 有益的
use.less	(a.)	tak berguna, tak bermanfaat	bù yòng dė 不用的, wú yì dė 无益的
us.er	(n.)	pemakai	shǐ yòng zhě 使用者

u.su.al	(a.)	yang biasa	píng cháng dė 平常的, tōng cháng dė 通常的
u.su.al.ly	(adv.)	biasanya	píng cháng 平常, tōng cháng 通常
u.ten.sil	(n.)	peralatan, perkakas	qì mǐn 器皿
u.til.i.ty	(n.)	faedah, kegunaan	xiào yòng 效用, gòng yòng 功用
u.til.ize	(v.)	menggunakan	lì yòng 利用
ut.most	(a.)	sepenuhnya	zùi dà xiàn dù dė 最大限度的
ut.ter	(a.)	sama sekali	wán quán dė 完全的, jué dùi dė 绝对的
	(v.)	mengucapkan	shuō 说, jiǎng 讲
ut.ter.ly	(adv.)	sama sekali	wán quán 完全
ut.ter.most	(a.)	sepenuhnya	zùi dà xiàn dù dė 最大限度的

V

va.can.cy	(n.)	kosong	kong 空, kòng bǎi 空白
		tempat kosong	kòng dì 空地
		waktu senggang	kòng xián 空闲, qīng xián 清闲
		lowongan	kòng quē 空缺, kòng wèi 空位
va.cant	(a.)	kosong	kòng dė 空的
va.cate	(v.)	mengosongkan	kòng chū 空出, téng chū 腾出
		meletakkan jabatan	cí qù zhí wù 辞去职务, lí zhí 离职
va.ca.tion	(n.)	liburan	jià rì 假日
		peletakan jabatan	cí zhí 辞职
vac.ci.nate	(v.)	mengvaksinasi	dǎ fáng yì zhēn 打防疫针
		mencacar	jiē zhǒng 接种
vac.ci.na.tion	(n.)	vaksinasi, pencacaran	yù fáng zhù shì 预防注射, yù fáng zhēn 预防针, jiē zhǒng 接种, zhōng dòu 种痘
vac.cine	(n.)	vaksin	yì miáo 疫苗, jūn miáo 菌苗, niú dòu miáo 牛痘苗
vac.il.late	(v.)	goyang, goyah	yáo bǎi 摇摆, yáo dòng 摇动
		bimbang	yóu yí 犹疑, chóu chú 踌躇
vac.u.um	(a.)	vakum	zhēn kōng 真空
vain	(a.)	sia-sia	bǎi fèi 白费, tú láo 徒劳
		kosong	kōng xū dė 空虚的
		sombong	zì fù dė 自负的
vain.ly	(adv.)	dengan sia-sia	bǎi bǎi dì 白白地, bǎi fèi di 白费地

val.id	(a.)	sah, berlaku	yǒu xiào dė 有效的
		benar	zhèng dāng dė 正当的,
			què shí dė 确实的
		kuat, sehat	qiáng zhuàng 强壮,
			jiàn kāng dė 健康的
val.ley	(n.)	lembah	shān gǔ 山谷
val.or.ous	(a.)	gagah berani	yīng yǒng dė 英勇的
val.our	(n.)	keberanian	yīng yǒng 英勇, yǒng méng 勇猛
val.u.a.ble	(a.)	berharga	yǒu jià zhí dė 有价值的,
			bǎo gùi dė 宝贵的
val.u.a.tion	(n.)	penilaian, penaksiran	gū jià 估价, píng jià 评价
val.ue	(n.)	nilai, harga	jià zhí 价值
		arti, pengertian	yì yì 意义, hán yì 涵义
	(v.)	menilai, menghargai	gū jià 估价, zhūn zhòng 尊重
val.ue.less	(a.)	tak bernilai, tak berharga	méi yǒu jià zhí dė 没有价值的
van	(n.)	mobil gerbong	dà péng huò chē 大蓬货车,
			yùn huò chē 运货车
		barisan depan	xiān tóu bù duì 先头部队,
			xiān fēng 先锋
van.guard	(n.)	barisan depan	xiān fēng 先锋
van.ish	(v.)	lenyap, hilang	xiāo shī 消失, xiāo sàn 消散
van.i.ty	(n.)	kesombongan	zì fù 自负, zì dà 自大
van.quish	(v.)	menaklukkan	zhēng fú 征服
		mengalahkan	dǎ shèng 打胜
		memperoleh kemenangan	dė shèng 得胜
		mengatasi	kè fú 克服
van.tage	(n.)	tempat yang menguntung-kan	yǒu lì dì wèi 有利地位
va.pour	(n.)	uap	qì 汽, shǔi zhēng qì 水蒸汽
va.pour-bath	(n.)	mandi uap	zhēng qì yù 蒸汽浴

va.pour.ize	(v.)	menguap	zhēng fā 蒸发
va.ri.a.ble	(a.)	berubah-ubah	yì biàn dė 易变的,
			cháng biàn dė 常变的
var.i.ance	(n.)	perubahan	biàn huà 变化
		perbedaan	bù tóng 不同, fēn qí 分歧
var.i.ant	(a.)	berbeda	bù tóng dė 不同的
	(n.)	yang berlainan	biàn zhǒng 变种, biàn xíng 变形
va.ri.a.tion	(n.)	variasi	biàn hùa 变化, biàn dòng 变动
va.ried	(a.)	bermacam-macam	gè zhǒng gè yàng 各种各样
		berbeda-beda	bù xiàng tóng dė 不相同的
va.ri.e.ty	(n.)	keanekaragaman	duō yàng xìng 多样性
		penggantian, perubahan	biàn zhǒng 变种
		jenis	
va.ri.ous	(a.)	berbagai macam	gè zhǒng gè yàng dė 各种各样的
va.ri.ous.ly	(adv.)	bermacam-macam	gè zhǒng gè yàng 各种各样,
			xíng xíng shì shì 形形式式
var.nish	(n.)	pernis	qīng qī 清漆
var.si.ty	(n.)	universitas	dà xué 大学
va.ry	(v.)	berubah, mengubah	biàn huà 变化, gǎi biàn 改变
vase	(n.)	jambangan bunga	huā píng 花瓶
vas.e.line	(n.)	vaselin	fán shì lín 凡士林
vast	(a.)	luas sekali	guǎng dà 广大
		sangat	feī cháng 非常
vast.ly	(adv.)	sangat besar, sangat	dà dà di 大大地, feī cháng 非常
veg.e.ta.ble	(n.)	sayur-sayuran	shū cài 蔬菜
	(a.)	nabati, tumbuh-tumbuhan	zhì wù dė 植物的
veg.e.ta.ri.an	(n.)	orang yang hanya makan	chī sù dė rén 吃素的人
		sayuran	
ve.hi.cle	(n.)	kendaraan, wahana	chē liàng 车辆

veil	(n.)	tudung, selubung	miàn shā 面纱
		tabir	mù 幕, zhàng 帐
		alasan	kǒu shí 口实, jiǎ tuō 假托
	(v.)	menyelubungi, menutupi	yǎn gài 掩盖, yǎn shì 掩饰
vein	(n.)	urat darah halus	jìng mài 静脉
vel.vet	(n.)	beledu, beludru	tiān é róng 天鹅绒
vent	(n.)	lubang angin	tōng fēng kǒng 通风孔
ven.ti.late	(v.)	memberi angin	shǐ tōng fēng 使通风
		tukar pikiran secara bebas	zì yóu tǎo lùn 自由讨论
		mengumumkan	gōng bù 公布, xuān bù 宣布
ven.ti.la.tion	(n.)	pemberian angin	tōng fēng 通风
		penukaran udara	huàn qì 换气
ven.ti.la.tor	(n.)	kipas angin	tōng fēng qì 通风器, diàn shàn 电扇
			kōng qì tiáo jié qì 空气调节器
ven.ture	(n.)	usaha yang mengandung risiko	mào xiǎn 冒险, mào xiǎn xíng wéi 冒险行为
ven.ture.some	(a.)	berani	dà dǎn dė 大胆的
		bertualang	mào xiǎn 冒险
verb	(n.)	kata kerja	dòng cí 动词
ver.bal	(a.)	mengenai kata-kata	cí jù dė 词句的, yán yú dė 言语的
		lisan	kǒu tóu dė 口头的
		mengenai kata kerja	dòng cí dė 动词的
verge	(n.)	pinggir	biān yuán 边缘
ver.i.fi.ca.tion	(n.)	verifikasi, pembuktian kebenaran	jiǎn yàn 检验, zhèng shí 证实
ver.i.fy	(v.)	menguji kebenaran, membuktikan kebenaran	jiǎn yàn 检验, zhèng shí 证实
ver.i.table	(a.)	benar, nyata	què shí 确实, zhēn shí 真实
ver.i.ty	(n.)	kebenaran	zhēn shí xìng 真实性, shì shí 事实

verse	(n.)	sajak, syair	shī 诗
	(v.)	membuat syair	zuò shī 作诗
versed	(a.)	benar-benar menguasai	shú liàn 熟练, jīng tōng 精通
ver.sion	(n.)	versi	kàn fǎ 看法, shuō fǎ 说法, dú tè jiàn jiě 独特见解
		terjemahan	fān yì 翻译, yì wén 译文
		cara menyampaikan pendapat	kàn fǎ 看法
ver.ti.cal	(a.)	vertikal, tegak lurus	chúi zhí dė 垂直的
ver.y	(adv.)	amat, sangat	hěn 很, feī cháng 非常
	(a.)	betul, sungguh	zhēn 真, zhēn zhèng 真正
ves.sel	(n.)	tong, bejana	tǒng 桶, róng qì 容器, qì mǐn 器皿
		kapal	chuán zhī 船只
		pembuluh	xuè guǎn 血管
vest	(n.)	rompi, kaus	hàn shēn 汗衫, bèi xīn 背心
	(v.)	memberi	gěi yú 给予, shòu yú 授予
vet	(n.)	dokter hewan	shòu yī 兽医
		veteran	lǎo zhàn shì 老战士
	(v.)	mengobati hewan	yī zhì dòng wù 医治动物
		memeriksa	jiǎn chá 检查, shěn chá 审查
vet.er.an	(n.)	veteran	lǎo zhàn shì 老战士
		kawakan	lǎo jiàng 老将, lǎo shǒu 老手, lǎo liàn dė rén 老练的人
ve.to	(n.)	veto	fǒu jué 否决
	(v.)	memveto	foǔ jué 否决
vex	(v.)	menyusahkan	shǐ rén fán nǎo 使人烦恼
		menjengkelkan	shǐ rén shēng qì 使人生气
vex.a.tion	(n.)	kekesalan	fán nǎo 烦恼
via	(prep.)	melalui	jīng gùo 经过, qǔ dào 取道

vice	(n.)	kebiasaan yang tidak baik	huài xí guàn 坏习惯
		sifat buruk	è xí 恶习
		penjepit, pengapit	lǎo hǔ qián 老虎钳,
	(v.)	menjepit, mengapit	qián zhù 钳住, jiā zhù 夹住
vice-	(pref.)	wakil, muda	fù 副
vice-chair.man	(n.)	wakil ketua	fù zhǔ xí 副主席
vice-min.is.ter	(n.)	wakil menteri	fù bù zhǎng 副部长
vice-pres.i.dent	(n.)	wakil presiden	fù zǒng tǒng 副总统
vi.cious	(a.)	jahat	xié è dė 邪恶的
		bercacat	yǒu quē diǎn 有缺点
vic.tim	(n.)	korban	xī shēng zhě 牺牲者,
			shòu hài zhě 受害者,
			zaō nàn zhě 遭难者
vic.tor	(n.)	pemenang	shèng lì zhě 胜利者
vic.to.ri.ous	(a.)	menang	shèng lì dė 胜利的
vic.to.ry	(n.)	kemenangan	shèng lì 胜利
vict.ual	(n.)	makanan	shì wù 食物, shì pǐn 食品
	(v.)	memberi makanan	gōng yìng shì pǐn 供应食品
vid.e.o	(a.)	video, yang berhubungan dengan televisi	diàn shì dė 电视的
	(n.)	televisi	diàn shì 电视
vid.e.o.cast	(n.)	penyiaran televisi	diàn shì guǎng bō 电视广播
view	(n.)	pemandangan	fēng jǐng 风景, jǐng sè 景色
		penglihatan, pandangan	shì lì 视力, yǎn jiè 眼界
		maksud, niat	yì tú 意图
		pendapat	guān diǎn 观点, yì jiàn 意见
		peninjauan	guān chá 观察, shì chá 视察
		pameran	zhǎn lǎn 展览
		pertimbangan	kǎo lǜ 考虑
	(v.)	meninjau	guān chá 观察, shì chá 视察
		melihat, menonton	cān guān 参观, guān kàn 观看

view.er	(n.)	penonton	guān kàn zhě 观看者, guān zhòng 观众
		pemirsa	kàn diàn shì dė rén 看电视的人
		peninjau	guān chá zhě 观察者
view.less	(a.)	tidak kelihatan	kàn bù jiàn dė 看不见的
		tidak ada usul	méi yǒu yì jiàn dė 没有意见的
view-point	(n.)	sudut pandang	guān diǎn 观点, kàn fǎ 看法
vig.il	(n.)	jaga malam	shǒu yè 守夜, zhí yè 值夜
vig.i.lance	(n.)	kewaspadaan	jǐng tì 警惕
vig.i.lant	(a.)	waspada	jǐng tì dė 警惕的, jiè bèi dė 戒备的
vig.or.ous	(a.)	giat, penuh semangat	shēng qì bó bó dė 生气勃勃的, chōng mǎn jīng lì 充满精力
vig.our	(n.)	kegiatan, tenaga, kekuatan	húo lì 活力, jīng lì 精力
vile	(a.)	hina, memalukan	bēi bǐ 卑鄙, kě chǐ 可耻
vil.la	(n.)	vila	bié shù 别墅
vil.lage	(n.)	desa, dusun	xiāng cūn 乡村
vil.lag.er	(n.)	orang dusun	xiāng xià rén 乡下人
vil.lain	(n.)	penjahat, bajingan	huài rén 坏人, è gùn 恶棍
vine	(n.)	pohon anggur	pú táo shù 葡萄树
vin.e.gar	(n.)	cuka	cù 醋
vine.yard	(n.)	kebun anggur	pú táo yuán 葡萄园
vi.o.la	(n.)	biola	tí qín 提琴
vi.o.late	(v.)	melanggar	wéi fàn 违犯, wéi bèi 违背
		memperkosa	diàn wū 玷污, qiáng jiān 强奸
		menggangu	fáng ài 妨碍, qīn fàn 侵犯
vi.o.lence	(n.)	kehebatan	méng liè 猛烈, jī liè 激烈
		kekerasan	bào lì 暴力, qiáng bào 强暴
		kekejaman	bào nùe 暴虐, cán bào 残暴
vi.o.lent	(a.)	hebat	méng liè 猛烈, jī liè dė 激烈的
		keras, bengis	qiáng bào dė 强暴的, cán bào dė 残暴的

vi.o.lent.ly	(adv.)	dengan keras	qiáng liè di 强烈地
		dengan hebat	jī liè di 激烈地
vi.o.let	(n.)	warna lembayung, warna violet	zǐ sè 紫色
		bunga violet	zǐ luó lán 紫罗兰
vi.o.lin	(n.)	biola	tí qín 提琴
vi.o.lin.ist	(n.)	pemain biola	tí qín jiā 提琴家
vi.o.lon.cel.lo	(n.)	selo	dà tí qín 大提琴
vir.gin	(n.)	perawan	chū nǚ 处女
vir.tu.al	(a.)	sebetulnya, sebenarnya	shí ji shàng 实际上
vir.tue	(n.)	kebaikan, kebajikan	shàn xíng 善行, měi dė 美德
		kesucian	zhēn cāo 贞操
vi.rus	(n.)	virus, racun	bìng dú 病毒, dú sù 毒素
vi.sa	(n.)	visa	wài jiāo qiān zhèng 外交签证
vis.i.ble	(a.)	kelihatan, tampak	kàn dé jiàn dė 看得见的, yǒu xíng dė 有形的
vi.sion	(n.)	penglihatan	shì lì 视力, shì jué 视觉
		pandangan	yǎn guāng 眼光
		impian, khayalan	huàn xiǎng 幻想
		pemandangan	jǐng xiàng 景象
vis.it	(v.)	berkunjung, mengunjungi	bài fǎng 拜访, fǎng wèn 访问
		bertamu	zuò kè 作客
vis.i.tant	(n.)	pengunjung, tamu	kè rén 客人, lái bīn 来宾
vis.i.ta.tion	(n.)	kunjungan resmi	fǎng wèn 访问
vis.i.tor	(n.)	pengunjung, tamu	fǎng wèn zhě 访问者, lái bīn 来宾, kè rén 客人
vi.tal	(a.)	vital, hidup	húo dė 活的, shēng mìng dė 生命的
		mematikan	zhì mìng dė 致命的
		penting sekali	zhòng yào dė 重要的
vi.tal.i.ty	(n.)	daya hidup	shēng mìng lì 生命力

vit.a.min	(n.)	vitamin	wéi tā mìng 维他命, wéi shēng sù 维生素
viv.id	(a.)	terang sekali	xiān yàn dė 鲜艳的, xiān míng dė 鲜明的
		hidup	shēng dòng dė 生动的
		bersemangat	húo pō 活泼, shēng qì bó bó 生气勃勃
viz	(abbr.)	yakni, yaitu	jí 即, jiù shì 就是
vo.cab.u.la.ry	(n.)	perbendaharaan kata, kosa kata	cí hui 词汇
vo.cal	(a.)	mengenai suara	shēng yīn dė 声音的
		yang bersuara	yǒu shēng dė 有声的
vo.cal.ist	(n.)	penyanyi	gē chàng jia 歌唱家
vo.ca.tion	(n.)	bakat	tiān cái 天才, cái néng 才能
		pekerjaan	zhí yè 职业
vogue	(n.)	kepopuleran, mode	fēng qì 风气, shí shàng 时尚
voice	(n.)	suara	shēng yin 声音, yì jiàn 意见
voice.less	(a.)	tak bersuara	wú shēng dė 无声的
vol.can.ic	(a.)	mengenai gunung berapi	hǔo shān dė 火山的
vol.ca.no	(n.)	gunung berapi	hǔo shān 火山
vo.li.tion	(n.)	kemauan	yì zhì 意志
vol.ley.ball	(n.)	bola voli	pái qiú 排球
volt.age	(n.)	voltase	diàn yā 电压
volt.me.ter	(n.)	alat pengukur voltase	fú tè jī 伏特机, diàn yā biǎo 电压表
vol.ume	(n.)	jilid	cè 册, juàn 卷
		banyak	dà liàng 大量
		volume	tǐ ji 体积, róng ji 容积
		kerasnya suara	xiǎng dù 响度, yīn liàng 音量
vol.ume-pro.duce	(v.)	memproduksi secara besar-besaran	dà liàng shēng chǎn 大量生产
vo.lu.me.ter	(n.)	alat pengukur volume	tǐ jī jì 体积计

vol.un.ta.ry	(a.)	sukarela	zì yuàn dė 自愿的, yì wù dė 义务的, zhì yuàn dė 志愿的
		sengaja	gù yì dė 故意的
		sekehendak hati	rèn yì dė 任意的, sŭi yì dė 随意的
		dengan sokongan sukarela	lè juān dė 乐捐的
vol.un.teer	(n.)	sukarelawan	zhì yuàn zhě 志愿者
	(v.)	sukarela	zhì yuàn 志愿, zì yuàn cān jiā 自愿参加
vom.it	(v.)	muntah	oŭ tù 呕吐
vote	(n.)	suara	biǎo jué 表决, tóu piào 投票
	(v.)	memberi suara	tóu piào 投票
		memutuskan	biǎo jué 表决
vot.er	(n.)	pemilih, pemberi suara	xuǎn jŭ rén 选举人, tóu piào zhě 投票者
vot.ing	(n.)	pemungutan suara	biǎo jué 表决, tóu piào 投票
vouch.er	(n.)	surat bukti	zhèng shū 证书
		bon, tanda bukti pembayaran	píng dān 凭单
vow	(n.)	janji, ikrar	shì yuè 誓约
	(v.)	bersumpah	fā shì 发誓
vow.el	(n.)	huruf hidup, vokal	yuán yīn 元音
voy.age	(n.)	pelayaran	háng hǎi 航海, háng xíng 航行
	(v.)	mengadakan pelayaran	háng hǎi 航海, háng xíng 航行
voy.ag.er	(n.)	orang yang berlayar, pelaut	háng hǎi zhě 航海者
vul.gar	(a.)	umum	dà zhòng dė 大众的
		kasar	cū sú dė 粗俗的
		biasa	tōng sú dė 通俗的
vul.gar.i.ty	(n.)	kekasaran	cū sú 粗俗, cū yě 粗野

vul.gar.ize	(v.)	menjadikan umum	yōng sú huà 庸俗化
		menjadikan biasa	píng mín huà 平民化

W

wade	(v.)	mengarungi	shè 涉, shè shŭi 涉水
wage	(v.)	melakukan, menjalankan	jìn xíng 进行
		berperang	zùo zhàn 作战
	(n.)	upah, gaji	gōng zī 工资
wag.on	(n.)	kereta barang	yùn hùo chē 运货车
waist	(n.)	pinggang	yāo 腰
waist-band	(n.)	sabuk, ikat pinggang	yāo dài 腰带, kù dài 裤带
waist.coat	(n.)	rompi, baju kaus	bèi xīn 背心
wait	(v.)	menunggu, menanti	děng 等, děng hòu 等候, děng dài 等待
wait.er	(n.)	pelayan	zhāo dài yuán 招待员
wait.ress	(n.)	pelayan wanita	nǔ zhāo dài yuán 女招待员
wake	(v.)	bangun, membangunkan	xǐng 醒, xǐng lái 醒来, nòng xǐng 弄醒, huàn xǐng 唤醒
wake.ful	(a.)	sadar	jué xǐng dė 觉醒的
wak.en	(v.)	membangunkan	huàn xǐng 唤醒
walk	(v.)	berjalan	zǒu 走
walk.er	(n.)	pejalan kaki	bù xíng zhě 步行者
walkie-talkie	(n.)	alat woki-toki	bù tán jī 步谈机, bù huà jī 步话机
walk.ing	(n.)	berjalan kaki	bù xíng 步行
		berjalan-jalan	sàn bù 散步
walk.ing-stick	(n.)	tongkat	shǒu zhàng 手杖
walk-out	(n.)	pemogokan	bà gōng 罢工
wall	(n.)	dinding, tembok	qiáng bì 墙壁
	(v.)	memasang tembok	zhù qiáng 筑墙

wal.let	(n.)	dompet	pí jiā zi 皮夹子
wall.paper	(n.)	kertas dinding	qiáng zhǐ 墙纸, bì zhǐ 壁纸
wal.nut	(n.)	kenari	hu táo 胡桃
wan.der	(v.)	mengembara, berkelana	liú làng 流浪, pái húai 徘徊
		berkeliling	màn yóu 漫游
wan.der.er	(n.)	pengembara	liú làng zhě 流浪者
want	(n.)	kebutuhan	xù yào 需要
		kekurangan	bù zú 不足, quē shǎo 缺少
	(v.)	ingin, mau, hendak	yào 要, xiǎng yào 想要
		membutuhkan, memerlu-kan	xù yào 需要, bì yào 必要
want.ing	(a.)	kurang	quē shǎo 缺少, quē fá 缺乏
war	(n.)	peperangan, perang	zhàn zhēng 战争
	(v.)	berperang	zuò zhàn 作战, dǎ zhàng 打仗
ward	(n.)	penjagaan, perlindungan	jiān shì 监视, bǎo hù 保护
		orang yang di bawah per-walian	shòu jiān hù rén 受监护人
		kamar pasien	bìng fáng 病房
	(v.)	melindungi, menjaga	bǎo hù 保护, shǒu wèi 守卫
		mencegah, menghindari	fáng zhǐ 防止, bì kāi 避开
		menangkis	dǎng zhù 挡住
ward.robe	(n.)	lemari pakaian	yī chú 衣橱
ware	(v.)	awas	dāng xīn 当心
	(n.)	barang dagangan	shāng pǐn 商品, hùo pǐn 货品
		periuk, belanga	qì mín 器皿
ware.house	(n.)	gudang	cāng kù 仓库
war.i.ly	(adv.)	waspada, hati-hati	jǐng tì 警惕, jǐn shèn 谨慎
war.i.ness	(n.)	kewaspadaan, sikap ha-ti-hati	jǐng tì 警惕, jǐn shèn 谨慎
war.fare	(n.)	perang, peperangan	zhàn zhēng 战争

war.like	(a.)	mengenai peperangan	zhàn zhēng dė 战争的
		suka berperang	hào zhàn dė 好战的
warm	(a.)	panas, hangat	rè 热, nuǎn 暖
		ramah, hangat	rè chén dė 热忱的, rè liė dė 热烈的
		bersemangat	jī áng 激昂, xīng fèn 兴奋
	(v.)	memanaskan, menghangatkan	shǐ wēn nuǎn 使温暖
		menjadi panas	biàn rè 变热, biàn nuǎn 变暖
war.mon.ger	(n.)	penghasut perang	zhàn zhēng fàn zi 战争贩子
warmth	(n.)	kehangatan, keramahan	wēn nuǎn 温暖, rè xīn 热心
warn	(v.)	memperingatkan	jǐng gào 警告
warn.ing	(n.)	peringatan	jǐng gào 警告
war.ren	(n.)	tempat memelihara kelinci	yǎng tù chǎng 养兔场
war.ri.or	(n.)	pejuang, prajurit	zhàn shì 战士
war.ship	(n.)	kapal perang	jūn jiàn 军舰
war.time	(n.)	waktu perang	zhàn shí 战时, zhàn zhēng shí qī 战争时期
wa.ry	(a.)	waspada, hati-hati	jǐng tì 警惕, xiǎo xīn 小心
wash	(v.)	mencuci	xǐ 洗
wash.a.ble	(a.)	dapat dicuci	kě xǐ dė 可洗的
wash-board	(n.)	papan cuci	xǐ yī bǎn 洗衣板
wash.er	(n.)	mesin cuci	xǐ yī jī 洗衣机
wasp	(n.)	tawon	huáng fēng 黄蜂
wasp.ish	(a.)	cepat marah, tidak sabar	yì nù dė 易怒的, jí xìng 急性
		menyengat	jiān kè 尖刻, kè bó 刻薄
waste	(a.)	yang disia-siakan	huāng fèi dė 荒废的
		tak berguna	méi yǒu yòng dė 没有用的
	(v.)	memboroskan	làng fèi 浪费
		menghabiskan	xiāo hào 消耗
	(n.)	pemborosan	làng fèi 浪费
		buangan, sampah	fèi wù 废物

waste-bask.et	(n.)	keranjang sampah	fèi zhǐ lǒu 废纸篓, lā jī lǒu 垃圾篓
watch	(n.)	arloji	shǒu biǎo 手表
		jaga	kàn shǒu 看守
	(v.)	menjaga	kàn shǒu 看守
		mengawasi	jiān shì 监视
		menonton	guān kàn 观看
watch-dog	(n.)	anjing penjaga pintu	kàn mén gǒu 看门狗
watch.er	(n.)	orang yang berjaga	kàn shǒu rén 看守人,
			kàn hù rén 看护人
watch.ful	(a.)	penuh perhatian	zhù yì dė 注意的
		waspada	jǐng tì dė 警惕的
watch.word	(n.)	semboyan	kǒu hào 口号, biāo yǔ 标语
wa.ter	(n.)	air	shǔi 水
	(v.)	menyirami	jiāo shǔi 浇水
wa.ter.fall	(n.)	air terjun	pù bù 瀑布
wa.ter.ing	(n.)	penyiraman	sǎ shǔi 洒水
wa.ter-melon	(n.)	semangka	xī guā 西瓜
wa.ter.proof	(a.)	tahan air	nài shǔi dė 耐水的,
			bù tòu shǔi dė 不透水的
wa.ter.tow.er	(n.)	menara air	shǔi tā 水塔
wa.ter.way	(n.)	jalan air, terusan	shǔi dào 水道
wave	(n.)	gelombang	bō 波
		lambaian	huī dòng 挥动
		ombak	bo làng 波浪
	(v.)	melambai, melambaikan	piāo yáng 飘扬, zhāo shǒu 招手
		mengombak	qǐ bō làng 起波浪
wax	(n.)	lilin	là 蜡
way	(n.)	jalan	dào 道, lù 路, dào lù 道路
		cara	fāng fǎ 方法
		arah	fāng xiàng 方向
we	(pron.)	kita, kami	wǒ mėn 我们

weak	(a.)	lemah	rùo 弱, shuāi rùo 衰弱
weak.en	(v.)	melemahkan	xùe rùo 削弱
		menjadikan lemah	biàn rùo 变弱
weak.ness	(n.)	kelemahan	shuāi rùo 衰弱, rùo diǎn 弱点
wealth	(n.)	kekayaan, harta	cái fù 财富
wealth.y	(a.)	kaya	fù yù 富裕, fù yǒu 富有
weap.on	(n.)	senjata	wǔ qì 武器
wear	(v.)	memakai	chuān 穿, dài 戴
		kelihatan	biǎo xiàn 表现, chéng xiàn 呈现
		tahan pakai	nài yòng 耐用
		mengauskan, memakai (pakaian) sampai lusuh	mó sǔn 磨损, mó pò 磨破
	(n.)	pakaian	yī zhúo 衣著
		pemakaian	chuān zhúo 穿著, pèi dài 佩戴
wear.er	(n.)	pemakai	pèi dài zhě 佩戴者
		pembawa	xī dài zhě 携带者
wea.ry	(a.)	letih	pí juàn dė 疲倦的
wea.ri.ness	(n.)	kelelahan	pí juàn 疲倦
weath.er	(n.)	cuaca	tiān qì 天气
weath.er.cock	(n.)	penunjuk angin	fēng biāo 风标
weave	(v.)	menenun	fǎng zhī 纺织
		menganyam	biān 编
weav.er	(n.)	penenun, penganyam	fǎng zhī gōng rén 纺织工人, zhī gōng 职工
web	(n.)	jaringan	wǎng 网
wed	(v.)	mengawini, mengawin-kan, kawin	qǔ 娶, jià 嫁, jié hūn 结婚
wed.ding	(n.)	perkawinan	hūn lǐ 婚礼, jié hūn jì niàn 结婚纪念
Wednes.day	(n.)	hari Rabu	xīng qī sān 星期三
weed	(n.)	rumput liar	zā cǎ 杂草, yě cǎo 野草

week	(n.)	minggu, pekan	xīng qī 星期, zhōu 周
week-day	(n.)	hari kerja	gōng zuò rì 工作日, píng cháng rì zi 平常日子
week-end	(n.)	akhir pekan	zhōu mò 周末
week.ly	(a.)	mingguan, tiap minggu	měi xīng qī dė 每星期的, měi zhōu dė 每周的
	(adv.)	tiap minggu	měi zhōu yī cì 每周一次
weep	(v.)	menangis	kū 哭, liú lèi 流泪
weigh	(v.)	menimbang	chèng 称
		mempertimbangkan	kǎo lù 考虑
weight	(n.)	berat, bobot	zhòng 重, zhòng liàng 重量, qīng zhòng 轻重
weight.y	(a.)	berat	chén zhòng 沉重
		penting	zhòng yào dė 重要的
wel.come	(n.)	sambutan, selamat datang	huān yíng 欢迎
	(v.)	menyambut	huān yíng 欢迎
wel.comed	(a.)	yang disenangi	shòu huān yíng dė 受欢迎的
weld	(v.)	mengelas	hàn jiē 焊接
wel.fare	(n.)	kesejahteraan	fú lì 福利
well	(n.)	sumur	jǐng 井
		mata air	quán 泉
	(adv.)	baik	hǎo 好
	(a.)	sehat	jiàn kāng 健康
well-be.ing	(n.)	kesejahteraan	fú lì 福利
well-bred	(a.)	sopan	yǒu lǐ mào dė 有礼貌的, yǒu jiào yǎng dė 有教养的
well-ground.ed	(a.)	mempunyai dasar	yǒu jī chǔ dė 有基础的
well-known	(a.)	terkenal	yǒu míng dė 有名的
well-meant	(a.)	dengan maksud baik	hǎo yì dė 好意的
well.nigh	(adv.)	hampir	jī hū 几乎

well.off	(a.)	kaya	fù yù dė 富裕的, fù yǒu dė 富有的
well-to-do	(a.)	kaya, mampu	fù yù dė 富裕的, xiǎo kāng dė 小康的
were	(v.)	ada, adalah	zài 在, shì 是
west	(n.)	barat	xī 西, xī bù 西部, xī fāng 西方
	(a.)	barat	xī fāng dė 西方的
	(adv.)	ke barat	xiàng xī 向西
west.ern	(a.)	barat	xī fāng dė 西方的
west.ern.ize	(v.)	mewesternisasikan	yáng huà 洋化
west.ern.most	(a.)	paling barat	zùi xī dė 最西的
west.ward	(a.)	ke barat	xiàng xī dė 向西的
wet	(a.)	basah	shī 湿, cháo shī 潮湿
wet-nurse	(n.)	inang	nǎi mā 奶妈
whale	(n.)	ikan paus	jīng yú 鲸鱼
wharf	(n.)	dermaga	mǎ tóu 码头
wharf.age	(n.)	bea tambak	mǎ tóu fèi 码头费
what	(pron.)	apa	shén mė 什么
	(a.)	apa, berapa	shén mė 什么, dūo shǎo 多少
		betapa	dūo mė 多么
	(conj.)	seperti, bagaikan	hǎo bǐ 好比
what.ev.er	(pron.)	apa pun	wú lùn shén mė 无论什么
what.not	(n.)	rak barang antik	gǔ dǒng jià 古董架
wheat	(n.)	gandum	xiǎo mài 小麦
wheel	(n.)	roda	lún zi 轮子, chē lún 车轮
when	(adv.)	kapan	shén mė shí hòu 什么时候
	(conj.)	ketika	dāng ... dē shí hòu 当…的时候
whence	(adv.)	dari mana	cóng nǎ lǐ 从哪里
whence.so.ev.er	(adv.)	dari mana pun	wú lùn cóng nǎ li 无论从哪里
when.ev.er	(adv.)	kapan saja, sewaktu-waktu	wú lùn shén mė shí hòu 无论什么时候, suí shí 随时
where	(adv.)	di mana, ke mana	zài nǎ lǐ 在哪里

where.fore	(adv.)	mengapa	wèi shén mė 为什么
wher.ev.er	(adv.)	ke mana saja	wú lùn dào nă lĭ 无论到哪里
whet	(v.)	mengasah	mó 磨
wheth.er	(conj.)	apakah	shì fŏu 是否, hùi bù hùi 会不会
whet.stone	(n.)	batu asahan	mó shi 磨石
which	(pron.)	yang mana	nă gè 哪个, nă yī gè 哪一个
which.ev.er	(pron.)	mana saja	wú lùn nă gè 无论哪个,
			súi biàn nă gè 随便哪个
while	(n.)	sebentar	yī hùi ér 一会儿
	(conj.)	walaupun	suī rán 虽然
		ketika	dāng ... dė shí hòu 当…的时候
whip	(n.)	cambuk	biān zi 鞭子
	(v.)	mencambuk	biān dă 鞭打
whirl	(v.)	berputar, memutar	xuán zhŭan 旋转,
			shĭ xuán zhŭan 使旋转
whis.ker	(n.)	cambang	xū 须
whis.per	(v.)	berbisik	ĕr yú 耳语
	(n.)	bisikan	ĕr yú 耳语
whis.tle	(v.)	membunyikan peluit	chuī shào 吹哨, chuī dí 吹笛
		bersiul	chuī kŏu shào 吹口哨
	(n.)	peluit	shào zi 哨子, dí 笛
		bunyi peluit, bunyi siul	dí shēng 笛声, shào shēng 哨声
white	(a.)	putih	băi 白
whit.en	(v.)	memutih	piăo băi 漂白, nòng băi 弄白
		memutihkan	biàn băi 变白
white.wash	(v.)	mengapuri dinding rumah	fĕn shuā 粉刷
whith.er	(adv.)	ke mana	dào nă lĭ 到哪里
whit.tle	(v.)	meraut	xuē 削
who	(pron.)	siapa	shéi 谁

who.ev.er	(pron.)	siapa pun	wú lùn shéi 无论谁, bù guǎn shéi 不管谁
whole	(a.)	seluruh	quán bù dė 全部的, zhěng gè dė 整个的
whole-heart.ed	(a.)	tulus, sepenuh hati	quán xīn quán yì dė全心全意的
whole.sale	(n.)	penjualan grosir	pī fā 批发
whole.some	(a.)	sehat	wèi shēng dė 卫生的, jiàn kāng dė 健康的
		berfaedah, bermanfaat	yǒu yì dė 有益的, yǒu yòng dė 有用的
whol.ly	(adv.)	sama sekali, secara kese- luruhan	wán quán 完全, tǒng tǒng 统统
whom	(pron.)	siapa	shéi 谁
whoop	(v.)	berteriak	jiào hǎn 叫喊
whose	(pron.)	kepunyaan siapa	shéi dė 谁的
who.so.ev.er	(pron.)	siapa pun	wǔ lùn shéi 无论谁, bù guǎn shéi 不管谁
why	(adv.)	mengapa	wèi shén mė 为什么
wick	(n.)	sumbu lampu	dēng xīn 灯心
		sumbu lilin	là zhú xīn 蜡烛心
wick.ed	(a.)	jahat, nakal	xié è dė 邪恶的, huài dė 坏的
wick.ed.ness	(n.)	kejahatan	xié è 邪恶
wick.et	(n.)	loket tempat penjualan karcis	shòu piào chuāng 售票窗
wide	(a.)	lebar, luas	kuān 宽, kùo 阔, guǎng kùo广阔
wide.ly	(adv.)	luas	guǎng 广, guǎng dà 广大
wid.en	(v.)	melebarkan, memperlebar	nòng kuān 弄宽, kùo zhāng 扩张
wide-open	(a.)	terbuka lebar	zhāng kaī dė 张开的
wide-spread	(a.)	tersebar luas	pǔ biàn dė 普遍的
wid.ow	(n.)	janda	guǎ fù 寡妇

wid.ow.er	(n.)	duda	guān fū 鳏夫
width	(n.)	lebar	guǎng kùo 广阔
wife	(n.)	istri	qī zī 妻子
wig	(n.)	rambut palsu	jiǎ fà 假发
wild	(a.)	liar	yě 野
		buas	yě mán 野蛮
		gila	fēng kuáng 疯狂
	(n.)	daerah liar	yuán yě 原野, huāng yě 荒野
wild.ly	(adv.)	liar	yě 野, yě mán di 野蛮地
		ribut	hú luàn di 胡乱地
wil.ful	(a.)	keras kepala	gù zhi dė 固执的, wán gù dė 顽固的
will	(v.)	akan, hendak	yào 要, xiǎng 想
		dapat	hùi 会
	(n.)	kemauan	yì zhì 意志
will.ing	(a.)	mau, sudi, sukarela	yuàn yì dė 原意的, zì yuàn dė 自愿的
win	(v.)	menang, memenangkan	shèng 胜, dé shèng 得胜, dǎ shèng 打胜
	(n.)	kemenangan	shèng lì 胜利
wince	(v.)	bergerenyit, menggerenyit	tuì suō 退缩
wind	(v.)	memutar	zhuǎn dòng 转动
		membelitkan, melilit	chán ráo 缠绕
		berbelok belok	wān wān qū qū 弯弯曲曲
		menggulung	juǎn lǒng 卷拢
	(n.)	angin	fēng 风
		napas	hū xī 呼吸
		bau	qì wèi 气味
		omong kosong	kōng tán 空谈
wind.bag	(n.)	tukang bual	kōng tán jiā 空谈家
wind.mill	(n.)	kincir angin	fēng chē 风车

win.dow	(n.)	jendela	chuāng 窗, chuāng hù 窗户
win.dow-pane	(n.)	kaca jendela	chuāng bō lí 窗玻璃
win.dow-shop	(v.)	jalan-jalan ke pertokoan	guǎng shāng diàn 逛商店
wind.pipe	(n.)	batang tenggorokan	qì guǎn 气管
wind.y	(a.)	banyak angin	dūo fēng dė 多风的
wine	(n.)	anggur	pú táo jiǔ 葡萄酒
wing	(n.)	sayap	chì bǎng 翅膀
wink	(v.)	mengejapkan mata	zhǎ yǎn 眨眼
win.ner	(n.)	pemenang	shèng lì zhě 胜利者,
			hùo jiǎng zhě 获奖者
win.ter	(n.)	musim dingin	dōng tiān 冬天
wipe	(v.)	menghapus	chá 檫, kaī 揩
wire	(n.)	kawat	tiě xiàn 铁线, tiě sī 铁纱
		telegram	diàn bào 电报
	(v.)	mengikat dengan kawat	yòng tiě xiàn bǎng 用铁线绑
		menelegram	dǎ diàn bào 打电报
wire.less	(a.)	tanpa kawat	wú xiàn dė 无线的
	(n.)	radio	shōu yīn jī 收音机
wire.pho.to	(n.)	foto telegraf	chuán zhèn zhào piàn 传真照片
wis.dom	(n.)	kebijaksanaan, kearifan	zhì hùi 智慧, míng zhì 明智
wise	(a.)	bijaksana	cóng míng dė 聪明的,
			míng zhì dė 明智的
wish	(v.)	mengharapkan	xī wàng 希望
		menginginkan	yuàn wàng 愿望
		menghendaki	xiǎng yào 想要
	(n.)	keinginan	yuàn wàng 愿望
wit	(n.)	kecerdasan	zhì lì 智力, caí zhì 才智
		orang yang sangat cerdas	caí zi 才子
witch	(n.)	perempuan tukang sihir	nǚ wū 女巫, wū pó 巫婆
witch.craft	(n.)	ilmu sihir	yaō shù 妖术, mó fǎ 魔法

witch.er.y	(n.)	ilmu sihir	yaō shù 妖术, mó fã 魔法
with	(prep.)	dengan, bersama	gēn 跟, tóng 同
		pakai	yòng 用
with.draw	(v.)	menarik kembali	shōu húi 收回, chè húi 撤回
		menarik diri	tùi chū 退出
with.er	(v.)	layu	kū wĕi 枯萎
		menjadikan layu	shǐ kū wĕi 使枯萎
with.hold	(v.)	menahan	zhì zhǐ 制止, kòu liú 扣留
with.in	(prep.)	di dalam	zài nèi 在内
		tidak lebih dari	bù chaō gùo 不超过
with.out	(prep.)	tanpa	méi yǒu 没有, háo wú 毫无
		luar	zài wài 在外
	(adv.)	di luar, bagian luar	zài wài 在外, wài miàn 外面
with.stand	(v.)	menentang, melawan	dǐ kàng 抵抗, fǎn dùi 反对
wit.ness	(n.)	saksi	zhèng rén 证人
		bukti	zhèng jù 证据
		saksi mata	mù jī zhě 目击者
	(v.)	menyaksikan	zùo zhèng 作证
		membenarkan	zhèng shí 证实
wolf	(n.)	serigala	láng 狼
wom.an	(n.)	wanita	nǚ rén 女人, fù nǚ 妇女
wom.an.hood	(n.)	kewanitaan	nǚ xìng 女性
wom.an.kind	(n.)	kaum wanita	fù nǚ 妇女
wom.an.ly	(a.)	kewanitaan	nǚ xìng dė 女性的
womb	(n.)	kandungan	zǐ gōng 子宫
wom.en.folk	(n.)	kaum wanita	fù nǚ 妇女
won.der	(n.)	keheranan, kekaguman	jīng qí 惊奇
		keajaiban	qí jī 奇迹, qí shì 奇事
	(v.)	ingin tahu	jí xiǎng zhī dào 极想知道
		merasa heran	gǎn dào qí guài 感到奇怪

won.der.ful	(a.)	ajaib, mengherankan	lìng rén jīng qí dė 令人惊奇的, qí guài dė 奇怪的
		sangat bagus	jīng cǎi 精采, miào jí lė 妙极了
won.der.land	(n.)	kahyangan, negeri ajaib	xiān jìng 仙境
won.der.ment	(n.)	keheranan	jīng qí 惊奇
won.drous	(a.)	menakjubkan	qí miào 奇妙
woo	(v.)	meminang	qiú hūn 求婚
wood	(n.)	hutan kecil	shù lín 树林
		kayu hutan	lín mù 林木, mù cái 木材
		kayu bakar	mù chái 木柴
wood.craft	(n.)	kerajinan kayu	mù cái jiā gōng 木材加工
wood.cut	(n.)	ukiran kayu	mù kė 木刻
wood-cut.ter	(n.)	penebang kayu	fā mù gōng rén 伐木工人, qiáo fu 樵夫
wood.en	(a.)	dari kayu	mù dė 木的, mù zùo dė 木做的
wood.land	(n.)	daerah hutan	sēn lín dì 森林地
wood.peck.er	(n.)	burung pelatuk	zhuó mù niǎo 啄木鸟
wood.work	(n.)	barang yang terbuat dari kayu	mù zhi pǐn 木制品
woo.er	(n.)	peminang	qiú hūn zhě 求婚者
wool	(n.)	bulu domba	yáng máo 羊毛
		kain wol	máo zhī pǐn 毛织品
wool.len	(a.)	dari wol	yáng máo dė 羊毛的, máo zhī dė 毛织的
	(n.)	pakaian wol	máo yī 毛衣, máo zhī pǐn 毛织品
word	(n.)	kata	cí 词
		janji	nùo yán 诺言
		kabar	xiāo xī 消息
		perintah	mìng lìng 命令
word-build.ing	(n.)	cara pembentukan kata	gòu cí fǎ 构词法

word.i.ness	(n.)	kepanjanglebaran	lūo sūo 罗索
word.ing	(n.)	pilihan kata, diksi	yòng cí 用词, cùo cí 措词
work	(n.)	pekerjaan	gōng zùo 工作, láo dòng 劳动
		karya	zùo pǐn 作品, zhù zùo 著作
	(n.)	pabrik	gōng chǎng 工厂
	(v.)	bekerja	gōng zùo 工作
		mengolah, mengusahakan	jīng yíng 经营
		berefek	qǐ zùo yòng 起作用
		menimbulkan	zào chéng 造成, chǎn shēng 产生
		memecahkan, menyelesaikan	jiě jué 解决
		menjalankan mesin	cāo zùo 操作, kāi dòng 开动
work.a.ble	(a.)	dapat dikerjakan	kě cāo zùo dė 可操作的, kě jīng yíng dė 可经营的
work.a.day	(a.)	hari kerja	gōng zùo rì dė 工作日的
work.day	(n.)	hari kerja	gōng zùo rì 工作日
work.er	(n.)	pekerja	gōng rén 工人, láo dòng zhě 劳动者
work.man.ship	(n.)	kemahiran, keterampilan	jì qiǎo 技巧
		hasil dari suatu kerajinan tangan	gōng yì pǐn 工艺品
work.shop	(n.)	bengkel	chē jiān 车间
		ruang kerja	gōng chǎng 工场
world	(n.)	dunia	shì jiè 世界
world-wide	(a.)	seluruh dunia	quán shì jiè dė 全世界的
worm	(n.)	cacing	chán chóng 肠虫, húi chóng 蛔虫
worm.y	(a.)	bercacing	dūo chóng dė 多虫的, shēng chóng dė 生虫的
worn-out	(a.)	usang	pò jiù dė 破旧的
		letih sekali	feī cháng pí fá 非常疲乏, hěn pí juàn 很疲倦

wor.ry	(v.)	susah, menyusahkan	fán nǎo 烦恼, shǐ fán nǎo 使烦恼
		cemas, mencemaskan	dān xīn 担心, shǐ rén dān xīn 使人担心
		mengganggu	dǎ rǎo 打扰
	(n.)	kesusahan, kecemasan	fán nǎo 烦恼, dān xīn 担心
worse	(a.)	lebih buruk	gēng huài 更坏
	(adv.)	lebih buruk	gēng huài 更坏
		lebih hebat	gēng lì hài 更厉害
		keadaan yang memburuk	qíng kuàng è huà 情况恶化
wor.ship	(n.)	sembahyang	jìng shén 敬神, bài shén 拜神, lǐ bài 礼拜
		pemujaan	chóng bài 崇拜
	(v.)	menyembah, memuja	chóng bài 崇拜, zùo lí bài 做礼拜
wor.ship.per	(n.)	pemuja	chóng bài zhě 崇拜者
worst	(a., adv.)	paling buruk	zùi huài 最坏
worth	(n.)	harga, nilai	jià 价, jià zhí 价值
	(a.)	bernilai, bermanfaat	zhí dé 值得, yǒu jià zhí dė 有价值的
worth.less	(a.)	tidak bernilai	wú jià zhí dė 无价值的, bù zhí dė 不值的
wor.thy	(a.)	bernilai	yǒu jià zhí dė 有价值的
		patut dihormati	kě zūn jìng dė 可尊敬的
	(n.)	orang yang terkemuka	jié chū rén wù 杰出人物
would	(v.)	mau, hendak	yào 要, xiǎng yào 想要
		dapat	hùi 会, néng 能
wound	(n.)	luka	shāng 伤, shāng kǒu 伤口, chuāng shāng 创伤
	(v.)	melukai	shāng hài 伤害
		terluka	shòu shāng 受伤
wrack	(n.)	kebobrokan	pò làn 破烂, pò miè 破灭

wran.gle	(v.)	bertengkar, cekcok	zhēng lùn 争论, chǎo zǔi 吵嘴
wrang.ler	(n.)	orang yang bertengkar	zhēng chǎo zhě 争吵者
wrap	(v.)	membungkus	bāo 包
		membelitkan, melilitkan	chán 缠
		menyelubungi	lǒng zhào 笼罩
	(n.)	selendang	wéi jīn 围巾
		selubung	pī jiān 披肩
wrap.per	(n.)	tukang bungkus	bāo gǔo zhě 包裹者
		kertas pembungkus	bāo zhuāng zhǐ 包装纸
		sampul	bāo shū zhǐ 包书纸
wrath	(n.)	kegusaran, kemurkaan	dà nù 大怒, bào nù 暴怒
wreak	(v.)	melampiaskan	fā xiè 发泄
		membalas dendam	bào chóu 报仇
wreath	(n.)	rangkaian bunga	huā huán 花环
		karangan bunga	huā quān 花圈
wreathe	(v.)	menganyam lingkaran	biān quān 编圈,
		menjalin lingkaran	biān huán 编环
		membelitkan, melilit	huán rǎo 环绕, pán rǎo 盘绕
		menghias	zhuāng shì 装饰
wreck	(n.)	kapal karam	fèi chuán 废船
		kecelakaan kapal	chuán zhī shī shì 船只失事, hǎi nàn 海难
		barang rongsokan	cán hái 残骸, fèi wù 废物
	(v.)	kecelakaan	shī shi 失事
		mencelakakan	shǐ zāo nàn 使遭难
		menghancurkan, merusakkan	pò huài 破坏
		mengaramkan, mengandaskan	shǐ chuán chén mò 使船沉没
wrest	(v.)	merebut	duó 夺

wres.tle	(v.)	bergulat	shuāi jiǎo 摔角
	(n.)	pergulatan	shuāi jiǎo 摔角, dòu zhēng 斗争
wres.tler	(n.)	pegulat	shuāi jiǎo yùn dòng yuán 摔角运动员
wretch	(n.)	orang yang malang	bù xìng dė rén 不幸的人
wrig.gle	(v.)	menggeliat	rú dòng 蠕动
wright	(n.)	pembuat, tukang kayu	gōng jiàng 工匠, mù gōng 木工
wring	(v.)	memeras, memilin	jiǎo 绞, niǔ 扭
		menyusahkan, menyiksa	shǐ rén kǔ nǎo 使人苦恼, shǐ rén tòng kǔ 使人痛苦
		memeras orang	lè sǔo 勒索
wring.er	(n.)	orang yang memeras	lè sǔo zhě 勒索者
wrin.kle	(n.)	kerut, keriput	zhòu wén 皱纹
	(v.)	berkerut, kusut	qǐ zhòu wén 起皱纹
		mengerutkan, mengusut-kan	nòng zhòu 弄皱
wrist	(n.)	pergelangan tangan	wàn 腕, wàn guān jié 腕关节
write	(v.)	menulis	xiě 写
		mengarang	xiě zùo 写作
		mengubah	gǎi xiě 改写
writ.er	(n.)	penulis	chaō xiě yuán 抄写员, shū jì 书记
		pengarang	zùo jiā 作家, zùo zhě 作者
writ.ing	(n.)	tulisan	shū xiě 书写, xiě zì 写字
		karangan	zùo pǐn 作品, zhù zùo 著作
writ.ten	(a.)	tertulis	shū miàn dė 书面的
wrong	(a.)	salah	cùo 错, cùo wù dė 错误的
		tidak beres, ada gangguan	yǒu máo bing 有毛病
wrong.do.ing	(n.)	perbuatan salah	zùo è 作恶
		pelanggaran	fàn zùi 犯罪
wrong.do.er	(n.)	orang yang salah, penjahat	fàn cùo wù dė rén 犯错误的人, zùi fàn 罪犯, dǎi tú 歹徒

wrong.ly	(adv.)	salah, tidak sah	cùo wù di 错误地, bù fă di 不法地

X

Xmas = Christmas	(n.)	hari Natal	shèng dàn jié 圣诞节
X-ray	(n.)	sinar X	X guāng xiàn X 光线
	(v.)	menyinari dengan sinar X	X guāng tòu shì X 光透视
xy.lo.graph	(n.)	gambar ukiran kayu	mù kè huà 木刻画
xy.log.ra.phy	(n.)	seni cetak dari ukiran kayu	mù kè shù 木刻术
xy.lo.nite	(n.)	gading buatan	jiǎ xiàng yá 假象牙
		seluloid	sài luò lù 赛珞璐

Y

yard	(n.)	pekarangan	tíng yuàn 庭院, yuàn zi 院子
		yard	mă 码
yard.man	(n.)	tukang kebun	yuán dīng 园丁
yard.stick	(n.)	meteran yard	mă chĭ 码尺
yarn	(n.)	benang	shā 纱, xiàn 线
		cerita yg aneh-aneh	gù shi 故事, qí tán 奇谈
yawn	(v.)	mengangop, menguap	dă hē qiàn 打呵欠
		membuka lebar	zhāng kaī 张开, liè kaī 裂开
	(n.)	angop	hē qiàn 呵欠
year	(n.)	tahun	nián 年, nián jì 年纪
year-book	(n.)	buku tahunan	nián jiàn 年鉴, nián bào 年报
year.ly	(a.)	tahunan, sekali setahun	měi nián dė 每年的, yī nián yī dù 一年一度
	(adv.)	tiap tahun	měi nián 每年, nián nián 年年
yearn	(v.)	rindu akan	xiăng wàng 想望, kě wàng 渴望
	(n.)	rindu, kerinduan	xiăng wàng 想望, kě wàng 渴望
yeast	(n.)	ragi	xiào mŭ 酵母
yell	(v.)	berteriak	jiào hăn 叫喊
	(n.)	teriakan	jiào hăn 叫喊
yel.low	(a.)	kuning	huáng 黄, huáng sè dė 黄色的
		cemburu, iri	yí xīn 疑心, dù jì 妒忌
	(n.)	warna kuning	huáng sè 黄色
		kuning telur	dàn huáng 蛋黄
yel.low.ish	(a.)	kekuning-kuningan	dàn huáng dė 蛋黄的, dài huáng sè dė 带黄色的

yen	(n.)	mata uang Jepang	yuán 元
yes	(a.)	ya	shì 是, shì dė 是的
yes-man	(n.)	pak angguk, penjilat	hǎo hǎo xiān shèng 好好先生
yes.ter.day	(n.)	kemarin	zuó tiān 昨天
yet	(adv.)	masih	hái 还, réng rán 仍然
		sudah	yǐ jīng 已经
		tetapi	suī rán 虽然, kě shì 可是
Is breakfast ready yet?		- Apakah sarapan sudah siap?	zǎo cān yù bèi hǎo lė mȧ ? 早餐预备好了吗？
It is strange, and yet it is true.		- Itu aneh tetapi nyata.	qí guài kě shì zhēn dė 奇怪可是真的
yield	(v.)	menghasilkan	shēng 生, shēng chǎn 生产, chǎn shēng 产生
		menyerah, mengalah	tuì ràn 退让, ràn bù 让步
	(n.)	penghasilan	shōu hūo 收获
		banyaknya penghasilan	chǎn liàng 产量, shōu hùo liàng 收获量
yield.ing	(a.)	mudah dibengkokkan	yì wān qū dė 易弯曲的
		mudah terpengaruh	yì shòu yǐng xiǎng dė 易受影响的
		mau mengalah	kěn ràn bù dė 肯让步的
yolk	(n.)	kuning telur	dàn huáng 蛋黄
yon.der	(a.)	di sana	nà biān dė 那边的, nà lǐ dė 哪里的
	(adv.)	di sana	zài nà biān 在那边
you	(pron.)	kamu, engkau, anda	nǐ 你, nǐ mėn 你们
young	(a.)	muda	nián qīng 年轻, yòu xiǎo 幼小
	(n.)	anak	xiǎo hái zi 小孩子
young.ster	(n.)	anak, pemuda	shǎo nián 少年
your	(adj.)	kepunyaanmu, milik anda	nǐ dė 你的, nǐ mėn dė 你们的
yours	(pron.)	kepunyaan anda	nǐ dė 你的, nǐ dė dōng xī 你的东西,

			nǐ mėn dė 你们的,
			nǐ mėn dė dōng xī 你们的东西
your.self	(pron.)	kamu sendiri, anda sendiri	nǐ zì jǐ 你自己
youth	(n.)	masa muda	qīng nián shí dài 青年时代
		pemuda	qīng nián 青年
youth.ful	(a.)	muda	qīng nián dė 青年的
		kelihatan muda	qīng nián sì dė 青年似的
yu.an	(n.)	mata uang RRC	yuán 元
yule	(n.)	hari Natal	shèng dàn jié 圣诞节

Z

zeal	(n.)	kegairahan, semangat	rè qíng 热情, rè xīn 热心
zeal.ot	(n.)	orang yang fanatik	kuáng rè zhě 狂热者
zeal.ous	(a.)	bersemangat	rè xīn dě 热心的
		giat	jī jí dė 积极的
ze.bra	(n.)	zebra	bān mǎ 斑马
ze.ro	(n.)	nol	líng 零
zest	(n.)	rasa	zī wèi 滋味
		animo	xìng qù 兴趣
		semangat	rè xīn 热心, rè qíng 热情
zig.zag	(a.)	berliku-liku, zig-zag, berkelok-kelok	pán xuán 盘旋
zinc	(n.)	seng	xīn 锌
zo.di.ac	(n.)	rasi bintang	huáng dào dài 黄道带
zone	(n.)	daerah	dài 带, dì dài 地带, qū yù 区域
the frigid zones		daerah iklim dingin	hán dài 寒带
the temperate zones		daerah iklim sedang	wēn dài 温带
the torrid zones		daerah iklim panas	rè dài 热带
the danger zone		daerah bahaya	weī xiǎn dì dài 危险地带
zoo	(n.)	kebun binatang	dòng wù yuán 动物园
zo.o.log.i.cal	(a.)	mengenai ilmu hewan	dòng wù xué dė 动物学的
zo.ol.o.gist	(n.)	ahli hewan	dòng wù xué jiā 动物学家
zo.ol.o.gy	(n.)	ilmu hewan	dòng wù xué 动物学

BIBLIOGRAPHY

Echols, John. M. & Hassan Shadily. *Kamus Inggris-Indonesia*. PT Gramedia. Jakarta. 1976.

Hornby, A. S. et al. *The Advanced Learner's Dictionary of Current English*. Second Edition. Dong Hua Publisher (東華書局印行). Taipei (臺北). 1962.

Hornby, A. S. & E. V. Gatenby & H. Wakefield. *The Advanced Learner's Dictionary of Current English*. Second Edition. Oxford University Press. London. 1973.

Hornby, A. S. *The Advanced Learner's Dictionary of Current English*. Fourth Edition. Oxford University Press, London. 1989.

Kamus Besar Bahasa Indonesia, Edisi Kedua, cetakan Kesepuluh, Penerbit PN Balai Pustaka, Jakarta. 1999.

Webster's Third New International Dictionary of the English Language Unabridged. G. & C. Merriam Company. Massachusetts. USA. 1966.

BIOGRAPHY

Wiliting was born in Fuqing town, in Fujian Province, China, on November 11, 1932. In 1938, he followed his mother who emigrated to Indonesia to join his father. The family lived in Kalibaru, Eastern Java. In 1943, they moved to Pekalongan, a coastal town in north Central Java.

In 1955, Wiliting graduated from Hua Chiao Middle School in Bandung. He then took further study by applying for Overseas Correspondence College of Amoy University in China, the People's Republic of China, majoring in Chinese Language and finished his study in 1960.

Between 1955-1961 he taught at Nan Hua Middle School in Bandung. Between 1962-1966 he taught at Hua Chiao Middle School in Pekalongan where he was appointed as headmaster. From 1970 he worked as a writer. His first book, *A Dictionary of English Idiom*, was published by Penerbit Dinastindo, Jakarta; his English grammar series (26 books) are published by Penerbit Grasindo, Jakarta. Beside that, more than his twenty other books were published by his own publishing house, Penerbit Harapan, Pekalongan.

生 平 简 介
shēng píng jiǎn jiè

黄礼枨—1932年十一月十一日出生于中国福建福清市.1938年,随母亲来印尼,定居于东爪哇的加里巴如村.1943年,随父母迁居中爪哇北加浪岸市.

学历:初中毕业于北加浪岸市中华学校(北华).高中毕业于万隆华侨中学(侨中).1957年攻读中国厦门大学华侨函授部语文系,1960年毕业.

工作经历:1955—1961年在万隆南北学校执教.1962—1966年在北加浪岸市华侨中小学执教.后当该校校长.十年执教期间,在百忙之中,他以强烈的兴趣,孜孜以求,自修英文,积累了一定的英文知识,打下了以后编写英文的基础.

1970年开始编著工作.先后共编写了50多本书种.其中有26本是《英语语法丛书》,由雅加达 GRASINDO 出版社(GRAMEDIA 集团)出版.《英印成语字典》,由雅加达 DINASTINDO 出版社出版,《英语动词时态的应用》,由北加浪岸 HARAPAN 出版社出版.(以上各书全用印尼语阐述).其他还有二十多本不一一介绍了.